I DO SOLEMNLY SWEAR

What conduct should the people expect from their legal officials? This book asks whether officials can be moral and still follow the law, answering that the law requires them to do so. It revives the idea of the good official – the good lawyer, the good judge, the good president, the good legislator – that guided Cicero and Washington and that we seem to have forgotten. Based on stories and law cases from America's founding to the present, this book examines what is good and right in law and why officials must care. This overview of official duties, from oaths to the law itself, explains how morals and law work together to create freedom and justice, and it provides useful maxims to argue for the right answer in hard cases. Important for scholars but useful for lawyers and readable by anybody, this book explains how American law ought to work.

Steve Sheppard is the William Enfield Professor of Law at the University of Arkansas School of Law. He has written articles in legal history, legal philosophy, international law, and the practice of law. With George Fletcher, he wrote *American Law in a Global Context: The Basics*. He is the editor of the *Aspen Bouvier: A Law Dictionary*, *The Selected Writings of Sir Edward Coke*, *The History of Legal Education in the United States*, Karl Llewellyn's *The Bramble Bush*, Allen Farnsworth's *Introduction to the Legal System of the United States*, and several series of law books, and has also contributed introductions to the revived works of John Selden, Sir William Jones, and Francis Lieber, among others. He clerked and practiced law in Mississippi and throughout the South and lives with his family in the Ozarks. He completed his doctorate in the science of law at Columbia University and holds other degrees from Columbia, Oxford University, and the University of Southern Mississippi.

I Do Solemnly Swear

The Moral Obligations of Legal Officials

Stephen Michael Sheppard
University of Arkansas School of Law

CAMBRIDGE UNIVERSITY PRESS
Cambridge, New York, Melbourne, Madrid, Cape Town, Singapore, São Paulo, Delhi

Cambridge University Press
32 Avenue of the Americas, New York, NY 10013-2473, USA

www.cambridge.org
Information on this title: www.cambridge.org/9780521735087

First published 2009

Printed in the United States of America

A catalog record for this publication is available from the British Library

Library of Congress Cataloging in Publication data

Sheppard, Steve, 1963–
I do solemnly swear : the moral obligations of legal officials / Stephen Michael Sheppard.
    p.   cm.
Includes bibliographical references and index.
ISBN 978-0-521-51368-5 (hardback) – ISBN 978-0-521-73508-7 (pbk.)
1. Legal ethics – United States.   2. Law – Moral and ethical aspects – United States.   3. Law and
ethics.   4. Administrative responsibility – United States.   I. Title.
KF306.S52   2009
174′.30973–dc22   2008044180

ISBN   978-0-521-51368-5 hardback
ISBN   978-0-521-73508-7 paperback

Before he enter on the Execution of his Office, he shall take the following Oath or Affirmation: – "I do solemnly swear (or affirm) that I will faithfully execute the Office of President of the United States, and will to the best of my Ability, preserve, protect and defend the Constitution of the United States."

U.S. Constitution, Article II, Section 1

The Senators and Representatives before mentioned, and the Members of the several State Legislatures, and all executive and judicial Officers, both of the United States and of the several States, shall be bound by Oath or Affirmation, to support this Constitution; but no religious Test shall ever be required as a Qualification to any Office or public Trust under the United States.

U.S. Constitution, Article VI, Clause 3

Each applicant shall sign the following oath or affirmation: I,............, do solemnly swear (or affirm) that I will comport myself as an attorney and counselor of this court, uprightly and in accordance with the law, and that I will support the Constitution of the United States.

Rule 5.4 of the U.S. Supreme Court

I do solemnly swear: I will support the Constitution of the United States and the Constitution of the State of Florida; I will maintain the respect due to courts of justice and judicial officers; I will not counsel or maintain any suit or proceedings which shall appear to me to be unjust, nor any defense except such as I believe to be honestly debatable under the law of the land; I will employ for the purpose of maintaining the causes confided to me such means only as are consistent with truth and honor, and will never seek to mislead the judge or jury by any artifice or false statement of fact or law; I will maintain the confidence and preserve inviolate the secrets of my clients, and will accept no compensation in connection with their business except from them or with their knowledge and approval; I will abstain from all offensive personality and advance no fact prejudicial to the honor or reputation of a party or witness, unless required by the justice of the cause with which I am charged; I will never reject, from any consideration personal to myself, the cause of the defenseless or oppressed, or delay anyone's cause for lucre or malice. So help me God.

Oath of Admission to the Florida Bar

Contents

Preface: Moral Officials, Retail Justice, and Three Caveats

This book examines a very basic idea: Officials must be moral, not just legal. In other words, legal officials ought to carry out their offices according to moral obligations, not just narrowly defined legal rules.

This idea is not popular in the United States: many people do not believe it, and many more are scared by it. In the media and cafe discussion, the idea spooks the left, who think it is code for religious judges, school boards, and legislators to stealthily bend the law to ban abortion, lead forced prayer in schools, arrest homosexuals, and tax the poor while ending liberty, community, and rights. And it scares the right, who think it is code for liberal feminist Black activists, who will coddle terrorists, immigrants, homosexuals, and the homeless while trampling freedom, property, and rights. Both the left and the right worry about a White House claiming ever greater powers, not least through a perpetual wartime license, using the language of moral certainty.

Meanwhile, academics and lawyers mistrust the whole idea of morality, in particular the idea of morality in the law. American society has changed from the days when Abraham Lincoln could argue with Stephen Douglas that the very bases of the law must be moral.[1] We don't trust "morality" until we know whose morality is under discussion. Morality is too contentious and unpredictable, and we have lost our common vocabulary for talking about it.[2] Rather than consider the idea of morality in law, with its broad

---

[1] Harold Holzer, *The Lincoln–Douglas Debates: The First Complete, Unexpurgated Text* (Fordham University Press, 2004). On the difference between Douglas's morality in procedure and Lincoln's morality in substance, see David Zarefsky, *Lincoln, Douglas, and Slavery: In the Crucible of Public Debate* (University of Chicago Press, 1993).

[2] See, for example, Hannah Arendt, "Some Questions of Moral Philosophy," in *Responsibility and Judgment* 139 (Jerome Khon, ed.) (Shocken Press, 2003), and Gertrude Himmelfarb, *The De-Moralization of Society: From Victorian Virtues to Modern Values* (Vintage, 1996).

and public connotations of duty, lawyers prefer the safer ideas of professional ethics.[3]

What has been lost?

Defining the moral obligations of officials is an ancient problem, and the line of philosophers and lawyers who have considered it is formidable. Plato and Aristotle argued strongly for the idea of the good official. The great Roman lawyer Cicero argued for truth and justice as the first duties of officials,[4] his ideas capturing the views of his predecessors and echoing for a thousand years in the princely letters of medieval bishops and in St. Thomas Aquinas's moral concept of law. Machiavelli, for all that he is read to encourage power at any price, recognized that the better alternative was the prince who was just and right in his actions. Indeed, his admonitions accord with the ideas of many observers of law in the early modern state. Writers who did much to frame our ideas of government and law after the medieval period, such as Elyot, Coke, Grotius, Pufendorf, Thomasius, Locke, and even Hobbes (after a fashion), all argued that real moral limits applied to the holders of office in the state. Hume, Kant, and Bentham, as well as some in our own time, notably Dworkin and Hampshire, have argued similar questions with similar positions.

More to the point of the American political experience, the framers of the Declaration of Independence and the U.S. Constitution, as well as abolitionists such as Garrison and Douglass and, ultimately, Lincoln and Martin Luther King, Jr., rooted their arguments for law and official conduct in what was good or right. This is what it meant to argue that governments must derive their "just powers" from the consent of the governed.[5]

To base a government on the consent of the governed and to base government on the good or the right do not ensure a stable or a peaceful result, though, and many serious controversies have arisen over what is wanted by the polity or what is good for the polity. The most serious of these, the claims for the protection or the abolition of slavery, were rooted in claims of morality and religion on both sides, leading even the abolitionists to mistrust such arguments after the war.[6]

Public discourse in political ethics has declined in popularity and coherence in the twentieth century: public disasters, the Holocaust, unpopular wars,

---

[3] See George P. Fletcher, *Basic Concepts of Legal Thought* 139–41 (Oxford University Press, 1996).

[4] Cicero could hardly be said always to have lived and practiced what he later preached, particularly in the wonderful book of letters to his son, *De Officiis*. On Cicero, see the very readable Anthony Everitt, *Cicero: The Life and Times of Rome's Greatest Politician* (Random House, 2001).

[5] The Declaration of Independence is available at http://www.archives.gov.

[6] For a nice illustration, see the discussion of the views of young Oliver Wendell Holmes, Jr., in Louis Menand, *The Metaphysical Club: A Story of Ideas in America* 3–72 (Farrar, Straus, and Giroux, 2001).

public corruption, and the divisive religious claims to the public space have diminished confidence in political leaders as arbiters of morality, have diminished any sense of agreement on a single view of morality, and have increased alienation from communal notions of the good and the right. As ethics have become less rooted in religious convention, ethical duties have been more cabined into specialized notions in philosophy or limited by professional codes, and it has become ever harder to locate a common vocabulary of ethics or morality in American culture.

At the same time, government has grown so powerful in the lives of its subjects that the State and its officials seem beyond morality. The will of politicians seems so unaffected by the anger or needs of citizens that the moral claims of critics seem as nothing compared to the whims of those with authority. The bureaucracy is so complex that officials appear to be ciphers beholden only to politics, leaving the corporate state as the only seeming personality. The notion that officials should be moral became first quaint and then laughable to a polity who knew through its press and politics the foibles of its elected and appointed officials.

Public debates have crowded one another through a boggling array of apparently immoral acts by officials – in the last decade including President Clinton's scandals and the extraordinary efforts to impeach him; the litigious mess of the 2000 election; the "wedge" polices of Karl Rove; the decisions and justifications to invade Iraq; the holding of U.S. detainees for years without a hearing; the endorsement of torture by Attorney General Alberto Gonzales and his lawyers, as well as the attorney general's apparent refusal to abide by the laws governing domestic spying; the firing of prosecutors for failing to use their powers for political ends, and the cover-up of those involved in the decisions; the influence of lobbyists; the bribes and misconduct of senators, congressmen, judges, governors, and aides; the failures of government to protect or assist the victims of Hurricane Katrina; the claims of a president to be above the laws through executive signing statements; and the deliberate lies regarding policy in lieu of science forced on the EPA – not to mention legal questions arising from policies on energy and the environment, the wars in Iraq and Afghanistan, the Global War on Terror, and the ever fuzzier lines among intelligence, war, criminal law, and police.[7]

---

[7] Attentive readers might infer from this list a partisan bias, one in which this book presents an otherwise unspoken assumption that the misuse of office is more likely by members of one political party than another in the United States. To an extent, this inference by the reader might seem supported by a plurality of examples from the party with executive power, which in 2008 is the Republican Party and has been for some years. I do not intend any partisanship here. Misuse of power is possible for any officeholder and for the members of any party, but it is most likely by those who happen to be the holders of the greatest power at any given time.

We need a vocabulary to discuss these affairs and many incidents less prominent yet equally troubling, and there is room yet to root this vocabulary in some notions of moral duty and right conduct. Few people now argue that there are no moral obligations at all, or that agreement cannot be found for them – sometimes.

The language of morals was invoked, for instance, by both sides during President Clinton's impeachment. The articles of impeachment were laden with words of moral significance. Impeachment article I stated that Mr. Clinton "willfully corrupted and manipulated the judicial process . . . [by] his corrupt efforts to influence the testimony of witnesses and to impede the discovery of evidence in that civil rights action . . . [so that he] has undermined the integrity of his office, has brought disrepute on the Presidency, has betrayed his trust as President, and has acted in a manner subversive of the rule of law and justice, to the manifest injury of the people of the United States."[8] His lawyers' response was in the same vein: "As the President himself has said, publicly and painfully, 'there is no fancy way to say that I have sinned.'"[9]

Still, there is an unease about such discussions. We find ourselves distracted in trying to prove the unprovable, and we fear being entangled in controversies manufactured for false purposes and misleading reasons. Still, within the great realm of arguments over what conduct is right or is good or is neither, the question usually evolves from whether any obligations exist into what such obligations are. And this question is hard for us for two very different reasons. First, our recent discussions have had very little firm ground shared among the contestants. Second, our arguments about what is good and right are nearly always colored by the fear that we will be held to a standard we will not meet. Our candidate, our leader, our favorite might break a moral precept that we embrace, to our embarrassment. And so we prefer to claim there are no moral limits that apply rather than to accept the inevitable breach of such limits from time to time. We not only lack the tools to agree on the moral obligations that would bind our officials, we are uncomfortable examining what it will mean when they break them.

It is past time for new thinking about all this. Though there are useful foundations for such thoughts in the works of great modern theorists such as Max Weber and H. L. A. Hart, these were not written to answer questions about what officials do and what they ought to do with laws today.

Answers to these questions might be expected to come from perennial debates about the nature of justice – or about what the law should be. In its grandest forms, we could think of these debates as questioning whether law should reflect one or another view of morality in the law's commands to

---

[8] U.S. House of Representatives, Committee on the Judiciary, Articles of Impeachment against William Jefferson Clinton, Article I, December 12, 1998.

[9] Submission by Counsel for President Clinton to the Committee on the Judiciary of the U.S. House of Representatives, December 8, 1998.

those subject to the law. In most lights, the fuss about justice usually concerns what should be demanded from citizens – whether the rules of law should establish equality or fairness among people in society (which often conflict), or whether the rules should promote property rights or corporate development over security or privacy (which also conflict with each other and with equality and fairness). Other than an implied obligation to enact or enforce the rules required by one outcome or another, the recent innings of these debates teach us only a little about the moral obligations of officials.

When debates over the grand meanings of justice turn from the citizen to the official, they sometimes have an unhelpful focus on the judge, somehow leaving out the legislator, the governor, the administrators, the police, or even the lawyers. Judges – especially judges in the United States who labor in the lights and the shadows cast by cases like *Dred Scott v. Sanford* and *Brown v. Board of Education* – are expected to make great choices and to decide great issues in the complex realms of human affairs. We have come to accept that such management is less likely or less honest in the political environments of the legislature or the executive.[10] However, an emphasis on the judge as the essential form of legal official is not just incomplete, it skews many of our notions of law, not least in creating the false impression that the decision of the official is usually an individual and isolated action, rather than a collaborative one made deep within a great nest of institutions.[11]

There is a greater problem with this idea of justice on the grand scale: understanding an idea so big usually raises very abstract questions that are hard to understand, much less to solve – such as whether equality is more important than individual right, or whether the right is more important than the good. Yet the real problem is that it is often quite hard to see how an answer to questions of justice on the grand scale would answer questions arising in the law as it is practiced by lawyers or relied on by ordinary people. Most problems under the law are so particular that any answer to the grand questions might still be applied variously in a particular issue, and so it is hard to see the practical value of justice in the grand answers.

THE IDEA OF RETAIL JUSTICE

The more compelling questions in the particular are whether the result in a particular case is fair, or right, or good; whether justice is done in each instance; or whether a person encountering the law has more or less confidence in the institutions of law as a result of the encounter. This retail application of justice echoes the grand considerations of justice, yet it is not the same.

---

[10] But see Jeremy Waldron's example to the contrary. Jeremy Waldron, *The Dignity of Legislation* (Cambridge University Press, 1999); and compare Alexander Bickel, *The Least Dangerous Branch: The Supreme Court at the Bar of Politics* (Bobbs-Merrill, 1962).

[11] See Jeremy Waldron, *Law and Disagreement* 203 (Oxford University Press, 1999).

Once reduced to individual cases, the questions shift in specificity, and the focus becomes very much on the conduct of individuals who use the law, not merely on the law writ large: Have the legislators in a given instance acted well or badly? Have the lawyers framed the questions of law in a dispute accurately from the facts that gave it rise? Has the judge chosen which rules to apply and applied them correctly? Have the lawyers cheated or acted well? How should we assess the actions of the jailors or court clerks? Who lied, or hid evidence, or filed a pleading without any investigation, research, or knowledge, or even care for what unfair burdens it might bring on the other side of the case? Who was too stupid, bored, or disinterested to realize they were being deceived?

To ask whether the officials – the lawyers, the jurors, the judges, the legislators, the police, the clerks, even the voters – have done their best in each case, indeed to ask whether *justice* has been done in each case, is different from asking grand questions of what justice is, although admittedly there is a relationship between the two approaches. This retail view of justice turns on how laws are applied to the common person, not just on how the law as a whole is defined.

To consider retail justice in the making and application of law in a given circumstance is to examine the justice in the conduct of individual officials: the legislators who enact a statute; the judge or administrator who decides to (or fails to) enforce a rule; the lawyer who brings forward a suit; the opposing lawyer who aids (or fails) in providing the court the evidence that is sought; the juror who goes along with the majority to get out of court by lunchtime; the juror who votes on a belief formed from careful thought about all the evidence.[12] All of these people are the actors whose conduct must somehow be assessed. Granted, the judge is an important player on this stage, yet the stage is crowded, and every player is a part of the play.

Today, we tend to think of "Justice" as something done by institutions – such as society as a whole or the state[13] – as if it is a playing piece found only in a political game. But, institutional justice is not the only sense in which we can think of justice.

---

[12] Someone unused to juries might think it is easy to be the heroic holdout who alone sees the truth of the case and defends it against all comers, like the fictional Juror Number 8 in Sidney Lumet's 1957 movie *Twelve Angry Men*, whose quiet confidence turned eleven wrongheaded votes toward justice. More common would be Sir John's experience in Alfred Hitchcock's 1930 *Murder!* in which the knowing holdout's doubts are pushed aside by the majority, and he votes to convict an innocent defendant. Nearly all potential holdouts follow Sir John's path and conform to the will of the majority. See research collected in Jason D. Reichelt, "Standing Alone: Conformity, Coercion, and the Protection of the Holdout Juror," 40 University of Michigan Journal of Law Reform 569 (2007).

[13] This is the sense of justice in John Rawls's famous project, which pretty much painted the barn for justice discussions for forty years. See John Rawls, *A Theory of Justice* (Harvard University Press, 1970).

Justice has traditionally been considered mainly as a personal obligation. In one of the more famous religious proclamations of justice, the minor Israelite prophet Micah, in the seventh century B.C.E., reminded the wayward Israelites of their personal obligations: "What does the Lord require of you but to do justice, and to love kindness, and to walk humbly with your God?"[14] Or, "It has been told thee, O man, what is good, and what the Lord requires of you: Only to do justice, And to love goodness, and to walk modestly with your God."[15] Justice as a personal aspect of religious duty is a recurrent theme in both the law and the prophets in the Jewish and Christian traditions.[16] We have, however, long been schooled to think of justice as institutional, and we think of individuals as acting (or not acting) morally, ethically, or even efficiently, rather than justly.[17] Furthermore, there are some messy problems in defining justice, which could allow us to simplify matters and merely to say that what is just is what is lawful.

So, this book is about the retail ideas of justice. In this sense, *all* of the things a good official ought to do, including understanding and following the law, are the same as justice by that official. That is to say that justice is what officials ought to do. Therefore to understand justice we must understand officials and their jobs. In doing so, we learn not only how tough these jobs are, but also how we can assess them. Indeed, we might come some way toward restoring our own sense of discernment over our officials, which is the heart of democracy.

CAVEAT EMPTOR: WE WILL TALK ABOUT MORALITY

This book is about justice and moral obligations, and so it reflects an assumption that it makes sense to talk about moral obligations. In other words, we

---

[14] Micah 6:8 (Revised New Standard Version).

[15] The last phrase may also translate as "it is prudent to serve your God." *TANAKH: The Holy Scriptures* 1051 (Jewish Publication Society, 1985).

[16] *Strong's Concordance* records nearly 500 verses incorporating a word for righteousness or justice in judgment, including 197 for *tsaddiyq*, or righteous judgment (Strong's 06662); 40 verses with a form of *tsadaq*, or justification by God's law (Strong's 06663); 116 of *tsedeq* (Strong's 06664); 1 of *tsidqah* (Strong's 06665); and 150 of *tsadaqah*, or justice in judgment (Strong's 06666). See James Strong, *The New Strong's Exhaustive Concordance of the Bible* (Nelson Reference 1991). See, for example, Leviticus 19:15; Proverbs 21:3; Isaiah 5:7, Isaiah 9:7. Some of these references are justice that only a prince or magistrate might bestow, but most are justice by each person toward others, regardless of station.

[17] Notwithstanding the ideas of justice promoted since Rawls, the idea of justice as inherently the product of the leader of a polity arose with Aristotle. See Aristotle, *Politics*, Books IV and XIII; and Fred D. Miller, *Nature, Justice, and Rights in Aristotle's Politics* (Oxford University Press, 1997). There are, of course, modern examples, most notably Sandel's powerful argument to focus moral civic engagement to the betterment of the individual, rather than merely seeking values across the polity. See Michael Sandel, *Democracy's Discontent* (Harvard University Press, 1996).

start with a belief that there is something meaningful in talking about a person's conduct as being right or good (or not). At this level of generality, there is little difference between morality as a whole and ethics as a whole.

This assumption does not require us to accept any one of the many competing theories about morals or ethics or about their fundamental nature. One could believe that morals arise from customs and habits, or from a social contract, or from the natural conditions of mankind in community, or as underived facts about the world, or from the divine will of almighty God whether defined within an ancient canon or by a modern whimsy.[18] In general, this book excludes none of these explanations; it does not require the choice or rejection of any one of these approaches. One can accept that there is morality but not care where it comes from.

Those who believe ethics or morality to be based on a single view of reality, or nature, or vocabulary, or whatnot will find much in the book to be irrelevant. People who embrace radical notions of individualism or objectivism that reject any notion of morality or other concepts of involuntary responsibility of the individual to others will find the book dissatisfying.[19]

A SECOND CAVEAT: THE SOURCES ARE UNTIDY

Some readers will find another source of disquiet here. It is the fashion in the modern academy to ground books in the criticism of one or a few prior books. By asserting (or presuming) the authority of a book of the moment, the author can skip the job of explaining the underlying principles of the new argument and move on. The reader is expected either to know the older book or to accept its importance, and no further justification of its premises is usually required in the new book.

In our case, this book might have offered as foundations Herbert Hart's *A Concept of Law*, Isaiah Berlin's *Crooked Timber of Humanity*, John Rawls's *A Theory of Justice*, Ronald Dworkin's *Law's Empire*, John Finnis's *Natural Law and Natural Rights*, Stuart Hampshire's *Justice Is Conflict*, Michael Sandel's *Democracy's Discontent*, or any of the works on professional or legal ethics by

---

[18] The Church of the Flying Spaghetti Monster arose during an argument over a Kansas state school-board rule for public schools that teach evolution also to teach "intelligent design," the argument being that the believers in the Flying Spaghetti Monster (called "pastafarians") have as much claim for their theories in state school science books as do literal Christians. Pastafarians have a moral code based on meatballs and sea piracy, among other things. See Bobby Henderson, *The Gospel of the Flying Spaghetti Monster* (Random House, 2006); *Cf.* "Review: The Editors Recommend The Gospel of the Flying Spaghetti Monster," 294(6) Scientific American 94 (2004).

[19] See, for example, Ayn Rand, *The Virtue of Selfishness* (Signet, 1964). Even so, the preceding arguments include several that are entirely voluntary, and in those arguments, the followers of Rand might find room for agreement.

Deborah Rhode, Dan Coquillette, William Simon, Arthur Isak Applbaum, or other mavens of professional responsibility. These works have large followings of clever readers, they are benchmarks in the current landscape of law and morals, and their extended criticism would have added an aura of authority to my project.

Yet these books were not written to answer the exact questions posed here, and their criticism for these purposes would have been aside from the points those authors intended to make. Though some of these books will be helpful in the questions here posed, the books that are more to the point for these questions are not as well known now. Most, like the works of Cicero, Gottfried Leibniz, Christian Thomasius, Francis Lieber, and even David Hume, have aged into obscurity. Others, such as the works of Lon Fuller, failed to acquire a wide audience, or like the statements of St. Paul or of the Prophet Mohammad, presented a view that not everyone would consider authoritative.

So, this book does not ground its arguments in a handful of prior books but presents a bricolage, an aggregation of stories and ideas from many works in jurisprudence, many moments in history, arguments in many religions and cultures, and many cases in the law. The arguments depend less on an authority assumed from others' books than upon the reader's decisions to accept or reject the conclusions drawn from these illustrations. In short, the reader has little netting from familiar texts and must walk alone the moral tightrope over law.

THIRD CAVEAT: WE ARE TALKING ABOUT MORALS AS A BASIS FOR OFFICIAL CONDUCT

Many smart people think there is no reason to ask what morality there is in the acts of a legal official. The idea that officials have moral obligations when making decisions or committing legal actions has lost interest for a century, and many lawyers and judges might argue that the idea does not even merit discussion. For some, it is a fool's errand.

For instance, the very scholarly and influential Judge Richard Posner has argued strenuously that there is nothing for the law to gain by basing legal decisions in ideas of morality. Morality, as he sees much of it, is just "dominant public opinion," which he believes neither influences behavior nor increases the justification of the law.[20] If he is right in all three conclusions,

---

[20] Richard Posner, *The Problematics of Moral and Legal Theory* 3–90 (Harvard University Press, 1999). The quote is from his handy summary of his views in a more recent blog. Richard Posner, "Faith-Based Morality and Public Policy," December 27, 2004, in *Guest Blogger: Richard Posner*, http://leiterreports.typepad.com/blog/2004/12/faithbased_mora.html (last visited July 17, 2007). Judge Posner distinguishes the morality he criticizes from other forms of normative and ethical theory, including moral theory in the vein of Adam Smith and David Hume, to reject anything smacking of moral realism that can serve as a touchstone for judicial decision-making, preferring instead a professional and pragmatic approach.

there is precious little benefit in discussing moral obligations for officials of the law.

Several reactions suggest possible objections or limits to this view, though. The first is this: even if we agree with Judge Posner that there is nothing to gain from considering *what* moral ideas might justify legal decisions, that alone does not tell us whether moral ideas guide *how* decisions of law are made.

We could imagine that it does not matter whether the law is fair, right, or just, but we would not, from that alone, have imagined that it would not matter if the laws were created or applied unfairly, wrongly, or unjustly. We might still think that making the rules in an unfair or bad way, or applying them wrongly or unjustly, could have dreadful repercussions for the legal system as a whole and for the people it regulates.

There is a second reaction. By reaching outside the law to certain moral concepts, such as fairness, liberty, and justice, the people and officials might prevent officials from lawfully running cruel and unjust regimes that are allowed by the narrowly written rules of the law. This is the heart of the matter. There is no *legal* protection against tyranny, because laws may always be changed by law. The only successful protection is a refusal by officials and the people to tolerate it. Likewise, there is no lasting assurance of legal protection against brutality and evil by legal officials; the only assurance that can guard such protections is the refusal by other officials and the people to support or allow it.

This practical moral limit on officials' actions is a problem of ancient concern. Montesquieu, the great French historian, put the matter nicely when he summarized how the Roman emperor Tiberius corrupted the Senate and cowed the judiciary so that his unjust excesses were carried out according to the law, a law altered to his liking: "No tyranny is more cruel than the one practiced in the shadow of the laws and under color of justice – when, so to speak, one proceeds to drown the unfortunate on the very plank by which they had saved themselves."[21] Such a statement echoes to us through the shadows of legal slavery, of the legality of the regime of Nazi Germany, of *de jure* discrimination in the United States, and of the writings of American lawyers excusing torture.

A third reaction may occur if we agree with Judge Posner's idea of morality as public opinion. His view is that morality is invented by people (rather than morality being inherent in the nature of mankind or of the world, positions he rejects). If we think this, we still do not have to believe that the law, which also

---

This distinction could mean that Judge Posner would agree with some of the possibilities presented on this page and the next several. More of Judge Posner's argument is discussed in Chapter 3.

[21] Charles de Secondat, Baron de Montesquieu, *Considerations on the Causes of the Greatness of the Romans and Their Decline* 130 (David Lowenthal, trans.) (Free Press, 1965). Montesquieu's view of Tiberius was, of course, strongly influenced by Tacitus, whose portrait of Tiberius was before him. See Tacitus, *The Annals* (David Lowenthal, trans.) (Franklin Library, 1982).

is invented by people, could not benefit if legal officials applied these invented moral ideas to invent legal standards of conduct. We might have to agree that a legal decision based on a wholly invented moral notion would be vulnerable to the criticisms to which the invented moral notion becomes vulnerable.

If we base a law on a moral idea and the morality changes, the law is likely to change as well.[22] This is exactly what happened when, thankfully, the Jim Crow laws[23] that were initially based on arguments of racial hierarchy, privilege, and paternalism fell under the scrutiny of new moral arguments for liberty and equality that America promoted for other countries during World War II and the Cold War.[24] Laws based on moral ideas can also encourage acceptance of those ideas, as was the case initially with racial desegregation in America, which was considered by many people (and not just in the Southern states) to be an immoral imposition until social mores grew somewhat more egalitarian.[25] This dynamic of the influence of morals on laws is, perhaps, more easily seen in the illustration of private dueling, which was long prohibited by law but fell from favor among the upper classes only when it came into ridicule among the social elites who had once embraced it.[26]

---

[22] This statement begs the questions of how morals change, who must accept or reject changed beliefs, and how norms develop or decline in society generally. The answers vary a great deal from case to case. All we need now is to acknowledge that some morals do change. See Crane Brinton, *A History of Western Morals* (1959) (Paragon House, 2000); *Sextus Empiricus: Outlines of Scepticism* (Julia Annas & Jonathan Barnes, eds.) (Cambridge University Press, 2000). Centuries ago, the common law was more confident in its reliance on social custom and morality as its source of law, giving rise to the legal fiction that laws did not really change. See Sir Henry Maine, *Ancient Law: Its Connection with the Early History of Society, and Its Relation to Modern Ideas* (1861) (Everyman's Library, 1972).

[23] See Douglas A. Blackmon, *Slavery by Another Name: The Re-Enslavement of Black Americans from the Civil War to World War II* (Doubleday, 2008). Blackmon illuminates the shamefulness of "Jim Crow laws" in even its name: "Imagine if the first years of the holocaust were known by the name of Germany's most famous anti-Semitic comedian of the 1930's." New York Times Book Review (June 22, 2008).

[24] The American civil rights movement has many historians. For the influence of the rhetoric of the United Nations see C. Vann Woodward, *The Strange Career of Jim Crow* (1954) (Oxford University Press, 1991). For the egalitarian rhetoric of Christian religion, see David Chappell, *A Stone of Hope: Prophetic Religion and the Death of Jim Crow* (University of North Carolina Press, 2003). For a reasonably complete telling of the tale, see Michael Klarman, *From Jim Crow to Civil Rights: The Supreme Court and the Struggle for Racial Equality* (Oxford University Press, 2004).

[25] See, for example, Stephan Thernstrom & Abigail Thernstrom, *America in Black and White: One Nation, Indivisible* (Touchstone, 1997).

[26] See Robert Baldick, *The Duel, A History* (Barnes & Noble Books, 1965). The duel follows a familiar pattern, descended from primitive fights through judicial combat to private arguments for honor to a waste of life. Legal prohibitions were nearly universal for centuries before its demise. See also John Selden, *The Duello* (1610), in John Selden, *Opera Omnia* (2d ed.) (Lawbook Exchange, 2008); Selden wrote appropriately for his time, accepting the duel as a legitimate means for determining both matters that could and matters that could not have been resolved by the law.

Thus, we learn that our third possible response to Judge Posner must take seriously the risks he poses for morals in law. The law is vulnerable to rejection or change if the morals are vulnerable to rejection or change. This does not mean that there might not be benefits to law – perhaps benefits essential to the law – in this relationship.

A fourth reaction, the last to be considered here, may be the most important. Those subject to the law might believe that the law is immoral (in many different senses) and for that reason act to evade or destroy the legal system. Citizens[27] have a choice to obey the law; they might prefer to risk punishment rather than to obey. Officials,[28] too, may choose how or if they will carry out their duties. As long as "fair," "good," or "right," "just," or "helpful" or similar notions matter at all, then citizens and officials may use such notions to assess the rules of the law, the means of their enactment and enforcement, and the significance of laws not enacted or not enforced.[29] Such assessments occur broadly as a matter of fact from time to time in a legal system, and there is no benefit to denying that they do. The United States resulted from a revolution that followed British law's failure in such a test.

These four reactions suggest that Judge Posner's objections, although very important, are not so broad as to end our inquiry. Even so, his argument at least challenges the study of moral obligations and the law to demonstrate that such studies fit within the traditions of law, its creation, its practice, its adjudication, and its influence in society.

---

[27] Throughout this book, "citizen" must stand in for a host of roles, and I use it interchangeably with the word "subject" and even "any person not acting as an official," as well as "official acting not within the role of office." Obviously, not every nonofficial in a country is a citizen. Many countries have aliens or native noncitizens, and of course, monarchies such as the United Kingdom use not "citizen" but "subject." Unless the context makes it clearly otherwise, "citizen" and "subject" here are meant to include every person who is subject to the law of the state, including officials when not acting in their official role.

[28] "Official" represents any of the many roles in the legal system, each of which shares one defining characteristic. An official is a person who is given authority by a law to act, whether individually or in a group, and that act affects another person, whether directly or indirectly, through the apparatus of the legal system. See Chapter 1.

[29] See, for example, Peter Coss (ed.), *The Moral World of the Law* (Cambridge University Press, 2000). A classic, if dated, argument for the interaction of a legal system and its moral climate is in Arthur L. Goodhart, *English Law and the Moral Law* (Stevens and Sons, 1953).

Acknowledgments

Many people have supported this book over its long life. Study at Columbia was aided by a benefaction honoring Augustus Newbold Morris, thanks to the Graduate Committee under the chairmanship of Peter Strauss. For the Columbia Center for Law and Philosophy Fellowship, as well as his many kindnesses, I am grateful to Jeremy Waldron. The project continued with help from the Dean's Scholarship Fund at the University of Arkansas School of Law, and from Richard Atkinson, Howard Brill, and Cyndi Nance. I am especially grateful for the generosity of Judge William Enfield, whose professorship I now hold and whose far-sighted gift to the School of Law supported the final years of this research.

Helpful as the money has been, even greater value has come from the opportunity I had to study with a wonderful committee, Jeremy Waldron, Kent Greenawalt, and George Fletcher, who were joined in my exam by the helpful and merciful Robert Ferguson. Their kindness in time and criticism had made better the ideas in this work and my thinking in general. It might be obvious to any who know these four scholars, but it should be noted that the materials they approved for doctoral work did not include some of the wilder arguments included here. In any event, they should not be blamed for my errors, which they tried so hard to correct.

Over the years, I have benefited particularly from discussions about this work and its antecedents (some of which are now long past but were still essential) with Andy Albertson, John Baker, Brian Barry, Barbara Black, John Berger, Peter DeMarsh, Michael Dorf, Ronald Dworkin, John Finnis, Brian Gill, Patrick Glenn, Phil Hamburger, Herbert Hart, Richard Helmholz, Michael Hoeflich, Mark Kelman, Anthony Lewis, David Lieberman, Lance Liebman, Frank Michelman, Alberto Mora, William Nelson, James Penner, Thomas Pogge, Andrzej Rapaczynski, Ed Rubin, Bernard Rudden, Oscar Schachter, Ned Snow, Jim Stoner, Peter Strauss, Brian Tamanaha, Richard Tuck, and

Mark Tushnet. A list cannot do justice to the particular help that each has given me, but there it is.

In the final throes of this work, the guidance, friendship, and leadership of two people was essential to it ever reaching your hands. John Berger at Cambridge University Press and Mary Cadette at Aptara, Inc., were each essential, and I am grateful for their efforts.

My family has suffered the traditional perils of living with a book that grew from a dissertation, and I am grateful that they never threw me out of the house. When this project started, my greatest debt was to Bill and Martha Sheppard, whose gentle persistence and support have never flagged, but the debt has extended very much to Christine in particular and to Maggie, Katie, and William, who supply a new inspiration for this work.

Introduction: Seven Questions about What Is Fit for an Official to Do

In the early 1600s, America was young, and England was enjoying the golden age of its common law. This was an important time for what has become the law of the United States. England was in transition from the feudal to the modern order; the economy was driven less by produce from ancestral lands and more by money, trade, colonies, and technology. The monarchy was becoming more bureaucratic, and the English law courts and Parliament, which had long been more independent of the Crown than were their counterparts on the continent, asserted again and again their authority as the guardian of the liberties of the subject. The colonists leaving England for America brought with them these models of state and law and these ideas of legal order.

The great expositor of these ideas was the English lawyer, judge, and parliamentary leader Sir Edward Coke, who had consolidated the powers of the courts and written the case reports and textbook institutes that would be brought to American shores, rooting there a notion of what would later be called the Rule of Law.[1] In one of this notion's first tests, King James I of England asked Coke whether he would submit to hearing the king's opinion before deciding a case. Coke refused, replying he would "do that which should be fit for a judge to do."[2]

By this act, Coke condemned himself to retirement from the bench, but he also created an enduring symbol of the independence of the law from political power, an independence built on a complex understanding that officials *of* the law have special duties *to* the law. Such duties may range widely in their origin and in their meaning.

---

[1] See Steve Sheppard, "Introduction," in 1 *The Selected Writings of Sir Edward Coke* xxii (Steve Sheppard, ed.) (Liberty Fund, 2004). On the Rule of Law, see Brian Z. Tamanaha, *The Rule of Law: History, Politics, Theory* (Cambridge University Press, 2005).

[2] "Commendams and the King's Displeasure," 3 *Selected Writings of Sir Edward Coke* 1320. (The spelling above is modernized, and "which" is added for clarity.)

Not one law, but the law as a whole, gave rise to Coke's belief that he had an obligation to defy the King. His decision to do so was based on a broad understanding of the requirements upon him as judge. Only some of these requirements arose from the written legal materials; requirements from the unwritten law – the *lex non scripta* – were every bit as real to him and were acknowledged by many others of his time.[3]

WHAT SHOULD BE FIT FOR AN OFFICIAL TO DO?

Of course, there is a long tradition that the officials who create and carry out the law ought to perform their duties with particular care. Only a portion of this care is explained or written as law, and even less is enforceable according to law.

The sources for this care are neither law nor are they not law. They are essential to law but do not arise from the same sources of law in the ordinary way. They arise from our understandings of moral obligation – both those understandings that are grounded in the traditional discourse of morality and those understandings that arise from sources particular to this question of care by officials, including the law itself.

These requirements are controversial. In the case of Sir Edward Coke, the judge hardly persuaded James I at the time, though James had heard and accepted much more powerful statements of Coke's views before.[4] In our own day, the idea that officials might have any authority other than the law for their actions conflicts with one of the most basic doctrines of legal philosophy, that there is a fundamental rule in every legal system, according to which all other rules of law are recognized. Yet Ronald Dworkin has convincingly argued that the rules of the legal system may themselves provide for authority that does not wholly depend on the law.[5] Still, when we thread among such fierce arguments, we will, I think, find plenty of evidence that such requirements – requirements for officials to do the right thing that arise from sources besides the law alone – are indeed meaningful and are appropriate bases for thought and action.

Therefore, this book examines the question, "What are the moral obligations of legal officials?" by considering essential abstract principles as they can be understood in actual moments of practice in the law, echoed in our understandings of professional responsibility, official responsibility, the idea of the state, and the nature of law itself. The book seeks such answers in the

---

[3] See J. H. Baker, *The Law's Two Bodies: Some Evidential Problems in English Legal History* (Oxford University Press, 2001).

[4] See Steve Sheppard, "Editor's Note," in Sir Edward Coke, "Prohibition del Roy" (1607), in 1 *Selected Writings of Sir Edward Coke* 478.

[5] See Ronald Dworkin, *Law's Empire* (Duckworth, 1986).

same manner in which Coke did, by resorting to ancient and modern writers from whom we can find principles and ideas with which to resolve our practical difficulties, and then by threading that knowledge through cases and examples. Coke read the ancients, including Aristotle, Cicero, and Tacitus, as well as contemporaries such as Sir Thomas More, Selden, and Bacon, yet he juxtaposed their ideas with real cases and problems in the law.[6] He would not have imagined a lawyer to be learned in the law without such knowledge, both in its sources and applied to law cases. Neither should we.

SEVEN QUESTIONS

So, let us then consider what an official should do, considering both ideas in the literature of the law and of office and illustrations that arise from practical situations. There are innumerable approaches one might take to such a consideration, but for this book, I've chosen a progression of seven questions:

1. What are legal officials, the law, and the legal obligations of officials?
2. What is at stake? Why, or how, is it helpful to consider any obligations of officials other than those imposed exclusively by the laws?
3. Do officials have obligations arising from more than law alone?
4. If so, what is the content of these obligations upon legal officials?
5. How do obligations arising from the laws interact with those that do not?
6. What does it mean when an official breaches these obligations?
7. What tools assist an official to do justice and discourage injustice?

This book follows these questions. The arguments developed in response to them are very briefly summarized in the overview that follows.

A GUIDE TO THIS BOOK

An Overview of the Arguments Introduced

1. *What Are Legal Officials, the Law, and the Legal Obligations of Officials?*

Officials and laws are essential to each other, and understanding one requires understanding both. To consider "what law is," in the context of officials' obligations, we look to how officials see law and to how citizens see it, each

---

[6] See John Marshall Gest, "The Writings of Sir Edward Coke," 18 Yale Law Journal 504, 516–18 (1909). Readers of Coke will recognize references to Tully as references to Cicero. Moreover, Coke was fond of quoting Cicero in epigraphs at the start of his *Reports*, a practice that is followed here in each chapter of this book.

giving rise to certain understandings. Officials see the law as a set of rules arising from an archive created by earlier acts of officials, interpreted and applied according to the culture of contemporary legal officials. Subjects see a host of signs in the law that are to an extent amorphous and to an extent the result of individual acts, whether by identified individuals or by anonymous actors working through a corporate body. From these we can synthesize a single view of the legal official, in which legal officials are the individuals in whom all of the powers of the state are allocated, divided among many roles, in each of which the role is both empowered and limited by some archival statements of law and by legal customs and cultural expectations, but within which the official has the sole discretion to act or not to act.

Every legal official has a wide range of discretion. Although that discretion is bounded by the rules that give the office its powers as well as by a legal culture that creates a set of expectations, how the official exercises that discretion is largely a matter left to that official. The rules of law do not control how discretion is exercised.

Officials act with very few controls or penalties, other than their access to promotion or image. The selection of officials and culture of officials are therefore the most likely external influences on how an official exercises discretion.

2. What Is at Stake? Why, or How, Is It Helpful to Consider Any Obligations of Officials Other than Those Imposed Exclusively by the Laws?

The actions of legal officials, both individually and as part of a collective act, produce many distinct and profound effects in the lives of others. A perfect inventory of these effects is impossible, but they are here represented by a group of nine metaphors for ease of use: the sword (the monopoly of force), the shield (the duty to protect from others), the balance (the power of judgment), the coin (the power to alter the economy), the commons (the title to public goods), the guide (the signal of good and evil in private life), the mirror (the representation of the people and their identity), the seal (superior authority with little or no real oversight), and the veil (the anonymity of identity and lack of direct accountability to those harmed). Those who are subject to the law depend upon legal officials for everything in each of the domains these metaphors signify. Some of these powers, such as the power of the sword, the balance, and the coin, represent needed but dreadful powers that are prone to misuses that risk direct harm to those who are affected by bad acts and decisions made in the name of the law. Some, such as the shield, the coin, the commons, and the mirror, represent opportunities for a good life for the subjects that are either prudently exercised or negligently lost. Some, such as the guide and the mirror, represent indirect conditions of life that frame identity and opportunity. Some, such as the seal and the veil, represent the danger of authority both to those who are subject to it and to the institutions (and other officials) that depend upon it to perform these functions.

3. Do Officials Have Obligations Arising from More than Law Alone?

Considering the relationship of the official to the law and also to the people regulated by law, it becomes easier to answer the question of whether official obligations arise from more than the law alone. Of course they do, particularly from the promises made in oaths of office, from the special risks created by office, from the expectations created by professional culture, from the implications of volunteering, from the reliance of others they have thus knowingly accepted, and from general principles of morality.

Understanding the extent of this responsibility is complicated because officials have a share of personal responsibility for every collective decision of the system as a whole. Although this responsibility matters most for actions or duties within a range of discretion, or within the boundary of the powers of every official, the obligations are greater than that and may require an official to alter the scope of discretion in order to satisfy very important obligations.

In this way, officials may be bound not only to carry out the law but also to do right by law. In this way, too, arguments from grand theory for fairness and justice in the law can be restated as arguments for actions not by "the state" or "the law" but as arguments for retail justice by individual officials. Arguments of justice, such as to be free of prejudice or bias, or to pursue freedom or economic justice, are much clearer seen in this light. Indeed, in this light, it appears that there can be no meaningful argument for any definition or claim of justice, unless that argument can sensibly be applied as an obligation of officials.

4. If so, What Is the Content of These Obligations upon Legal Officials?

Officials must use their discretion in certain manners and toward certain ends. What these manners and ends are is deeply controversial, and in the controversy, just discerning which voices one should hear can be difficult. After considering this difficulty, the chapter then inventories different forms of moral obligation, including obligations arising from institutional sources of personal moral obligation that underpin the law itself. These obligations take personal, institutional, procedural, and substantive forms, and like all ideals are nearly impossible to fully satisfy. This book cannot fully explore any (much less all) of these obligations, but the personal obligation of charity, the oldest in the literature, is considered in a little more detail.

5. How Do Obligations Arising from the Laws Interact with Those that Do Not?

The problem of official action is easiest when the official's legal and moral obligations are compatible. This is the case fairly often, a fact that is largely overlooked by many observers. The more dramatic questions that arise when they conflict give rise to a limited number of choices, which are first explored here by looking at the more familiar grounds of conflict among obligations for citizens. Officials have a greater range of choices than one might think. The patterns between incompatible obligations must result in changing the obligations, in changing one's role, in breaching one or the other, or in resignation from office.

6. What Does It Mean When an Official Breaches These Obligations?

There is very little legal oversight of officials, and yet officials inevitably breach their duties under both the law and morality. The problem of dirty hands, the condition in which immoral decisions are unavoidable, arises because the demands of moral behavior are so extensive that they cannot be satisfied completely: they are ideals that can only be partially met in the practical world of human affairs. Thus, the best one can hope for in most instances is that the official will reach the least unjust result possible.

The problem of remedies for breach is difficult, mainly because the remedies in law are so rarely available or used, and the remedies for immorality are social and psychological, not legal or physical. Other officials, or (less likely) the citizenry, may condemn an immoral official like any bad person, and one tool that is out of fashion is shame, which is more important but less likely now than offense.

The most significant remedy is for those aware of moral breaches by an official to interfere with the advancement or reappointment of that official. This form of interference occurs in the realm of politics, and those with the power to decide or influence the decision to appoint one person or another to office are morally obligated to make moral judgments in doing so, which is to say to promote those who use their powers for the good rather than for the sake of power alone. This is the moral basis for the exercise of the vote by the people governed by officials.

7. What Tools Assist an Official to Do Justice and Discourage Injustice?

There is no perfect calculus that can relieve an official of the duty of discretion. Each official must work to act in the least immoral manner in every opportunity for action. Traditionally, moral obligations have been distilled into aphorisms that allow assessment of a decision or action, and the book presents several maxims, with illustrations of their manifestation and of their breach. Yet tools for assessment need to be both positive and negative, and fallacies, illustrations of false or misleading reasoning, are also catalogued.

The Severability of These Questions

These questions are answered here with some attempt at an overview of a single problem. That does not really mean that the answers developed from one question are essential to the next. It is quite likely that you will find one argument, or several, unpersuasive but find some merit in the others. This is to be expected, and you could, for instance, accept the usefulness of the maxims and fallacies at the end of the book having rejected all of the arguments that led me to them. A lawyer might think of this book as a series of severable arguments; even if some fail, the merit of the others might be sufficient for them to work. A philosopher might consider it all either as a structured system of rational conclusions derived from observable premises or as a jumble of aphorisms, but in either case the aphorisms or the conclusions must stand on their own.

1
Law and Office

The administration of the government, like the office of a trustee, must be conducted for the benefit of those entrusted to one's care, not of those to whom it is entrusted.

Cicero, *On Duties*, Book I, Chapter XXV[1]

At the outset, we must deal with two fundamental questions: what is the law, and what are officials? We must have a common understanding of the law and the people who work with it, if we are to consider what implications there are for us, and for them, in what they do. Thus, we must consider what we imagine when we think of laws and officials.

There is a tension between two visions of the law in America, and these views of law color our view of the official. On the one hand, we see the law as a Romantic ideal. Two lawyers stand like gladiators, each fighting for a cause before a judge who decrees a winner and a loser. A president or a senator stands like a Roman of old, pronouncing the law. In each picture, the individual appears as the source of the law, the person acting upon the law and the law acting through the person.[2] Yet we also see a classical ideal, our laws framed and shaped by famous institutions in vast marble buildings, great armies of experts in which the efforts of each individual are only a portion of the whole.[3]

[1] Marcus Tullius Cicero, *De Officiis* 87 (Walter Miller, trans.) (Loeb edn.) (Cambridge, MA: Harvard University Press, 1913).

[2] This thin depiction is taken from George Fletcher's meditations on Isaiah Berlin's model of Romanticism. See George P. Fletcher, "Liberals and Romantics at War: The Problem of Collective Guilt," 111 Yale Law Journal 1499, 1505 (2002), developed further in –, *Romantics at War: Glory and Guilt in the Age of Terrorism* (Princeton University Press, 2002).

[3] This model benefits from Mary Ann Glendon's contrast between the classical and the Romantic model of judges. Her classical judge is objective and rule-centered, whereas her Romantic judge is passionate and above legal technicalities; she prefers the first ideal. See Mary Ann Glendon, *A Nation under Lawyers: How the Crisis in the Legal Profession Is Transforming American Society* (Farrar, Straus, and Giroux, 1994). I suggest that both the classical and the Romantic aesthetics are needed in all legal systems, across all offices (including each judgeship). I think it is better not to consider the Romantic individual overly isolated from the professional institutions and culture that give that individual's

The classical model understands the law to act through "the process," a system of competing groups of officials working among many institutions.[4]

Both visions are accurate to an extent, but each depends on the other for completeness. It is impossible to think meaningfully of the institution without thinking of the individual officials, just as it is impossible to think meaningfully of the officials without considering their institutions. When seen in this light, neither the individuals nor the institutions can disappear. The officials have roles in the institution, and how each person carries out those roles gives the institution meaning.

The institutions of the law are the apparatus of the modern state. They are the bureaucracy, a corporate enterprise, in which every official must act (but within a particular domain) and in which no one official has a claim – or should have a claim – to final authority.[5] Bureaucracy in its fullest sense includes all offices – those who make laws, administer them, adjudicate them. It is the means by which the state achieves anything. Thus judges are a type of bureaucrat, and "legal official" includes a wide variety of administrators, including those who administer the law for individuals, the private attorneys.

With the demise of the traditional kingdom and the rise of the modern state, an evolution that happened in most of Europe and America between about 1450 and 1800, the identification of law, states, and officials became complete. The nature of offices, which in Europe had decayed from the civil service of the Roman Empire to hereditary kingships and personal agents, became robust, independent, and defined by law.[6] Further, the law was created more often by

actions subjective meaning. See Steve Sheppard, "Passion and Nation: War, Crime, and Guilt in the Individual and the Collective," 78 Notre Dame Law Review 751 (2003). Conversely, it is a mistake to pretend an official should make decisions that are dispassionate toward those who are affected by them; that way lies efficiency over right conduct.

[4] "The process" became the popular label for the institutional aspects of the long-running investigation and impeachment of President Clinton in 1998. See, for example, G. B. Trudeau, *Buck Wild Doonesbury* 63 (Andrews McMeel Publishing, 1999). The term was corrupted from a more noble tradition in U.S. law. See, for example, Henry M. Hart, Jr., & Albert Sacks, *Hart & Sacks' The Legal Process: Basic Problems in the Making and Application of Law* (William Eskridge, Jr., & Phillip Frickey, eds.) (Foundation Press, 2001).

[5] The description of the legal system in this section is built on the bureaucratic model of the state developed by Max Weber, influenced by both Aristotelean ideas of the law and Dicean notions of the rule of law. See Max Weber, *Economy and Society* 212–26, 956–63 (Guenther Roth & Claus Wittich, eds., 1978); Jeremy Waldron, *The Law* (Routledge, 1990); Albert V. Dicey, *Introduction to the Study of the Law of the Constitution* (9th ed.) (Macmillan, 1939). See also Steve Sheppard, "The Rule of Law," in *UNESCO Encyclopedia of Life Support Systems* (EOLSS, 2002).

[6] The kings were officials, as were their counselors. See Fritz Kent, *Kingship and Law in the Middle Ages* (Greenwood Press, 1985); Ernst Kantorowicz, *The King's Two Bodies: A Study in Medieval Political Theology* (Princeton University Press, 1997). The primary distinction, which Weber discusses at length, is the move from a charisma to bureaucracy, in which the official no longer is thought to own an office as a grant or patrimony. Yet even the notion of ownership was never without considerable duties and limits implied upon it.

those in legal offices than by those in personal service to an overlord, and by the eighteenth-century dawn of the United States, nearly everything done by the state was done and described through law. Indeed, it was such an increase in legalization of the state that led to a written constitution intended to structure the whole of the new government by law. In America, as in Europe, laws were created and enforced by acts of officials in the name of the people or the prince or the state, even as the prince himself had decreasing influence on their content or their enforcement.

The increase in official management corresponded with a rise in official populations – lawyers, sheriffs, clerks, and other assistants became more specialized and professional, and the officials whose offices were hereditary or honorific increasingly relied on these professionals or accepted some training in their roles. The law became more complicated, particularly given that it was required more often to regulate ever more complicated human activity as trades, technology, and the economy grew and evolved.

The growth in the population of legal officials did not, however, mean that the rules of the law were divorced from the wider culture. Indeed, officials relied then (as now) on the subjects themselves as sources of legal obligation. Laws evolved to enforce private agreements and to recognize customary understandings of reasonable care in what we would now call tort. Some portion of these customary or deliberate extralegal obligations became routinely accepted by officials on behalf of the state from sources among states, as in the treaties and customs of international law. Yet all of it was ratified or created by officers, and everything the officers did was governed by laws.

The offices of contemporary legal systems are public; no official owns the office or may use it with unlimited discretion. With rare exception, there is no sovereign person, no last word. Every decision must be made in accord with the mechanisms of the legal bureaucracy, and every decision is subject to reversal, amendment, or rejection, if not at the time of one dispute then later. The ability to act within the whole of the system is fragmented among hosts of officials, each official having obligations that must be carried out in order for the system to accomplish its goal, and every decision is revisited again and again over time. What defines an official is the holding of an office with this type of power to carry out a function within the bureaucracy of the legal system; and these powers are inherently corporate, contributing to an act by a collective of officials, or acting upon powers conferred by a collective of officials, or directing others among the collective of officials.

Seen this way, the building blocks of a modern legal system are offices, and the essential purpose of offices is to fulfill tasks of the legal system. As Karl Llewellyn quite forcefully put it in explaining that the best way to understand the rules of law was to understand how officials use those rules,

"What . . . officials do about disputes is the law itself."[7] In this way, defining the official is important in the definition of the law, and vice versa. We must do more work to understand how offices interact with laws, particularly the role of rules, discretion, professional culture, and the like, but that the legal system depends on offices, and offices are part and parcel of the system, is essential to any modern understanding of law. Thus, how we see law is essential to how we see offices, and how we understand each will influence how we understand the other.

PERCEPTIONS OF LAW

It is surprisingly difficult to describe the law, and there have been many widely varying descriptions over the centuries.[8] In all events, no single idea about the law will help us to understand the problem of officials, because we understand already that there is more than one viewpoint about the law that will matter. This problem was confronted in the 1950s by the great legal philosopher H. L. A. Hart, who argued that the most influential definitions of law that existed then were limited by one perspective or another, which he described as the internal or external points of view. He rather convincingly showed that neither alone made sense but that any full understanding of law must include both.[9] For the purposes of understanding the role of officials in the legal system, we must consider at least some ways in which the law is perceived by officials and those subject to their authority.[10]

---

7   Karl N. Llewellyn, *The Bramble Bush: The Classic Lectures on Law School and the Law* (Steve Sheppard, ed.) (Oxford University Press, 2008). This line is very often misinterpreted. He is not saying that the law is what officials say it is; he is saying that the way to understand rules of law is by studying how the rules are applied. See the introduction in *id.*

8   For a brief summary see Steve Sheppard, "Jurisprudence and Critical Legal Studies," in *The International Encyclopedia of Political Science* (CQ Press, 2009).

9   Hart's requirement to fully perceive law is to see it as it is seen by those who understand and accept the rules of law, while at the same time to see it as it is seen by those who do not understand but accept the law as a source of rules. Someone who sees a red light and comes to expect people to stop, without much worrying why, has an outsider's view. The insider understands the reasons inherent in the system of rules; the insider knows that the people stop because they are signaled by the red light, which communicates a reason for them to stop. The red light cannot be fully understood as a legal sign except from both perspectives. See Hart, *The Concept of Law* 90 (Oxford University Press, 2d ed., 1997).

10 This division between perspectives differs a bit from Hart's division. Here, we observe officials and subjects rather than insiders and outsiders, so it is a four-square problem: as a matter of fact there are people who hold office with an outsider's view, just as there are citizens who have an insider's view. Often, officials have an insider's perspective, and subjects have an outsider's perspective. See Jeremy Waldron, "Normative (or Ethical) Positivism," in *Hart's Postscript: Essays on the Postscript to The Concept of Law* 411, 424–25 (Jules Coleman, ed.) (Oxford University Press, 2001).

The Law as Perceived by Officials: Archive and Professional Culture

One of the most frequent arguments between officials over the law was whether the king may make judgments of law or if he should fully delegate the royal power over justice to specialists. This was one of the central arguments over the nature of English law, and its settlement has dramatically influenced law in the United States. The argument arose between Sir Edward Coke and James I, in which the judge warned the king that the monarch could not decide a legal dispute, because the king lacked the understanding of the law essential to apply the law accurately:

> Then the King said, that he thought the Law was founded upon reason, and that he and others had reason, as well as the Judges: To which it was answered by me, that true it was, that God had endowed his Majesty with excellent Science, and great endowments of nature; but his Majesty was not learned in the Lawes of his Realm of England, and causes which concern the life, or inheritance, or goods, or fortunes of his Subjects; they are not to be decided by naturall reason but by the artificiall reason and judgment of Law, which Law is an act which requires long study and experience, before that a man can attain to the cognizance of it; And that the Law was the Golden metwand and measure to try the Causes of the Subjects; and which protected his Majesty in safety and peace: With which the King was greatly offended, and said, that then he should be under the Law, which was Treason to affirm, as he said; To which I said, that Bracton saith, *Quod Rex non debet esse sub homine, sed sub Deo et Lege.* (That the King ought not to be under any man but God and the law.)[11]

There is much in this, not the least that the law governs all officials, even the king, governing him so fully that even he could not rightly decide a case except by the law. Once Coke had established that – rather dangerous – point, he'd won the day. He did so not by claiming a mere privilege for his profession, even though this was implied in the argument.[12] He did so by arguing the need for the decisions of law to be made by someone with an insider's skill, an insider's perspective, which Coke and the lawyers had but that the king did not have. James I's perspective was based on a general idea of reason, making him, though the prime official, genuinely an outsider to law as it was understood and practiced in the courts and the private affairs of his subjects.

---

[11] Sir Edward Coke, "Prohibition del Roy" (1607), in 1 *The Selected Writings of Sir Edward Coke* 478, 481.

[12] This cultural subdivision is the hallmark of all professions. Legal institutions are integrated with the profession of law, which is perhaps defined less by the model of the public servant and more by the model of the warring advocate. See Anthony Kronman, *The Lost Lawyer: Failing Ideals of the Legal Profession* (Harvard University Press, 1995). Even so, the profession is still demarcated by common training and culture. See William F. May, *Beleaguered Rulers: The Public Obligation of the Professional* (Westminster John Knox Press, 2001).

Thus, from the dawn of American law, we can see an argument of what law must be, including a tension between the Romantic view of the official, acting alone and from reason, and the institutional, acting within an institutional framework established by laws and customs set down and debated.[13]

The United States has inherited both perspectives. Today there are insiders who understand the latter-day "artificiall reason" of the law. Some of these insiders hold office and some do not. Likewise, most officeholders and most subjects understand the law through actions in the name of law, lacking any general notion of the law but judging its effects in their lives through their "naturall reason." The mix of competing perceptions can thus give rise not only to an identification of the laws that happen to exist in a given system at a given time but also to a definition of laws in general.[14]

Within Coke's arguments we can find the seeds of a very professional under-standing of the law, one concerned specially with the offices that carry it out, and one that reflects his lifetime of study and performance of its many roles.[15] It is, indeed, a model that works well in the present hour. Although the law has changed in its scope and complexity in the United States over four centuries, the basic ideas of law we know today were remarkably apparent to Coke, whose opinions in such modern fields as environmental law, administrative law, cor-porations, criminal procedure, and monopolies, no less than his views on the limits of executive power by law, still offer much for the modern student. It would, in some regards, be odd if the very nature of the law had changed so much in American history that a model of law from its dawn would not work at midday.

---

[13] Of course, the entire legal system does not participate in the lawyer's culture, though the lawyer's culture influences the host of subcultures that compose the cultures of the law. Administrators, civil servants, legislators, clerks, police officers, even chief executives participate in unique subcultures that share identity, belief, and practice with the other subcultures of the law. See, for example, Steven Maynard-Moody and Michael Musheno, *Cops, Teachers, Counselors: Stories from the Front Lines of Public Service* (University of Michigan Press, 2003).

[14] On the internal and external points of view, see Hart, *Concept of Law* 89–91 (2d ed.). There are as many theories dividing the internal and external view of the law as there are legal philosophers. See Brian Z. Tamanaha, *Realistic Socio-Legal Theory: Pragmatism and a Social Theory of Law* 153–4 (Oxford University Press, 1997). The external view, associated with the "bad man" of Holmes's speech, has caused problems, both because the bad man does not always view the law with the detachment that the external point of view requires, and because Holmes does not advocate only an external point of view, even in that speech. See William Twining, "Holmes's Influence on Modern Jurisprudence: Holmes and English and German Jurisprudence: Other People's Power: The Bad Man and English Positivism, 1897–1997," 63 Brooklyn Law Review 189, 208–22 (1997).

[15] Coke served as lawyer to a vast array of clients; was reader in the Inns of Court, Solicitor General, Attorney General, municipal judge, trial judge, Chief Justice of Common Pleas, Chief Justice of King's Bench, Member of Parliament (both as Speaker and as de facto leader of the opposition), Member of the House of Lords, and Member of the Privy Council; was a prolific author of legal texts; and was a not infrequent litigant himself. See Sheppard, "Introduction," in Coke, *Selected Writings*.

Coke argued that the law is a product of man-made reason and judgment of a body of law, which requires long study of its materials and experience in its practice before anyone can understand it. We know from the unusual breadth of Coke's writings what he understood that archive to embrace: the records of parliaments and councils, the reports of cases and the oral arguments of lawyers and judges, the customs of the realm as represented in histories and records, and the natural limitations on law and conduct that arise in interpretation.[16] We know, too, what study and practice he had in mind: the study of students under their masters, the participation in the arguments and conferences of lawyers, and the actual practice of the law, integrating rules with the claims and needs of clients and their antagonists. So, using this quite traditional view, we can reduce these ideas into a statement about the law.

Law is an archive of rules synthesized in a professional culture that manages those rules, and to which everyone in the state is bound.[17] The archive contains the rich array of rules created by officials in the past that regulates the power of the state and records the acts of past officials as they related that power to the lives of citizens then. The archive's rules arise from many sources in many forms, whether they are generated in constitutions, codes, statutes, ordinances, and the like or enunciated in opinions by judges, presidents, or administrators.[18] In a process more clearly seen in the doctrine of sources in international law, the archive is rich with sources whose authority might in truth depend on the nature of the forum addressing a particular question, as well as on that question.[19]

Legal culture is the sum of the cultures of those who act as officials, particularly those who apply the rules for individuals – the lawyers.[20] The practitioners

---

[16] See *id*.

[17] The notion of archive and culture owes a debt to Professor Cover's model of law as *nomos* and narrative. See Robert Cover, "1982 Term – Foreword: Nomos and Narrative," 97 Harvard Law Review 4 (1983), reprinted in *Narrative Violence, and the Law: The Essays of Robert Cover* 95 (Martha Minnow, Michael Ryan & Austin Sarat, eds.) (University of Michigan Press, 1995). It differs in many ways, though.

[18] In the sense of Hart's concept of the law, the archive embraces both primary rules, which apply to citizens, and secondary rules, which apply to officials.

[19] See, for example, Article 38 of the Statute of the International Court of Justice, which ranks sources of law. First are treaties, then custom, and then the "general principles of law recognized by civilized nations"; second are "judicial decisions and the teachings of the most highly qualified publicists of the various nations, as subsidiary means for the determination of rules of law." The *Restatement of the Law of Foreign Relations* gives a different hierarchy, with custom first, then treaties, then general principles common to the major legal systems of the world, though rules from such sources may be divined from international judicial and arbitral tribunals, national courts, the writings of scholars, or generally unchallenged state pronouncements. Restatement of Foreign Relations, 3d §§ 102, 103.

[20] More specifically, it is the sum of the subcultures of officials. Police, the bar, the bench, court reporters, court clerks, legislators, and other groups form distinct subcultures that share a unique cultural form, each arising from their frame of action based on secondary rules

of the culture depend on the archive, in the same way that any culture depends on its narratives, but the culture of any given moment includes both more and less than the archive.[21]

Astute readers will recognize in the idea of legal culture an echo of the old doctrine of the *lex non scripta*, the unwritten law, and there is something to that.[22] The legal culture intersects with the archive, synthesizing it to produce a particular rule or mandate or outcome justified by the application of materials in the archive.[23] The application of different materials into a particular scale of authority, as well as the means of generating new materials, might be subject to rules or practices memorialized in the archive, but such a memorialization will depend on continued understanding and behavior by officials and those who are understood as influential members of the legal culture.

Accordingly, most acts of an official are based to some degree upon rules that can be read from the archive. The meaning and application of those rules – the rules' relationship to the official's action – will depend on the official cultures, some aspects of which are reflected in other rules, and some of which are not; but in every case, the official must apply cultural practices and personal judgment to select and apply rules to a given situation.[24]

of law. See, for example, Pierre Bourdieu, *Distinction: A Social Critique of the Judgement of Taste* (Harvard University Press, 1987).

[21] There has been a continuing study of legal culture over the past century. In its local and social aspects, see, for example, Thomas L. Shaffer and Mary L. Shaffer, *American Lawyers & Their Communities: Ethics in the Legal Profession* (University of Notre Dame Press, 1991); John Henry Merryman, "Law and Development Memoirs II: SLADE," 48 Journal of the American Society of Comparative Law 713 (2000); and Gad Barzalai, *Communities and Law-Politics and Cultures of Legal Identities* (University of Michigan Press, 2003) (considering law among Israeli and Palestinian communities). In its national aspects see H. Patrick Glenn, *Legal Traditions of the World* (Oxford University Press, 2000); Friedrich Karl von Savigny, *Of the Vocation of Our Age for Legislation and Jurisprudence* (Abraham Hayward, trans.) (Batoche, 1999). In its international aspects, see, for example, Brian Z. Tamanaha, A *General Jurisprudence of Law and Society* (Oxford University Press, 2001).

[22] Many people assume that the law must be wholly written to be the law, that "law derives from nothing unwritten." Henry de Bracton, 2 *De Legibus et Consuetudinibus Angliae* 19 (George E. Woodbine, ed., & Samuel E. Thorne, trans.) (Harvard University Press, 1968). Later writers have disagreed. See, for example, William Blackstone, 1 *Commentaries on the Laws of England* *17, *63; Matthew Hale, *The History of the Common Law of England* 22–3 (3d ed. 1739) (Charles M. Gray, ed.) (University of Chicago Press, 2002). The hope that law is reducible to a set of simply written rules is condemned as childishness in Jerome Frank, *Law and the Modern Mind* (Coward-McCann, 1936).

[23] The similarity of the archive to rules and of the culture to interpretation in the debates over open texture and legal indeterminacy is briefly considered in Chapter 3.

[24] The acceptance by other officials of an idea or rule of law is particularly significant in sources of the archive that are either sufficiently new or sufficiently ambiguous that no custom has yet evolved to determine the significance of their statements as law. This might be the best explanation of presidential signing statements. They aren't law in the sense of the statutes they attempt to interpret or explain; they are a part of the archive that has significance only when given it by other officials. See Steve Sheppard, "Presidential Signing Statements: How to Find Them, How to Use Them, and What They Might Mean," 2006 Arkansas Law Notes 87.

Law Perceived by Citizens: Signs and Acts, Impersonal and Personal

The officials' understanding of the law cannot describe how it or its officials are perceived by the people. The typical person subject to the law is unlikely to worry about archives or cultures but will see the law as a homogeneous form, with bits of an archive barely perceived that are applied somehow, by members of a culture that renders the archive more mysterious and more potentially dangerous. For most subjects, the idea of law has two aspects, quite different from the division between archive and culture. The citizen sees the law as at once both personal and impersonal.

As so far described here, the law is impersonal. "The Law" in people's lives is chiefly represented in signs and in narratives. It is in signs, manifestations of the abstraction, as well as in specific commands (or potential commands) in courthouse architecture, police cars, traffic signs, and tax forms. Though the signs are significant, and their perception by the citizenry is important, their use will not be much considered here beyond their contribution to the anonymity of the law.

People fear or trust the abstraction that is the law, as well as the things that are done in its name. Yet these things that happen in people's lives will not be done by some abstraction such as a poem, or by some manifestation such as the Archangel Gabriel. The subject understands too that these things will be done, or not done, by real human beings. Granted, these human beings have a professional culture that in some ways encourages an impersonal aspect. They have a distinct culture within the larger polity; they populate a network of organizations that are largely hierarchical, and many decisions that these people make are only partial or are collaborative. None of these caveats alters the obvious truth that everything that is done or is not done by law is done by individual people. These people are the legal officials.

This is no revelation as a matter of legal scholarship, in which the need to see the human in the system seems to be a recurrent theme. American legal philosophy for the past century has remained fascinated by the individual official. A central aim of writers identified with legal realism and later with critical legal studies, among others, has been to strip away the veneer of impersonal law and to recognize the very personal role played in the law by lawmakers and judges, including their interests and biases.[25]

---

[25] See, for instance, the high-water mark of individualist realism, in Jerome Frank, *Law and the Modern Mind* (Coward-McCann, 1935). The demystifying banner of critical legal studies – law is politics – is defended in Frank Michelman, "Bringing the Law to Life: A Plea for Disenchantment," 74 Cornell Law Review 256 (1989). Pierre Schlag makes a more radical, and wonderfully entertaining, critical statement, in *Laying Down the Law: Mysticism, Fetishism, and the American Legal Mind* (New York University Press, 1996). On the critical observation of the identity of the individual official lost in hierarchy, most associated with Duncan Kennedy, see Steve Sheppard, "The Ghost in the Law School: How

The individual official is most clearly seen in the narratives. There – whether the narrative is a news report of an arrest or a trial, or any of the myriad stories of legal fiction, television, and movie scripts that have captured the popular fancy for the past century – the individual official tends to be the focus of the institution in the narrative. We may be unconscious of the degree to which we vest people with the symbolism of the law, but we do so. In Harper Lee's *To Kill a Mockingbird*, the law is seen in its glory in Atticus Finch, in its uselessness in his judge, in its evil in the biased witnesses and jurors, and even in its rejection by the mob.[26]

Yet, the citizenry echo the language of officialdom, and individual subjects talk of the acts of officials in their aggregate and in the impersonal in the same way the officials do. We speak of "The Law" in an anthropomorphized way. We speak of a judge's opinion as "the opinion of the court." Even the decisions of jurors are collected and rendered as a corporate verdict: "We, the jury." We talk of old opinions not just as John Marshall's opinion but as "the precedent."

In the language of Judge John Noonan, Jr., we have grown used to the masks worn by the lawyers, judges, and administrators, and in doing so, we have dangerously endowed impersonal rule with a false appearance of personality.[27] In considering Justice Holmes's famous edict about "the life of the law," Noonan saw this endowment "attributed to an abstraction the action of living men and women. The Scarecrow was given life."[28] The danger he saw in this was to mistake not only the nature of the law but also the effect on its people. Holmes, Noonan said, "overlooked the actual people in the process. The jar and motion of their experience was replaced by the imaginary adventures of the law."[29] Noonan's observations remain as vital today as when he published these lines in 1976.

It is a mistake to confuse the archive with the culture, but it is an even greater mistake to confuse the culture with the acts of an individual within it. This confusion, although made by officials, reflects the view of the law directed to the citizens, and the view the citizen receives, from personal experience and from cultural depiction, is deeply colored by it. The point of shaking up this confusion – that each act of the law is made, in whole or in part, by an individual – bears restatement from time to time.

Duncan Kennedy Caught the Hierarchy *Zeitgeist* but Missed the Point," 55 Journal of Legal Education 94 (2006).

[26] See, for example, Claudia Johnson, "Without Tradition and Within Reason: Judge Horton and Atticus Finch in Court," 45 Alabama Law Review 483 (1994).

[27] John T. Noonan, Jr., *Persons and Masks of the Law* 1 (Farrar, Straus, and Giroux, 1976). Judge Noonan blamed Oliver Wendell Holmes, Jr., for the personification of the law, but it would misread Noonan not to see he knows the practice is not far older, as Noonan's examples from the dawn of the republic make clear.

[28] *Id.* at 2, criticizing "The life of the law has not been logic: it has been experience." Oliver Wendell Holmes, *The Common Law* 1 (Little Brown & Co., 1881).

[29] *Id.*

Thus, to ask what subjects see in the law is to ask what each subject sees not just in specific signs, such as a speed limit at a given place on a road, or the abstraction as a whole. It is also to ask what subjects understand from the action and inaction of officials: how they trust this person or that person, fear them, need them, rely on them, hope for them, or just encounter their work.

The same can be said for officials themselves, who are, after all, also subject to the law. We can look for meaning in the law by examining the life, the growth or pain or satisfaction in the individual official – the reaction of that individual to the acts of others, whether in horror, admiration, or indifference. Looking to both subjects and officials, we can see in them all the hopes and fears that each has about other people, and we can more comprehensively examine the acts of officials through this lens.

Having settled down to such an observation, the terrifically wide scope of the task of doing so in any useful or interesting manner becomes more apparent. The archive of rules in the law is too large, its rules too numerous and varied – encompassing too many arenas of human conduct and official action – to be organized in any but a summary fashion.

THE CONCEPT OF THE LEGAL OFFICIAL

"Who is a legal official?" might now seem like a question with one obvious answer, but there is little agreement about it among theorists. In part, this is because the definition can be manipulated like other variables in a theory to provide more or less support for different theories about the law. Many theories of law or the legal system are concerned exclusively with judicial behavior, and the conduct of presidents, senators, and legislators is consigned to the world of politics.[30] Some of these theories appear concerned only with appellate judges and not even with trial courts.[31] Others are directed toward the police or agency administrators.[32] Yet there are tools for a theoretical perspective drawn from across the landscape of these varying offices in the late-nineteenth-century work of Max Weber.

---

[30] The classic example is the venerable model of law by John Chipman Gray, *The Nature and Sources of the Law* (1909) (Gaunt, 1999). This distortion of the role of the judge, as if the judge were outside of the bureaucracy, is common in judicial criticism but skews our view of the law as a whole. See, for example, Robert Bork, *A Country I Do Not Recognize: The Legal Assault on American Values* (Hoover Institution Press, 2005); Ran Hirschl, *Towards Juristocracy: The Origins and Consequences of the New Constitutionalism* (Harvard University Press, 2004).

[31] See Alexander Bickel, *The Least Dangerous Branch: The Supreme Court at the Bar of Politics* (Yale University Press, 1986).

[32] See, for example, Edwin J. Delattre, *Character and Cops, 4th Edition: Ethics in Policing* (AEI Press, 2002); A. Fleming Bell II, "Ethics in Public Life," adapted from *Ethics, Conflicts, and Offices: A Guide for Local Officials* (North Carolina Institute of Local Government, 1996).

Weber's careful study of the state accepted the distinctions then prevalent between public law and private law, between government and administration, and between traditional and modern sources of law, but all of these divisions were subsumed in the modern state into his model of bureaucracy.[33] Weber described a complex bureaucratic system, defined by laws, with officials in many distinct roles, none of whom have an ownership interest in their offices, and all of whom are necessary to the comprehensive accomplishment of bureaucratic tasks.[34]

Most important for anyone who would think about the obligations of officials, Weber recognized that officials must be in a morally ambiguous position and could not achieve their tasks without moral compromises.[35] The boundaries of bureaucracy, at least as it defines who is an official within it, are porous. Politics, for instance, is sometimes within and sometimes without, including "all the efforts as a whole made in order to share in the power, or to influence the distribution of power either among the States or among the various groups inside one and the same state."[36]

So, again we see that to consider the roles of all officials is to consider the legal system as a whole, albeit with a priority of concern for the individual over the corporate. Looking at this scale, in the Romantic and classic perspectives at once, allows a multifaceted view of the official that can perceive the working of the system as a whole (including its successes and its failures), a perception that is not possible at a lesser scale. At this scale, we also see a different view of the responsibility of officials for the system.

DEFINING THE OFFICIAL

Returning to the perspectives of the official and of the subject, we can see certain complementary elements in the theory of bureaucracy. The official is

[33] In this, he varies from most American approaches, which treat the bureaucracy as no more than the agencies in the executive branch. See, for example, James Q. Wilson, *Bureaucracy: What Government Agencies Do and Why They Do It* (Basic Books, 1989). There are many other definitions, such as a bureaucracy being any system of limiting management in a manner not affected by profit. See Ludwig von Mises, *Bureaucracy* (Center for Futures Education, 1983).

[34] See Max Weber, "Bureaucracy," in 2 *Economy and Society: An Outline of Interpretive Sociology* 956 (Guenther Roth & Claus Wittich, eds.) (University of California, 1968). Weber included the judge within his model of bureaucracy. See *id.*, 961. Though my understanding of bureaucracy is strongly rooted in Max Weber's initial work, Applbaum's much more accessible essay knits Weber's successors into a new and important narrative, which I have relied on in part in considering the role as a defining element of the official. See Arthur Isak Applbaum, *Ethics for Adversaries: The Morality of Roles in Public and Professional Life* (Princeton University Press, 2000).

[35] See Max Weber, "The Profession and Vocation of Politics," in *Political Writings* 309, 310–11 (Peter Lassman & Donald Speirs, eds.) (Cambridge University Press, 1994).

[36] This translation is from Max Weber, *The Profession of Politics* 2 (Simona Drachici, trans.) (1920) (Plutarch Press, 1989).

likely to consider the archive to define offices through constitutions, statutes, regulations, and the like.[37] They are also, and less clearly defined, roles that are defined functionally and come to be recognized as legal offices through custom. This process, by which the royal *witan* emerged into a divided system of Crown courts, occurs still.[38] It is usually observable in the treatment of assistants assigned to offices already recognized by the archive, as their independence and scope of discretion evolve and enlarge.[39]

The citizen who is subject to the power of officials, however, will consider how the law appears to operate in the nonofficial world. The citizen knows from the many signs in the culture that there are obligations in law that in principle apply to everyone, yet sees all too often that these laws apply selectively, infrequently, with exceptions. What the citizen must do or not do is limited in the law both by the signs the citizen can interpret – the stop sign or the bank guard – but also by the unsolved murder and the foreclosure notice. What the citizen cannot interpret is how or when these signs will be replaced by concrete actions that change the immediate future. The law is a limit, and its manifestation is in officials and the signs they make in general and the acts they take in particular that alter peoples lives, for the better or for the worse.

When these approaches are combined, a definition of the official becomes clear: Legal officials are the individuals in whom all of the powers of the state are allocated, divided among many roles. In each role the official is both empowered and limited by the law, expressed in archival statements of law and by legal customs and cultural expectations, but within this role the official has the sole discretion to act or not to act.

So each person who creates, interprets, applies, or changes the law is – to that degree – a legal official. Thus, a senator is a legal official, but so are members of the senator's staff, whether working on legislation or providing constituent services under the laws. The president and members of the cabinet and their staffs are legal officials not only when passing executive orders and rules but also in creating policies that are enabled by statutes and treaties, or by acting or failing to act to carry out powers given to their offices.[40] Police

---

37 For instance, the U.S. Constitution requires the president to appoint "Officers of the United States, whose Appointments are not herein otherwise provided for, and which shall be established by Law: but the Congress may by Law vest the Appointment of such inferior Officers, as they think proper, in the President alone." U.S. Constitution, Article II, section 2. Custom has dictated and the courts have interpreted who is a principal officer and who is an inferior officer. See, for example, *Morrison v. Olson*, 487 U.S. 654 (1988).

38 See, for example, Daniel Coquillette, *The Anglo-American Legal Heritage*, Chapters 2–10 (2d ed.) (Carolina Academic Press, 2004).

39 A fine current illustration is the judge's secretary or, increasingly, office administrator. See, for example, Stephen L. Wasby, "A Judicial Secretary's Many Roles: Working with an Appellate Judge and Clerks," 7 Journal of Appellate Practice & Process 151 (2005).

40 Policymakers in office cannot avoid their responsibility as legal officials under the law by saying that they are not lawyers or tasked as lawyers. They do, after all, make policy that

officers are legal officials, but so are bailiffs, jailors, and executioners. Lawyers are legal officials, both because they are technically officers of the courts and because they are interpreters of the law for their clients and the public. Jurors are legal officials, and so, when they vote on initiative legislation, are voters.

There are times when an official is acting according to this role and other times when the official is acting as subject. Likewise, there are times (at least in the United States) when a citizen acts in the role of an official, in the limited sense of selecting officials and in the more robust sense of acting as a juror. In this sense, the official is like the medieval king, who was said to have two bodies: the person of the monarch and the office of the monarchy.[41]

This definition does not yet answer one of the enduring questions for officials, which is to what degree conduct in office may be based on the morals, or desires, or conscience of the individual.[42] Still, it must define the office according to power that affects others, those subject to the law. It also provides a scope of personal action that cannot be reduced, one that allows engagement in an archive and a culture but that leaves the individual in a particular role distinct from all other officials, within which the individual official must act or fail to act, which is the scope of the discretion of the office.

Discretion and the Definition of the Legal Office

Every office within the legal system is defined by the legal obligations embedded in that particular office by the rules of law. The definitions of office, both in the obligations to act in the role and in the limit of action within it, are usually signaled by substantive rules that are to be applied by the holder of that office. These are the elemental bases for the rule of law, the idea that no person may govern without being bound by law.[43] Yet, the office also has sufficient authority to carry out its objectives according to the independent will of the

---

arises from law and further applies the law. For instance, when former Undersecretary of Defense for Policy Douglas Feith argued to a House Judiciary Subcommittee that he relied on legal counsel in making his policies allowing humane torture, he could not absolve himself of legal responsibility. It was an odd statement by any lights for an attorney with a J.D. from Georgetown. See Dahlia Lithwick, *Feith in the System*, Slate.com, July 15, 2008.

[41] See Ernst Kantorowicz, *The King's Two Bodies: A Study in Medieval Political Theology* (Princeton University Press, 1997).

[42] See, for example, Stuart Hampshire, "Public and Private Morality," in *Public and Private Morality* (S. Hampshire, ed.) (Cambridge University Press, 1978); Arthur Isak Applbaum, *Ethics for Adversaries: The Morality of Roles in Public and Professional Life* (Princeton University Press, 1999). Officials' definition through roles is a well-established idea. *See*, for example, Woodrow Wilson, *The State: Elements of Historical & Practical Politics* (1889); Max Weber, "Politics as a Vocation" in *From Max Weber* 115 (H. H. Gerth & C. Wright Mills, eds.) (Oxford University Press, 1946).

[43] See Steve Sheppard, "The Rule of Law" (Subject Article 6.31.1), in *UNESCO Encyclopedia of Life Support Systems* (EOLSS, 2002) (available at http://www.eolss.net).

official: there is an inevitable discretion governing the acts of office that is not explained by the rule of law alone.

Isolating Discretion within the Role

Every official role can be understood as the acts to be executed by the official in that role within the legal system. The source and content of these obligations vary among roles. They range from the simple to the complex: from few obligations that are clear, consistent, and unvarying, to many obligations that are vague, conflicting, and mutable.

The content of the whole set of legal obligations may be inchoate – potential only until exercised – and never known for many offices. Many obligations arise as a matter of incompletely articulated custom or as rarely observed written statutes or rules, themselves contingent on rare circumstances. Even so, there tends to be very little confusion or ambiguity apparent in the daily activities of most legal officials, who tend to behave both according to a variety of enacted written rules and according to the customary examples of colleagues and predecessors.

For example, the legal obligations of a justice of the U.S. Supreme Court could be seen as the amalgam arising from the text of the U.S. Constitution of 1789, the precedents of prior Court majorities, the various statutes that enact the jurisdiction for the Court, and the various rules and precedents adopted by the Court, as well as the customs arising from the habits of current and former justices. Similarly, the legal obligations of a New York City police officer arise from the federal and state constitutions, the state statutes, city ordinances, departmental regulations, and, perhaps most often, the customs and oral tradition of current and former officers.[44]

Each of these offices – Supreme Court justice and city beat cop – share certain elements of definition in their legal obligation. The most essential is that both offices have powers that are circumscribed so that they can only be used toward certain ends at certain times and in certain ways. This circumscription is established by the same legal obligations that, within these boundaries, describe

---

[44] Custom is an ancient and constant source of law. Customs ground many forms of legal obligation, for the Joe on the street and for arcane professionals. The law of negligence turns on what the ordinary person might reasonably expect, which is a standard based on custom. Customs and practices provide standards for liability under the common law and admiralty. See, for example, *The T. J. Hooper*, 60 F.2d 737, 740 (2d Cir. 1932) (L. Hand, J.).

For legal officials, the idea of custom as a basis for legal obligation is just as pervasive. For instance, the very idea that courts will follow their precedents is a custom about customs. On a more particular scale, the customs and practices of a police department are considered legal obligations for the purposes of defining police regulations as state laws under the federal laws protecting civil rights. See *Monell v. New York City Department of Social Servs.*, 436 U.S. 658, 694 (1978). These customs have a strong practical influence on the daily operations of a police officer. See Michael Lipsky, *Street-Level Bureaucracy* (Russell Sage Foundation, 1980).

the powers the official controls to act according to the official's substantive discretion. (The duty to do X does not extend beyond doing those things essential to accomplishing X.)

The term "discretion" here may mislead, in that it includes certain obligations that are required by the archive and customs of law (and will be enforced by other officials), some thought good or bad by other officials but not the law (and so will be used as a basis for reputation and preferment by other officials) and some that are optional (and will not be disturbed by other officials). For instance, we say that a prosecutor exercises discretion in bringing indictments against a criminal suspect, but within that discretion there is a host of legal limits on its exercise, limits that arise both from custom and from law.[45] We say that a magistrate has the discretion to grant or deny an extension of a filing deadline, but that discretion has boundaries on its use. For example, allowing unjustified extensions of time to one side in an administrative proceeding may be an abuse of discretion.[46] Even the decision of a deputy clerk in a county courthouse to allow the filing of a court document at a minute or two past the office's closing hour may be seen as an act of discretion that in some situations would be expected as a matter of good conduct; in some instances the same favor would be seen as the illegal abuse of discretion, and in some instances, that favor falls somewhere in between.[47] There are also limits on the exercise of substantive discretion over matters clearly within the powers of the official to act, matters that are committed by the rules of the system to the official.

Role Discretion and the Definition of the Legal Official

There is a trick in defining the role of an official, in that one of its defining aspects is how much the occupant of an office defines the office. In other words, the boundaries of every role are a bit fuzzy, and roles differ in the degree to which the official may define them. It is a matter of history that officials enter roles defined by others and, through their conduct, alter the role. These alterations are sometimes enduring and sometimes not. The role of the U.S. Supreme Court Justice was altered forever by the conduct of Chief Justice

---

[45]　See Kenneth C. Davis, *Discretionary Justice: A Preliminary Inquiry* 189–214 (University of Illinois Press, 1969); Richard Bloom, "Twenty-Eighth Annual Review of Criminal Procedure: II. Preliminary Proceedings: Prosecutorial Discretion," 87 Georgetown Law Journal 1267 (1999).

[46]　For example, in an oversight against abuse of discretion, Congress amended the labor law, 5 U.S.C. § 706, to provide judicial review for extensions of time to unions to comply with demands for explanations of alleged election irregularities. *Hodgson v. International Asso. of Machinists & Aerospace Workers*, 454 F.2d 545, 552 (7th Cir. 1971).

[47]　Clerks' offices have a wide variety of largely customary powers over setting rules and interpreting them. See, for example, Michael D. Webb & David Bird, "The Clerk's Office: An Underutilized Resource," 21-10 American Bankruptcy Institute Journal 32 (2002–2003).

John Marshall, but the role of the Texas trial judge was little altered by Judge Roy Bean.[48]

There are therefore intricate problems created by the borders of discretion, problems that are the defining elements of the office, which we can describe as "role discretion." Role discretion operates like jurisdiction; matters outside the power of an official are for that reason beyond the influence of an official act by the official. (We can leave aside for the moment the problem of how the official might act indirectly by influencing other officials through unofficial channels.) However, these borders of role discretion are themselves set according to a variety of forms of law. Some are set by the dictates of other officials, some according to written rules from various sources of law, and some merely by custom. Some limits are geographic, some are by subject matter, and some turn on other factors such as the person who would be subject to the official's orders.

Consider the discretion, as a matter of substance and of role, of a municipal policeman to make an arrest. In the United States, the limits of a policeman's discretion to arrest are set by city ordinances, including both those that define crimes and those that dictate the policeman's authority to arrest, which they bound by geography (for instance, only within the city limits). The power of the city to enact such ordinances is set by state statutes, which might in themselves constrain the scope of the ordinances. All of these might be restricted in scope by federal law, both in constitutional provisions (such as limits on unreasonable search and seizure) and in statutes (such as those conferring certain immunities), or even treaties (such as a convention recognizing the immunity of ambassadors).

Although this web of sources and limits of discretion might seem to create a fixed wall of role discretion, this appearance is misleading. Many limits are customary, such as the understanding of what is reasonable in many circumstances, which is largely a statement of what has been done in the past in similar circumstances. Not only do the customs change, but also the rules themselves change as new ordinances and statutes are passed, new treaties are entered, and new understandings of the Constitution emerge. These changes all turn on actions of legal officials other than the official who might exercise discretion at a given moment, such as the policeman who might make the arrest.

---

[48] The many paeans to John Marshall as the model of an influential judge include R. Kent Newmyer, *John Marshall and the Heroic Age of the Supreme Court* (Louisiana State University Press, 2002). Roy Bean, a justice of the peace on the Texas frontier, was a more dubious character. See Jack Skiles, *Judge Roy Bean Country* (Texas Tech University Press, 1996); Ruel McDaniel, *Vinegaroon: The Saga of Judge Roy Bean, Law West of the Pecos* (Kessinger Publishing, 2004). Judicial influence on the substance of the law, and the means by which it is acquired, takes many forms; four are explored in Michael Hoeflich & Steve Sheppard, "Legal Scholarship and the Courts in the United States," 28 Zeitschrift für Neuere Rechtsgeschichte 20 (2006).

There are often cases, however, in which either the substantive or role discretion of the official is altered by the action of the official. Indeed, the action of an official might lead to expansion or contraction of the discretion of all similar officials in the future. The critical determinant in an official's alteration of discretion is the acceptance by other officials of the change.[49]

For example, a state judge might find in a case of first impression that a city policeman who arrests a person whom the policeman observes to violate an international law has an implied power to enforce federal laws, even in the absence of a state law specifically conferring that authority. If this decision is upheld by other judges on appeal, and by federal judges on review, the discretion of the policeman may be said to have been increased to allow this act. Prior to the arrest, one might have said, plausibly, that the city officer had no role discretion to arrest an international offender. After the arrest, one might say that the officer's role discretion was in doubt. After judicial approval, one could say, plausibly, that the city officer has this discretion.

This illustration, of course, is of a rare event, and yet the alteration of discretion remains an ongoing affair of significance. Decisions of judges to refuse jurisdiction to hear certain cases, as when the U.S. Supreme Court ruled it would not hear most cases brought against a state by its own citizens, act as limits of discretion for the official.[50] Decisions by Congress to act in new areas expand legislative jurisdiction, and thus expand the discretion of congressional representatives to vote in new areas. These sorts of decisions, however, are just as subject to the later approval of other officials as were the decisions of the policeman to arrest the international crook, imagined above. If other officials determine that the Court must hear cases brought by citizens against their states – for instance, to redress a state denial to those citizens of the equal protection of the laws – they may enact a constitutional amendment, again expanding discretion.[51] And if other officials determine that Congress has expanded its jurisdiction too far, they may refuse to enforce the resulting laws.[52]

---

[49] There are many illustrations, but one is paramount in U.S. history. Judges opposed to slavery who exercised their discretion to free slaves on various pretexts despite the Fugitive Slave Act generally succeeded or failed based on the acceptance or rejection of their decisions by other officials. See Robert M. Cover, *Justice Accused: Antislavery and the Judicial Process* (Yale University Press, 1975).

[50] The court in *Hans v. Louisiana*, 134 U.S. 1 (1890), held that the Eleventh Amendment enshrined state sovereign immunity, even against suits not enumerated in its prohibitions.

[51] See U.S. Constitution, Amendment XIV. Of course, the Fourteenth Amendment does allow actions to be created by Congress for its enforcement, the Eleventh Amendment notwithstanding.

[52] This is the notion behind constitutional judicial review. In *United States v. Morrison*, 529 U.S. 598 (2000), the court ruled that Congress could not enact the Violence Against Women Act under the Commerce Clause, because violence against women involves neither economic activity nor interstate commerce. Like all such decisions, the decision could have been otherwise.

In some cases, an official's exercise of discretion in one office becomes the basis for evaluation by other officials who might promote or remove the official based on their view of the official's performance. This is common enough in administration, but something like it happens when voters consider candidates for office, and it happens when officials with powers of appointment consider potential appointees. When such decisions are made enhancing the authority and prestige of an official for certain forms of conduct, other officials are likely to emulate that conduct, and vice versa.

Thus role discretion is both a complex and a fluid idea. Its very alterability for any given official may be affected both by that official's actions and by the perception of the validity of those actions by later officials. In a democracy, this might be influenced, albeit more indirectly, by the electorate.

The Legal Official in the Culture of the Legal System

The legal system is a network of offices. Each office has a particular role in the network, and the role of that office is usually defined not by the holder but by the existing archive and culture of the legal system. So we say that each official is but a cog in the machine; the machine defines the cogs.

The roles that the archive and the culture of the system play in defining the office were briefly considered earlier. But there is another implication of the legal system in defining an office and its obligations: the official is a member of the culture of the system as a whole, and much of the official's view of the office will be ascertained from the professional and social culture within which that office is framed.

There is nothing surprising in this. Judges tend to be part of a judicial culture. Police culture is the object of endless popular novels and entertainments. Legislators have their own clubs, ranging from the shared experiences of a village council to the lobbyists' restaurants of Washington, D.C.

The fact of official culture gives rise to informal expectations and pressures on every official. What is to be expected from a police officer is not defined as much by a manual or even training programs as by associations, friendships, peer groups, and supervisor's reports. What is expected of legislators is what is defined, usually by what is done by legislative leaders and predecessors. The implications for an official of legal culture, as a culture, can be profound, leading to a moral ecology of officials.

The Moral Ecologies of Legal Officials

The moral ecology is the whole set of norms in a community that are the public consequences of private and public actions, from which every person in the community learns what is accepted as right and good in that community.[53] "Community" in this sense is usually thought of as the public community, the community of all of the people who are subject to the laws. Yet there is no reason not to examine the moral ecology of smaller communities.[54] Like the metaphor from environmental science, ecology can describe a variety of scales from the biosphere to specific biomes to ecosystems of scales running to the microscopic.[55]

"Moral ecology" can apply in discussing human communities, so long as the community is a unit in which common beliefs of what is moral can influence people within the unit in a manner distinct from their effect on those without. In this instance, the legal system is both a single unit and also a cluster of units; it is something like an ecosystem with a variety of interconnected subsystems: the police, courts, judiciary, legislators, administrators, prison guards, and so on each have substantial communities within which a rich moral life continues, and there is a broad, if looser, moral community as their various communities interact in the management of the legal system as a whole. Ideas of what is forbidden or allowed for a police officer will be most developed among police officers in a moral system, yet they will be influenced both by the example of other groups, such as the prosecutors and judges, and by their direct communications of encouragement or discouragement on specific matters.[56] The manner in which these moral ideas affect the members of the community ranges from the highly nuanced forms of communication in which some assent or consensus is developed to very pointed actions in which individuals in the community encourage behavior consonant with the moral ecology and discourage dissonant views and actions. Tools for such encouragement and discouragement range from the small indications of social status that are

[53] Steve Sheppard, "Passion and Nation: War, Crime, and Guilt in the Individual and the Collective," 78 Notre Dame Law Review 751 (2003), citing, among others, Robert P. George, *Making Men Moral: Civil Liberties and Public Morality* (Oxford University Press, 1993).

[54] A nice laboratory for variation among moral ecologies in a single culture may be the differences in hierarchically valued traits that range among summer camps for children; though some attributes – such as athletic prowess for boys and beauty for girls – were universal among middle-class American children in the late twentieth century, different camps, even different cabins, developed different values and created different bases for status. Roger Bennett and Jules Shell, *Camp Camp: Where Fantasy Island Meets Lord of the Flies* (Crown Publishing, 2008).

[55] See, for example, Michael Begon, Colin R. Townsend, & John L. Harper, *Ecology: From Individuals to Ecosystems* (Blackwell Publishing, 2005).

[56] Moral ecology describes both the relationship among norms in a single group and the exchange of ideas about norms with other groups. A full discussion of this idea would be distracting here, but it would include arguments about whether moral realism or moral progress exists along the lines meant by C. S. Lewis when discussing changing morality for the better in *Mere Christianity* (1943) (Touchstone Books, 1996).

common among groups to preferment or rejection from appointments and jobs in the community.

In general, what is done within the particular community of a shared moral ecology will be considered by its participants to be acceptable, to be good for the reason that it is done as part of the culture, part of the tradition: what is done is what should be done. Only a critical perspective, usually from without but occasionally from within, will allow an evaluation of the strength or weaknesses of the morality implied by the beliefs and actions within a single moral ecology.[57]

Understanding this personal and sociological aspect of the legal community and its subgroups is essential in understanding the practical world in which officials develop their understanding both of their legal obligations and of how to carry them out. If there are other obligations, they must arise within this context and have meaning within the context of the group within which the official works.

The Personal Motivation of Officials

Moral ecology is by no means the only source of an official's motivations and goals, and understanding the official requires at least a glancing appreciation of the other influences that led the person to seek office or perform it in one manner or another. To consider this potentially very esoteric question, we can look to something a bit elementary but still essential – why do citizens seek to become officials?[58]

Although the motives of would-be officials and officials themselves are as complicated as those of people in any other profession, the peculiar activities of governance add rare opportunities.[59] A legal official has exceptional chances to pursue a variety of motives that are not available in many careers or life

---

[57] In his role as armchair religious sociologist, C. S. Lewis described such small moral ecosystems as "pockets":

> [M]any of us have had the experience of living in some local pocket of human society – some particular school, college, regiment, or profession where the tone was bad. And inside that pocket certain actions were regarded as merely normal ('Everybody does it') and certain others as impractically virtuous and Quixotic. But when we emerged from that bad society we made the horrible discovery that in the outer world, our 'normal' was the kind of thing that no decent person ever dreamed of doing, and our 'Quixotic' was taken for granted as the minimum standard of decency.

C.S. Lewis, *The Problem of Pain* 56 (1940) (Harper, 1996).

[58] For now, we ignore the involuntary official, particularly the juror, although many of these observations may apply in the venire and the jury rooms as well.

[59] As sociologist C. Wright Mills put it, "The higher politicians do not constitute one psychological type; they cannot be sorted out and understood in terms of any standard set of motives. Like men of other pursuits, politicians, high or low, are sometimes driven by

projects: *Noblesse oblige*, or a sense of a moral responsibility to use one's talents for others.[60] Creativity, or the desire to solve problems, to do something.[61] The fear that one's opponents, or those less capable, will take office.[62] Ambition, or the quest for power for its own sake.[63] Image, respect, or status, the quest for advancement and praise from others.[64] Honor, or a sense of inner satisfaction from acting rightly.[65] When the satisfaction of such motives is an end in life, the roles of governance can take on a peculiar allure. On the other hand, for

technological love of their activities . . . more frequently than others, they are drawn to politics by the prestige that their success brings them. . . . Rarely is it the money. . . . " C. Wright Mills, *The Power Elite* 227 (Oxford University Press, 1956).

[60] Responsibility as a motive to govern is central in the literature, often mingled with other motivations. Cicero believed service was required by both the nature of personal responsibility and the chance for personal attainment. "[T]hose who are equipped by nature to administer affairs must abandon any hesitation to winning office and engage in public life. For only in this way can either the city be ruled or greatness of spirit be displayed in public life." Cicero, *On Duties* 29 (M. T. Griffin and E. M. Atkins, eds.) (*De Officiis*, Book I, v. 72) (Cambridge University Press, 1996). U.S. Senator Paul Simon located this responsibility in Jesus's parable of servants who are rewarded only when they are good stewards of the master's resources. See Paul Simon, *The Glass House: Politics and Morality in the Nation's Capitol* 2 (Continuum, 1984), citing Matthew 25, vv. 14–30. For *noblesse oblige*, see the entry in 3 *International Encyclopedia of Public Policy and Administration* 1500-02 (Jay M. Shafritz, ed.) (Westview Press, 1998). See also David Selbourne's excellent and passionate essay *The Principle of Duty* (Notre Dame Press, 2001).

[61] Creativity, problem solving, and responsibility are all found in the catch-all hope of officials to "make a difference." Among many examples, see Senator Joseph Lieberman's answer to "Why choose public life?" Joseph Lieberman and Michael Dorso, *In Praise of Public Life* 16 (Simon & Schuster, 2000).

[62] This is a motive often masked in modern politics by the notion of qualifications. See, for example, the public basis for Senator Orrin Hatch's campaign for president in 2000: his opponents were "less qualified." See Dana Milbank, *Smashmouth: Two Years in the Gutter with Al Gore and George W. Bush: Notes from the 2000 Campaign Trail* 162 (Basic Books, 2001).

[63] This might be thought of as an authentic will to power. See Friedrich Nietzsche, *The Will to Power* (Walter Kaufman and R. J. Hollingdale, trans.) (Vintage, 1968). A popular contemporary defense of the ambition to govern is in James Champy and Nitin Nohria, *The Arc of Ambition: Defining the Leadership Journey* (Perseus Books, 1999).

[64] Good reputation remains important in modern culture, even if it is less valued and its loss less feared than in the early days of the Republic. Certainly, the dangerous allure of reputation was a centerpiece of discussions of government from classical times to the seventeenth century. See, for example, Sir Walter Raleigh, *The Arts of Empire and Mysteries of State Discabineted in Political and Polemical Aphorisms, Grounded on Authority and Experience, and Illustrated with the Choicest Examples and Historical Observations* (John Milton, 1692).

[65] This sense of honor is both an aspect of duty and a form of image. Pliny the Younger wrote to his son-in-law, Pompeius Falco, answering whether he should practice law while serving as the tribune for the plebeians; Pliny said that this decision, to avoid a conflict of loyalties, required a balance of effects on reputation and honor. See Pliny, *The Letters of the Younger Pliny* (John B. Firth, trans.) (Walter Scott 1900) (Epistulae 1.23). See also A. N. Sherwin-White, *The Letters of Pliny: A Historical and Social Commentary* 138–41 (Oxford University Press, 1985).

some, it may be no more than a job, the simple quest for employment and income.[66]

These motives are complicated. For any one person to decide to serve as an official or to commit an act of office may invoke a group of conflicting emotions and beliefs, as well as assessments of concrete events and their significance.[67] To turn from these motives to an effect derived from the participation in legal office, the question is what conditions are needed for these motivations to appear to the official to be realized in the official's life.

Achievement

The first condition is achievement. *Noblesse oblige*, making a difference in people's lives, creativity – all of these ideals turn upon the ability of the official to engage in some conduct that results in a state of affairs that the official believed was contingent on the official's actions. For at least some of these motives to be satisfied, the official must perform some deeds in office that satisfy the official's ambitions.

Achievement is, however, only a small part of this alloy of ambitions. For many ambitions to be realized will depend on the image created by the official in office. That image may well vary as it is perceived by the official contemplating his or her conduct, by the family and friends of the official, by other officials, and by subjects.[68]

Image

Self-image: How the official perceives herself or himself in the role of office depends predominately on the judgment of the official alone. Of course, opinions of others, as well as cultural artifacts, may reinforce, challenge, or refine the official's own judgment, in what is known to psychology as the reflected

---

[66] That someone pursues an office for its salary or employment does not bar that person from wanting to do good by it. Indeed, most often these goals are probably complementary, allowing personal benefit while promoting the good of others. See Kathleen Nott, *The Good Want Power: An Essay in the Psychological Possibilities of Liberalism* (Basic Books, 1977).

[67] Professionals in philosophy and in psychology see motives differently. Motive to a philosopher tends to be predominately a rational enterprise. Motive to a psychologist is likely to be significantly emotional, based on questions of cognition and tendency. See, for example, Eva Dreikurs Ferguson, *Motivation: A Biosocial and Cognitive Integration of Motivation and Emotion* (Oxford University Press, 2000).

[68] Durkheim evaluated the moral and juridical links between the professional and the entities through which morals must be interpreted – the self, the family, the profession, and the political group. My evaluation roughly corresponds to Durkheim's, with some differences (such as a wider scope for private image than the family rules Durkheim explored). I suspect judgment affects image a bit like Hart's notion of social facts, which comports with Durkheim's moral and civic rules. See Emile Durkheim, *Professional Ethics and Civic Morals* (Cornelia Brookfield, trans.) (Routledge, 1957).

self.[69] Even so, whether an official has fulfilled a duty, or acted responsibly, or been creative, or maintained a sense of personal honor, or not done these things can be judged, at least in the first instance, by the official, through comparison to some benchmarks of behavior. These benchmarks are likely to be complicated, but they will in essence be the combination of motivations, examples, and morals that the official personally accepts as appropriate guides for self-evaluation. For now, we can at least imagine that concepts of morality, ethics, and religion and other standards for right action compete with less noble inclinations as well as self-serving rationalizations, including some degree of sloth, thoughtlessness, repetition, and conflict avoidance. This complexity is increased owing to the effects of time. One's self-image is hardly based on one's immediate actions alone. It is the cumulative result of the evaluation of actions remembered. We also must accept the possibility that for many people this process is not fully understood, much less articulated.

Reflected Image: Image in the judgment of others is essential to the realization of some motivations for office. By definition, ambition and power are satisfied through the acquiescence of others. But more subtle aspects of image and status also must depend on the judgment of others. Good reputation is sought by most officials regardless of the motives that excited their interest in office.[70]

[69] The reflected self is constructed for and among intimates, as opposed to a social comparison or social self, which is constructed for public consumption. Compare Dianne M. Tice and Harry M. Wallace, *The Reflected Self: Creating Yourself as (You Think) Others See You*, with David Dunning, "The Relation of Self to Social Perception," in *Handbook of Self and Identity* (Guilford Press, 2003). Examples of social identity occur when an official might find ideals of office through its popular depiction. For a laugh, see David Ray Papke, "Crusading Hero, Devoted Teacher, and Sympathetic Failure: The Self-Image of the Law Professor in Hollywood Cinema and in Real Life, Too," 28 Vermont Law Review 957 (2004). There are lots of arguments at the margins on these questions. See, for example, Bernard Crick, "Reading Nineteen Eighty-Four as Satire," in *Essays on Politics and Literature* 133, 140–2 (Edinburgh University Press, 1989).

[70] We might suppose some officials feel there is no one whose respect they care to maintain, no one from whom they fear shame. Such arrogance is precisely the basis for the corruption of power. When penning his famous aphorism, Acton was talking of standards of moral judgment for popes, kings, and other absolute rulers, arguing their actions are appropriately to be judged by a higher standard than would apply to ordinary subjects.

> Historic responsibility has to make up for the want of legal responsibility. Power tends to corrupt and absolute power corrupts absolutely. Great men are almost always bad men, even when they exercise influence and not authority: still more when you superadd the tendency or the certainty of corruption by authority. There is no worse heresy than that the office sanctifies the holder of it.

John Emerich Edward Dalberg-Acton, *Essays on Freedom and Power* 364 (Beacon Press, 1948). The paradigmatic case may be Emperor Tiberius after the death of his mother, Agrippina. Tacitus seems to believe that his unanswerable power drove him insane. Tacitus, *Annals*, Book XIV in *Complete Works of Tacitus* (Alfred John Church and William Jackson Brodribb, trans.) (Random House, 1942) (available in Latin and English at www.perseus.org).

The roster of those whose judgment could matter to an official will vary, contingent on both the person and the office, but there is another dimension of image among others in its narrowest domain – the official's private image. This is the image of the official held by one's friends, family, mentors – those in whom some bond of loyalty or similar personal investment makes opinion particularly distinct and significant to the official. It is likely, though, that some of those people will be in a position to judge, and have their judgments count with the person being judged, owing to relationships with the official that arose through some form of respect or dependence, as a child respects a parent, or a student respects a teacher.[71] While the respect of peers, elites, and even the people may matter greatly to the official, the form of reliance from which a private image has meaning may be different. The private image may be of particular significance in the refinement of self-image.

Private Image: Private image will be subject to all of the potential sources of rules for judgment that personal image is, although these sources will be applied through two distinct lenses. The first lens is the nature of judging others rather than oneself. We do not always judge others by the same standards of conduct we expect of ourselves, and the variation may be more or less harsh or stringent, depending on the individual. The second lens is that of loyalty. The very nature of the private image requires that it be one that is held within a small community of friends and family, those who are defined by their relationship and whose relationship will alter how they see one another. This lens can also alter the standards of evaluation that might be applied otherwise.[72] Neither the judgment of others nor loyalty will necessarily result in a more benign form of judgment by the officials' friends and family than they might make of their own acts, but experience suggests that this will often be the case. In such instances, though, a condemnation within that community, a criticism of that private image by those who form it, may be particularly significant to the official.

Public Image: At the next larger extent of community one finds a public image, which may vary considerably to the degree an official has a reputation or image among other officials or among subjects. Officials are often deeply interested in how other officials perceive them.

---

[71] Aristotle was interested in the people before whom we might feel ashamed. They are people "whom we admire, or who admire us, or by whom we wish to be admired, or from whom we desire some service that we shall not obtain if we forfeit their good opinion." Aristotle, *De Rhetorica* 1384b in *Complete Works of Aristotle* 2152, 2205-06 (W. Rhys Roberts, trans.) (Jonathan Barnes, ed.) (Princeton University Press, 1984).

[72] My views of loyalty developed in the shade cast by George Fletcher's book *Loyalty: An Essay on the Morality of Relationships* (Oxford University Press, 1995).

Officials assess other officials not only according to the statements in the archive but also according to the norms of the legal culture. More particularly, perhaps, officials assess others according to the subculture that predominates within each community of officeholders. The archive of laws provides the rules for work, for certain ground rules for success, in the official's employment. The secondary rules of the law – the constitution and procedures of the legal system – provide the particular dimension of both law creation and compliance, which generally only other officials know. Necessarily, the ways in which an official complies with the laws are different from those of the subject, and the forms of judgments by other officials are more complex and less tied to the risk of punishment.

The communities of officials within the legal system operate like other communities. Social rules evolve within the subculture, and deviation from these rules is the basis of criticism by its members.[73] Some few of these rules are reflected in or derived from the laws themselves. So officials assess themselves and other officials according to standards of conduct within the community that operate as social rules, not only according to legal rules. Only a few of those social rules are likely to be reflected in the constitution, rules of the law, or official codes of conduct. None of them need to be recognized as laws must be, although they can be and are, if haphazardly.

For instance, some courts have attempted to use rules to speed judges along to issue opinions.[74] Rules in this context may be laws, but their injunctions are hardly more than the stuff of social rules. The judges have life tenure and only very rarely face any formal sanction. The rules reflect preexisting culture or at least its ideals – social expectations before the rules were adopted. Variations from the written rules are as subject to criticism as deviation from the social

---

[73] Hart distinguished culture, or social rules, from mere habits. When social rules set a standard,

> not only is such criticism in fact made but deviation from the standard is generally accepted as a good reason for making it. Criticism for deviation is regarded as legitimate or justified in this sense, as are demands for compliance with the standard when deviation is threatened. Moreover, except by a minority of hardened offenders, such criticism and demands are generally regarded as legitimate, or made with good reason, both by those who make them and those to whom they are made.

Hart, *Concept of Law* 54–5 (2d ed.).

[74] See, for example, the U.S. Court of Appeals for the Seventh Circuit's Operating Procedures, Presumptive Times for Action. The flow of an opinion is choreographed with times, punctuated with admonitions on the hierarchy of job duties, with judges to research and draft an opinion in 90 days or no more than 180 days, with responses in 10 days, and further opinions in 28. Seventh Circuit Rules, Appendix 9 (2005). As an example of judges making rules for themselves, note the conditional language, intermingled with the declarative. This rule is unusual in its detail as well as its didactic prose. More typical is the Eighth Circuit rule, which is more informative to the lawyers than demanding of the judges. Eighth Circuit Rules, Appendix Rule IV.A describes the opinion-writing process and concludes, "The court strives to issue all opinions within ninety days after argument."

rule had been before. Judges who are thought by their colleagues to take just a bit too long to write their opinions may be criticized by them for that reason. The slow-moving judge could lose reputation. Of course, speed is not the only measure by which judges evaluate one another. The quality of a judge's writing and reasoning in opinions, the sense that the opinion is accurate in its summary of the record and use of the precedent, that it is fair and wise – such criteria are rarely reduced to rules. (At least such criteria are not rules in the Seventh Circuit.) But, they are at least as likely to be the basis for the reputation of a judge as is speed.

In all, the bases for criticism of an official by other officials are rather like professional reputation generally. Officials in each subset of the legal institution – administrators, judges, legislators, police officers – belong to communities with social rules that are the basis for reputation and criticism.[75] Some of these rules are also enacted as formal rules of law, usually as procedures, but sometimes as quasi-primary rules that are limited to apply to the official, such as liability standards for harms to others from violations of law within the scope of one's office.[76]

The public image of an official held by a subject, or the subjects as a group, will vary widely according to the subjects' knowledge of, or at least perception of, the individual as well as of the legal system as a whole. It will also vary according to the perceived role of the particular official. Certainly, some officials have a public image among subjects, formed by the subjects' observation of or awareness of officials' actions. The policeman on the street corner is known and judged by passersby; the judge is known and judged by litigants and lawyers in the courtroom, the administrator by petitioners, and so on.

A relatively few officials have a specific public image formed by secondhand accounts filtered from observers to others. Presidents and governors receive particular attention in the press for their official actions, and occasionally other officials develop a public persona in that manner. This is especially the case for elected officials, which in many states include judges and agency heads.[77]

---

[75] Durkheim recognized that the members of the public would not be bothered by violations of distinct norms within a profession but would nonetheless criticize violations of general civic morals. Emile Durkheim, *Professional Ethics and Civic Morals* (Cornelia Brookfield, trans.) (Routledge, 1957). Even so, one of the hallmarks of a profession is the development of a specific ethical culture, which often varies from more general morals. See John Kultgen, *Ethics and Professionalism* (University of Pennsylvania Press, 1988).

[76] This is the point of 42 U.S.C. § 1983, which establishes federal civil liability only for people who violate rights secured by the Constitution and certain statutes, if those people are acting "under color of state law," which means they are either officials or in a quasi-official capacity.

[77] For example, in 2004 in North Carolina, voters elected the governor, lieutenant governor, attorney general, auditor, commissioner of agriculture, commissioner of insurance, commissioner of labor, secretary of state, superintendent of public instruction, members

Candidates for election or reelection must create a public image in their election campaigns, although for many offices, garnering sufficient attention for the image to have any detail is quite difficult.

Still, much of the subject's perception of any given official is partial and impersonal, aggregated over many different individuals, and then parceled back to the image of an agent of a corporate mass. It is the expectation we have of the policeman known only by the uniform, not by the conduct of the individual. In many instances, this corporate image is often secondhand, based not just on the perceptions of others but on perceptions that may range from the truthful to the inaccurate to the grossly false, marketed for the political benefit of those who would influence the law or politics of the state.[78] On the other hand, that image may also reflect the accumulated wisdom of personal experience of many subjects with officials as a group over time.[79]

Aggregated Image: The image formed by such aggregated perceptions is almost beyond the official's influence, but not quite. The subjects' image of the official is likely to be anonymous, owing to the corporate nature of many actions by officials. The law is the product of many officials in their different

---

of the two houses of the state legislature, and the county commissioners, and in each county the registrar of deeds, all on a straight party ticket. Voters were allowed choices without regard to party affiliation for supreme court justices, appeals court judges, superior court judges, district court judges, and the County Soil & Water Conservation Board. Sample Ballot, Wake County, North Carolina, at http://msweb03.co.wake.nc.us/bordelec/downloads/2004_nov_composite_bal.htm. This list does not account for state offices elected in staggered years, which in 2002 included the district attorney, clerk of the superior court, members of the county board of education, and the soil and water conservation district supervisor. Sample Ballot, Forsythe County, North Carolina, at http://www.forsyth.nc.us/elections/0041102/041102GenElecSampleBallot.pdf (last visited July 19, 2008).

[78]   In recent years, America has been beset with tales of "activist judges," "out-of-touch judges," and "runaway juries." The public has grown to accept these labels, based usually on rare and exceptional cases, without much noticing that the labels are used toward a political end of limiting liability for corporate defendants. Neither has the public noticed that the data do not support these labels generally, nor has it recognized the contradictions in these depictions, such as the significance of seeking to have judges that are "in touch." See, for example, Mary R. Rose and Neil Vidmar, "Commentary: The Bronx 'Bronx Jury': A Profile of Civil Jury Awards in New York Counties," 80 Texas Law Review 1889 (2002); Theodore Eisenberg & Martin T. Wells, "Trial Outcomes and Demographics: Is There a Bronx Effect?" 80 Texas Law Review 1839 (2002). For the effect on officials', or at least judges', public image from these attacks, see Dahlia Lithwick, "Needles and Threats," *Slate*, April 5, 2005 (available at http://www.slate.com/id/2116256/) (last visited July 19, 2008).

[79]   Perceptions of unfair treatment, particularly unfair treatment by race, are widely held among members of some racially defined communities in the United States. These anecdotal perceptions are widespread and may not be statistically unfair depictions of official action. See, for example, Adero S. Jernigan, "Driving While Black: Racial Profiling in America," 25 Law and Psychology Review 125 (2000); Sherri Sharma, "Beyond 'Driving While Black' and 'Flying While Brown': Using Intersectionality to Uncover the Gendered Aspects of Racial Profiling," 12 Columbia Journal of Gender & Law 275 (2003).

tasks. In this sense, the law is managed rather in the way that a car used to be the result of many laborers on a production line. Each is the result of a division of labor, and so the labor of an individual is difficult to disaggregate from the whole, particularly for a subject who lacks detailed knowledge of the legal system.

Even so, this image is the one that is most likely to be capable of alteration by the official. Influencing others to improve or diminish the image of officials in the perception of the subject may improve or degrade the official's image itself.

One aspect of official image, whether perceived by oneself, one's friends, or one's official colleagues, but particularly by the polity at large, is the response of the official to the law. We can reconsider the effects of the law on the subject, recognizing that in the modern legal system, officials are subjects in all regards outside their official role.[80]

Even so, the subject's perception of the official will be influenced by an understood asymmetry in both responsibility and opportunity. The official must take this understanding into account as well, when considering not only the official's own image but also the official's share in the aggregate image of the community of legal officials. Thus, it is understood that officials will often be treated differently for violations of law than would subjects, no matter how often officials themselves might repeat that no one is above the law. The fact that the lawbreaker is an official will reduce the potential for mistaken or negligent treatment by other officials. That the official knows the procedures of the legal system will reduce fear of the unknown. On the other hand, the need to demonstrate fairness to all may result in prosecutions of officials for acts that would be ignored if done by a subject. Political loyalties and conflicts that beset many legal officials may exacerbate these distortions of treatment as well.

But the difference in treatment by the law is less essential to the official's own image than is the difference in responsibility to the law. The image of the official in the eye of the subject turns most on the activity of the official in managing

---

[80] A few anachronistic exceptions persist, such as the monarch of England, who is effectively immune from some laws. Other immunities persist because of the role of office, such as the immunity given to foreign heads of state, although this custom may be somewhat in decline. See *United States v. Noriega*, 117 F.3d 1206 (11th Cir. 1997); *Regina v. Bow St. Metropolitan Stipendiary Magistrate and Others, ex parte Pinochet Ugarte* (No. 3), 1 A.C. 147 (H.L. 1999).

This customary immunity is subject to the loss of recognition by legal officials owing both to changes in the formal laws, such as the Torture Convention, and to more fundamental changes in culture that do not allow sovereignty to excuse certain actions of great evil that would contradict the justifications for a sovereign existence. See Winston P. Nagan and Craig Hammer, "The Changing Character of Sovereignty in International Law and International Relations," 43 Columbia Journal of Transnational Law 141 (2004). In essence, the idea that the king can do no wrong is in decline. See Guy I. Seidman, "The Origins of Accountability: Everything I Know about the Sovereign's Immunity, I Learned from King Henry III," 49 Saint Louis University Law Journal 393 (2005).

the effects of the law in the subject's life. Officials are the people who bring the fear of the law into the subject's life, who satisfy needs and fears (whether created by officials, other subjects, or circumstance), who create the norms and alter the identity. In each decision by the legal official, the law will either directly or indirectly alter these effects, producing new results for the subjects affected, for the community of subjects as a whole, and for the institutions of law.[81] Accordingly, each official will gain satisfaction, praise, condemnation, or untroubled obscurity according to how that official and others perceive the effects of the law in the citizen's world.

Thus, at its core, the image of the official among subjects turns on the nature of the law itself, as it affects the subjects. The fears, needs, norms, and identity of the subject are influenced by what the official does and how the official does things. If the subject believes that only those subjects who have truly committed crimes are arrested and tried for them, then the innocent subject is likely to trust the official, the criminal is likely to fear the official, and neither is likely to hate the official. The converse is also true, and variations on this theme are legion.

Anxiety

In this initial survey of the effects of law upon officials, one additional aspect deserves mention. For most competent people, authority brings anxiety. It is hard to make the right decision, confronted with difficult problems and usually with inadequate resources. As Chief Justice John Roberts said in 2005, after a lifetime of appearing as a lawyer before courts: after becoming a judge he discovered that "deciding the cases was a lot harder than I thought it would be.... I've found that I had to spend a lot more time than I thought I would just getting to the first step of what the right answer would be.... As a judge you actually do have to decide."[82]

The need to exercise authority brings with it the difficulty of decision. That decision is made in the light of all of the consequences each decision carries for the official in that official's sense of honor and self-perception, and every decision risks a loss of reputation in some manner or another. The procedures for decision, the social rules of the community of legal officials, the hopes and fears of the subjects are all affected by every action. The anxiety of doing the job well is, for many officials, a constant feature of office.

---

[81] This is one way of understanding Kelsen's idea that the basic norm of the legal system changes with changes in the law. See Hans Kelsen, *General Theory of Norms*, especially 144–6 (Michael Hartney, trans.) (Oxford University Press, 1991); J. W. Harris, *Legal Philosophies* 74–80 (2d ed.) (Butterworths, 1997).

[82] John G. Roberts, Speech at Wake Forest University School of Law, February 25, 2005, recording at http://www.npr.org/templates/story/story.php?storyId =4795796 (last visited July 19, 2008).

Personal Motivation and Moral Ecology

If an official perceives that the way to achieve goals in office and to have a comfortable self-identity, an acceptable public identity, and a diminished degree of anxiety is to conform to a particular mode of behavior in office, that is likely to be how the official will behave. There is nothing, at least in this series of motives (we are leaving aside a personal sense of morality), that would require that mode of behavior to be written in a book brought down through time from other officials. Rather it will be the culture in which the official carries out the office: the agreement, praise, and respect garnered from certain acts, or the resistance and shame that come from others. The motivations of individuals applied to given cases are thus influenced by moral ecology, and moral ecology sets parameters for not only the likely realization of a given motivation but even its formation. Both the motivations of individuals and the moral ecology of officials as a collective influence the culture of the law.

Moral ecology is, in this sense, part and parcel of the culture of the legal officials. Insofar as that culture is integral to the interpretation, application, and understanding of the law, the moral ecology of legal officials is itself a defining element of the law, influencing the way in which officials make decisions and carry out (or don't carry out) actions of office.

THE LEGAL OBLIGATIONS OF LEGAL OFFICIALS

The nature of a legal official is to be responsible for a set of duties and powers that are – at least in some degree – derived from the archive and the culture of the law. The manner in which these duties and powers are carried out is also – again at least in some degree – defined or derived from law. To the degree that the powers and duties of officials and the manner in which they are exercised are derived from laws, these are the legal obligations of the officials.

It is important to remember that, though we often think of laws as strictly what is written, this is not really true. It has never been true.[83] Written requirements of the law can only form the archive, and the practice of the law – the customs and culture that individual officials learn and emulate – is rarely written down. Indeed, what few writings there are tend to be either broadly phrased codes of conduct or specific cases in which officials are found to violate the customs.

The laws – both culture and archive; both unwritten and written – are a preeminent source of officials' legal obligations, but further obligations

---

[83] On the problems of divining legal practice from the written record, see, for example, J. H. Baker, *The Law's Two Bodies: Some Evidential Problems in English Legal History* (Oxford University Press, 2001).

arise from conditions derived from their position in the legal system. So, officials have many obligations to act when someone else performs or fails to perform a legal obligation. Some officials have the power to act within their broad powers limited to actions approved or allowed by supervisors. Some officials have broad obligations of investigation or action that cannot be seen as specific obligations to investigate or act on one matter or another, which imply obligations on that official to choose among possible investigations and actions, according to that official's understanding of the duties of office.

Regardless of whether an official acts in response to the conduct of others, at the moment in which any official acts, there is a complex range of legal obligations that could dictate that action. This range, even for a single official act, may encompass a host of obligations, some of which are clear and unambiguous, but some of which are ill defined and vague, and some of which conflict in ways that are difficult or impossible to reconcile.[84]

This conflict is a pervasive element of the common law, and it is most often seen in the distinctions between majority and dissenting opinions on appellate courts, which often do not reflect disagreements over the application of a given standard but reflect disagreement over which of two conflicting standards applies. Given stark consequences in applying one analysis or another, the answer is thus ordained by the question. Was the constitutionality of a sodomy statute in *Bowers v. Hardwick* a question of the right to privacy or of police powers?[85] Was the legality of a presidential election's recount in *Bush v. Gore* a question of equal protection or of federalism?[86] Choices between conflicting bases for judicial analyses tend to be the basis for the most enduringly important dissenting views from the bench. Even so, it remains the legal official's responsibility not only to recognize the existence and nature of all of these obligations but also to choose the obligations that will be the basis for the legal action.

Within that responsibility to the law, as seen in this sort of breadth, officials have a critical responsibility in deciding to obey or to reject the law. Official obedience to the laws that govern officials is a requirement for the continuation

---

[84] See Anita S. Krishnakumar, "On the Evolution of the Canonical Dissent," 52 Rutgers Law Review 781 (2000).

[85] See 478 U.S. 186 (1986), in which Justice White analyzed sodomy laws as a matter of valid state police powers, but Justice Blackmun dissented, seeing the question as one of privacy. Blackmun's view carried the day in *Lawrence v. Texas*, 539 U.S. 558 (2003).

[86] In 531 U.S. 98 (2000), a majority found that Florida violated the Equal Protection Clause by using different vote-counting methods in different counties, and that no recount could be completed by a state-imposed deadline for recounts. Justice Stevens and three others argued that the state courts could interpret state election laws to craft an appropriate remedy in a state matter. The effect of the majority opinion was to uphold a contested certification of George W. Bush as the winner, making him president of the United States.

of a legal system. When a body of officials rejects the legal system, the system fails just as surely as if the subjects revolt against the state.[87]

The Sources of Officials' Legal Obligations to Act

We might consider that the sources for a legal official's actions are direct and simple. For instance, a police officer's decision to cite a driver for speeding might be based on the comparison of one legal source to one practical fact: a legal speed zone sets a maximum speed, and the officer observed the driver exceeding that speed in the zone.

The sources of an official's action might appear more complex but still be based on practical reasons for action. For example, a legislator's decision to vote to pass legislation setting a given speed limit might turn on a complicated balance of perceived political concerns and federal highway regulations. Or, the decision of a judge to free an arrested speeder might rely on ideas of the basic requirement that laws be specific, or it could rely on the powers of states, or even the public good.[88]

These views, though, are rather incomplete. It is true that the discussion of legal discretion in the Anglo-American tradition is preoccupied with the judge as the official exercising discretion, as well, perhaps, as fears of the use of that discretion.[89] The problem of discretion throughout the whole of the legal system is much broader, and in its breadth illustrates further the problem of discretion even in the judicial case.

Some observers distinguish the freedom of decision of a judge from that of a legislator or executive official, reserving the idea of discretion only to one office or another. The differences between these offices are described as differences in the forms of constraint in the sources of legitimate action, the relative breadth of sources of legitimate action, or the type of official who could countermand an act or discipline the official.[90] This type of political hair-splitting can be depicted by an irregular verb: "I act in my discretion; you act on extralegal principles; he exceeds his authority." Such moves have yet to gain enough ground in the language, however, to allow the usage of the term "discretion"

---

[87] This problem is considered further in Chapter 2.

[88] For instance, in *State v. Stanko*, 974 P.2d 1132 (Mont. 1998), a state speed limit of "reasonable and prudent" was void as unconstitutionally vague. See Robert E. King and Cass R. Sunstein, "Doing Without Speed Limits," 79 Boston University Law Review 155 (1999).

[89] See, for example, R. Kent Greenawalt, "Discretion and Judicial Decision: The Elusive Quest for the Fetters That Bind Judges," 75 Columbia Law Review 359, 363, 378 (1975).

[90] See George C. Christie, "An Essay on Discretion," 747 Duke Law Journal 753–4 (1986). Discretion is sometimes categorized, usually dividing between the manner in which an official is to exercise independent judgment and the reasons for allowing the exercise of independent judgment. See Carl E. Schneider, "Discretion and Rules: A Lawyer's View," in *The Uses of Discretion* 47 (Keith Hawkins, ed.) (Oxford University Press, 1991).

to be committed to one type of office or another.[91] Once we consider the full legal bases for a decision, the whole set of such bases includes these ideas of practical reasons from legal sources, but it must include much more as the implications of these sources become more apparent.

Officials' Discretion Regarding Sources of Obligations to Act

The complex network of any one legal official's interrelated obligations is created by hosts of officials, working over time. Officials work in many groups (some of these individuals and groups having philosophically or politically opposed interests) to produce the artifacts of legal materials. These materials run the gamut of statutes, judicial opinions, agency rules, treaties, ordinances, executive orders, constitutional provisions, scholarly writings, and customary practices, multiplied beyond number over time and across jurisdictions.

This mass of laws leads to well-known problems of fit and of conflict. Despite such a plethora of laws, experience quickly shows that it is quite rare for a single legal obligation to perfectly answer many questions, leaving the ever-present difficulty of "legal interstices," the gaps between obligations caused by the imperfect fit between an obligation described or applied to one situation when considered in the light of a new, slightly different situation. This is sometimes called the open texture of law, in which its obligations are refined as needed over time.[92] Further, so many obligations from so many sources lead very often to conflict among obligations, or among the potential consequences of satisfying or failing to satisfy an obligation.

An official who acts at a juncture of legal obligations in which the fit between action and legal obligation is not perfect, or in which there is an appearance of conflict among obligations, is often said to be exercising discretion. Many ideas are packed into the term "discretion" here, which Dean Ed Rubin described as "a musty old term redolent of palace intrigue" that remains central in our descriptions of bureaucratic processes of supervision and policymaking, despite being of little value in describing how these processes are carried out.[93] In this sense, it is very much a generic term for the power or authority of an official to select the outcome of a particular decision and the reasons for it.[94] In order to distinguish this sense of discretion from another

---

[91] Illustrations of the irregular verb are in two superb manuals of legal administration. See Jonathan Lynn and Anthony Jay, eds., *The Complete Yes Minister: The Diaries of a Cabinet Minister by the Right Hon. James Hacker, M.P.* (BBC Publications, 1984); *Yes, Prime Minister: The Diaries of the Right Hon. James Hacker* (Salem House, 1986).

[92] See Hart, *The Concept of Law* 124–55 (2d ed.) (1994).

[93] See Edward L. Rubin, "Discretion and Its Discontents," 72 Chicago-Kent Law Review 1226, 1229, 1336 (1997).

[94] This definition might seem insufficient because it is too general to account for Ronald Dworkin's early division of weak from strong discretion, or discretion that is more or less

to be discussed later, we might describe this sense of discretion as "substantive discretion," to represent the discretion to select the substantive grounds for action. The other form of discretion, which I have been calling here "role discretion," is the ability of the official to affect the definition of the official's own office.[95]

Derivatively it follows that substantive discretion is the tool by which officials may select among sources of obligation to ascertain the obligations according to which they will act. The exercise of substantive discretion affects both the action taken and the obligations that were potentially and actually acted upon. When an official chooses to act in a given situation according to one obligation, that action is evaluated by other officials in the light of that obligation as opposed to others. Further, when other officials are later confronted with the decision to act in similar situations, the earlier selection of one obligation by a predecessor is likely to influence the later officials to act in accordance with that same obligation.

Patterns in the Applications: Conflict and Reconciliation

Lawyers and scholars battled throughout the twentieth century over the existence and significance of the problems of conflict among legal obligations and fit between obligations and actions. At this stage, the question is not so much whether these problems exist, but rather what practical consequences there are when such problems are identified in the legal system.

Resolving Legal Obligations upon the Official as Official

The most important effect one might observe is that conflicts among legal duties tend to be reduced over time. In other words, when confronted by conflicting legal obligations, legal officials will tend to employ substantive discretion to reconcile these conflicts. Officials act over time to change duties, either through the substantive alteration of one obligation or another, or through the evolution of privileges, immunities, or exceptions from various

---

constrained by prior legal rules. See Ronald Dworkin, *Taking Rights Seriously* 31–2 (Harvard University Press, 1978). The definition here is nearer to Dworkin's sense of strong discretion, which he believed in 1978 did not occur in the process of judging. See *id.* 81–130. Dworkin seems to have abandoned this division in his later writings. See Ronald Dworkin, *Freedom's Law: The Moral Reading of the American Constitution* (Harvard University Press, 1996). Discretion as used here is meant to be seen not as a rigorously defined set of conditions but as obligations more or less met by circumstance.

[95] The distinction here between substantive discretion and role discretion comes from Maurice Rosenberg's taxonomy of discretion; substantive discretion is like his primary discretion, whereas role discretion is a slightly limited form of his secondary discretion. See Maurice Rosenberg, "Judicial Discretion of the Trial Court, Viewed from Above," 22 Syracuse Law Review 635 (1971).

obligations.[96] The result, at least among obligations of any longevity, is usually an increasingly tidy system of mutually compatible and reinforcing official obligations.

One can see efforts at such reconciliation through the processes of *stare decisis* in the common law and of statutory codification.[97] In large part these efforts of reconciliation among the obligations binding upon citizens are necessary in order to promote coherence among the legal obligations of citizens. Conflicting obligations lead to less obedience and to less confidence by the citizen in the legal system, as well as, of course, to greater injustice.

Such reconciliation also benefits the official. Applying one choice from a set of coherent obligations reduces the effort necessary to reach a result that will find agreement by other officials. Each official finds making a decision and acting upon it to be more efficient and less troubling. There is usually an added bonus, in which officials are kept effectively immune from citizens' legal actions for mistakes the officials make in the exercise of official legal obligations.[98] Thus, officials maintain a near-monopoly on their ability to affect legal decisions made by other officials.

Resolving Conflict between Obligations as Official and Citizen

Some obligations that apply to an official may result in potential conflicts with general legal duties of the citizen. In part these conflicts arise because the role requires actions that are within the monopoly of law. These actions are forbidden to citizens but required of certain officials. In part these conflicts arise merely as a result of status.

Officials tend to seek to reconcile the conflicting duties over time, often by developing more privileges or immunities or exceptions to general legal duties. For example, police are excepted from ordinary regulations on the carrying of weapons, the use of force, and the restraints against trespass. Similarly, actions that are performed by an official are not subject to ordinary standards of care

---

[96] The whole sordid history of the federal assurance of sovereign immunity as a barrier to citizens' suits against the states, even in state courts, is described in *Alden v. Maine*, 527 U.S. 706 (1999), which held that state officers cannot sue a state in state court for violating federal wage and hours laws.

[97] For the idea that *stare decisis* provides a method to reconcile conflicts between the original intent of the drafters in 1789 and later constitutional doctrines, see Henry Paul Monaghan, "*Stare Decisis* and Constitutional Adjudication," 88 Columbia Law Review 723 (1988). For *stare decisis* as a method of reconciling conflicting rulings of law, and a critique of both the method and the goal, see Christopher J. Peters, "Foolish Consistency: On Equality, Integrity, and Justice in *Stare Decisis*," 105 Yale Law Journal 2031 (2000). For a gentler treatment of the modern incarnations of the Benthamite project of statutory codification as a method of resolving conflicts, see Gunther A. Weiss, "The Enchantment of Codification in the Common-Law World," 25 Yale Journal of International Law 435 (2000).

[98] See Barbara E. Armacost, "Qualified Immunity: Ignorance Excused," 51 Vanderbilt Law Review 581 (1998).

that might apply to a citizen, even if a citizen might be liable as negligent for similar conduct. Instead, officials are cloaked with sovereign immunity, or at least qualified immunity.[99]

Lingering Problems of Conflict and Fit

This process – the creation of laws, followed by reconciliation of the new laws with other laws resulting, in effect, in new laws, which in turn require reconciliation – goes on for every obligation created by law, whether it is an obligation of citizens or of officials. From those patterns, macro-patterns sometimes emerge, in which certain sets of obligations arise, are widely integrated into the system of obligations as a whole, and provide a critical mass against which other laws are reconciled. Some of these macro-patterns persist for a long time, and others are short-lived.[100]

Legal officials thus create these patterns and macro-patterns of evolving legal obligations. They are likewise bound by the obligations created, but only in the dynamic sense that the obligations are in the process of flux themselves. The transitory nature of such an obligation may be no more apparent at the time of a single official's single action than is the evolution of all species apparent in the life of a single mayfly. The plasticity of this process is not terribly apparent in most single acts.

One of the most important mechanisms of the legal system – one of particular importance in the process of the creation and reconciliation of obligations – is the definition of offices. Through this process the degree of influence any one official will have is ascertained, and so too is the degree to which an official will affect and be affected by the evolution of legal obligations. The essential tool for such definitions is discretion, particularly in its form of role discretion.

OFFICIAL ACTIONS, REASONS, AND CORPORATE ACTIONS

It is fine, in theory, to talk about why officials do things, how officials act within their discretion, and whether they satisfy their obligations to act or not to act. In practice, it can be really quite hard to assess these things. Perhaps

---

[99] Such exemptions may reach an extreme unjustifiable by any basis other than the power, such as Congress's exemption of its own employees from most labor laws. See Organization of the Congress, Final Report of the Joint Committee on the Organization of Congress 131-48, S. Rep. No. 215, vol. II & H.R. Rep. No. 413, vol. II, 103d Cong., 1st Sess. (1993); Harold H. Bruff, "That the Laws Shall Bind Equally on All: Congressional and Executive Roles in Applying Laws to Congress," 48 Arkansas Law Review 105 (1995).

[100] These observations were provoked by the Roman law theorist Alan Watson in his *Sources of Law, Legal Change, and Ambiguity* (University of Pennsylvania Press, 1984).

the greatest difficulty with such assessments is that we are not well equipped to assess motive. Or, to put it another way, it can be very hard to know the causes of anyone's actions, including officials' actions, including, even, our own actions.

There are writers who believe that everything an official does is done for a reason.[101] This can confuse things pretty thoroughly, at least if we expect to understand the law from the officials' reasons. First, just because individuals might have a reason to do something does not suggest that they understand their reasons, that they can accurately depict them, that they would want to do so, or that they would not prefer to present some other reasons that had nothing really to do with their decision but that they think would sound more appropriate to other people.

It seems quite likely that an individual who seeks a particular outcome through exercising power over others might engage in a bit of self-deception as to the true motivation for that exercise. We know that a sense of certainty becomes a justifying basis regardless of the evidence that might or might not support the conclusion that seems so certain.[102] We know that the creation of false moral excuses is a common practice in the rationalization of human action.[103] So, although we might act from reasons that we understand, and we might be able to describe those reasons, we might also have no specific reason or have beliefs about our reasons that are incorrect − and yet the rules of law require the assignment of some articulable reasons for our decisions. This is a topic that has been dealt with in very slight detail already.[104] For now, we can consider the following observations.

---

[101] Legal theorists tend to associate a moral obligation with a type of reason. This tendency is based on a view of human action that presupposes all human desires to arise from reasons, or at least on a view of norms as reasons for action. See, for example, Joseph Raz, *Engaging Reason: On the Theory and Value of Action* (Oxford University Press, 1999). These theorists rarely incorporate the increasingly rich experimental research of neuroscientists and psychologists, such as that by Caroline Palmer, few of whom agree with the theorists, and most of whom agree more with David Hume that there is some form of integral relationship between reasons and emotions as causes of most actions. See, for example, Kenneth R. Hammond, *Judgments under Stress* (Oxford University Press, 2000).

[102] See Robert A. Burton, *On Being Certain: Believing You Are Right Even When You're Not* (St. Martin's Press, 2008).

[103] See Cordelia Fine, *A Mind of Its Own: How Your Brain Distorts and Deceives* (W. W. Norton, 2006). Fine builds on Milgram's experiments to argue that a basic reason for self-deception is a distorted sense of justice: we blame the victim because we want to believe that the world we live in is sufficiently just that the victim wouldn't be hurt unless the harm was justified. *Id.* 66–78. See also Carol Tavris and Elliot Aronson, *Mistakes Were Made (but Not by Me): Why We Justify Foolish Beliefs, Bad Decisions, and Hurtful Acts* (Harcourt, 2007).

[104] On the shift from confidence to reasons in jury instructions, see Steve Sheppard, "The Metamorphoses of Reasonable Doubt: How Changes in the Burden of Proof Have Weakened the Presumption of Innocence," 78 Notre Dame Law Review 1165 (2003).

Officials are part of a system, and for the person subject to the law, the ultimate meaning of most official acts is achieved only through the act's ratification by other officials. Those officials must be able to evaluate the rationale for the decisions they review, which gives rise to requirements for public statements of reasons for actions by legal officials. These reasons are significant in isolation, but they are particularly meaningful through reference to the official statements of the factual contexts in which they arise.

Those reasons are capable of evaluation, of comparison, of logical analysis, even of extrapolation to reach new conclusions. The transposition of ambiguous references into reasons for legal actions and the comparison of legal actions to official statements of facts in which reasons may support a rule of law – these two practices comprise the art of legal reasoning.[105]

For instance, why an officer begins to investigate a person whom the officer suspects of a crime might be difficult for the officer to assess. Instincts and emotions, inarticulable feelings and hunches, play a significant part in such decisions.[106] Yet once the officer makes an arrest, for the arrest to be valid, the officer must be able to rely on sufficient reasons for other officials to accept those reasons as a legitimate and sufficient basis for the arrest. Otherwise, the other officials ought to act to free the suspect.

The same is true for legislators, who might or might not initially have a good reason for wanting to pass or repeal a statute, but must eventually offer sufficient reasons to persuade other legislators to do so. Moreover, there must appear to judges and officials sufficient reasons to uphold the statute if it is challenged.

No official should expect to be able to exercise discretion under the law without eventually providing a sufficient rationale for other officials to review the decision (or at least without a sufficient rationale being apparent when others review it). In other words, in a legal system under the rule of law, no official can act without explaining why.

This requirement of explanation, coupled with what we know of the dangers of mistake and deception in the assignment of reasons, creates difficulties for the subject and for other officials in assessing public statements of the reasons for law. Officials must be willing to second-guess the assigned

---

[105]   See Antonin Scalia and Bryan A. Garner, *Making Your Case: The Art of Persuading Judges* 39–56 (Thomson-West, 2008).

[106]   This is what David Hume meant when he warned, "Since reason alone can never produce any action or give rise to any volition, I infer, that the same faculty is incapable of preventing volition.... Reason is, and ought only to be the slave of the passions, and can never pretend to any other office than to serve and obey them." David Hume, *A Treatise of Human Nature* 414–15 (Book 2, Chapter 3, Section 3) (L. A. Selby-Bigge & P. H. Nidditch, eds.) (Oxford University Press, 1989).

rationales of other officials.[107] Subjects encounter in every decision, once it is finally made, a raft of actions for apparently different reasons, sometimes quite divorced from appearances, made by seemingly a gray mass of people.

In this way, from the subject's view, the law is always somewhat impersonal. The results of the law, the effect in the subject's life, come from the actions of legislators, executives, clerks – countless people whose actions affect the burden or the benefit felt by the subject, but whose identity and reasons for action are unknown. Only a few people, a sheriff's deputy, a bailiff, a judge, represent the whole of this congregation of officials to the subject. To the subject, the rationale of these officials is probably all the rationale there is, to the degree that such a rationale is communicated to or divined by the subject at all.

Problems arise when we begin to assess the reasons provided (or available when they are not provided). The most important question is fitting the reasons provided to the act: Are these actually the reasons that motivated the decision, or are the reasons offered a mere sham? If some reasons are forbidden and others are acceptable, how do we know that acceptable reasons do not mask forbidden reasons?

Officials must act independently, and yet they are constantly working in the aggregate on corporate decisions, made in part by other officials. This requires not only that each official assess the actions taken by other officials, but also that each independently assess the reasons other officials give for that action. Every act by an official that endorses or furthers an act by another official is, to some extent, endorsing or furthering the reasons for the earlier act. The same is true if an official fails to act when he or she has the power to overturn another's decision. This means that when a judge holds a prisoner after a sheriff has arrested the prisoner, the judge is, at least to a degree, endorsing both the prisoner's arrest and the sheriff's reasons for the arrest. It also means that when Congress fails to overturn an executive order, it is – and every member is – to some extent endorsing that order and its reasons. If the reasons given by the sheriff or the president are false, either for the arrest or for the presidential order, then the judge in the one case and Congress in the other have endorsed those false reasons.

The need for officials to assess actions for such knowledge and the need for the polity in a democracy to make such assessments are both very real. When officials will not offer information on how decisions are made, both

---

[107] The canonical illustration is *Yick Wo v. Hopkins*, 118 U.S. 356 (1886). San Francisco's lawyers failed to convince the Supreme Court that a ban on wooden laundries was to reduce the risk of fires, when all white-owned laundries were made of brick but all Asian-owned laundries were built of wood.

other officials and the people who are subject to these decisions are very likely justified in their fears of the silent officials.

None of this means that there is always a legal means to require an exercise of authority or honesty in its exercise, although there often is. In the United States, we might be more aware of a legal or moral responsibility of an official to act than of a responsibility not to act, but there are also tools of law such as mandamus and injunction to demand an official carry out at least the most fundamental duties of office.[108]

---

[108] The writ of mandamus is an ancient order for an official to act when a citizen has a right to the official's action. See, for example, *Porter v. Florida Parole & Probation Com'n*, 603 So.2d 31 (Fla.App. 1 Dist. 1992). A few provisions in the law allow a more tailored enforcement, such as a provision of the Civil Rights Act of 1871, or the Ku Klux Klan Act, which grants the victim of a conspiracy to deprive civil rights an action in federal court against any public official who knew of the conspiracy, had the power to intervene in it, and failed to do so. 42 U.S.C. § 1986. See, for example, *Clark v. Clabaugh*, 20 F.3d 1290 (3d Cir. 1994).

2
The Stakes: The Interests of Others in Official Actions

Those who propose to take charge of the affairs of government should not fail to remember two of Plato's rules: first, to keep the good of the people so clearly in view that regardless of their own interests they will make their every action conform to that; second, to care for the welfare of the whole body politic and not in serving the interests of some one party to betray the rest.

Cicero, *On Duties*, Book I, Chapter XXV[1]

Chapter 1 presented one way to understand the law as the result of the actions of officials, in which the law is an archive of rules created by past officials, applied in a current culture of official expectation and practice, in which individual officials carry out their offices with sole discretion yet as part of a corporate whole. A working definition of the official follows from that, which is both formal and functional: an official of the law is any person who holds an office that is given authority by law to act in a way that can alter the opportunities or condition of another person through the apparatus of the legal system. That is hardly a revelation, but it is a necessary foundation for asking what interests different people have in the actions that are taken by anyone holding that office.

There are two broad answers. The first is that the law requires that others care about officials' actions because others must do what officials say. The laws are written, and offices given authority, to demand that other people obey the acts of officials. The second is broader, in that the law has a wide-ranging and complicated effect on people's lives, hopes, and even identities. Understanding both answers, but especially understanding the scope of that second answer – the effects of officials' acts in others lives – provides an essential context for considering the moral significance of official conduct.

---

[1] Marcus Tullius Cicero, *De Officiis* 87 (Walter Miller, trans.) (Loeb edn.) (Harvard University Press, 1913).

That the law requires obedience is clear to anyone who has ever been in a car when the blue lights flash from the car behind. What is less obvious, perhaps, is that the law must require such obedience, and it must demand it from every citizen and every official.

H. L. A. Hart very usefully argued that the very existence of a legal system depends both on an obedient behavior of citizens and on an obedient attitude of officials toward the law. This is a twofold requirement of obedience. Citizens must usually obey those laws that govern their behavior in general, and officials must generally accept the rules that govern their acts as officials.[2] If they don't, the legal system will simply fail.

The Obedience of Subjects

Citizens do not need to worry about why they obey the law, or even know that they obey it. For the law to work, it is only necessary that they obey most of the time, without regard to the reasons why. Still, as Hart noted, the reasons why they might obey or not obey laws may well be based on morality or custom. Granted, in a minimally effective legal system, it does not matter why subjects obey the rules of law: "in a healthy society they will in fact often accept these rules as common standards of behaviour and acknowledge an obligation to obey them or even trace this obligation to a more general obligation to respect the constitution."[3] This acknowledgment, like the subject's obedience, may be based on "a variety of different reasons and among them may often, though not always, be the knowledge that it will be best for him to do so."[4]

There are many reasons why the law depends on citizens' obedience, but the most important is the approach typified in the argument of the social contract. In its simplest form, the social contract is bilateral: I will surrender some of my natural liberty because it is in my interest for you to do the same; I won't steal from you if you won't steal from me. In its statist form the contract recognizes that I have few means of enforcing my bilateral agreement, and so it is trilateral: I will obey the state and let it punish me for stealing in order to ensure that you are punished if you steal from me.[5] But, I won't accept my loss of independence from the state for long if the state won't punish you when

[2] H. L. A. Hart, *The Concept of Law* 110–23 (2d ed.) (Oxford University Press, 1997). Hart, of course, was extrapolating from John Austin's famous observation that law requires a habit of obedience by the subjects to the sovereign. See John Austin, *The Province of Jurisprudence Determined* 299–300 (1832) (Franklin Press, 1970).
[3] Hart, *Concept of Law* 116–17.
[4] *Id.* 114.
[5] For a nice introduction to the tripartite model of law, see George Fletcher, *Basic Concepts of Law* (Oxford University Press, 1999).

you steal from me. My obedience to the state depends on your obedience to the state, and if you, or if enough people, don't obey the state's laws, then it becomes unlikely that I will.[6]

My obedience, of course, depends on other things as well. It is contingent on a trust in the values and fairness of the law, although fairness independently requires equal and sufficient enforcement.[7]

My obedience is likely also to depend on a personal fear of enforcement. If I believe I am likely to be punished for disobedience, I am likely to obey. When fear of enforcement is not high, my obedience depends on my beliefs that I am better off by obedience, or that I have to do this, or that it is right to do this; and if others seem better off by disobedience, or seem free to disobey, or seem not to accept a duty to obey, it is less likely that I will continue to obey. If there is a wholesale practice of disobedience, then the tools of enforcement are likely to be overwhelmed, and I will have less fear of enforcement at precisely the moment that others' disobedience is a practical argument against my own obedience. This dynamic of lawlessness is the source not only of revolutions, but also of riots and looting by subjects, of corruption and abuse by officials.[8]

The Obedience of Officials

Official obedience to the law is the key to Hart's second condition for the successful existence of a legal system. The rules governing the legal system, which Hart calls "secondary rules,"[9] "must be effectively accepted as common public standards of official behaviour by its officials. . . . They must regard these as common standards of official behaviour and appraise critically their own and each other's deviations as lapses."[10]

Official behavior must be based on the law and empowered and limited by the law, and officials must carry out those powers and conform to those limits,

---

6 There is an immense literature on the contractarian model of laws, an ancient argument recurringly made new by the like of Hobbes, Locke, Rousseau, and Rawls. See Sir Ernest Barker's introduction to *Social Contract: Essays by Locke, Hume, and Rousseau* (Oxford University Press, 1971).

7 See Tom R. Tyler, *Why People Obey the Law* (Princeton University Press, 2006).

8 See Stuart P. Green, "Looting, Law, and Lawlessness," 81 Tulane Law Review 1129 (2007).

9 Hart called these the system's "rules of recognition specifying the criteria of legal validity and its rules of change and adjudication." Hart, *Concept of Law* 116. These three forms of secondary rule would translate into the language of the practicing lawyer, roughly, as the constitution and procedures of the legal system. The ultimate rule of recognition can be difficult to identify, but in the U.S. Constitution, the Ratifying Clause is a good candidate. See Kent Greenawalt, "The Rule of Recognition and the Constitution," 85 Michigan Law Review 621 (1987). The whole of the secondary rules, including secondary rules of adjudication and change – as well as other rules such as those for the definition of role and the power of appointment – are broader, amounting nearly to the whole of constitutional, administrative, and procedural law.

10 Hart, *Concept of Law* 116.

or there is no law at all, only a system of power.[11] Official obedience to law is, therefore, the central underpinning of the rule of law.[12]

It is not enough for officials merely to conform to the system as citizens might. For the system to exist, officials must treat deviations from the rules by other officials, particularly conduct in violation of rules that are designed to be recognized as law, as serious lapses from standards. Implied in this is that, when the officials do not do so, at some scale or degree, the legal system is likely to cease to exist.[13]

The official, just like the citizen, has a choice to comply with the constitution and rules of the legal system; there is no good in suggesting that this choice is foregone by becoming an official. Hart recognized that the system depends on acceptance but requires also the treatment of lapses as deviance. When officials do not regard a lapse as deviance, then what follows? The system is altered, and perhaps it will fail.

The Unanswered Questions of Obedience

The mere fact that laws exist explains neither why citizens would obey them nor why officials would carry them out. Something more is needed.[14]

---

[11] See Aristotle, *Politics*, Book 4.

[12] See Albert V. Dicey, *Law of the Constitution* 150 (Macmillan, 1950).

[13] Hart does not explore this implication, although it follows from his statements on the necessity of official acceptance of the validity of the rule of recognition and other secondary rules. Hart recognizes that the "Janus-faced" requirement of the legal system demands acceptance by both subjects and officials. *Id.* 117. That is the point of this passage, that the officials' acceptance is as important to the persistence of the legal system as was the then-well-known point that a system depended on the general obedience of the subjects.

[14] In a wonderful sense, Hart's positivism here echoes Wittgenstein's early philosophy: when Wittgenstein says, "The world is all that is the case" he makes no claims for why it is the case or whether it is a good thing. Ludwig Wittgenstein, *Tractatus Logico-Philosophicus* 5 (1922) (C. K. Odgen, trans.) (Dover Publications, 1999). Neither does Hart: when he describes what the concept of law is, he is not describing how it comes to succeed, merely what it looks like when it does. See Hart, *Concept of Law* 240–1.

   Some think Hart meant more, who make normative claims for either his positivism or their own positivism. See Stephen Perry, "Hart's Methodological Positivism," 4 Legal Theory 427 (1998). Tom Campbell argues that positivism demands certain moral conduct from its officials. This book concludes similarly because of the nature of law; it does not do such because of the nature of positivism. I am not sure that it follows that his "ethical positivism" really breaches the wall he accepts with "legal positivism" because of how he defines rules. See Tom D. Campbell, *The Legal Theory of Ethical Positivism* (Dartmouth Publishing, 1996).

   Some senses of this criticism are right, as in arguing that there is a value to having a structure of rules that operate as a rule of law. See Jeremy Waldron, "Normative (or Ethical) Positivism," in *Hart's Postscript: Essays on the Postscript to the Concept of Law* 411, 424–53 (Jules Coleman, ed.) (Oxford University Press, 2001). These senses in which the critics are right do not seem to me to alter the underlying value of the separability thesis.

   This might all seem like a technical argument of little merit outside the tiny world of jurisprudes, but I think it has a great parallel in the world of American politics, which I hope

To determine what is needed, we can examine the relationship between the law and the people whose acceptance or conformity it needs. We can examine the law to determine what people see in it, how they trust it, fear it, need it, rely on it, hope for it, or just encounter it. We can look to the expectations and fears people bring to the law, and if we understand them well enough, we might be able to determine when those expectations and fears are sufficient to make their acceptance and obedience to law more or less likely.

THE SCOPE OF THE LAWS IN EVERYDAY AFFAIRS

The law is immense. To inventory it fully is simply beyond the scope of this book. Just the law in the United States of the early twenty-first century is overwhelmingly vast in scope, detail, and complexity. Quite likely, the laws in the United States (in all its many jurisdictions combined) are the most comprehensive, detailed, and complicated set of legal rules ever devised in a single country. Laws govern almost every arena of human endeavor, so much so that even those arenas that may not be governed by law must be defined by law. Just measuring the archive of U.S. law is hard.[15] If, however, we attempt to look to a smaller, less economically complex community, in which there are archives of law similar to ours, we might learn something at least of what officials believe was required of the law.

Subjects and Their Stakes in the Law

In order to understand our stakes in the law, despite the complexity of law, we have to assess its benefits and burdens somehow. An example of law that resonates with the culture but that is easier to study might give some indication of what the citizen and the official believe happens when laws are created and applied.

to develop throughout this work. For now, let me just say that it helps to see the difference between the glass and the drink.

[15] In 2005, a minimal set of U.S. laws requires the *United States Code*, whose 35 volumes do not even contain all of the acts of Congress in force (those are in the *Statutes at Large*). The *Code of Federal Regulations*, which sets norms for subjects' behavior in particularly small print, is 216 volumes, depending upon how it is counted. Picking a middling-sized jurisdiction out of 51, the annotated code of Arkansas runs 54 volumes. To these we add 4,300 volumes of published decisions from the federal courts and 456 volumes of Arkansas appellate reports. This list ignores state regulations, municipal laws, county ordinances, laws from the like of water districts, and private organizations' standards that form the basis for liability; nor does it consider the additional law arising from treaty, foreign law, or international custom. And, the whole notion presumes that the law is only what is written.

By way of comparison, the entire 1989 edition of the *Oxford English Dictionary* fits its 291,500 entries into a nicely printed 20 volumes.

A Case Study from Colonial Massachusetts, Part One

As an example, we will try something from the dawn of the American experience, and we will consider the laws of an early American community, focusing on one part of its archive, the rules in one of the first sets of laws compiled in the English colonies in America, the 1648 *Book of the General Lawes and Libertyes of Massachusetts.*[16] Its fifty-nine pages, roughly alphabetized for the easy use of official and freeman alike, depict in 121 topics what seemed essential to the officials of the twenty-five-year-old colony,[17] a colony of just fourteen thousand people.[18]

Puritan Law: The Lawes and Libertyes *as Partial Archive:* Like most codes, the writing and proportions of this portion of the colonial Massachusetts legal archive hint at the application of the law in the community at the time. For instance, the modern reader might be troubled to learn that the Massachusetts colonists decreed that rebellious adolescents could be put to death.[19] Yet, there

---

[16]   All of the English colonies had laws before 1647, from charters to companies and proprietors, from proprietor's instructions or governor's orders, from pronouncements of colonial councils or general courts, and from the background of English law. The earliest homegrown code was probably Sir Thomas Dale's harsh 1611 code in Virginia, *Lawes Divine, Morall and Martiall.* See generally, Peter Charles Hoffer, *Law and People in Colonial America* (Johns Hopkins University Press, 1992); *Foundations of Colonial America: A Documentary History* (W. Keith Kavenagh, ed.) (6 vols.) (Chelsea House, 1973).

   Lawes and Liberties, completed in 1647 and promulgated in 1648, was the most comprehensive homegrown codification of the law enacted up to then, an attempt to fill some of the gaps in earlier enactments that were perceived by a study of general English law and custom (especially Michael Dalton's 1635 *The Countrey Justice* and the works of Coke); about a third of its rules were enacted before the code was published. See George Lee Haskins, *Law and Authority in Early Massachusetts: A Study in Tradition and Design* 135–40 (University Press of America, 1960).

   The 1647 code was not the first Massachusetts code. *The Body of Liberties,* written in 1641, emphasized liberties of the subject and limits on official conduct. The bulk of *Body of Liberties* was rendered into the 1647 code, which was more thorough in covering matters of private dispute. *Id.* The code was distributed free throughout the colony to magistrates, and it appears to have been immediately employed, even in the western courts. See Joseph H. Smith, ed., *Colonial Justice in Western Massachusetts, 1639–1702: The Pynchon Court Record, an Original Judges' Diary of the Administration of Justice in the Springfield Courts in the Massachusetts Bay Colony* (Harvard University Press, 1961).

[17]   *The Lawes and Liberties of Massachusetts: Reprinted from the copy of the 1648 edition in the Henry E. Huntington Library* (1647) (Thomas G. Barnes, ed.) (Legal Classics Library, 1982).

[18]   The population of Massachusetts colony in 1650 was 14,037 with Plymouth holding an additional 1,566. Growth was rapid, the population of each having been a third less in 1640. *Estimated European Population of American Colonies 1620 to 1780,* transcribed by D'lin Clark from Series Z-19 U.S. Census.

[19]   The thirteenth and fourteenth capital crimes were:

   13. If any child, or children, above sixteen years old, and of sufficient understanding, shall CURSE, or SMITE their natural FATHER, or MOTHER; he or they shall be put to death: unles it can be sufficiently testified that the Parents have been very unchristianly negligent in the eduction of such children; or so provoked them by

is no record of these offenses ever being thus punished.[20] Even so, a close reading of the text suggests some rough categories into which these laws could be organized, and a comparison to judicial practice suggests that there is something to be gained in considering the code as a whole.[21]

If *The Book of the General Lawes and Libertyes* is organized topically (rather than alphabetically) it can be given eleven headings. By that organization, the categories of laws directly affecting the citizen, from the longest texts to the shortest, are (1) the regulation and taxing of commerce, (2) regulation of property and family, (3) definition and trial of crimes, (4) law of the person, (5) regulation of religion, (6) debt collection, and (7) regulation of natural resources. Those laws that most affected officials were (1) obligations to the commonwealth, including military action; (2) court procedures; (3) definitions of office and official obligations including oaths of office; and (4) rights of the person.[22]

This elemental code established the greatest portion of the rules governing the lives of a legal system. Given that the colony's laws concerning legal process, freemen, voting, and the politics of the selection of the colonial deputies reflected the tension between royal and ecclesiastic authority as well as Puritan recognition of the individual, the *General Lawes and Libertyes* reflected the expectations not only of the leaders of the colony but also of its leading subjects.

> extream, and cruel correction; that they have been forced therunto to preserve themselves from death or maiming. Exod. 21. 17. Lev. 20. 9. Exod. 21. 15.
>
> 14. If a man have a stubborn or REBELLIOUS SON, of sufficient years & understanding (viz) sixteen years of age, which will not obey the voice of his Father, or the voice of his Mother, and that when they have chastened him will not harken unto them: then shal his Father & Mother being his natural parents, lay hold on him, & bring him to the Magistrates assembled in Court & testifie unto them that their Son is stubborn & rebellious & will not obey their voice and chastisement, but lives in sundry notorious crimes, such a son shal be put to death. Deut. 21. 20. 21.

Lawes and Libertyes 5–6.

[20] Haskins, *Law and Authority* 81. Haskins has found a few cases in the judicial records in which children were whipped or made to stand on the gallows, the harshest penalties for children recorded. *Id.* 253 n.157. Massachusetts colonial courts often remitted children accused of offenses to their families for punishment. *Id.* 81.

[21] Appeals were brought in every subject, but mainly in capital cases and larger cases in debt. My inventory of work in the colonial Supreme Judicial Court fifty years after the adoption of the still then-current *Lawes and Libertyes* is in Steve Sheppard, "Paul Dudley: Heritage, Observation, and Conscience," 5 Massachusetts Legal History (2000). By then the work of the court had changed in its procedures but little had changed in substance from the work that preceded the SJC's founding in 1692. See Barbara A. Black, "The Concept of a Supreme Court: Massachusetts Bay, 1630–1686," in *The History of the Law in Massachusetts: The Supreme Judicial Court 1692–1992* 43 (Russell K. Osgood, ed.) (Supreme Judicial Court Historical Society, 1992).

[22] The survey of the specific laws describing this organization is included in this book in the appendix.

Many of these expectations are found not in the laws alone but in the two-page prefatory epistle, which presents a nice series of justifications for the laws the General Court was then promulgating. First was the precedent that God had given laws to the Israelites, described in a metaphor of special practical force for the recently arrived colonists, "a Common-wealth without lawes is like a Ship without rigging and steeradge."[23] Yet, though the people moved from the law of God to corruption, "if they had walked according to the light & law of nature they might have been preserved from such moral evils and might have injoyed a common blessing in all their natural and civil Ordinances." The laws of Massachusetts thus enjoyed the twin powers of both ecclesiastic and civil authority, the church elders helping to draft the laws, and the freemen voting to have them published. Most fascinating are the arguments made not only to the freemen to enforce the laws, but also to strangers and nonfreemen to obey them.

> You have called us from amongst the rest of our Bretheren and given us power to make these laws: we must now call upon you to see them executed: remembring that old & true proverb, The execution of the law is the life of the law. If one sort of you viz: non-Freemen should object that you had no hand in calling us to this worke, and therfore think yourselvs not bound to obedience &c. Wee answer that a subsequent, or implicit consent is of like force in this case, as an expresse precedent power: for in putting your persons and estates into the protection and way of subsistance held forth and exercised within this Jurisdiction, you doe tacitly submit to this Government and to all the wholesome lawes therof, and so is the common repute in all nations and that upon this Maxim. *Qui sentit commodum sentire debet et onus.*[24]

The contractarian arguments of the officials to the subjects could hardly be clearer: you have implied your consent to the commonwealth, and in any event you receive the benefit of its laws as a whole; you have a duty to obey them all. These claims, of course, rest as much on the Biblical exegesis that preceded them, but the claims also rest on a consent theory that is, as are many other arguments in these laws, shot through with modern arguments about why they should be obeyed.

---

[23] *Lawes and Libertyes*, Preface, recto.

[24] *Id. verso.* The maxim is here intended to mean, "Who takes the benefit ought also bear the burden." It is taken from *Shelley's Case*, at 9 Coke 99b, in 1 *Selected Writings of Sir Edward Coke* 20, where its meaning is the reverse, that he who bears the burden is entitled to the benefit. We can be relatively certain that Coke is its source, not least owing to Coke's omission to add "et e contra," the stinger found in other usages that hew closer to its canon origins. See *Regula* 55 in *Regulae Iuris Bonifacii VIII* in *Libro Sexto Corporis Iuris Canonici* (1298), in *De Rechtsregels Van Bonifatius Viii Uit Het Zesde Boek Van Het Corpus Iuris Canonici* (1298) (Ton Meijers, trans., 1999), www.rorate.com/rorate/scripts/kr_print.php? t=ro_kerkrecht&id=71. (Last visited December 3, 2005.)

The similarity between this brief colonial artifact and the vast modern American legal system is striking. These Puritan colonists engaged in a considerable regulation of commerce within the colony, with other colonies, and with native tribes: they passed laws ensuring fairness in sales and constant weights and measures for the inspection of goods, as well as humane laws governing the collection of debts. They promoted education by law, establishing a college and schools, as well as laws threatening bad children but requiring their education and temperance. They built roads and schools, and they banned public intoxication and smoking in houses.

Puritan Law: Official Culture: Colonial legal officials, though they saw themselves as most regulated by the Bible, were carefully regulated by the laws, which specified, for instance, which offices were elected and which few appointed, who could stand for what offices, the scope of duties, and the rights of subjects to freedom from official actions.[25] They were careful about procedures in both criminal and civil law and, even in the time of Cotton Mather, still forbade arrest by the civil authorities for offenses against religion, unless the offenses were also enacted by statute. On the other hand, religion was regulated, the servants and nonfreemen were beholden to the freemen, and relations with the natives were highly regulated. Still, the main differences were, perhaps, in the shortness of their list of criminal laws, all of which were based on Biblical injunctions, including five offenses against church dogma, the most notorious to us being witchcraft.[26] Many of these laws, of course, are no longer on the books in the Commonwealth of Massachusetts, although others persist, such as the prohibitions of murder and fraudulent conveyances.[27]

The legal culture in Massachusetts Bay was closely linked with the culture of its surrounding community. Both were Puritan, but both the wider community and the legal community included individuals who were not of the same religion. The officials were generally people of comparative wealth, general education, and religious learning. A few lawyers had trained in the Inns and immigrated, but most attorneys were homegrown, having taught themselves or

---

[25] A fine description of Winthrop and other colonial officials as legal officers is in Haskins, *Law and Authority* 141–62.

[26] See the lists in the appendix. Prosecutions of witchcraft were not unknown but still rare in Massachusetts in the middle of the century, the trials at Salem not occurring until 1692. See the section entitled "Officials and Their Stakes in the Law."

[27] 26 Annotated Laws of Massachusetts, General Laws, chapter 265 (2005), prescribes the death penalty for murder with deliberately premeditated malice aforethought or with extreme atrocity or cruelty. That statute, last amended in 1982, remains on the books but was declared unconstitutional in *Commonwealth v. Colon-Cruz*, 393 Mass. 150 (1984). The statute, if reinstated, would likely be subject to the Massachusetts Model Jury Instructions for Homicide (1999), which could drastically curtail use of the sentence.

Fraudulent conveyances are still voidable in Massachusetts, per 15 Annotated Laws of Massachusetts, General Laws, chapter 109A § 9 (2005).

been taught by others from law books published in England, and learning the crafts of representation, legislation, or adjudication through practice alongside others already engaged in such pursuits. Although patterns of practice and legal custom were increasingly evident as the colonies grew and matured, processes of argument from the archive were not yet complicated or long-winded. Even so, by this time there was a strong recognition that, although religion could justify the legal system as a whole, and although it might illustrate the justice of the civil definition of crimes, the culture limited criminal definitions to acts made in the legal archive rather than strictures in the Bible. The judges, assistants, and legislators were drawn from the propertied classes, which were also the best educated. There was also an expectation that males in such families would serve as leaders in the community.[28]

This culture of duty is reflected in the archive. As written by the freemen of the General Court, justice, tranquility, defense, welfare, and liberty were the objects of the law, whether the subjects liked it or not. The law, applied more broadly than the form in which it was codified, had a comprehensive and often controversial effect in the lives of Massachusetts colonists. It was no accident that the members of the General Court felt obliged to explain that the law applied to all and not just to the freemen. The decade before, the colony had experienced a revival of antinomianism, the rejection of ecclesiastic and legal authority in favor of authority by direct grace.[29] The revival had been a heresy that nearly became dogma, and after its tide had ebbed, the government built its dams. Anyone who rejected the authority of the law or of the church, or defamed a court judgment, could be exiled.[30] And many were.[31] To keep this

[28] The literature on colonial law is not extensive, particularly on that of the seventeenth century. The references in the other notes in this and the next section nearly exhaust the field of general histories, although there are other studies on particular judges and courts. See Loretta A. Norris & Larry M. Boyer, *American Colonial Courts and Lawyers: An Annotated Bibliography* (Library of Congress, 1976). For two compelling recent colonial legal histories, see Mary Sarah Bilder, *The Transatlantic Constitution: Colonial Legal Culture* (Harvard University Press, 2004); Daniel J. Hulsebosch, *Constituting Empire: New York and the Transformation of Constitutionalism in the Atlantic World, 1664–1830* (University of North Carolina Press, 2006).

[29] Antinomianism had by then been linked, often dubiously, with Puritanism for at least a century, but thanks to the sermons of John Cotton and Anne Winthrop, the argument nearly became the governing doctrine of the colonial church. See David B. Hall, *The Antinomian Controversy, 1636–38: A Documentary History* (Wesleyan University Press, 1968). It has never died out. See Alan Norrie, *Law And the Beautiful Soul* (International Specialized Book Service, 2005); "From Law to Popular Justice: Beyond Antinomianism," 5 Social & Legal Studies 383 (1996).

[30] Besides the argument in the preamble, the law provided for the banishment of Anabaptists, a group closely associated with antinomianism. *Lawes and Libertyes* 2.

[31] The code restated precedent. Anne Hutchinson, the leader of the cause, and her closest followers were exiled. Others in the opposition were banned from carrying arms, and occasionally jailed or flogged, though many of her followers recanted. See Emery Battis, *Saints and Sectaries: Anne Hutchinson and the Antinomian Controversy in the Massachusetts Bay*

controversy in perspective, it is important to remember that not all colonists were Puritans; from the arrival of the *Speedwell*, the first ship in the Puritan fleet, a majority had been "strangers" (almost always Anglicans), not known to the congregation.[32]

The judges were, though, concerned with much more than religious crimes. The colony's attorneys prosecuted crimes great and small – murder, piracy, robbery, rape, battery, and libel, as well as quarreling and violating the sumptuary laws.[33] Although private wrongs such as trespass and theft were generally dealt with as crimes, judges also resolved breaches of various private obligations.[34] Contracts were enforced in court, as were claims to property through death or descent.[35] Marriage was carefully regulated, and the civil magistrate replaced the preacher as the officiant for matrimony.[36] In contrast

Colony (University of North Carolina Press, 1962). A brief and lively account is in Edmund S. Morgan, *The Puritan Dilemma: The Story of John Winthrop* (Little, Brown & Co., 1958).

Everyone's favorite antinomian must be Anne Oliver, who would harangue new immigrants at the dock and called the governor a wretch for fining her for stealing goats. She was intermittently jailed, flogged, and subject to a bond by her long-suffering husband; she accepted banishment in lieu of a fine in 1650. See John Winthrop, *The Journal of John Winthrop, 1630–49* 275–6 (Richard S. Dunn, James Savage, & Letitia Yeandle, eds.) (Harvard University Press, 1996); George F. Dow, *Every Day Life in the Massachusetts Bay Colony* 214–18 (Benjamin Blom, 1935). The third most common cause before the Court of Assistants, the colonial high court, was vilifying authorities, for which whipping or a fine was imposed. Edwin Powers, *Crime and Punishment in Early Massachusetts, 1620–1692: A Documentary History* 408 (Beacon Press, 1966).

[32] After the Puritan fleet had finished, there were 133 strangers to 100 Puritans. See George F. Willison, *Saints and Strangers: Being the Lives of the Pilgrim Fathers & Their Families, with Their Friends & Foes; & an Account of Their Posthumous Wanderings in Limbo, Their Final Resurrection & Rise to Glory, & the Strange Pilgrimages of Plymouth Rock* (Reynal & Hitchcock, 1945). The law of 1648 still regulated "Strangers." *Lawes and Libertyes* 49.

[33] Charles J. Hilkey, *Legal Development in Colonial Massachusetts, 1630–86* 96–111 (Studies in History, Economics and Public Law 37:2, no. 98, Columbia University Press, 1910). Murder and manslaughter were the most frequently prosecuted offenses in the Court of Assistants, although cases of fornication and public drunkenness were often brought before the county and town courts. See Powers, *Crime and Punishment.*

[34] The best example is the 1642 dispute of Sherman v. Keayne, the great case of the stray sow, in which Keayne killed the swine, which was claimed later by Sherman's wife to be hers. She sued him for it, twice. Resolving the disputes eventually resulted in the division of the General Court into separate legislative and judicial bodies. See Jonathan Winthrop, *Journal of the Transactions and Occurences in the Settlement of Massachusetts and the Other New England Colonies* in 2 *Winthrop's History of New England* 64–6, 116–20 (April 22, 1642) (James Kendall Hosmer, ed.) (Charles Scribner's Sons, 1908). For context, see Arthur Prentice Rugg, "A Famous Colonial Litigation: The Case between Richard Sherman and Capt. Robert Keayne, 1642," 30 Proceedings of the American Antiquarian Society 217 (1920). For the influence of the case on the development of the general structure of law in the colony and on the framing of the *Lawes*, see Richard B. Morris, "Massachusetts and the Common Law: The Declaration of 1646," 31 American Historical Review 443 (1926).

[35] See Hilkey, *Legal Development* 112–40, collecting cases, predominantly from the *Essex County Court Records.*

[36] *Id.* 127–31. One of the most prosecuted laws required consent of the bride's parents or guardian, or a court order. *Lawes and Libertyes* 38–9. There were other prosecutions under

to their later reputation, the Puritans did not expect much of the regulation of morals (with the exception of public intoxication) to be done through the laws, relegating those functions to the church and community.[37]

In all, there is a rough but reasonable correlation between the 1648 *Lawes*, the work of the courts, and the apparent expectation of the citizenry. The archives, both the *Lawes* and some written expositions of the English common law, were available and employed by the officials to guide their conduct; to provide reasons to identify, arrest, and punish malefactors; and to resolve local disputes.

The culture of the officials who applied that law was described by particular habits and identity derived less from the rules of the law than from social circumstances generally. The division of the wealthy from the poor was not so vast in the colonies as it had been in England. The greater divide in many instances, at least in Massachusetts, was the strength of apparent adherence to Puritanism.

The Perception of Colonial Subjects. Governor Winthrop, or one of the freemen who formed the committees that promulgated the code, might see it quite differently from, say, Anne Oliver, who as a woman and an antinomialist (and a falsely accused goat thief) certainly felt neither responsibility for the code nor any special compunction to obey it.[38] Even so, her argument against her arrest for theft was not that the law was wrong but that there was no evidence against her.[39]

What of the natives, and the strangers, or the servants, and women? The law was enforced against them all, and they appear to have expected it to be. The churches and communities established their memberships, according to law. The constables sought and arrested suspected criminals, and victims expected them to do so, just as the juries expected to hear evidence and order some

---

the marriage laws, not least for bigamy. See Hilkey, *Legal Development* 106, citing the cases of James Luxford and John Richardson.

[37] See William E. Nelson, "Introductory Essay," in *Plymouth Court Records: 1686–1859* (David Konig, ed.) (Pilgrim Society, 1978). The seventeenth-century records bear this out. See *Historical Records Survey, Division of Professional and Service Projects, Work Projects Administration Abstract and Index of the Records of the Inferiour Court of Pleas (Suffolk County Court) Held at Boston, 1680–1698* (Historical Records Survey, 1940).

[38] Of course, feelings in such a case need not be all or nothing. Anne might have felt respect for certain rules or have abided by ideas reflected in them, such as Biblical crimes, or she might have accepted certain ideas, such as the need for barrel-stave inspectors, without embracing the authority of the governor.

[39] See Dow, *Every Day Life* 216. She might have been right. In the midst of Anne's troubles with the law, she recovered a ten-shilling judgment for false imprisonment for a different offense. *Id.* The most famous woman in the colonies was probably brought her involuntary prominence by a similar course of disagreement with religious and legal authority. See Michael Paul Winship, *The Times and Trials of Anne Hutchinson: Puritans Divided* (University Press of Kansas, 2005).

hanged and others released. The General Court enshrined certain ordinances of the Bible (but by no means all of the Mosaic code) into the colony's laws, underscoring the obligation of the people to obey divine command while limiting the state from judging all sins against God. Certain laws were passed to create economic opportunities, others to ensure fairness among people, and others still to ensure punishment for wrongdoing.

Much in the 1648 *Lawes and Libertyes of Massachusetts* and its enforcement seems familiar to the modern eye. Granted, this short code, taken from a colony three and a half centuries ago, is hardly a perfect comparison to the laws of a modern constitutional federal republic that separates church from state. Few legal systems today are as overtly based on religious edicts, and the idea of the general welfare has altered with modern technology and knowledge, particularly of public health.[40] Even so, there are obvious contemporary analogs to all of these concepts and concerns derived from the colonial law. Moreover, with such caveats, we have at least some idea of the whole scope of the laws of a legal system relevant to the modern American experience.

The question for the contemporary observer, then, is what meaning we can ascribe to this scope in the lives of those subject to the law. There are a variety of ways in which we can generate a practical and logical framework of categories within that scope, of what the laws do in people's lives.

Legal philosophers call rules that direct subjects to do or refrain from specific acts by various names, according generally to the role the laws play in their theory – primary rules, legal norms, individuated laws, and so on. Each of these has a theoretical difference, and there are considerable arguments over their meanings.[41] For the purpose of this discussion about how the subject knows the law in practice – how the subject resorts to it or is subjugated by it – "law" roughly means all of these things from theory. "The law" means the sum of the laws and the institutions through which laws are promulgated and enforced. The point is that we can, roughly, map the effects

---

[40] In the era of the faith-based initiative, one might be excused from wondering how far American law had moved from the Puritan code's prohibition of idolatry. There are other, older reasons to wonder. See Robert C. Post, "Cultural Heterogeneity and Law: Pornography, Blasphemy, and the First Amendment," 76 California Law Review 297 (1988). Other legal systems are more comfortable with such laws, at least for now. Kathryn A. O'Brien, "Ireland's Secular Revolution: The Waning Influence of the Catholic Church and the Future of Ireland's Blasphemy Law," 18 Connecticut Journal of International Law 395 (2002).

[41] All of these are terms are much argued. For short, primary rules are the rules as enacted by the legal system that are intended to govern a subject's conduct. They might be either individuated laws, which would be how the citizen best understands them, or real laws, which is how a lawmaker understands them. See A. M. Honore, "Real Laws," in *Law, Morality and Society* 100 (P. M. S. Hacker & J. Raz, eds.) (Oxford University Press, 1977). Norms are any rules providing an individual with a reason for action, whether arising from social custom or from law alone. See Georg H. Von Wright, *Norm and Action: A Logical Enquiry* (Routledge, 1963).

of the law, attempting to understand what the effects of the law are in citizens' lives.

Modern Reflections on the Colonial Subject's Perspective. Consider again the example of colonial Massachusetts. Imagine ourselves in that small world in 1650. We can observe one thing immediately. To be a subject means to be at the mercy of an official armed with the law.

To imagine ourselves in the position of a subject to the colony's laws can be helpful:

The law can arrest us bodily. It can take our property, for what the officials call a public wrong or for a debt they say that we owe. The law can make us go to court and defend ourselves, sometimes over and over. The law demands our taxes, and it can take our liberty if we don't pay. The law can order us to serve on juries. It can make us be soldiers and go to war. If we are found drunk, it will whip us in public. It can order us to go to church, and not to say certain things in public. It can exile us. It can take our children, and it can force us to pay for schools where children are taught new ideas that we don't hold. The law can banish us for saying a court was wrong in convicting an innocent man.[42]

The law is fearsome, and it claims its power as a monopoly.[43] The Governor, the deputies, the judges and constables, see to it that no one but they can do all these things. The only limits on the law are that officials act according to rules that divide the law; deputies have to write those rules, freemen must approve them; constables carry them out, and judges rule on them.

Of course, who but the officials judge whether the officials are following the laws? As Juvenal the Roman asked, who guards the guardians?[44] Only

---

[42] Although hardly a Puritan, and with a more particular notion of the sovereign than the General Court might have agreed, Thomas Hobbes summarized many of these burdens at about the same time. "Those Levies therfore which are made upon mens estates, by the Soveraign Authority, are no more but the price of that Peace and Defence which the sovraignty maintaineth for them." Thomas Hobbes, *De Corpore Politico, or, the Elements of Law, Moral and Politick with Discourses upon Severall Heads, as of the Law of Nature, Oathes and Covenants, Several Kinds of Government: With the Changes and Revolutions of Them* 104 (T. R. for J. Ridley, 1652).

[43] This monopoly of law over state power is not a necessary claim for the law. It is merely how we tend to see it now in the West. The example of colonial Massachusetts is one in which this claim is weaker than we are used to making today. The church was a separate source of law over church matters, as it was throughout Europe. The early modern state, however, including Massachusetts, had divided the power over the sword and the cross, and the effect of Protestantism in Europe was especially pronounced in limiting ecclesiastic access to punishments beyond church privileges. The fights of Sir Edward Coke with the church courts are documented in Coke, *Selected Writings*. The same transition occurred in Catholic Europe, although it took longer; the last Inquisition in Spain did not end until 1834. Contemporary Iran and other states that accept *shari'a* as state law are similar. Religion is not the only alternative source of cultural norms that smack of law.

[44] *Sed quis custodiet ipsos custodes?* Juvenal, *Satires VI*, 347–8. The tag has taken on a life of its own, and yet Juvenal's rant is instructive. In talking of protecting the virtue of a daughter from an insinuating seducer, the common advice is to lock the daughter away under guard,

after the guardians broke into different teams, with some on the legislative court and others on the judicial court, was there anyone overlooking the guardians but God almighty and, maybe, the freemen. After all, we don't select these people, though if we could, we would select the best, wouldn't we? Or, would we pick those who would just feather our nests?

Anyway, the constable is only human, and whom will he arrest for the riot we walked past – the merchant's son who started it or the strangers who were there? Speaking of being human, sometimes they take evidence of spirits, testifying in court through live human beings; it is what we believe. Could anyone complain of a conviction for a crime witnessed by such a ghost?

The law claims to fulfill certain of our needs, particularly our safety from things we fear even more than the law. Without the militia, who will save us from the Indians, the French, the Dutch, and the pirates? Without the constables and the watch, who will punish the murderers, the robbers, the rapists? Can you or I be trusted to do it on our own?

Without the law, would anyone punish my murderer? You would not be allowed to, even if you have the courage and strength. What then would restrain a murderer? The officials do all of this; so we have only to do what they say, and we must help them when we are needed, or when we know something.

Without the law, how will I know you will sell me fair wood for my barrels, or pay me what you owe me after I deliver them? Without the officials, who will collect the tax to build the roads or maintain the harbor quay? Without the road or quay, how can we sell our goods? If you built one, could I use it?

On the other hand, if there is trouble, do we know the watch will come, or the constable or the judge will listen to us? How fair will the judge be? What if one of us is murdered by the magistrate's brother? Will the constable really arrest him? What if it was the merchant? Will he go to the gallows without bribing a soul? If the stave-wood inspector takes a few shillings from the stave-maker, will he approve the staves even if they are dried and useless? If I and my neighbor quarrel over whether I owe more for a mare that was about to foal, who will decide for us?

The law orders our money. It sets our interest rates, our rights to property, the means of our contracts. And, it requires our education and ensures our poor will not starve. If I would make money otherwise, or if I need help but am not favored, will I be protected by the law? Will I be allowed to earn my living as I want?

The law decrees our contributions toward common enterprises. The village green, the quays, the roads, the town warehouse, the schools, even the town well exist through the joint efforts of us all, organized by the

---

so then who will guard the guardians? Juvenal, *The Sixteen Satires* 45 (Peter Green, trans.) (Penguin, 1998). Thus the folk maxim of setting the fox to guard the henhouse. These and other maxims of distrust for the guardians turn on the natural inclination of the guards to betray their tasks to satisfy personal desires.

officials. Without the law, how rich must I be to be sure of access to clean water?

The law gives some answers itself. It tells us what we should do. The felonies of the colonial laws echo the language of God for the offences like idolatry, rape, and murder, though no divine command sends the inspector to check that the wood is good enough for barrels. Some laws send the children to school; some forbid lying and cheating, and they give our neighbors the power of remedy if we lie to them or cheat them. Even the tax laws tell us we must support the public works. These laws are all given to us as a lump, and we are told they are needed for the Commonwealth.

We have the benefit and must accept the burden; we have the law's protection and must give it our assistance. Officials might claim it is right for us to do what they say, not just because they say it but because what they order would be what we ought to do anyway. If we would be good citizens, we would do what it says. If not, the power of the law could be brought to us, and others will judge us even if the magistrate does not. We might even judge ourselves as disappointments to our family or to ourselves for being bad citizens, bad people, scofflaws. We hope then, that what the law requires of us is really right and good. The law requires us to denounce witches, after all. If we do not, who would stop them? Who could punish them?

The law defines us. The Commonwealth is us, even if we are not freemen. We are the people, beholden to the officials, but in some small way we are parts of their enterprise. The law tells not only us what to do but also all of our neighbors, and we all thus act the same. We judge others, and we are judged by others, by these standards, without even waiting for the constable or the judge. To live here, even the servants must swear an oath of fidelity.[45] When the Commonwealth puts someone to death, it is done in the name of God and the Commonwealth. We are God's people; the law says so. We cannot feed a Jesuit priest; the law says that, too. So we are people who are Christian but refuse shelter to Christians. It is who we are under the law.

---

[45] The oath of fidelitie specified

> I (A B) being by Gods providence an Inhabitant within the Jurisdiction of this Common-wealth, doe freely and sincerely acknowledge my selfe to be subject to the Government thereof. And doe heer swear by the great and dreadfull name of the Ever-living God, that I will be true and faithfull to the same, and will accordingly yield assistance therunto, with my person and estate, as in equitie I am bound: and will also truly indeavour to maintein and preserve all the Liberties & Priviledges therof, submitting my selfe unto the wholsom Laws made & established by the same. And farther, that I will not plot or practice any evil against it, or consent to any that shall so doe: but will timely discover and reveal the same to lawfull Authorie now heer established, for the speedy preventing thereof. So help me God in our Lord Jesus Christ.

Lawes and Libertyes 56.

Summary: Contemporary Echoes of the Subject's Experience. In short, to consider the colonist's view of the law, we see it in many dimensions, which for the moment we could label fears, protection, decision, norms, economy, common goods, personal identity, group identity, official selection, and the anonymity of corporate acts. It is a powerful force and to be feared, a force that can take lives, wealth, liberty, and peace from the subject. It is a means of securing what the colonists need for protection – against violence, dishonesty, theft, even bad behavior by others, and for some, starvation. It provides a referee for disputes that cannot be resolved otherwise. It is a source of ideas about the good and the right, telling the colonist what a good or right-thinking person would do. It defines in part the identity of the colonist not only by assisting in creating an identity for the individual but also by identifying the community through common purposes and conduct. The law acts on the colonist's behalf, and the colonist bears a sense of indirect responsibility leading to some measure of pride or shame in what the colony does. And, the law determines the means for selecting some colonists to bear this power, leaving others to be subject to it through their actions.

Officials and Their Stakes in the Law

If we are to consider fully the stakes various people have in how the law is carried out, the effects of the law are important to officials in both what the law does and (even more, perhaps, than for the subject) the manner in which the law is created and applied. Particularly, what are effects of the law that would lead to a greater or lesser likelihood that officials will obey, or at least accept, the constitution and procedures of the law?

A Second Case Study from Colonial Massachusetts

We can consider the effect of law upon officials, as well as upon subjects, by returning to the case study by which we considered the scope of law and its reach into the lives of the subjects. Here we can examine one of the more famous instances of the effects of the law in Massachusetts colonial history.

In 1692, twenty people were put to death by judicial order in Salem, Massachusetts, following charges of witchcraft.[46] This was hardly an isolated

---

[46] Witchcraft was a crime at common law, defined in 1604 under an act of Parliament, "against conjuration." Witchcraft Act, 1 Jac. I, c. 12 (1604). The Salem trials applied the common law and this statute, as witch's trials had been in England since Henry VIII had begun them during the schism with Rome. See Gregory Durston, *Witchcraft and Witch Trials: A History of English Witchcraft and Its Legal Perspectives, 1542 to 1736* (Barry Rose Law Publishers, 2000). Although witchcraft was an offense in the 1648 *Lawes and Libertyes*, that code was suspended, at least formally, with the loss of the colony's charter in 1684.

affair: nearly the whole legal system of the colony was engaged in the trials, which were overseen by the colony's chief justice and lieutenant governor, and which led to the arrest of hundreds throughout Essex County and to charges against 144, mostly women.

The Salem Trials: The story is well documented and still well known, or at least elements of it remain well known.[47] The Plymouth minister's young daughter and a few of her friends, including several evacuated from villages attacked in the ongoing Indian wars, began having fits. The local doctor could cure the fits of neither the girls nor their friends who copied them, concluding that the girls (eventually seven girls) must be the victims of supernatural disorders. The fits, after all, resembled Cotton Mather's recent depiction of bewitched children in Boston.[48] When a warrant was issued to arrest Tituba, a Barbadan slave who had told them stories of witchcraft, the girls began to denounce other villagers as witches and wizards. The girls not only said they had seen the villagers commit acts of magic but also related statements told them by spirits that the villagers had done so. The initial accusations were against Tituba and two other social outcasts, whose trials before the local court were *causes célèbres*. Tituba confessed in court, and the girls gained in credibility. The girls denounced more villagers, including prominent members of the community, whom County Judge John Hathorne jailed for trial.

The colonial governor, Sir William Phips, created a special Court of Oyer and Terminer to hear the charges against all the accused. The court's seven judges were chaired by Lieutenant Governor William Stoughton. Accepting Cotton Mather's advice, the court allowed "spectral evidence" testimony by accusers who claimed that they were speaking for ghosts and witnessing demons. Faced with such evidence, and knowing that all of the accused had been found guilty and hanged, fifty-five of the accused confessed (and were freed) and five fled into exile. Of the nineteen who argued their innocence, nineteen were found guilty and hanged, as were two dogs that were convicted of complicity. The twentieth defendant, seventy-five-year-old Giles Corey, refused to accept the jurisdiction of the court and was pressed to death with stones.[49] Among those

---

[47] The story has been researched in much detail, perhaps the best recent work being by Hoffer and Norton, upon which this narrative relies in general. See Mary Beth Norton, *In the Devil's Snare: The Salem Witchcraft Crisis of 1692* (Alfred A. Knopf, 2002); Peter Charles Hoffer, *The Salem Witchcraft Trials: A Legal History* (University Press of Kansas, 1997); *The Devil's Disciples: Makers of the Salem Witchcraft Trials* (Johns Hopkins University Press, 1996). See also the now slightly dated but still powerful Bernard Rosenthal, *Salem Story: Reading the Witch Trials of 1692* (Cambridge University Press, 1995).

[48] Cotton Mather, *Memorable Providences, Relating to Witchcrafts and Possessions* 2–5 (R.P. 1689).

[49] 1 *The Salem Witchcraft Papers: Verbatim Transcripts of the Legal Documents of the Salem Witchcraft Outbreak of 1692* 239–46 (Paul Boyer & Stephen Nissenbaum, eds.) (Da Capo

hanged were the minister George Boroughs, who recited the Lord's Prayer from the scaffold, and several who had denounced the trials, including the tavern keeper John Proctor, who wrote from jail to Increase Mather and other colonial leaders, describing the torture used to extract confessions and the dangers of spectral evidence.[50] Also punished was deputy constable John Willard, who refused to continue arresting the innocent and denounced the trials, after which he was accused himself and hanged.[51]

Following Proctor's letter, a meeting was held in Boston of leading intellectuals in the colony, after which Increase Mather, Cotton Mather's father, wrote *Cases of Conscience*, denouncing the use of spectral evidence in court.[52] Throughout the summer of 1692, public condemnations of the trials grew. Sermons were preached against them, and the anger of the public toward the Court of Oyer and Terminer increasingly echoed dissatisfaction with the disastrous colonial management of the Indian war. Further, accusations began to surface against Governor Phips's wife and perhaps himself.[53]

By October, with one hundred and fifty in jail and hundreds more accused, prisoners were dying in their shackles. Phips asked the legislative General Court to disband the Court of Oyer and Terminer, which it did in a close vote, sending the remaining cases to the newly created Supreme Judicial Court, which was barred from hearing spectral evidence and which acquitted all but three of the remaining cases.[54] Phips pardoned those.[55] From the first child's fit to the last hanging, the Salem trials lasted only seven months, with gubernatorial pardons following nine months later.

Three Salem Officials: Today we can assess the whole episode with horror, but the reactions of three of the leading officials in the immediate aftermath are of particular interest to our study.

Press, 1977). Corey was tortured under the old common law rule of *peine forte et dure*, which at least prevented his estate from being seized in attainder, as happened to those who were convicted and hanged.

[50] 2 *Witchcraft Papers* 667–80. There was other evidence as well. See Wendel D. Craker, "Spectral Evidence, Non-Spectral Acts of Witchcraft and Confessions in Salem in 1692," 40 *Historical Journal* 331 (1997).

[51] 3 *Witchcraft Papers* 819–52; Marion Starkey, *The Devil in Massachusetts* 148 (Alfred A. Knopf, 1948).

[52] See Increase Mather, *A Farther Account of the Tryals of the New-England Witches with the Observations of a Person Who Was upon the Place Several Days When the Suspected Witches Were First Taken into Examination: to Which Is Added, Cases of Conscience Concerning Witchcrafts and Evil Spirits Personating Men / Written at the Request of the Ministers of New-England by Increase Mather* (J. Dunton, 1693). There were other denunciations of spectral evidence, from both within and without the colony. See Starkey, *Devil* 224–7.

[53] Emerson W. Baker and John G. Reid, *The New England Knight: Sir William Phips, 1651–1695* 146–52 (University of Toronto Press, 1998). Phips is also spelled "Phipps."

[54] 3 *Witchcraft Papers* 903–94.

[55] 3 *Witchcraft Papers* 863–5.

Phips. Governor Sir William Phips was initially a whole-hearted supporter of the witchcraft tribunal he had established.[56] Yet he dithered increasingly over the matter, distracted from the issue and by it while fighting a frontier war that was not going well.[57] After creating the capital court to try all of the accusations, he left for a month in the battlefield, returning to find his original policy increasingly unpopular among all of the social classes, particularly the religious and intellectual elite. The policy was, though, in the hands of the politically independent court, which was controlled by Stoughton, the former chief judge and the lieutenant governor, and Phips did not intervene for some time. Only when the trials began to threaten his own hearth did he act to end the proceedings, placing most of the blame for them on Stoughton.[58] For Phips, the matter was a political embarrassment, but there seems little evidence of genuine remorse for the damage done to the lives of the victims, or for that matter to the reputation of the courts or the law.

Stoughton. Chief Justice William Stoughton, certain in the righteousness of his cause and bent on destroying a nest of witches, appears to have suffered no doubts over the truth of the evidence before him, regardless of its illogic or contradictions, whether it came from those accused who thereby escaped punishment, from the tortured defendants themselves, or from invisible spectres conjured up by teenagers. By all accounts (including Phips's), he resented Phips's taking away the power to hear spectral evidence and fought the dissolution of the Court of Oyer and Terminer. Still, giving him his due, Stoughton presided over the new court, and without spectral evidence he rightly dismissed most of the remaining unconfessed indictments with little more than pro forma hearings. His later years were spent in continued public service until his death, and despite others' broad denunciations of the witchcraft trials over which he presided, he never renounced his own part in them.[59]

---

[56] The Court of Oyer and Terminer was an extraordinary institution in the colony, with broad penal authority, established at Phips's request by the General Court. It was not required in the crisis, and indeed it was an overreaction. Not only could the usual courts have heard the criminal matters before them, but the accusations themselves could have been treated to a more sober and cautious appraisal.

[57] Mary Beth Norton has proved that the hysteria behind these executions, and the willingness of leaders such as Phips and Stoughton to believe their troubles were caused by Satan, resulted from official war rhetoric and losses in the ongoing Indian wars. See Mary Beth Norton, *In the Devil's Snare: The Salem Witchcraft Crisis of 1692* (Alfred A. Knopf, 2002).

[58] See Baker & Reid, *New England Knight* 134–55.

[59] See Emory Washburn, "William Stoughton," in *Sketches of the Judicial History of Massachusetts From 1630 to the Revolution in 1775* 242–7 (Little and Brown, 1840). Stoughton died in 1701, after a wave of public apologies by the accusers had been already made, along with condemnations of the trials' use of spectral evidence, published by both Cotton Mather and his philosophical opponents Thomas Brattle and Robert Calef. Stoughton said nothing. In 1711, the Commonwealth reversed all attainders from the Salem convictions and paid more than seven hundred pounds in reparations to the survivors. 3 *Witchcraft Papers* 945–1046.

Sewall. Judge Samuel Sewall reacted quite differently. Appointed as a judge of the Court of Oyer and Terminer, he initially carried out his judicial duties with diligence, he being somewhat in the shadow of Stoughton and the other, more senior judges.[60] He appears, for instance, to have accepted the truth of the charges against silent old Giles Cory when Thomas Putnam, the wealthy father of Ann, Cory's chief accuser, wrote him that witches were crushing his daughter at the time the bailiffs were crushing Giles. Indeed, as late as September 1692, Sewall was assisting Stoughton and Cotton Mather in preparing to publish a defense of the trials.[61] In October, though, Sewall's doubts were stirred by a meeting with Judge Thomas Danforth in Cambridge, who denounced the trials.[62] Meanwhile, the General Court passed a bill calling for a fast and a convocation of ministers "that they may be led in the right way regarding the Witchcrafts."[63] In November, he prayed for guidance and for the Lord to "save New England as to Enemies and Witchcrafts and vindicate the law Judges, with his Justice and Holiness."[64]

In December, Sewall was selected as judge of the new Supreme Court of Judicature, which would sit over the remaining trials in 1693. Though he sat through weeks of trials exonerating the remaining accused, Sewall noted little of it in his voluminous diaries.[65] The years after the trials were hard in the colony, particular so for Sewall. Hannah, his wife, had delivered a stillborn child in 1696, and the colony remained mired in war, plague, and economic depression. In December, the General Court ordered January 14, 1697, to be the day to atone for the colonists' unspecified sins, which had brought on such divine wrath. The Sewalls's two-year-old daughter died and was buried on Christmas Day. Sewall's diary shows him alternately engulfed in his private grief, recalling his part in the grief of others, and considering the perhaps divine retribution it provoked. On Christmas Eve, he recorded his son Samuel reciting from the Gospel of Matthew, " . . . I will have mercy and not sacrifice, ye would not have condemned the guiltless," which did "awfully bring to mind the Salem Tragedie."[66]

On January 14, Sewall was still deep in mourning for the loss of his children. The parish of Boston's Old South Church, including many of the officials of

---

[60] See Emory Washburn, "Samuel Sewall," in *Sketches of the Judicial History of Massachusetts From 1630 to the Revolution in 1775* 258–63 (Little and Brown, 1840); N. H. Chamberlain, *Samuel Sewall and the World He Lived In* (De Wolfe, Fiske & Co., 1897).

[61] 1 *The Diary of Samuel Sewall, 1674–1729* 297 (M. Halsey Thomas, ed.) (Farrar, Straus, and Giroux, 1973).

[62] *Id.* 298.

[63] *Id.* 299.

[64] *Id.* 301.

[65] *Id.* 304–9.

[66] *Id.* 364.

the General Court, had assembled for the fast when Sewall gave to his minister, Samuel Willard, a bill to read. Willard read the bill while Sewall stood with his head bowed.

> Samuel Sewall, sensible of the reiterated strokes of God upon him self and family; and being sensible, that as to the Guilt contracted, upon the opening of the late Commission of Oyer and Terminer at Salem (to which the order for this Day relates) he is, upon many accounts, more concerned than any that he knows of, Desires to take the Blame and Shame of it, Asking pardon of Men, And especially desiring prayers that God, who has an Unlimited Authority, would pardon that Sin and all other his Sins; personal and Relative: And according to his infinite Benignity, and Soveraignty, Not Visit the Sin of him, or of any other, upon himself or any of his, nor upon the Land: But that He would powerfully defend him against all Temptations to Sin, for the future; and vouchsafe him the Efficacious, Saving Conduct of his Word and Spirit.[67]

This was no idle prayer, and in later years Sewall set aside days for private fasting and atonement for his actions in the trials. He remained on the colony's new Supreme Judicial Court, becoming Chief Justice in 1717, which he remained until two years before his death in 1730.[68] As the legal historian Peter Hoffer has summed him up, "Sewall was a pious man and a conventional one. He believed in witches and feared the Devil. He was also a man of exceeding good sense, a practical man, and he realized, if belatedly, that somehow God's people had become the Devil's disciples."[69]

A Contrast to Salem: Before leaving the story of Salem, particularly as a case study for the purpose of considering the role of law in people's lives, a coda is required.

Salem did not have the only witch trials in New England in 1692. Not far from Salem, in Stamford, Connecticut, a similar story had begun, with an accusation of bewitchment raised by a young woman, Katherine Branch. Her accusations led to what would be known as the Fairfield Witch Panic, resulting in the arrest of a half dozen and eventually in the trials of two people, Goody Elizabeth Clawson and Goody Mercy Disborough, who were held for trial under the procedures for witchcraft, which required careful experimentation to prove the claims raised against the defendant.

Jones. Preliminary hearings were held by a Stamford magistrate and his colleagues, who gathered what evidence they could with meticulous records before

---

[67]   *Id.* 367. The particular drama of that day is nicely depicted in Richard Francis, *Judge Sewall's Apology: The Salem Witch Trials and the Forming of an American Conscience* (Fourth Estate, 2005).

[68]   See Emory Washburn, "Samuel Sewall," 258–63.

[69]   Hoffer, *The Devil's Disciples* 198.

binding the accused over to a special Court of Oyer and Terminer appointed in Connecticut, following a procedure similar to that of Massachusetts. The Connecticut tribunal was chaired by Deputy-Governor William Jones, who prepared a manual of procedure in witchcraft cases from the available books. Jones wrote over the requirement that conviction follow only upon "good and sufficient proofs" and listed a variety of evidence that would be insufficient.[70] Aided by the meticulous evidence gathered by the magistrates, the procedures of the court appear to have been carefully followed, leading ultimately to the dismissal of charges against all of the accused but for two defendants, followed ultimately by the acquittal of both Clawson and Disborough, Clawson being dismissed by the trial jury and Disborough released on appeal.[71]

There were many differences between Stamford and Salem, not the least being that Connecticut was not then in a fierce and precarious war but also being that it was a far less puritanical culture and more prone to skepticism in the face of such claims. None of these diminish the effect of Jones's persistent application of the forensic and legal procedures, which led to such a different result.

Four Models of Legal Official

There is a useful comparison among Phips and Stoughton, on the one hand, and Sewall and Jones, on the other, as officials generally of the problem in the trials. Each took the danger of witchcraft seriously – and before we laugh, we should recognize that we would almost certainly have agreed with them, had we lived in the English world of the seventeenth century.[72] The problem was not the existence of the crime but whether there was sufficient evidence that the people accused had committed it. Lives were lost, homes were shattered – fortunes, reputations, and friendships were destroyed, all based on the evidence invented in the imaginations of young accusers and the desperate accused, buttressed occasionally by chance.[73] Only more thorough skepticism by the judges, more

---

[70]   Richard Godbeer, *Escaping Salem: The Other Witch Hunt of 1692*, 91–109 (Oxford University Press, 2005).

[71]   The records are reproduced in *Witch-Hunting in Seventeenth Century New England: A Documentary History, 1638–1693* 315–54 (2d ed.) (David D. Hall, ed.) (Northeastern University Press, 1999).

[72]   The twentieth century has had its share of enemies within, whose treatment by the multitudes was hardly better than that dealt out to witches: Indians; union leaders; Jews; Catholics; Cajuns; immigrants from Ireland, Asia, and Mexico; black community organizers and freedom riders; communists; feminists; homosexuals; and now perhaps Muslims.

[73]   The crisis in the judgment evolved from a mistake in procedure. Reviewing the Salem witchcraft trials "brings strongly to light the way in which the security afforded by legal forms and solemnities for the accurate investigation of facts may wholly break down when the men who are to do the judging have their minds saturated with certain sorts of opinion." James Bradley Thayer, "Trial by Jury of Things Supernatural," in *Legal Essays* 329, 341 (1908) (Rothman, 1972).

careful thought of the results as well as the means by which they were produced could have saved them, and that care, that skepticism, that hesitation born of doubt needed to avert such a horrible injustice, was not to be had in the mix of personalities then on the bench.

Stoughton, from this distance at least, appears never to have perceived the problem in his efforts. He believed in his cause and in his convictions. He was certain. All of the problems he could see were the fault of enemies, skeptics, and unbelievers – all of whose obstruction was to be swept aside for the benefit of the colony. As much as anyone else, his certainty led to the death and despair of his innocent countrymen, but he never believed it. His confidence, reinforced by Mather's, surely bolstered the less confident, younger Sewall to accept the court's rulings. Phips's political angling, and his distraction brought about by his poor management of the war, led him to delay intervention until well past the point of crisis.

The effects upon the subjects were horrible. Not only were many killed, many others were marred forever. Confidence in the government, not high to begin with, plummeted as the people came to believe that their officials were incompetent and that God had abandoned them.[74]

The effects of the trials upon the officials themselves were less severe but instructive. Though he no doubt discounted its effects, Stoughton was harmed considerably then, and posthumously, by the erosion of his reputation. He would have been reviled by many of the subjects who might be brought before him, but this is little compared to his reputation for centuries as a symbol of injustice and intemperance.[75] The effect of his certainty, though, was not nearly as pronounced upon him as it has been on other officials. The charge of holding a Salem witch trial is not one a modern judge is likely to hear without an emotional response, and it is largely Stoughton we have to thank.

Phips realized the danger to his reputation that grew from several threats arising out of the trials. On the one side was growing discontent in the polity, driven by fear and anger over the increasingly obvious injustice of the trials. This discontent was reflected not only in popular concern but in the growing disaffection of the intellectual and social leaders of the colony. On the other side was the increasing risk that Phips himself would be caught in the net he had cast in setting up the courts. There is little evidence of remorse for the harm his policy had caused – we have no evidence of him passing more than a moment in worry over the innocents his court had sent to die – but there was a practical need to reduce the risks for his reputation and his authority in office.

In Sewall we find a cipher who became a hero, initially following in the steps of others, then moved to question his own conduct and find it wanting. While

---

[74] See, for example, Larry Gragg, *The Salem Witch Crisis* 161–77 (Praeger, 1991).
[75] See Emory Washburn, "William Stoughton."

we might be tempted to parochially discount his fears that God had punished his children for his transgressions, such a fear of the Puritan God was normal, and in any event, it is hardly Sewall's only reason for renouncing his earlier judgments. He had seen case after case fail when tried by fair evidence. He had heard the accusers of the executed recant their testimony. He knew that the people he had sent to hang had been innocent, and that knowledge brought sorrow and remorse, compounded by his personal tragedies. The result was his public acknowledgment of his official error, which still stands as testament not only to the dangers of law unrestrained by skepticism but also to the possibility of its reform.

Jones is an almost accidental official, a person who is a judge as a result of other duties, but who takes the duties seriously and performs them with a particular care for their purpose and for the law. Jones is determined not to convict an innocent or to free a witch, and he uses the procedures with care to determine the result.

Stoughton and Phips, Sewall and Jones each represents a type. Stoughton, the certain and self-confident official, whose image of his office was unflinching not only in the face of his critics but also in the face of the evidence. Phips, the practical but responsive politician, whose concern for his public image was such that it drove his management of the law to both start and end the travesty. Sewall, the reflective and open-minded judge, who learned both from the subjects before him and from the circumstances around them, whose self-image was harmed most by his mistakes and who responded with courage to acknowledge his errors in public. Jones, the careful plodder, reserved judgment, followed the rules, and did the work, as a result of which justice was done.[76]

In their time, each survived the trials with his public image generally intact. They were after all, in roughly the same boat as were all of their fellow elites in the colony and in England. Yet history has judged the Salem judges harshly, even Sewall, for their participation in the tragedy in the courtrooms of Massachusetts. Sewall alone among the Salem three represents a saving grace, and it is his image that still stands, larger than life, head bowed, in the Massachusetts State House.[77] Jones and his colleagues in Connecticut have, by comparison, appeared little in history and then mainly as comparative heroes.[78]

[76] There is no limit to the personality types to be found in nearly any legal story, representing both ideal and perverse forms of human conduct. For instance, none of these three people seem to have been especially diligent or lazy, more or less intelligent, or more or less kindly to their families.

[77] A mural by Albert Herter depicts the public reading of the Repentance of Samuel Sewall in the chambers of the Massachusetts House of Representatives in the State House in Boston. See *Milestones on the Road to Freedom in Massachusetts: Ceremonies at the Presentation,* Boston State House, January 18, 1943.

[78] See, for example, Richard G. Tomlinson, *Witchcraft Trials of Connecticut* (Connecticut Research, Inc., 1978).

The judgment of history upon an official is rarely anticipated in its own time, and yet it does have its harbingers, particularly in the public image perceived by the subjects. An official's legacy – the potential judgment of history – is an aspect of the image of the official that the official may care about, may yearn to improve, or may hope to counterfeit, but it is as unpredictable for any individual as all of the other motives and aspects of a person's fulfilling an official role.

The effects of the injustice committed by these officials acting in concert were unpredictable for any one official. But it is quite likely that some effects will occur to some officials, and these effects will be the results of the judgments of the officials and others, all the more so when the effects of the law on the subject provoke harsh judgment.

In other words, there are Stoughtons and Phipses, as well as Sewalls and Joneses in most communities of officials. They are archetypes,[79] and people like each are likely to be found in nearly any community of officials. Indeed they each may represent an aspect of varying impulses even in a single individual. Their reactions of unwavering confidence, pliability to protect reputation, and fair-minded self-judgment are a sample of the range of responses to the apparent fact of unjustified effects of the law on the subjects.

Unlike some archetypes, however, these individuals' reactions cannot be assessed in isolation. The decisions of each official are significant only in their community of officials – the decision by one depends on its agreement and implementation by others – and it is here that their interaction becomes essential to understanding each role in the legal system as a whole.

Stoughton could not succeed in his authority without Phips. Once Phips lost confidence in their project, Stoughton's authority to punish these accused witches was itself destroyed. Sewall's confidence in the project was shaken not only by its end by Phips, but also by the patent injustice revealed over time, which finally doomed Stoughton, and others like him, never to regain this cherished authority. Jones could not have succeeded, and indeed did not succeed, without the support of his fellow magistrates and the appellate judges of the General Court.

The officials must share in the authority. Legal authority cannot persist long when exercised by one alone. To carry this authority, each official must act in

---

[79]   As an exercise in types, a trio similar to the Salem judges can be found among the German officials in Abby Mann's *Judgment at Nuremberg* (1961) (New Directions, 2002), the script for Stanley Kramer's astonishing movie. The movie is discussed in Chapter 4, but the parallels would be between Stoughton and the prosecutor Emil Hahn, Phips and the cooperative judge Werner Lammpe or perhaps the politic American General Merrin, and Sewall and the remorseful judge Ernst Janning. Jones has no parallel among the prisoners, and to the degree there is a parallel, it would be Chief Judge Dan Haywood.

concert with others. That is another effect of the division of labor. It is why there is, indeed, responsibility across the aggregate for each.

The Official and the Subject

We must be cautious in believing that any one set of motivations or any hierarchy of values, goals, or concerns is necessarily held by a given official or by all officials. The time-server, for instance, is fairly unbothered by all of these effects.

What is certain about these effects of law on the official is that most of the time, most of them turn, to some degree, on the effect of law on the subject. Even the social rules of the community of officials are deeply affected by them. The exercise of authority depends on the acts of the subject creating a circumstance for the fear, or fulfillment, of the law. The image of the official depends on how and what is done to or for the subject. The anxiety is, at least at times, affected by the accuracy of the official's actions in the lives of those subject to them.

Officials are inextricably tied to the subjects of the law. The effects of the law in the subjects' lives are significant not only in what the official does but also in the official's own identity. What the law does to the subject will alter how the official sees both the law and the office.

OFFICIAL INFLUENCE ON THE LIVES OF OTHERS: NINE METAPHORS

This chapter has considered the stakes that various people have in the law, not only in the archive of its rules, but also in its culture, the manner in which laws are created and enforced. We can discern a rough list, in which the effects on subjects include:

- The fearful aspects of law as a power in their lives.
- The dependence that the law engenders as the protection from harms by others (including other officials) as well as from harms by circumstances.
- The provision of arbiters for private disputes.
- The regulation of the economy and the provision of social goods.
- The normative functions of law as it tells us all what to do and not to do.
- The cultural functions through which we and our neighbors construct our identities and by which we are responsible, if indirectly, for what the officials do through laws.
- The selective mechanism by which some subjects are designated as officials and held responsible to carry out the laws.

- The anonymity with which many laws are created and executed among a community of officials.

The effects on officials derive primarily from these effects on the subjects but have certain aspects dependent on their role and on the others whose regard is meaningful to them in that role. Officials seek achievement, or doing some of the things the law is supposed to do in the lives of the subjects. They seek a good image of themselves for doing their jobs, both in their own eyes and in the sight of others, and they have recurrent concerns about performing their jobs successfully and maintaining their image with themselves, their friends, their colleagues, and the subjects. These pursuits by officials, however, depend largely on the effects of the law on the subject.

The most essential effects of the law in people's lives can be summarized by the effects of the law in the lives of the subjects. These effects can be generalized into concepts that are, of course, mere labels for series of complex and interrelated effects. In this summary fashion, they have a metaphorical utility, although the metaphorical aspect of the labels risks being lost in their seemingly descriptive nature.

Thus, to make obvious the representative nature of these concepts, which we will use throughout the argument to come, I propose discussing them by labels of more obvious metaphorical value. Taking the benefit not only of poetic language to evoke the unspoken but also of the traditions of symbols associated with the law, I will refer to them as the sword, shield, balance, coin, commons, guide, mirror, seal, and veil.

The power of officials over the subjects by which they can bring death, terror, and loss upon individual subjects, whether the subject deserves such punishment or not, we can identify as the sword. The law's putative monopoly on power to protect from others, which not only may fail to be exercised but forbids subjects from many forms of protection both of themselves and of their fellows, can be labeled the shield. The law's capacity to referee private disputes, and indeed disputes among some officials, we may refer to as the balance. The law's power to define civic notions of right and wrong, of the good and reasonable, and to encourage or coerce acceptance of these goals we can consider the guide. The peculiar claims of the law that subjects ought to construct their identity through law, that the governed are held to accept the morality or immorality of their state as their own – regardless of how little or how much participation, acceptance, or even knowledge of the subject they may possess in an official act, there is an inescapable association with it – this we can call the mirror. The concern that officials and subjects have in the selection of officials, and the image of officials *qua* officials, their conformity or rejection of the social rules that develop in the community of officials, we can call the seal. The inability of the subject to discern the origin of official action may be termed the veil, and the power of the law to create community assets and to guide the economy we can call the commons and the coin.

We might briefly note that these powers of law, these aspects of the authority of law that are here cloaked in these metaphors, differ from the usual justifications for those powers used in the academy. Since the days of Plato and Aristotle, political scientists have argued that the authority of the ruler, or in our case the body of officials, arises from the greater knowledge of the ruler, or the requirement that the ruler coordinate the polity to achieve some appropriate end. These ideas of knowledge and coordination have been mooted so that even when the end is to achieve goals in the interest of the subject, it is worthwhile for the subject to agree to the authority.[80] To an extent, these justifications are predicates to some of these powers, perhaps most notably the shield and the coin. But knowledge and coordination are not seen by the people, at least as they have been depicted so far, as justifications for the power; the successfulness of the use of the shield and of the coin are seen as what matters.

The Dangers of Metaphor

Law seems peculiarly drawn to metaphor. Lawyers are fond of imagery, describing concepts with evocative images from other dimensions of human knowledge, and metaphor is an age-old tool of legal discourse. The Egyptian balance of Ma'ath and Thoth.[81] Blind justice.[82] Justice with her scales.[83] The medieval

---

[80]   Aristotle, *The Politics*, Book 4. See, for example, Andres Rosler, *Political Authority and Obligation in Aristotle* 178–218 (Oxford University Press, 2005). Professor Raz describes this process, which he nominates the normal justification thesis, without the baggage of classical antecedents in *The Morality of Freedom* 53 (Oxford University Press, 1988). See also William Lucy, *Understanding and Explaining Adjudication* (Oxford University Press, 1999). The coordination thesis underlies most of the justifications of the social contract. See Sir Ernest Barker, "Introduction," in *Social Contract: Locke, Hume, Rousseau* (Oxford University Press, 1962). When knowledge is extended to moral knowledge, the idea of superior knowledge mattered as much to Kant as to Plato. See Immanuel Kant, *The Metaphysical Elements of Justice* (John Ladd, trans.) (Bobbs-Merril, 1965).

[81]   See the scenes from the Last Judgment in E. A. Wallis Budge, *The Egyptian Book of the Dead* (Gramercy, 1995). For more on the balance as a metaphor for law, see Steve Sheppard, "The State Interest in the Good Citizen: Constitutional Balance between the Citizen and the Perfectionist State," 45 Hastings Law Journal 969, nn.1–3 (1994).

[82]   "In Thebes there were set up statues of judges without hands, and the statue of the chief justice had its eyes closed, to indicate that justice is not influenced by gifts or by intercession." Plutarch, "Isis and Osiris," ch. 10, in 5 Moralia § 355 (Frank Cole Babbitt, trans.) (Loeb Classical Library, 1936); see also Diodorus, i.48.6.

[83]   This was Themis, goddess of harmony, but since Homer, she has represented justice. See Alice I. Youmans, Joan S. Howland, & Myra K. Saunders, "Questions and Answers (Blind

king's two bodies.[84] The spirit of the law in the enlightenment.[85] The Victorian seamless web.[86] The modern activist judge.[87] All of these images and phrases, and many, many more have been deployed to describe and to criticize the content and methods of the law. This practice has been embraced by scholars of the common law, who have recognized its utility as a tool both for depicting texts and for organizing complex data.[88] It seems that lawyers generally accept metaphors as nonliteral representations of categories that are somehow accurate or true, which is a contested point in modern philosophy.[89] This process may accelerate as more legal information enters the symbolically rich environment of the Internet.[90]

Justice)," 182 Law Library Journal 197 (1990), who date Themis's blindness like Plutarch's Theban judge only to Durer's fifteenth-century woodcut for *Ship of Fools.*

[84] See Ernst Kantorowicz, *The King's Two Bodies: A Study in Medieval Political Theology* (1957) (Princeton University Press, 1997).

[85] Charles-Louis de Secondat, Baron de la Brède et de Montesquieu, *The Spirit of the Laws* (1741) (Anne M. Cohler, Basia Carolyn Miller, & Harold Samuel Stone, eds.) (Cambridge University Press, 1989).

[86] Maitland famously noted of legal history, "Such is the unity of all history that any one who endeavours to tell a piece of it must feel that his first sentence tears a seamless web." Frederic W. Maitland, "A Prologue to a History of English Law," 14 Law Quarterly Review 13 (1898). The significance of the metaphor has changed over time, from its original sense of the interrelationship of historical data to sometimes representing the comprehensiveness of legal rules or theories of legal rules. See, for example, Lyrissa Barnett Lidsky, "*Defensor Fidei:* The Travails of a Post-Realist Formalist," 47 Florida Law Review 815 (1995).

[87] Admittedly, "activist judge" is not a metaphor but a stereotype, at best a synecdoche, in which one entity characterizes all related entities. See Sister Miriam Joseph, *The Trivium: The Liberal Arts of Logic, Grammar, and Rhetoric* 244–5 (Paul Dry Books, 2002).
   "Activist judge" and "judicial activism" arose in the backlash to the Supreme Court's acceptance of the New Deal, the tropes periodically given new life in reactions against judicial remedies of racial desegregation, privacy protection, labor law security, and product liability. The earliest use of the phrases I have found is in C. Herman Pritchett, *The Roosevelt Court: Study in Judicial Politics and Values, 1937–1947* 286 (Macmillan, 1947), though the phrases had reached beyond the New Deal agenda at least by the 1960s. See Alpheus Thomas Mason, "Judicial Activism: Old and New," 55 University of Virginia Law Review 385 (1969).

[88] See Bernard J. Hibbits, "Making Sense of Metaphors: Visuality, Aurality, and the Reconfiguration of American Legal Discourse," 16 Cardozo Law Review 245 (1994); Robert L. Tsai, "Fire, Metaphor, and Constitutional Myth-Making," 93 Georgetown Law Journal 181 (2004).

[89] See, for example, Richard Rorty, *Philosophy and the Mirror of Nature* (Princeton University Press, 1981). Davidson in particular has argued that metaphors have only a literal meaning, because there is no limit to what the metaphor represents. Donald Davidson, "What Metaphors Mean," in *On Metaphor* 29, 44 (Sheldon Sacks, ed.) (University of Chicago Press, 1979). At least some lawyers see the dangers of metaphor and recognize the epistemological fights over their use. See, for example, John Stick, "Can Nihilism Be Pragmatic?" 100 Harvard Law Review 332 (1986); Cass R. Sunstein, "On Analogical Reasoning," 106 Harvard Law Review 741 (1993). As I employ metaphors here, I believe that they signal categories with vague and contested boundaries, from which analogy to events in the real world can be reasonably and fairly made.

[90] See Stuart J. Kaplan, "Let Me Hear Your Web Sights: Visual and Aural Metaphors for the Internet," 40 Idaho Law Review 299 (2004); Jonathan H. Blavin & I. Glenn Cohen, "Gore,

Metaphor and its related tools seem to some to be inevitable in the common law, or at least in some legal texts.[91] Indeed, metaphor might be essential to any rich understanding of human knowledge, although we need not go so far here.[92]

Metaphors pose dangers, however, and philosophers have long mistrusted them.[93] Metaphors almost always label categories, and there are real potentials for distortion both in the definition of the category and in the fit of its label. The nature of the label is to highlight some aspect of the category, and so it emphasizes that aspect of all of the units that are associated with the category. That emphasis might distract from the aspects that are most common among the units or most essential in defining the category.[94]

This distraction is inherent in metaphors that are stereotypes.[95] Stereotypes define a group (whether of people, or ideas, or any other entities) and then label the group via a single dimension, whether or not that dimension

Gibson, and Goldsmith: The Evolution of Internet Metaphors in Law and Commentary," 16 Harvard Journal of Law & Technology (2002).

[91] Texts alone are probably not the basis for metaphor, but it is hard to imagine a text without the poetic. Mark Turner & George Lakoff, *More than Cool Reason: A Field Guide to Poetic Metaphor* (University of Chicago Press, 1989). Poesy is usually an aspect of individual creation, which may suggest that the degree to which we are drawn to the poetic in the law is the degree to which law in the common law tradition is the result of the writings of people in a frame of writing as individuals – judges and scholars – as opposed to being in a frame of writing for institutions – committees and legislatures. One finds little metaphor, indeed little poetry, in the Code of Federal Regulations, but much in the appellate reports.

[92] Psychologists, particularly David Grove and others engaged in symbolic modeling, incorporate all of semiotics and much of epistemology into the metaphorical. See Penny Tompkins & James Lawley, *Metaphors in Mind: Transformation through Symbolic Modeling* (Developing Company Press, 2000); David J. Grove & B. I. Panzer, *Resolving Traumatic Memories: Metaphors and Symbols in Psychotherapy* (Irvington Publishers, 1989).

[93] Compare John Locke's equation of metaphor with fallacy, in the *Essay on Human Understanding* (Book 3, Chapter 10), to Davidson's argument that metaphors have no meaning other than their literal significance. See Donald Davidson, "What Metaphors Mean," in *On Metaphors* 29, 30 (Sheldon Sacks, ed.) (University of Chicago Press, 1978). Still, Davidson's argument seems shallow compared to Ricoeur's semantic and psychological description. See Paul Ricoeur, *The Rule of Metaphor, Multi-Disciplinary Studies of the Creation of Meaning in Language* (Robert Czerny, trans.) (University of Toronto Press, 1975).

[94] See George Lakoff & Mark Johnson, *Metaphors We Live By*, 159–84 (University of Chicago Press, 2003). Lakoff and Johnson assess metaphor in a quite sweeping manner against "truth." They have stronger tools for assessing the correspondence of a metaphor to the category it represents, and if we focus on the problem of correspondence rather than on the nature of truth, such analysis of a given metaphor is both a guide to its structure and a tool for its criticism.

[95] Scholars studying stereotype and those studying metaphor seem not yet to have recognized the parallels in these studies. See, for example, *Stereotypes as Explanations: The Formation of Meaningful Beliefs about Social Groups* (Craig McGarty, Vincent Y. Yzerbyt, & Russell Spears, eds.) (Cambridge University Press, 2002). The essays in this collection make claims for stereotype as a universal form of categorizing information that are strongly resonant with the claims of Lakoff, Davis, and others for metaphor, and in places their analyses seem taken from an ur-source.

is manifest in all of the members of the group.[96] Particularly damaging to a fair understanding of the whole of the group or to each member of the group is when such labels fit preconceptions that are not or cannot be proved, or when an attribute of a few is used to describe the nature of the whole community.

The danger of the stereotype is equally strong in the narrative. Narrative has grown very popular as a device in recent decades in American legal theory, as a tool particularly to redress the inequities in legal theory drawn from bloodless utilitarian models that ignore the effects of law on the lives of those helped least by it. The tool is particularly embraced by critical scholars, feminist legal theorists, and race critical theorists to tell the stories of those marginalized by the law, to demonstrate the need for legal reforms that are not always justified in economic or utilitarian terms.[97] In this enterprise, the narrative is a metaphor, representing by implication a host of similar stories, and it runs the risks of stereotype, or exaggeration, and distraction. Even so, narrative remains a powerful and useful tool, as do all metaphors, in concentrating our attention on specific aspects of a problem that might otherwise be neglected.

One last danger of metaphor requires, perhaps, the gravest warning of all. There is a danger of losing the mundane in the metaphor. The small decisions of daily life might not seem related to idealized or famous events. They are, though. The same mistakes that led Samuel Sewall astray – or lead modern jurors to reach an unjust verdict – easily repeat on a daily basis, whether in a rush or through overconfidence or through a venal preference for money or status over truth or justice.

One response to these dangers is to emphasize the metaphorical nature of labels prone to confuse or mislead. Labels that appear more descriptive, narrative, or scientific might not arouse in the reader some skepticism over their accuracy. Labels that are obviously poetic more fairly signal their evocation of a loose set of defining aspects in the category they signify. Poetic metaphors

---

[96] In general, a stereotype may be justified, just as it may distort. Lakoff compares stereotypes used in recent politics, along such lines as "Liberals love bureaucracy, and conservatives love freedom," which he shows are only contingently distorting, because some may be compared validly to an ideal. George Lakoff, *Moral Politics: How Liberals and Conservatives Think* 310–21 (2d ed.) (University of Chicago Press, 2002). Yet the nature of a stereotype is inherently prejudicial in any given case. By definition, the stereotype is based on untested prior assumptions when applied to any given case, to which it will be applied based on some degree of cursory similarity to its general case. Considering only uses of stereotypes in the aggregate, Lakoff may have elided this danger in them; the aggregation hides the nearly constant process of reassessment of the prejudgment.

[97] See, for example, Kathryn Abrams, "Hearing the Call of Stories," 79 California Law Review 971 (1991); Alex M. Johnson, Jr., "Defending the Use of Narrative and Giving Content to the Voice of Color: Rejecting the Imposition of Process Theory in Legal Scholarship," 79 Iowa Law Review 803 (1994).

alert reader to their artifice, at least as long as they are vital aspects of poetic language.[98]

If we are to deploy our own labels for the effects of the law in people's lives, then, it seems, the fairest way of doing so is to adopt signals for them that are obvious in their metaphoric nature. It might be that all labels tend toward the metaphoric, or at least the metonymic, through usage over time. The most prosaic label has a potentially broader symbolic value that would allow it to stand for a wider range of propositions.

This creeping symbolism seems to happen when people signify a particular character, skill, or reputation, as in my uses of Stoughton, Phips, Jones, and Sewall. Such usage in colloquial American English objectifies the person with an indefinite article, while the definite article is reserved to refer to the person objectified, as in "*a* John Kennedy" versus "*the* John Kennedy."[99] The same objectification occurs with labels in politics and law. Snail darters, hot coffee spills, Love Canal, and Ford Pintos have entered the metaphorical legal lexicon with little regard for the cases from which they arose. So we can assign categories for the effects of law through labels that are clearly metaphorical.[100]

This selection should encourage doubt and criticism. Are there too few or too many? Are there overlooked aspects of the law in people's lives (which is likely), or confusions among quite different things bundled together confusingly or misleadingly (which is more likely)? The nine labels suggested beg to be refined by other critics, and spurring further refinement is more useful than attempting to construct a scheme that will need no further work.

As an initial encouragement to this criticism, we might recognize that asking different questions will almost certainly lead to different categories. Aristotle asked what types of justice should we expect and answered with just two categories: natural justice, which is unchanging, and conventional justice, which varies according to time and place.[101] John Locke asked what a legitimate state should do when it is formed of a compact among free people, and answered with three requirements to achieve two great goals – to preserve the rights to

---

[98]　"Language is vitally metaphorical; that is, it marks the before-unapprehended relations of things and perpetuates their apprehension, until words, which represent them, become, through time, signs for portions or classes of thought instead of pictures of integral thoughts: and then, if no new poets should arise to create afresh the associations which have been thus disorganized, language will be dead to all the nobler purposes of human intercourse." Percy B. Shelley, *A Defence of Poetry* 18 (1845) (Bobbs-Merrill, 1904).

[99]　There remains an ambiguous effect of the definite article when the phrase is the object of the gerund of the verb "to do," as in "doing a John Kennedy," which is semantically equivalent to the same phrase with a definite article, although both of which are very different from the same phrase when the noun is preceded by no article at all.

[100]　Such an assignment is, of course, largely done already. Much of this list adopts standard images of justice and law from historical sources. See Dennis E. Curtis and Judith Resnik, "Images of Justice," 96 Yale Law Journal 1727 (1987).

[101]　Aristotle, *Nicomachean Ethics* 1134b, in *Complete Aristotle* (Barnes, ed.) 1790–1.

property and pursue the public good – which require settled laws, an impartial judge, and the executive power to punish injustice and prevent invasion.[102] Judge Richard Posner asked what are the functions of law and found mainly three: defining the powers of government and the rights of citizens, keeping order, and providing the framework for dispute resolution.[103]

Indeed, for every question, there is a different list, no matter how similar the questions. Thomas Campbell asked how a state benefits its people to justify their acceptance of it; he found six state benefits (which are accomplished generally through laws): maintaining the physical necessities of survival, controlling harmful or wrong conduct, encouraging beneficial or right conduct, rectifying harms and wrongs, organizing public goods, and sustaining social convention and custom.[104] Asking what basic needs the state ought to promote yields yet a different list, more than likely along the lines of John Finnis's list of seven basic goods of human life: knowledge and aesthetics, skills in performance, self-integration, practical reasonableness, justice, friendship, and religion or access to the divine.[105] Finnis built his list in the Thomistic tradition, but a different perspective on the same questions can yield a different answer. Thus, Jim Griffin's different list of goods that the state ought to promote derives from his more Aristotelean and utilitarian analysis.[106]

Despite the range of lists and numbers of values, virtues, and goods on them, inconsistency among answers to varying questions is only one problem here, and there are methods by which these varied answers can be organized. Conscious of the many approaches that one might take both to asking the question and to defining an answer, we can consider again the stakes: what are the effects of law in people's lives that they should have an interest in how legal officials carry out their duties? These effects can be summarized in the

---

[102] See §§ 123–31 in John Locke, *Two Treatises of Government: A Critical Edition with an Introduction and Apparatus Criticus* 15–17 (Peter Laslett, ed.) (Cambridge University Press, 1967). For the legal context of Locke's argument for the public good, see Steve Sheppard, "The Common Law and the Constitution: John Locke and the Missing Link in Law," a paper delivered at the American Society of Legal History, November 2005. For the underlying religious doctrine essential to the equality in these claims, see Jeremy Waldon, *God, Locke, and Equality* (Cambridge University Press, 2002).

[103] Richard Posner, *Federal Courts: Crisis and Reform* 7 (Harvard University Press, 1985).

[104] Thomas D. Campbell, *The Legal Theory of Ethical Positivism* 18–19 (Dartmouth Publishing, 1999).

[105] John Finnis, *Natural Law and Natural Rights* (Oxford University Press, 1982). The captions do not nearly convey the subtlety of the categories in Finnis's list, particularly his notion of practical reasonableness, which incorporates a complicated set of prudential values that are both instrumental of other basic goods and good in themselves.

[106] See James Griffin, *Well-Being: Its Meaning, Measurement, and Moral Importance* (Oxford University Press, 1986). Griffin divides goods into basic and prudential goods, the basic goods being necessary to survive, and the prudential goods being needed to develop one's potential for accomplishment.

metaphors of the sword, shield, guide, balance, mirror, seal, veil, commons, and coin of the law.

The Sword

Through the law, officials have the power, often the duty, to direct violence toward other people. Violence is inherent in the law, necessary to bind willful and dangerous people to its commands.[107] Max Weber defined the state as a human community that successfully claims a "monopoly of legitimate physical violence within a certain territory," and politics, including law, is the means of the distribution of that power.[108] The law's violence is an object of fear, not only to the criminal but to the innocent, who know (or are intended by officials to know) that such power can be used through mistake or abuse.

In the examples of colonial Massachusetts, the power of the law's sword enforced laws against murder and theft, yet it also brought twenty people to death for no deliberate reason. Its force is personal and direct, as when it crushed Giles Corey or hanged John Proctor. Its threat is even more sinister, as when it scared the innocent into confession of wicked acts they had never dreamt of, much less performed. And its effects are indirect and farther felt than its direct force, frightening colonists far from Salem with the spectre of such inquisitions.

This is the official's sword, the ability to control and exercise violence against people in the state and to use that ability to determine how people must behave. When exercised with skill, restraint, and care, the power of the sword is the necessary means of officials, used to maintain order and encourage progress. It is not only the threat or use of physical force but the power to order, to command and expect obedience lest force appear. The sword is the means not only by which the burglar is restrained but also by which the taxes are collected and the proper forms are signed.[109]

Well used, the sword is a tool of order and justice. It is essential to the shield. Thus, it is a matter of real concern to most citizens that the sword be used, that it not be left sheathed when needed. American politics is rife with stories of "law

---

[107] See Michael Ignatieff, *The Lesser Evil: Political Ethics in an Age of Terror* (Princeton University Press, 2004).

[108] Max Weber, "The Profession and Vocation of Politics," in *Political Writings* 309, 310–11 (Peter Lassman & Donald Speirs, eds.) (Cambridge University Press, 1994).

[109] On the many ways in which violence occurs in the law, see *Law's Violence* (Austin Sarat & Thomas R. Kearns, eds.) (University of Michigan Press, 1992). The basic role of violence in the law, of course, is not to correct illegal acts but to encourage the habit of obedience. As Sarat and Kearns see it, violence enacts, affirms, and enforces the logic and superiority of a legal order. Violence in the successful legal system is not for "ferocious displays of force" but subtler "subjugating, colonizing, 'civilizing' acts of violence." *Id.* 3.

and order," a political agenda of some currency by which candidates for legal office promise the voters to use the power of the state to punish criminals.[110]

The exercise of the sword is a matter that must concern the subject. Exercised arbitrarily, this is the power of tyranny. Even wielded with less extreme results, it is the power of abuse and injustice to the victims of its use, as well as outrage and fear for those whom it does not touch directly. At its extreme, a poor use of this power may lead not only to tyranny but also to anarchy or revolution. The sword badly employed provokes revolt. This was, in essence, the charge brought by the framers of the Declaration of Independence, which is a litany of the abuses of colonists at the hands of the British government, as well as the Crown's failure to heed colonial petitions of complaint.[111] The chaos that follows in the wake of an event is itself an object of fear for those who must endure it.

The sword is a fearsome power still. For countless African Americans, it is the sense when police lights appear in a rear-view mirror that the standards of traffic enforcement for whites do not include the racial profiling of Driving While Black.[112] On a more individual and mundane level, the sword triggers a sense of dread when a taxpayer receives a notice of audit from the Internal Revenue Service, and for countless Americans, it is the anger that rises when they are brought to court in a dubious civil suit.

The Shield

The shield is the ultimate justification of the law. We tolerate the fear of the sword and the limits on our powers in return for protection and order. Other than through fear of the sword alone, the prospect that the state will protect our lives, our property, and freedom of action is the most rational reason to obey its officials. The shield is the fundamental purpose of the law.[113]

---

[110] "Law and order" was first associated with the Nixon–Agnew campaign of 1968, with an underlying connotation of racism. See Joe McGinniss, *The Selling of the President* (reissue ed.) (Penguin Press, 1988); Kathleen Hall Jamieson, *Packaging the Presidency: A History and Criticism of Presidential Campaign Advertising* (Oxford University Press, 1996). Similar ambivalence arising from the need for a policy but fear of its true purpose afflicts the use of racial indicators in police work, the danger of "racial profiling."

[111] Of particular interest for our purpose is that the colonists not only framed their complaints as abuses of the prerogatives of office, but presented them in a form more like a legal brief than a political platform. See Carl L. Becker, *Declaration of Independence: A Study in the History of Political Ideas* (Vintage, 1958); Barbara A. Black, "The Constitution of Empire: The Case for the Colonists," 124 University of Pennsylvania Law Review 1157 (1976).

[112] See David A. Harris, "The Stories, the Statistics, and the Law: Why 'Driving While Black' Matters," 84 Minnesota Law Review 265–326 (1999).

[113] It is no accident that the badges of police officers are often referred to as shields. See Raymond H. Sherrard, *The Centurions' Shield: A History of the Los Angeles Police Department, Its Badges and Insignia* (RHS Enterprises, 1996).

The shield is the heart of all ideas of the social contract, whether Hobbes's idea that we surrender forever our freedom in return for the shield's protection or Locke's idea that we surrender our freedom for so long as we receive the shield's protection.[114] It is even one way of viewing Rawls's principle of right, that it is proper we surrender our freedom to the extent that we receive the shield's protection.[115]

In recent years, the desire for the shield of law has grown ever greater, particularly as the means by which individuals are harmed by others have grown more complex. Individuals have become dependent on a complicated economy beyond the realm of mere self-reliance, through which both riches and poverty may flow with little control by the individual. Corporations and governments have a capacity now to alter human health and environment, both for good and ill, beyond the dreams of early Americans.[116] The forms of fraud and deceit, and the nature of harm, have all grown both more robust and more subtle.[117] Subjects seek the shelter of law from harms both from mankind and from nature.[118]

Returning to the examples from colonial Massachusetts, we see many illustrations of expectations of the shield that fit easily in our time, turning upon the threat of punishment as the means of prevention: officials are to bar acts of violence, poisoning, cruelty, fraud, and public bad behavior. Certain of these protections were prospective, as with bread regulations, barrel-stave inspectors, and gauge marks for coopers. As we see with the example of the Salem trials, however, a failure of the officials to provide one form of protection, protection against native attacks, encouraged a demand for protection against another threat, harm by witchcraft, a relationship made all the more powerful by official attribution of both to evil supernatural forces.

---

[114] Compare Thomas Hobbes, *Leviathan* (C. B. MacPherson, ed.) (Penguin Classics, 1982), with John Locke, *Second Treatise*, in John Locke, *Two Treatises of Government: A Critical Edition with an Introduction and Apparatus Criticus* 15–17 (Peter Laslett, ed.) (Cambridge University Press, 1967).

[115] See John Rawls, *Justice as Fairness, A Restatement* (Harvard University Press, 2001).

[116] Although the problem of environmental harm is more apparent in the metaphor of the commons, saving citizens from harm through private or public harms to the environment may be just as much a matter of the shield.

[117] The deception of investors by officers in the Enron Corporation was, at this writing, still the subject of ongoing criminal investigation, leading to the indictment and demise of its accounting firm, and to the conviction of some officers of that corporation, such as its treasurer, Ben Glisan, who pled guilty to conspiracy to commit wire and currency fraud.

[118] The 2005 disaster in New Orleans, made more through the errors of officials and their contractors than through the action of Hurricanes Katrina and Rita, echoes the disastrous flood of Johnstown, Pennsylvania, caused more by bad dam maintenance than by the rains that defeated it. See David McCullough, *The Johnstown Flood* (Peter Smith Publisher, 1987); Ted Steinberg, *Acts of God: The Unnatural History of Natural Disaster in America* (Oxford University Press, 2006).

The shield today, as ever, concerns the subject in the manner of its deployment. If the law does not provide such protection and yet holds the monopoly over the force needed to ensure it, then subjects have no other means to acquire it and remain at the mercy of those who harm them. This presents a circumstance not unlike self-defense, and it threatens the claim of the law to monopolize violence. Even so, officials must strive to protect but not to overprotect, such that the danger of the sword does not overwhelm its safety. The ideal manifestation of the shield would be that legal investigation and enforcement shall be so measured that all harm is deterred or punished but no one innocent is punished or threatened. This is the real meaning of the maxim, *Lex est tutissima cassis.*[119] Yet such a balance can never practically be achieved, and in that failing, our fear *of* the sword often outweighs our fear *for* the shield.[120]

The Balance

The balance is a recognition that we cannot always resolve our disputes ourselves, and we have historically resorted to the law to do so.[121] Whether among equals or unequals, a judge is needed to end disputes. What litigant can be objective, or expect objectivity from an opponent? Self-interest skews our recollections of events and the bases of our claims, and it powerfully limits our instinct toward truth if our lives, liberty, wealth, or reputation are at stake. Further, it is sometimes necessary to have a judge, in order to determine contested or unestablished facts needed to answer a question. But neutral arbitrators are not enough, because those who lose a dispute, no matter how fairly, are often inclined to avoid complying with its resolution.[122]

The need for an independent arbiter is all the greater when the state, or at least its legal officials, is one of the litigants. Segregation of judgment from

---

[119] When he was made serjeant, Sir Edward Coke had golden rings cast, as was the custom, bearing a motto for the occasion. He chose "Lex est tutissima cassis," an abbreviation for an older tag, *Lex Est Tutissima Cassis; Sub Clypeo Legis Nemo Decipitur* (Law is the safest helmet; under the shield of the law no one is deceived). See *Selected Writings of Sir Edward Coke* lxxxii.

[120] See Vidar Halvorsen, "Is It Better That Ten Guilty Persons Go Free Than That One Innocent Person Be Convicted?" 23 Criminal Justice Ethics 3 (2004). On the practical efforts of balancing evidence toward that end, see Steve Sheppard, "The Metamorphoses of Reasonable Doubt: How Changes in the Burden of Proof Have Weakened the Presumption of Innocence," 78 Notre Dame Law Review 1165 (2003).

[121] For a litany of balances used metaphorically in legal judgment, see Steve Sheppard, "The State Interest in the Good Citizen: Constitutional Balance between the Citizen and the Perfectionist State," 45 Hastings Law Journal 969, 1027 (1994).

[122] Even when the power to mediate claims is devolved from the courts onto litigants, many cases return to court either for adjudication or enforcement. See, for example, Peter N. Thompson, "Enforcing Rights Generated in Court-Connected Mediation: Tension between the Aspirations of a Private Facilitative Process and the Reality of Public Adversarial Justice," 19 Ohio State Journal on Dispute Resolution 509 (2004).

prosecution is one of the most fundamental distinctions of law from the raw assertion of power.[123] Indeed, whether the arbiter is a judge, a jury of peers, or even the mob of Athens, there is a nearly universal distrust for any system of laws that aggregates the powers to accuse, adjudge, and punish a person for a crime. The dangers of mistake and of abuse are all too obvious. Thus the law balances the claims even of the state against the claims of the subject.

Turning to the example of colonial Massachusetts, some manifestations of the balance are obvious, as in the creation of courts and juries and in the adjudication of various crimes and disputes. What is less obvious is the nature of the balance in the many different facets of the state. There is a balance inherent in determining which offenses to list as crimes and which not. The balance of interests between debtors and creditors, the listing of certain sins as crimes but not others, the dedication of money to support the faithful inspector of barrel staves – each of these required a balance to be made in the selection of those acts that would be required or forbidden, inspected or ignored.

The perils in the balance are also obvious. Acting as a judge requires skill and dedication, as well as an innate sense of judgment, and there is the ever-present risk of error. Usually, the errors are difficult to detect in themselves, because the final mistake in a decision results from a host of small, even partial, errors. In the Salem Court of Oyer and Terminer, the initial decision to admit spectral evidence in the witchcraft trials was in keeping with the idea of spectral conspirators, and that idea was unquestionable in the minds of the members of the court. Indeed, spectral evidence alone appears not to have been the cause of any conviction, although it altered the balance for all those convicted.[124] Moreover, there is a danger of corruption, in which the officials holding the balance will privilege the claims of one person over another for reasons other than evidence of historical truths. We may wonder if the proof of witchcraft abroad in the land around Salem did not look like a nice distraction from, and explanation for, the military failures in the Massachusetts war.[125]

The Coin

The regulation of the economy is an important and inevitable aspect of the law in individual lives. This is as true in the United States as it was in ancient Athens.[126] Whether the regulation takes the form only of taxes, which ever fall

---

[123] Although separation of powers is most often associated with Montesquieu, he saw himself as describing a condition that had already long existed in England. Charles-Louis de Secondat, Baron de la Brède et de Montesquieu, "The Spirit of the Laws" 70 (1741) (*Encyclopaedia Britannica*, 1952).

[124] See Wendel D. Craker, "Spectral Evidence, Non-Spectral Acts of Witchcraft, and Confession at Salem in 1692," 40 The Historical Journal 331 (1997).

[125] This is, again, the thesis convincingly argued in Mary Beth Norton, *In the Devil's Snare*.

[126] See Edward W. Harris, "Law and Economy in Classical Athens: [Demosthenes] 'Against Dionysodorus,'" in *Athenian Law in Its Democratic Context* (A. Lanni, ed.), republished

more on some than on others, or it takes the forms of commercial regulation, or it takes even the modern form of a guarantor of access to certain basic goods, the law determines what forms of conduct will be allowed and encouraged, what forms of failure will be ameliorated, and what limits on one's misfortunes will be shared among the community.

The coin is a particular aspect of the sword and shield, necessary to them not just for the funds needed to wield them, but further as the sword and shield have meaning in the regulation of commerce.[127] The state's power over the coin can protect against fraud and dangerous goods, just as it encourages new commerce for health and safety. Yet it also creates monopolies and stifles creativity, rewarding the commerce of the influential and creating dependents among the rest.[128]

The significance of the coin for the subject is complex. The most obvious is fear of the regulation, the tax in making one's life choices. For the person subject to this regulation, few decisions can be truly free. What job to take, what produce to make, whether to marry and whom, how hard to work, where one works, where one lives, what schools one pursues – all such questions and untold more are affected by the state. The fear that what one makes or earns will be lost is particularly acute when regulations change in their content or their enforcement. This is, however, the price to be paid for security from the threats of other people, for the maintenance of the commons, and for the coordination of projects deemed essential to the state, or to the people.

The coin, after all, matters as much for the fears it assuages as for the fear that it creates. The coin provides common protections, funding not only the night watch but also the orphanage and asylum. Both rebellion and famine are rare when social security and financial stability are a matter of law. When the law's power in the coin fails to keep the poor and desperate from utter alienation from the society regulated by law, the potential for anarchy increases. Food riots make sense to those without food, and neither love nor fear of the law will overcome the demand for food for oneself and one's family.[129]

---

at www.stoa.org (last visited June 5, 2008). For the same point in American history, see John Steele Gordon, *An Empire of Wealth: The Epic History of American Economic Power* (HarperCollins, 2004).

[127] Echoing Cicero and Tacitus, Sir Edward Coke noted that the public treasure "is the ligament of peace, the sinews of war, and the preserver of the honour and safety of the realm." Earl of Devonshire's Case, 11 Report 91b.

[128] Although much trade regulation is essential to safety of goods and markets, plenty has been raw favoritism. Congress once passed a law to ban additives in milk. See *United States v. Carolene Products Co.*, 304 U.S. 144 (1938). Despite health and safety arguments accepted, perhaps dubiously, by the Court in upholding the law, it was clearly market favoritism, which eventually faded away. See Geoffrey P. Miller, *The True Story of Carolene Products*, 1988 Sup. Ct. Rev. 397.

[129] See R. George Wright, *Does the Law Morally Bind the Poor? Or, What Good's the Constitution When You Can't Afford a Loaf of Bread* (NYU Press, 1996).

Although it is not as obvious in times of well-distributed plenty, the coin also represents the state's uses of law to alter the balance of economic distribution among the polity. The state, after all, has the power to ensure social security, and in the recent western tradition, the protections of private property and the freedom of contract are also forms of regulation of the coin. Property is protected by law, when the law does so. Private interests (and indeed public interests) can be created by private acts, whether by creation of property, grants of property, or entrance into contract. There is no inherent aspect of the concept of law that requires either private property or free contract, and indeed both have developed as a matter of history to succeed legal regimes of status.[130] That the law may give or deny such capacities is more easily seen, perhaps in the law of corporations or of antitrust. The limited liability company is wholly the creature of law, and only political will tolerates monopoly.

There is nothing to distinguish the dangers posed to individuals or the commonwealth by the use of money from the dangers of any other human activity. The risks of fraud, of theft, of deceit, indeed of social instability, poverty, and riot are not immunized from legal scrutiny because they affect wealth or property. The wholesale failure of regulation that preceded the failures of savings and loan companies in the 1990s, the Enron fraud of 2001, the debt crisis of 2008, and the astonishing fraud of Bernard Madoff discovered in the same year – all of these would have vexed the colonial leaders who inspected barrel staves, controlled monopolies, and regulated mills and markets.

This aspect of the coin bears special consideration, particularly in the degree to which the law allows concentrations of wealth or requires its redistribution. One might take a strict *laissez faire* view of the state's role, along the lines of Herbert Spencer, allowing it only such intervention in the market as required to protect the strong, or Arthur Laffer, that lower taxes for the rich benefit the poor.[131] Or, one might take a radical egalitarian view such as Pierre Prodhoun's assertion that private property is theft, or a softer view such as Johns Rawls's, that wealth is justified only so long as it benefits the poor.[132] Law as law does not require any choice on that continuum.

Even so, law that is justified by democracy does not have the luxury of such wide swings between the socialist or oligarchic economic commitments it will enshrine by laws. As nicely stated by Lyndon Johnson's one-time speechwriter Bill Moyers, "Extremes of wealth and poverty cannot be reconciled with a

---

130 See Sir Henry Maine, *Ancient Law: Its Connection with the Early History of Society, and Its Relation to Modern Ideas* (1861) (Everyman's Library, 1972).

131 See Herbert Spencer, *Social Statics: or, The Conditions Essential to Happiness Specified, and the First of them Developed* (John Chapman, 1851). Arthur B. Laffer, *The Laffer Curve: Past, Present, and Future* at www.heritage.org (last visited August 31, 2008).

132 See Pierre J. Proudhon, *What Is Property?* (Donald R. Kelley & Bonnie G. Smith, eds.) (Cambridge University Press, 1994); John Rawls, *A Theory of Justice: Original Edition* (Harvard University Press, 2005).

genuinely democratic politics" that challenge the egalitarianism asserted in the American Revolution, which "changed the lives of 'hitherto neglected and despised masses of common laboring people.'"[133] Legal officials in the United States have long seen the law as a steward of democratic values, asserting that legal institutions balance between the greatest economic interests and the common laboring people,[134] and this stewardship is an aspect of the coin as well.

The Commons

There are certain coordination problems in a state that cannot be managed except by acts of the state. Classically, these amounted to fortifications, ports, roads, and public buildings, but eventually they included parks and commons. In Massachusetts, Boston and Salem, for instance, each had customary regulations of their roads, ports, and commons, as well as regulations for shipping and transport and other activities that affected the common wealth.

The problem of legal protection of the commons is often now heard only as a motif in the fashionable lament of the "tragedy of the commons," which suggests that public management of common goods leads to destruction, or at least to less efficient management than would private ownership, though this proposition is heartily debated among scholars.[135] Yet to treat resources needed by all as public or private is, fundamentally, a decision the law must make, to preserve it as a public good managed by state officials, to dedicate it to private ownership, or to establish some intermediate trust or regulated entity.

It doesn't matter, at the metaphorical level, whether the state protects the commons through the laws of private property, the tools of public ownership, or the rules of regulation. What matters is that the state somehow ensures that the commons is protected for the benefit of all, because if it does not, then the likelihood of suffering by at least some and perhaps all of the people increases.

---

[133] Bill Moyers, *Moyers on Democracy* 4–5 (Doubleday, 2008), quoting Gordon S. Wood, *The Radicalism of the American Revolution* (Vintage, 1993).

[134] Paul D. Carrington, *Stewards of Democracy: Law as a Public Profession* (Westview Press, 1999).

[135] The commons intended in this phrase initially meant property held in common among the people, not the state, but that distinction, always a bit dodgy, had largely fallen away. That common goods are less managed than private goods is an old idea; Aristotle remarked that that which is common to the greatest number receives the least care. Aristotle, *The Politics* 1261b. The tragedy of the commons, in which the commons is destroyed by overuse, is a nineteenth-century observation made popular after Ronald Coase, "The Problem of Social Cost," 3 Journal of Law & Economics 1 (1960), and Garrett Hardin, "The Tragedy of the Commons," 162 Science 1243 (December 13, 1968), in support of privatization. See, for example, Ludwig von Mises, *Human Action: A Treatise on Economics* (Yale University Press, 1949). See Shi-Ling Hsu, "What Is a Tragedy of the Commons? Overfishing and the Campaign Spending Problem," 69 Albany Law Review 75 (2005–2006).

The implications of the commons are now seen to extend far beyond the physical construction or use of roads and ports or reserved lands for common grazing. The commons is now understood to include not only new goods such as certain forms of intellectual property and the electronic spectrum of telecommunications,[136] but also the human environment, natural resources such as whales, fish, and birds, and indeed the climate, seas, and planet as a whole.[137] In some regard, particularly when sheltering the commons from harm by one in order to protect the interests of another, the metaphor of the commons represents a special form of the shield.[138]

The most obvious problem of the commons is that the state may not protect it, either to allow access, to ensure preservation, or even to prevent harms through its abuse. Thus, if the state fails to preserve the commons and the commons is the habitable climate, all other purposes of law fail, too. Other problems abound, such as the definition of what is or isn't commons, allocations of monopoly, use of the commons that prevents innovation, and poor management of the commons that prevents progress. The stakes of the commons, however, are very real.

The Guide

The guide is the power of officials to define civic goals and to encourage acceptance or to coerce obedience by individuals to these goals. Officials have the power not only to act for the people but to cause the people to act for them. In its essence, much of the law is intended to alter the behavior of subjects, to cause people to do what the officials choose for them to do.[139] Officials lead, and subjects follow.

In many instances, the guide is an important means for maintaining public order, public health, fair access to scarce resources, and coordinating a host of other activities necessary in a community. It is the means by which drivers are told to drive on the left or the right side of the road. It is the reference by which subjects may tell other subjects the extent of their liberties, without relying on

---

[136] See, for example, Thomas W. Hazlett, "Spectrum Tragedies," 22 Yale Journal on Regulation 242 (2005).

[137] See, for example, Kirsten H. Engel & Scott R. Saleska, "Subglobal Regulation of the Global Commons: The Case of Climate Change," 32 Ecology Law Quarterly 183 (2005).

[138] For environmental problems that are problems of shield as much as of commons, see, for example, Rachel Carson, *Silent Spring* (Mariner Books, 2002); Lois Marie Gibbs, *Love Canal: The Story Continues* (New Society Publishers, 1998); Marc Reisner, *Cadillac Desert: The American West and Its Disappearing Water* (Penguin Books, 1993). For a high-stakes debate, see Sir John Houghton, *Global Warming: The Complete Briefing* (Cambridge University Press, 2004); Tim Flannery, *The Weather Makers: How Man Is Changing the Climate and What It Means for Life on Earth* (Atlantic Monthly Press, 2006).

[139] Hart denominated this domain as primary rules. Hart, *The Concept of Law* 86–99.

personal tastes or whims. It is the instrument by which parents are required to support and to educate their children.[140]

We see ample evidence of the role of the guide in 1648 in Massachusetts. The laws were deliberately and obviously drafted to establish a Puritan state, in which non-Puritans would conform to puritanical standards in public and in private, and many of the strict moral offenses are still with us. A freeman in a Puritan town could not be drunk in public or smoke within twenty feet of a dwelling. Such laws surely provoked some resentment then as they do occasionally today.[141]

There are serious problems for many people who are subject to the power of the guide, particularly when the law requires them to act contrary to their conscience. Religion and morality provide numerous grounds for conflict, and legal obligations frequently contradict one or another of the grounds in such conflicts. Parents, for instance, are prone to resist schools legally teaching their children ideas that the parents do not accept.[142] Even in more mundane settings, the power of the guide may require immense resources to be given by the citizenry; requiring education requires the funding of schools.

The Mirror

The power of the mirror is a more personal aspect of the powers of the law; it is the identity of the subject with the laws itself. This is more than an abstract notion. We identify ourselves through a host of frames in which we understand who we are based on our membership in a particular culture governed by and defined in part by the law.[143] A defining aspect of what it meant to be Jewish was that the tribes followed the laws given to them by Moses.[144] A defining aspect of being American is to be governed by the U.S. Constitution and the

---

[140] This does not always happen. The law in some states has devolved this power to parents. See Steve Sheppard, "Officials' Obligations to Children: The Perfectionist Response to Liberals and Libertarians, or Why Adult Rights Are Not Trumps over the State Duty to Ensure Each Child's Education," 2005 Michigan State Law Review 809.

[141] The regulation of smoking seems to have been a cyclic phenomenon in America, with lobbies from tobacco corporations as well as smokers and libertarians opposed to antismoking laws that were common in the nineteenth century, repealed early in the twentieth, and restored late that century. See Christopher Cobey, "The Resurgence and Validity of Antismoking Legislation," 7 University of California-Davis Law Review 167 (1974).

[142] See, for example Edward J. Larson, *Summer for the Gods: The Scopes Trial and America's Continuing Debate over Science and Religion* (Harvard University Press, 1997).

[143] The idea that law is a visible symbol of social solidarity has been at the root of many arguments. See, for example, Emile Durkheim, *The Division of Labor in Society* 24–6 (1893) (W. D. Halls, trans.) (Free Press, 1983). The argument is generally made in a vain attempt to retain by law symbols already fading in society. See, for example, Patrick Devlin, *The Enforcement of Morals* (Oxford University Press, 1965).

[144] See *Tanakh: The Holy Scriptures, The New JPS Translation According to the Traditional Hebrew Text* (Jewish Publication Society, 1985).

laws of the United States.[145] This is what Abraham Lincoln meant when he said that "A nation may be said to consist of its territory, its people, and its laws."[146]

When these laws are matters of respect and perceived as good, citizens take pride in this identity, as when many Americans think of their protections under the First Amendment. When these laws are matters of shame or perceived as dangerous or venal, citizens themselves may feel shame, as when most Americans think of the legal regimes in the United States allowing slavery or racial segregation.[147]

The mirror is the personal basis for both pride and guilt for acts done in the name of the state, or of its people, for they are in some definite senses inseparable. The responsibility for the mirror, to be sure, rests primarily with the officials. To the extent that a person can cause such orders, in any degree, that person must accept responsibility to at least that degree for the conduct of another person who acts as required. This responsibility is all the more grave because the substance of these orders, especially whatever morality may be contained in them, must become in some sense the morality of the citizen subject to the orders, perhaps even if the citizen is willing to accept the pain of punishment in order to reject them.[148]

There are fine illustrations of the mirror enforcing an individual identity through law in the example of colonial Massachusetts. The law established the rights of individuals according to age, gender, religion, and property, setting the social web of relationships for each person in the colony, and altering them according to judgments of the court.[149] The famously litigated cases of Ann Hutchinson and the Hutchinsonians and of Ann Oliver were instances not only of demanding conformity from the defendants but also of using those trials to strengthen the identity of good colonists. Good Puritans, good Bostonians, were not antinomians; the law said so. Thus those who accepted the authority of the divines were reinforced in their views, their understanding of who they are, their identity.

The dangers of the mirror are clear as well. The colonists were, indeed colonists in Salem still are, tarred by the brush of the injustice wrought by

---

[145] See, for example, George P. Fletcher, "Three Nearly Sacred Books in Western Law," 54 Arkansas Law Review 1 (2001).

[146] Abraham Lincoln, "Address to Congress, December 1, 1862," in 5 *Collected Works of Abraham Lincoln* 527 (Roy P. Basler, ed.) (Rutgers University Press, 1953).

[147] See, for example, Jonathan Kozol, *The Shame of the Nation: The Restoration of Apartheid Schooling in America* (Crown, 2005).

[148] This problem is explored further in Steve Sheppard, "Passion and Nation: War, Crime, and Guilt in the Individual and the Collective," 78 Notre Dame Law Review 751 (2003).

[149] This is probably a universal aspect of the law. See, for example, Daniel Lord Smail, *The Consumption of Justice: Emotions, Publicity, and Legal Culture in Marseille, 1264–1423: Conjunctions of Religion and Power* (Cornell University Press, 2003), in which a primary object of the resort to law was to gain social standing for oneself and diminish it for one's enemies.

a handful of judges, sparked by a handful of children, with the increasing complicity of many others, albeit some more or less under threat, to assist in the accusations and trials. Certainly, some were more guilty than others of that travesty, but it was difficult then for any to dissociate themselves utterly from responsibility. True, there were those, such the Stauntons and the Phipses, whose varying sense of responsibility did not seem to have led to the shame felt by the Sewalls, but the responsibility is broader than those who sense the guilt of it. That few of the Salem residents had any say in the decisions to hold the trials, or to give evidence, does not somehow avert the vague sense of personal identity from the corporate engagement with it.

In our own times, the power of the mirror of the law is apparent in the daily news. That laws should determine enough of our daily life that they are part of our identity ought to come as no surprise to Americans at the dawn of the twenty-first century. The law still determines the extent of our civic participation, even if those who are not burdened by it seldom recognize these limits.[150] Our liberal, tolerant culture is enforced in many laws in the United States, laws that ban censorship and allow nearly unfettered access to firearms. Yet, we live in one of the few developed nations that has the death penalty for criminals. The effects of these laws, their role in individual identity, are rarely felt within the culture in which such laws are largely accepted as the way things are. But once the American travels to other countries and discerns the differences in those legal systems, the identification with the American's native law becomes pronounced.[151] This nativism is more apparent at home when it appears to compete with another legal system, as in the competition with Cold War Communism or now that the culture of the liberal West is seen by many to be competing with the particular religious culture of Wahabbist Islam.

What is done by the officials becomes part of who the subjects are, how they each perceive themselves and others perceive them, whether the individual endorses what is done or not. The official thus holds the power of identity, the power of mirror.

The Seal

Having considered six broad ways in which the law alters people's lives – as threat, protection, referee, oracle, resource, and identity – a different form of

---

[150] See, for example, Gordon Bazemore & Jeanne B. Stinchcomb, "Social, Political, and Philosophical Perspectives on Felony Disenfranchisement in America: Civic Engagement and Reintegration: Toward a Community-Focused Theory and Practice," 36 Columbia Human Rights Law Review 241 (2004).

[151] George Fletcher nicely describes this effect in the Introduction, and regarding the French in Chapter 2, of George P. Fletcher & Steve Sheppard, *American Law in a Global Context: The Basics* (Oxford University Press, 2005).

the influence of the law in the lives of the subjects is important, in that the law bestows its seal upon a subject, designating the citizen as an official. The law segregates officials from fellow citizens, creating the roles by which some subjects not just are bound by the law but are its creators and enforcers.[152] The citizen who becomes an official accepts an array of additional duties that differ from those of subjects, but this acceptance is only part of the difference. The subject-turned-official accepts a new identity, becoming a member of the legal culture and being seen by other subjects as different from them for that reason. This difference has many dimensions, but none so obvious as the official's asymmetry in power: the official now may command the subject and be beyond response from the subject in return.[153]

By definition, the official has a deeper commitment to the law and its institutions than do subjects generally. In nearly all cases, the commitment is even one that is financially rewarded. For both reasons, mandated by law, the official acquires a responsibility to carry out an office, but that responsibility comes with a undefined commitment to the institutions of law as a whole. After all, a single office has no meaning without the other offices that make up the whole institution. It might well be that a person first venturing to hold an office is unaware of these implications, but that does not mean that they are not present; it merely suggests that the extent of the institutional commitments made by an official to the law might not be known fully, and therefore some aspects of those commitments do not depend on voluntary acceptance. The central commitment is voluntary, and these collateral commitments are implied and, to an extent, they may be inescapable. Certainly, there is a symbiotic relationship between the highest executives and the next levels of officials; the whole institution of the law depends on the complicity of individuals who commit themselves to the duty of the law, usually in return for their increased share of its authority.[154]

Indeed, in all but one instance in America, the office of the juror, office is voluntary. With the exception of the jury, all offices are held by people who have agreed to take them and continue to hold them by choice. That choice

---

[152] In a government of laws, the law must identify the governors. It is possible to have a state or government in which office is hereditary, but if such patrimonial offices exist, they will come to be enshrined in the law. Compare Max Weber, 2 *Economy and Society: An Outline of Interpretive Sociology* 956 (Guenther Roth & Claus Wittich, eds.) (University of California, 1968) with *id.* 1013–15.

[153] Of course, the nature of the official's power is to confer the ability of finality, not infallibility on official judgments. See H. L. A. Hart, *The Concept of Law* 140–7 (2d ed.) (Oxford University Press, 1994).

[154] This appears to be true even after the law has apparently become a bureaucratic enterprise, freed from the sense of ownership of office. Compare Part III of Étienne de la Boétie, *The Politics of Obedience: The Discourse of Voluntary Servitude* (1550) (Kessinger Publishing, 2004) with Max Weber, "The Profession and Vocation of Politics," in –, *Political Writings* 309 (Peter Lassman & Donald Speirs, eds.) (Cambridge University Press, 1994).

does not alter the law's power in isolating the official from the culture, nor does it change the official's implied commitment to the institution as a whole.

Turning again to colonial Massachusetts, the laws were very specific in the means by which officials could be selected, the groups from which they might be chosen, and the methods of selection. Care was taken to specify what oaths were required of each officeholder. The distinctions between offices were not terribly important; the duties of these officials were often broader in scope than we might consider wise today. Stoughton after all sat as judge while also serving as lieutenant governor. But the demarcations between official and subject, again with the exception of jurors, were considerable. As the travail of Samuel Sewell well illustrates, officials accepted not only the privileges but also the responsibility of their offices.

The effect of the law today in this manner is well known: individuals accept a range of offices, with more or less dependence upon the state – executives, legislators, judges, administrators, lawyers, police, clerks, jailers – all enter into offices set by law, and thus become responsible for the whole of the law, for some extent of the sword, the shield, and all the rest. These people become those specially responsible for the successes and failures of the law. That they are often elected by popular suffrage establishes a degree of responsibility for their action in others, but it does not diminish their personal and independent participation in the actions of the law.

Yet there are many reasons for concern regarding the operation of the seal. Most obviously, there is the danger of individuals taking or holding office for the benefit not of the subjects but of themselves alone or some group of allies.[155] This danger is greater than it might look owing to the sense of obligation many unelected officials feel toward their sponsors – those who appointed them to their office – in the same manner that elected officials may feel beholden to their political parties or their campaign donors. Such an obligation is likely to lead either to a betrayal of the subjects or to the betrayal of the sponsors.

Further, there are always real, if usually unspoken, questions of the fitness of the person for the office. Law demands at least some intellectual capacity, as well as the personal attributes necessary to perform the functions of the sword, shield, and balance, perhaps even with some understanding of the effects of office on the guide and the mirror. The operation of the seal in this manner is one to provoke concern whether it is done by selection by other officials or through election by voters.

---

[155] U.S. Congressman John Breaux is said to have responded to charges of corruption, "I can't be bought, but I can be rented." Quoted in Amitai Etzioni, *Capital Corruption: The New Attack on American Democracy* i (Harcourt, Brace, Jovanovich, 1984).

The Veil

The relationship between the seal and the other stakes of the subject in the law give rise to a further stake, which is the veil through which it is often difficult for the citizen to see who makes a decision harming that citizen's interests, or how it is made. The veil results from the diffusion of power over different offices, so that the identity of the source of power is hidden from its victim.[156] The veil confuses the responsibility of the seal and makes accountability for decisions difficult to assess. It also diminishes the confidence the subject has in the motives officials might have for their actions, an important facet of the subject's trust in the law and the state as a whole.[157]

A given official may be responsible for one slight aspect of a large and complex bureaucracy with highly specialized forms of knowledge, may be immersed in a legal culture with arcane and specialized vocabulary, or may be balancing competing interests on a scale in which the concerns of one citizen are very difficult for the citizen to measure. An official might, therefore, all too easily hide an operative motive for an official act, labeling it as based on another, more acceptable cause. The most likely reason for such secrecy is to increase the official's own power, usually at the expense of other officials.[158] Regardless of the cause, this imbalance of information makes it very difficult for a citizen accurately to see what has happened, or why, when that citizen has been ordered to, or limited from, some conduct by legal officials.

Distinctly, the official acts in a collective enterprise, which allows an official to disguise the responsibility for a particular action. The official might deliberately hide the degree to which that official acted on personal initiative rather than according to limits ascribed by lack of discretion or jurisdiction, or superior orders, or the political exigencies of a broader agenda, or countless other distractions. Perhaps more dangerously, the official may be unaware of the responsibility that attaches to the official's own acts, numbed by the smallness of the part that one person plays in the grand scheme of the law into

---

[156] See Paul Carrese, *The Cloaking of Power: Montesquieu, Blackstone, and the Rise of Judicial Activism* (University of Chicago Press, 2003). Carrese credits Montesquieu with first describing the benefit of separation of power as a way of hiding its true holders.

[157] See Tom R. Tyler & Yuen J. Huo, *Trust in the Law: Encouraging Public Cooperation with the Police and the Courts* 63–8 (Russell Sage Foundation, 2002).

[158] The "office secret" and its variants are probably inherent in all bureaucracies, not merely those in the state, but here it functions particularly to favor administrators. "Bureaucracy naturally prefers a poorly informed, and hence powerless, parliament – at least insofar as this ignorance is compatible with the bureaucracy's own interests." Max Weber, 2 *Economy and Society* 993. For its dangerous effects on group dynamics, see Irving L. Janis, *Victims of Groupthink* 32–3 (Houghton-Mifflin, 1972).

losing a critical sense of personal action.[159] This bureaucratic effect may even encourage a particular form of irresponsibility for the deliberate actions of a person with a considerable discretion and responsibility for acts that, but for the bureaucratic shell around the person, the actor would have been ashamed to perform.[160]

Besides these immediate dangers of legal authority, there are other reasons for concern about the official that arise from the nature of the system in which some people have power over others. This is the result of power wielded indirectly, through the bureaucracy, which dissipates responsibility and hides blame. The bureaucratic filters in no way lessen the dangers of the sword. If anything, the bureaucracy heightens the dangers of the seal through obscurity, complexity, and corporatism.[161]

Even so, the most troubling of such dangers is the problem of secrecy as a matter of policy, corporate as a matter of the system as a whole toward the citizens. In order to act on the behalf of the citizenry, it is not always certain that the fullest extent of information on the conduct, motives, and even misconduct of officials helps them to act to accomplish their tasks, no matter how appropriate those tasks are. In some domains of public safety, such as in matters of foreign affairs, military operations, and criminal investigation, deceit of the citizenry may be necessary to achieve the ends pursued.[162] There are lesser arguments for similar but fundamentally different deception, for the more domestic reasons of civic stability and public safety. These lesser arguments are often presented entwined with the arguments of necessity, and one often finds that they are actually mere smoke screens for self-serving or incompetent officials. Regardless of the cause, such intentional deception clouds even further the citizen's ability to gauge the morality of an official's

---

[159]   This "loss of critical sense" in a bureaucracy is one of the psychological consequences of bureaucratic management. See Ludwig von Mises, *Bureaucracy* 105 (1944) (Center for Futures Education, 1983).

[160]   Such an alteration in personal judgment partly explains the horrific results of the Stanford experiment, in which college students randomly assigned as guards rather than as prisoners in a psychology experiment quickly devolved to a shocking level of brutality. See *Quiet Rage: The Stanford Prison Study* (Stanford Instructional Television Network, 1991) (written by Ken Musen & Philip Zimbardo). This type of ethical decline in a bureaucratic setting occurs in private corporations, and the relationship between the bureaucracies of the corporation and state is longstanding. See, for example, Robert Heilbroner, *In the Name of Profit: Profiles in Corporate Irresponsibility* (Doubleday, 1972); Arianna Huffington, *Pigs at the Trough: How Corporate Greed and Political Corruption Are Undermining America* (Three Rivers Press, 2004).

[161]   It is the process at the heart of the banality that Hannah Arendt described in considering the conversion of the German state and legal machinery into the tool of Holocaust. See Hannah Arendt, *Eichmann in Jerusalem: A Report on the Banality of Evil* (Viking Press, 1963).

[162]   See Sissela Bok, *Secrets: On the Ethics of Concealment and Revelation* 191–209 (Vintage, 1983). Necessity in such matters, though, is much rarer than most officials believe.

conduct. Then again, secrecy is often employed for none of these reasons but merely out of habit, or to hide an official's mistakes or misdeeds from the sunlight.[163]

Colonial Massachusetts provides a particularly telling example here. The decision to introduce the evidence of spectral witnesses was made by Stoughton, in consultation with Cotton Mather. Mather had a quasiofficial role in the government owing to the influence of his ministry and his standing in society. There appears to be little or no public knowledge of his role in that decision, or indeed of the means by which the decision was reached. Who, then, could argue effectively against the decision before the court, not knowing its origin? Who would know to lobby Mather directly in an attempt to change his mind? Eventually, by dint of social organization and local culture, the question was raised by one person who would have known, Cotton's own father, whose views contrary to his son's were immediately influential. But the veil protected Cotton Mather's role, and indeed perhaps the roles of others on the court.

When it is hard to assess the conduct of some few acts that become known, the significance of these acts increases, as they become not merely acts in themselves: judgments in these matters may also serve as surrogates for the veiled and unknown actions for which no other judgment is possible.

HOLDING THE STAKES

The stakes in how the law is applied are immense. It is not enough to argue that observers have a stake in what the law is. The manner by which officials create it, carry it out, the whole of "the law in action" is a matter of significance in many ways.

It is not enough, however, to say that the law alone can govern itself. The law, after all, is what the officials make of it, its culture as well as its archive. And the acts of its culture very rarely expose the official to any risk of correction or even question by the subjects affected by their conduct.

The legal official is normally immune from any legal response to the exercise of authority. The legal rules protect legal officials from sanction for most forms of misconduct.[164] The law provides for sanctions against legal officials only for

---

[163]   Secrecy is not, however, a default position for all bureaucrats. At least some managers of federal agencies prefer their operations to be essentially public, both to avoid charges of favoritism and to encourage political support. See James Q. Wilson, *Bureaucracy: What Government Agencies Do and Why They Do It* 398–401 (Basic Books, 1989).

[164]   Kings have enjoyed immunity from judicial process through the simple device of not submitting to it unless it suited them to do so. From this flowed the doctrine of judicial immunity. Sir Edward Coke ruled in a Star Chamber decision in 1607: "[A] Judge, for any thing done by him as Judge, by the authority which the King hath committed to him, and as sitting in the seat of the King (concerning his justice) shall not be drawn in question before

rare acts in which the legal official exceeds the authority of office. It is practically a matter of definition, but the citizen who is harmed or wronged by the action of a legal official (that is valid according to the archive and the culture) almost never has recourse for the wrong or the harm through law.

Despite such immunity, official conduct remains inherently troubling, if not potentially frightening. Beyond the particular fears for various stakes, the general circumstances of officials with power over others should give us pause to consider the moral, as opposed to the legal, depictions of office.

The first is the recognition of corruption by the temptations of power, to recognize that many who enter the path of the legal official with high ideals may find all too many temptations to use power acquired to achieve those ideals for personal and ignoble ends. To recognize this temptation, however, cannot explain the actions of all officials, many of whom do resist it, nor can the temptation exonerate those who have succumbed to it. It is a problem that will be considered further in Chapter 3.[165]

The second factor, aggravating our more direct concerns, is a recognition of the unclean nature of the task. This is the knowledge that, regardless of the purity with which an official pursues certain ideals throughout a career, the practical exigencies of political and legal decisions require some choices that have no ideal choice. There are ethical paradoxes, in which the best one might hope is care in the choosing between two equally repugnant choices, or in selecting between immoral ends and immoral means.[166] Although such paradoxes might not be terribly frequent in the careers of some officials, they are certain enough to occur in a legal system. This condition, known as the problem of unclean hands, will be considered further in Chapter 5.[167]

Added to this factor is the closely related dilemma of the responsibility for making a decision in many domains of uncertain or deeply controversial morality. An official forced to choose simply cannot claim the luxury of a citizen who can hold contradictory views and never act in opposition to either.

These factors, themselves adding to a reasonable concern for the morality of legal officials' acts, point to one last reason for concern. In a sense, when officials act in moments of moral paradox or moral uncertainty, their decisions relieve the citizenry of the pain of choice, allowing the officials to act as a scapegoat,

any other Judge, for any surmise of corruption, except before the King himself" because the King "delegates his power to his Judges, who have the Custody and Guard of the King's oath." Floyd and Barker, 1 *Selected Writings of Sir Edward Coke* 431. As to the extent of official immunity today in the United States, see, for example, *Brosseau v. Haugen*, 543 U.S. 194 (2004) (describing qualified immunity of police officer in shooting a fleeing felon).

[165] See Chapter 3, the section entitled "The Stakes and the Special Temptations of Power."
[166] Thus the dirty hands of politics. See Max Weber, "The Profession and Vocation of Politics," in *Political Writings* 364–8 (Peter Lassman & Donald Speirs, eds.) (Cambridge University Press, 1994), described in Chapter 4 in the section entitled "Good Faith."
[167] See the first section of Chapter 5.

to whom much of the moral responsibility for the decision may be ascribed.[168] This sense, however, may also deepen the sense of incomplete exoneration with which citizens inclined toward this reaction may see themselves, masking as it does the mirror effect in which the officials' actions were, after all, made on their behalf.

Thus, we, as citizens, have much cause for concern regarding the moral obligations of our legal officials in carrying out their duties, concerns that arise from both the sword and the mirror, and our knowledge of the corroding effects of both: we hold hopes and fears for the obligations that officials will ascribe to us, from our knowledge both that we may be hurt by their decisions and that their actions are made in our name. It is a concern heightened by our knowledge not just of the corruptibility of anyone with such power but also of the potentially corrosive effects of inescapable choices associated with its exercise. Last, it is a concern made grave by the knowledge that officials perform horribly necessary tasks in making choices with moral effects for the citizenry, not only relieving the citizens of the requirement to make a difficult choice, but bearing a disproportionate degree of the blame for doing so on their behalf.

> The only means by which the stakes of the subjects can be protected, other than through resorting to other officials, or to infrequent elections of a handful of officials, is through private judgment of the officials. In this, the subject is free to judge the official by any criteria, including the subject's own view of the law. More to the point, though, the subject is likely to judge by other criteria, by the sense of judgment of right and good conduct in society at large.

---

[168] Scapegoats embody the evil and ill luck within a society. The scapegoat most familiar to Western culture is described in Leviticus 16. On the Day of Atonement, the high priest confessed the sins of the people of Israel to a goat, sometimes called the goat of Azazel, which was then sent into the wilderness. Leviticus 16:22. For the universal aspects of this metaphor, see Sir James George Frazer, 9 *The Golden Bough: A Study in Magic and Religion, Part VI,* "The Scapegoat" (Macmillan, 1913).

3

Officials' Obligations Arise from More Than the Law Alone

> For no phase of life, whether public or private, whether in business or in the home, whether one is working on what concerns oneself alone or dealing with another, can be without its moral duty; on the discharge of such duties depends all that is morally right, and on their neglect all that is morally wrong in life.
>
> Cicero, *On Duties*, Book 1, Chapter 2[1]

Having considered one view of what officials are, one in which the discretion to act is within a complex array of boundaries, we then considered some of the pervasive effects of officials' actions in the lives of others. The question now is whether there are meaningful arguments that the officials must exercise their discretion with such effects according to anything more than law or personal whimsy. This chapter examines that question and finds several independent sources of obligation binding officials that arise beyond the specific rules of law and the personal whims of the individual.

First, the very nature of the law demands that the individual act from a moral foundation beyond the law itself. This demand is explicit in the requirements and forms of oaths that are essential for any official to accept the powers of office, and it is inherent in the structure of the legal system itself. Second, there is no meaningful basis for believing, really, that officials are not supposed to be right or good, or that they are somehow exempt from the general obligations of moral behavior in society. Third, the positions are (with rare exception) voluntary and place the individual official in positions that demand responsiveness to the needs and demands upon the office occasioned by the powers of the office. Last, these are positions that run risks of corruption, of the abuse of power, of a special and dangerous arrogance that can endanger those subject to the power of the official and threaten the authority of the law

---

[1] Marcus Tullius Cicero, *De Officiis* 7 (Walter Miller, trans.) (Loeb edn.) (Cambridge: Harvard University Press, 1913).

itself; the holders of these positions bear an unusual burden not to succumb to these risks.

LEGAL DEFINITIONS OF OFFICE INCORPORATE NONLEGAL OBLIGATIONS

Every legal official has a set of obligations that pertain to that official's particular role in a legal system. To many observers, the most prominent – indeed the only – source of obligations is the law. The law defines the official, depicting not only the name of each office but also the duties assigned to it, the powers to carry them out, the circumscription of those duties and powers, and often the manner in which those powers must be exercised. We are used to the legal definition of office, and indeed we are accustomed to limiting our understanding of the office to its legal definition. We are so accustomed to this limited understanding of legal offices that we will go to some lengths to describe all obligations that attach to a legal office as being legal obligations. Claims that officials must act in ways that are not clearly bound by, controlled by, or defined by law are often greeted with skepticism or anger. Yet it does not follow that a person should be freed from basic moral obligations because there are also obligations of law; just because there is a homicide law does not mean that there is not also a moral bar to murder.

Thus one might see the controversy between Ronald Dworkin and Richard Posner, perhaps the two most influential American legal theorists of the past fifty years, played out through the 1990s as a fight over the extent to which the law alone defines, or ought to define, legal offices. Professor Dworkin has recurrently argued that judges properly rely on morality when acting within the scope of their legal office. Dworkin early argued for a reliance on moral principles, incorporated into the law not as results but as sources of principles – for instance, allowing a New York judge in 1889 to bar a murderer from inheriting through the will of his victim – and he lately argued that a moral reading of the U.S. Constitution was necessary in 1954 for the U.S. Supreme Court to decide *Brown*.[2] Judge Posner attacked Dworkin's position, claiming that neither moral theory nor any aspect of morality *per se* may appropriately serve as the basis for deciding a case at law.[3]

---

[2] Compare Ronald Dworkin, "The Model of Rules," in *Taking Rights Seriously* 14, 23 (Harvard University Press, 1977) citing *Riggs. v. Palmer*, 115 N.Y. 506, 22 N.E. 188 (1889), with Ronald Dworkin, *Freedom's Law: The Moral Reading of the Constitution* 13 (Harvard University Press, 1996), citing *Brown v. Board of Education of Topeka*, 347 U.S. 483 (1954).

[3] This is the argument mentioned in the preface. Judge Posner considered why "professional moralists" have been so persistent, offering two reasons. First, he argued that the experience of revulsion against Nazism "created a demand for a powerful vocabulary of condemnation" to express our anger, which led to an allure for claims of universal moral truth that the Nazis

This dispute is most easily seen as one in which the issue is, "What limits are there to the sources of law?" But this view is incomplete. It is also a dispute about the role of legal officials and whether or not the sole source of the obligations of officials is in the law itself. Seen in this light, Dworkin's argument is more than that the judge may rely on a personal understanding of what is moral in deciding a case. Posner's argument is more than that a claim that the judge may not. Both of them are also arguing over how one knows on what the judge may rely in deciding the case. They are arguing over how the judge ought to exercise judicial authority, not in ordering one litigant to do or not do something, but in deciding whether to issue such an order. They are arguing over how the judge should exercise role discretion as much as, or more than, they are considering substantive discretion.

This argument over how a judge uses discretion not just in applying a rule to facts, but in selecting from among competing sources of rules – that is, selecting the basis for judgment – is the central argument regarding judges in American history. It is the same argument, whether it is an argument raised against Joseph Story's invalidation of a state court intrusion on the commitments of a federal treaty, or against *Dred Scott, Lochner,* or the New Deal court, whether made arguing to limit judicial discretion through the anchor of neutral principles or made arguing to protect expansive discretion by the authority of the least dangerous branch.[4] The most telling characteristics of these arguments, however, are that they all must turn on more than just the claims of law. They also turn upon claims of what judges ought to do, claims that are not by any clear means rooted in the same notion of law.

had violated. He believed the more influential cause is that moralistic argument encourages solidarity among the like-minded, giving a means of identifying and encouraging a community of believers. See Richard Posner, *The Problems of Jurisprudence* 89–90 (Harvard University Press, 1990). And, he believed that moral philosophy is ever preaching to the choir, that no one is ever convinced by a moral argument to take up a position that they did not already hold. *Id.* 38–44. These beliefs are drawn from his earlier arguments, albeit he gives them more sting in his later writing. See, for example, *id.* 348–50; Richard Posner, *The Problematics of Legal Theory* (Harvard University Press, 1999).

    Judge Posner's target for much of his sting responded in Ronald Dworkin, "Philosophy & Monica Lewinsky," 47 New York Review of Books (2000). Dworkin lists those of Posner's arguments that are more personally directed toward his work, with his unrebutted responses at www.nyu.edu/gsas/dept/philo/faculty/dworkin/papers/posner.html (last visited July 28, 2005). For a nice summary, see James Ryerson, "The Outrageous Pragmatism of Judge Richard Posner," Linguafranca (May 2000) (available at http://linguafranca.mirror.theinfo.org/0005/posner.html) (last visited September 6, 2007) discussing Richard Posner & Ronald Dworkin, "'An Affair of State': An Exchange," Linguafranca (April 27, 2000).

4   There are, to understate, many approaches to the problem. Compare Herbert Wechsler, "Toward Neutral Principles of Constitutional Law," 73 Harvard Law Review 1 (1959) with Alexander M. Bickel, *The Least Dangerous Branch: The Supreme Court at the Bar of Politics* (Yale University Press, 1962).

Rather, these claims are rooted in arguments of the authority of the judge and how that authority should be exercised. In the defining moment of the definition of the judge in the modern state, Sir Edward Coke explained to King James that Coke's obligations to the King, to the law, to his judgeship, were that he must do what is "fit" for a judge to do.[5] Such a claim cannot be understood solely by resort to legal precedents or arguments. Such a claim can only be based in part on the rules of the law itself, whether as precedents of a court, customs of judges, dictates of statutes, or principles of a constitution. These are all limited by the very nature of the judge, who must resolve new cases and do so with a balance of legal authority and personal independence.

Oaths of Office

The oath of office has a distinct place in American experience. Recall that in colonial Massachusetts, distinct oaths were created for every office, including the office of freeman.[6] This practice continues today, governed as often by custom as by the rules of the archive.[7] In one variation or another, many legal officials are invested with their authority only after they subscribe to an oath, pledging loyalty and fidelity to the laws.[8] Archetypical of such oaths is that of the president of the United States, whose oath is set forth in Article II.

> Before he enter on the Execution of His Office, he shall take the following Oath or Affirmation: – "I do solemnly swear (or affirm) that I will faithfully execute the Office of President of the United States, and will to the best of my Ability, preserve, protect and defend the Constitution of the United States."[9]

Similar but more comprehensive language is required of all other federal officials, who must take an oath to "support and defend the Constitution of the United States against all enemies, foreign and domestic" and who must also promise to "bear true faith and allegiance to the same" so that the officer will "well and faithfully discharge the duties of the office on which I am about to

---

[5] See Chapter 1, discussing Coke's response to the King's demand for the power of royal consultation in law cases. This must be seen in the light of Coke's strong conception of allegiance to the crown. See "Calvin's Case," 1 *Selected Writings of Sir Edward Coke* 166 (Steve Sheppard, ed.) (Liberty Fund, 2004).

[6] See Chapter 1.

[7] The judges of many U.S. courts select the form of oath they choose to administer to attorneys being first admitted to practice in their courts. Two illustrations are on the back cover of Howard Brill, *Arkansas Professional and Judicial Ethics* (7th ed.) (M&M Press, 2006).

[8] See Brian Burrell, *The Words We Live By: The Creeds, Mottos, and Pledges That Have Shaped America* (Free Press, 1997).

[9] U.S. Constitution, Article II, Section 1, Clause 7. See also Robert F. Blomquist, "The Presidential Oath, The American National Interest and a Call for Presiprudence," 73 UMKC Law Review 1 (2004).

enter. So help me God."[10] Each oath is bound in words of fidelity, both toward the Constitution and toward the office. These oaths just as surely require the officer to determine the meaning of this fidelity as Sir Edward Coke believed he and he alone could determine what a judge must do.

These oaths require moral adherence to a constitution, perhaps even to a constitutional structure.[11] They do something more in creating a parallel moral obligation to act according to legal obligations.[12]

The very nature of an oath demands that the oath-taker make certain commitments, invoking other, prior commitments as assurance of the commitments of the oath. To "swear" or to "affirm" is a pledge that only has a significance as an application of some form of prior undertaking to do what one swears or affirms. In European and American history, such commitments have been based on a relationship to the divine.[13] The oath called upon God to observe the oath-taker's conduct, and the oath presumed divine punishment if it were broken. The drafters of the Constitution were sensitive to the theological objections by some to this divine invocation, notably the Quakers to invoking God for such a secular purpose, as well as recognizing that an obligation of swearing might be seen as an establishment of religion; thus they required that the presidential oath may be sworn or affirmed, allowing the undertaking to be moral but not sectarian and not necessarily religious.[14] Regardless, though, of

---

[10] 5 U.S.C.A § 3331 (2000).

[11] At least one observer believes that the oaths of constitutional fidelity may limit Article V. Note: "The Faith to Change: Reconciling the Oath to Uphold with the Power to Amend," 109 Harvard Law Review 1747 (1996).

[12] John Duke Coleridge, 1st Baron Coleridge, then Lord Chief Justice, wrote:

> It would not be correct to say that every moral obligation involves a legal duty; but every legal duty is founded on a moral obligation. When each of us took that first oath, we each assumed a legal duty that was founded on a moral obligation. We each declared, in an "appeal to God or a god or to some revered person," a determination to "keep a promise." I wonder how many of the problems that face our profession today might be answered in substantial part by revisiting our oaths and recognizing anew the promise that each of us has made.

R. v. Instan, L.R. 1 Q.B. 453 (1893). (Baron Coleridge had written, just a decade before, the famous opinion in Duley and Stephens, [1884] QBD 273 DC.) For a commentary on the role of the oaths taken by Bill Clinton in the events leading up to his impeachment trial, see James E. Pfander, "Presidential Oath-Taking," 16 Constitutional Commentary 549 (1999).

[13] The demand of an oath of particular wording was a common device in England and in the colonies for binding officials to particular policies, as well as ensuring personal allegiance, institutional allegiance, and a basis for prosecution for corruption. See, for example, Edward Vallance, *Revolutionary England and the National Covenant: State Oaths, Protestantism, and the Political Nation,* 1553–1682 (Boydell Press, 2005); David Martin Jones, *Conscience and Allegiance in Seventeenth Century England: The Political Significance of Oaths and Engagements* (University of Rochester Press, 1999); Charles Evans, *Oaths of Allegiance in Colonial New England* (1922) (Clearfield Press, 1998).

[14] See Matthew A. Pauley, *I Do Solemnly Swear: The Presidents' Constitutional Oath: Its Meaning and Importance in the History of Oaths* (University Press of America, 1999). This history casts

the presence or absence of the religious undertaking of an oath, oaths of office are inherently promises of future conduct. Oaths have long been understood to imply a promise to carry out the office to the best of one's ability, and oaths simply do not allow for reservations or partial commitments.[15]

There are several bases for the morality of that undertaking, not the least being that the oath represents a formal commitment in which the oath-taker intends other people to take reliance. Oaths are not taken alone; they must be administered, and the fact of the oath is generally one of public notice. They are said aloud, in a manner that ensures at least the appearance of being voluntary. The oath represents an assurance that invites reliance by the people subject to the official's authority. Such solemn promises have a distinct claim on the imagination, not unlike marital vows; for as long as the vow is not released, we perceive a strong moral duty to the people to whom an oath is given that it must be honored.[16] The oath is not, then, only to God, or only to oneself, or to one's own moral code; it is taken and so made to other individuals. There is one last basis for the oath, an idea that it represents a bond between the oath-taker and an abstract notion of the institution served or the law itself. This is, after all, the simplest meaning of a promise to "preserve, protect and defend the Constitution."

The meaning of oaths to protect the U.S. Constitution has had a profound effect on American law. Chief Justice Marshall's closing paragraphs of his opinion in *Marbury* based the obligation of judicial review on them. "Why otherwise does it [the Constitution] direct the judges to take an oath to support it? This oath certainly applies, in an especial manner, to their conduct in their official character. How immoral to impose it on them, if they were to be used as the instruments, and the knowing instruments, for violating what they swear to support!"[17]

in awkward light the intolerant responses to the statement in 2006 of Congressman-elect Keith Ellison, a Muslim, that he would take his oath on the Qu'ran. See Omar Sacirbey, "Conservatives Attack Use of Koran for Oath: Sacred and Secular Books Have Subbed for Bible," Washington Post B9 (December 9, 2006). The entire affair was based on false assumptions, however, as members of Congress don't use any book to take their oath of office. See Randy Hall, "Muslim Congressman Won't Use Koran When Taking Oath of Office," Canadian News Service (December 1, 2006).

15   See, for example, Francis Wayland, *The Elements of Moral Science* 294 (Gould, Kendall and Lincoln, 1842).

16   On this, see *The Oath*, a metaphorical novel by Elie Wiesel, describing the quest of an oath-taker to be released from an oath of silence meant to limit the effects of an old injustice, in order to save the life of an innocent boy. (Marion Wiesel, trans.) (Schoken Books, 1986).

17   *Marbury v. Madison*, 5 U.S. 137, 180 (1803). Marshall was himself following the custom of the law as he understood it, having observed his teacher George Wythe resolve a similar case by relying on his oath, in setting aside a Virginia law as unconstitutional. See *Commonwealth v. Caton*, 8 Va. (4 Call) 5 (1782).

The content of the oath makes clear that the judges, the jurors, the presidents, the officers, all who take these oaths are bound personally to determine for themselves how they are obliged to carry out their legal obligations. The laws alone are insufficient, in three regards. First, a personal understanding of these laws, and what it means faithfully to defend these laws, is also required.[18] Second, laws creating a legal office don't in themselves create a moral claim on the official; the laws create legal obligations. Yet the laws can require a moral undertaking as a condition of entering the office, which is the function of the oath.

Last, and most important, the oath acts in a manner that laws alone cannot, to the benefit of the rule of law. If laws that are alterable by one official or a group of officials are the whole source of obligations for all other officials, those other officials lack the independence necessary to ensure a just legal system under the rule of law. In other words, each official must have an independent obligation and power to function in the legal system, and the oath is sufficiently personal to provide that independence, whatever supervisory functions others might exercise over the official notwithstanding.[19]

The persistence of oaths as a prerequisite for holding many offices demonstrates at least a recognition by the archive of law that some application of moral notions defines the duties of office. Though oaths are not required of every official, particularly not as defined for the purposes of this discussion, there are very few who do not take one to commence their powers in office. Indeed, those who might like to avoid the obligations of an oath might be troubled to determine any other basis for the trust an office confers upon its holder.[20]

Even so, the archive requiring oaths could be changed, and the culture of oaths could decline. If that were to occur, it would be unlikely that a new formal obligation would not arise that would instill the personal commitments that

---

[18] For a powerful example of the influence of the oaths of lawyers in the Justice Department as a catalyst to civil rights reform, see Gary J. Greenberg, "Revolt at Justice," in *Inside the System* (Charles Peters & Timothy J. Adams, eds.) (Praeger, 1970), reprinted in Amy Gutman & Dennis Thompson, *Ethics & Politics: Cases and Comments* 79 (Wadsworth Publishing, 1984).

[19] This point is well developed as to judges in H. Patrick Glenn, "La responsibilité des juges," 28 McGill Law Journal 228 (1983). Glenn is aware of the danger posed by judges accountable only to judges but sees the true form of judicial accountability as a loyalty to the judicial function, requiring independent and neutral power exercised according to an ideal of good judging. *Id.* 280–3.

[20] This problem of an oath as the primary source of authority was recently considered in Quebec, where it was found that retired judges named by the chief justice for six months of postretirement activity could not function in the absence of an oath of office, since the judge's capacity flowed from the oath, notwithstanding that the judge had sufficient independence. *Williamson c. Mercier*, 2004 Jurisprudence Express 1402, [2004] RJQ 1933. I am especially grateful to Patrick Glenn for telling me of this case.

the oaths represent in some symbolic form that replicates the functions of the oath itself.[21]

Office and the Rule of Law: The Promise of Independence

There is a more fundamental aspect of every legal office, which also requires independence in assessing its role. Every office creates a duty of judgment beyond the description of the office in the archive. In the modern bureaucratic legal system, for the law to act – for the legal system to do anything – requires the coordination of many, many individuals, each of whom is responsible for a particular aspect of that manifestation, and without all of whom the act cannot take place.

The legal bureaucracy of the modern state depends on a division of labor, separating power not only among institutions but among individuals within them. This is not merely a device to increase the efficiency with which laws are produced or enforced, although this is one effect.[22] The legal system divides the power of the state among different individuals, each of whom is entrusted with one portion of a decision, and each of whom must decide to act before a single corporate act of the state through law may be committed.[23] A manifestation of law is, thus, a corporate decision made throughout the bureaucracy.

The manner by which a legal decision is made does not give anyone unlimited authority or power, however. Usually, each aspect of a decision is based on earlier decisions. Thus, a judge asked to apply a statute is relying on the decisions of the legislators in passing it. There is a very strong presumption that each official carries out that office correctly, and therefore most decisions, once taken, are not re-evaluated *ab initio* by other officials. A strong doctrine of deference often gives rise to situations in which one official has made a decision, and the next must decide to apply it or not. The nature of the bureaucracy is, generally, to give deference to the official first tasked with the decision, and in many instances, later officials are supposed to act to overturn that decision only under the most compelling of circumstances.[24]

---

[21] See L. T. Hobhouse, *The Metaphysical Theory of the State: A Criticism* 91 (1951) (Greenwood Publishing, 1984). The obligation to discern whether a valid law is moral, for Hobhouse, rests with individual officials.

[22] See Tom Campbell, *Separation of Powers in Practice* (Stanford University Press, 2004).

[23] See Brian Z. Tamanaha, *On the Rule of Law: History, Politics, Theory* 122–6 (Cambridge University Press, 2004).

[24] The classic statement of deference in American constitutional law was the opinion in *NLRB v. Jones & Laughlin Steel Corporation*, 301 U.S. 1 (1937), in which the Court determined that it should defer to congressional definition of the constitutional limits of interstate commerce in passing laws, and it should defer to agency interpretations of those laws. The court left for later evaluation the limits of that deference. Deference can describe the law governing many decisions within branches, such as the standards of appellate review, as well as between institutions, such as comity and the limits on the judicial review of agency

Within the scope of the discretion granted to each official, however, the official may also have a commitment described by law to act independently of the prior officials. The decision on review to determine whether there are indeed compelling circumstances to overturn a prior decision, for instance, is independent of what the decision is. This type of commitment of one task or another is evident when, for instance, a legislator votes on a bill offered for adoption by a legislative committee; the legislator is not bound by the committee's resolution, but will not usually perform again the work of the committee. A judge determining whether a plaintiff has demonstrated sufficient evidence sufficiently well to plead a case under a statute must assess the evidence and is not bound by the statute to rule either to grant or to allow the pleading; the judge must independently weigh the evidence (but will usually not analyze whether the legislature passed an unconstitutional statute). This form of independence is essential to perform the labor once it is divided, and the rule of law demands independence of each official in those tasks.[25]

In this manner, each office is subject to the rule of law, but each office also contributes to it. Unless each official exercises the discretion committed to that office with independence and judgment in the last analysis unbiased by other officials' decisions, the system of rule by law breaks down. A mere hierarchy develops, in which the official at the top speaks for all.[26]

As considered in Chapter 2, every office has discretion, and the manner in which this discretion is exercised cannot be fully dependent on the content of the legal archive. As to legislation, this discretion is considerable, and the

and state decisions. See Steven Alan Childress, *Federal Standards of Review* (Butterworth Legal Publishers, 1992); see also Rebecca L. Donnellan, "The Exhaustion Doctrine Should Not Be a Doctrine with Exceptions," 103 West Virginia Law Review 361 (2001). More on deference in U.S. law is in George P. Fletcher & Steve Sheppard, *American Law in a Global Context: The Basics* 69–70 (Oxford University Press, 2005).

[25] A fine example of this notion, also in U.S. constitutional law, is the interpretation of due process of law to require that a judge must have the power to deny a motion in order for a motion of forfeiture of property to be given an adequate judicial hearing. Thus a state law that required the judge to grant a motion for an order of replevin based on a plaintiff's allegations was void. *Mitchell v. W. T. Grant Co.*, 416 U.S. 600 (1974).

[26] This complaint is the basis for most arguments against judicial review, that the rest of the government becomes merely the servant of the courts. For example, in *Judicial Tyranny: The New Kings of America* (Mark Sutherland, ed.) (Amerisearch, 2005), essays discuss the perils of allowing judges to alter law to vary from the common-law tradition, or the will of the people, or the social traditions of the country. That these arguments are all opposed to one another does not seem to trouble the essayists, any more than that the flaws of legislators manifest on the same grounds of variance with tradition; nor do they seem troubled by similar limits of the legislative will by the executive. One is tempted to judge these essays consequentially and politically; the essayists do not like the results the courts have made, and they seek to change them; their instrumental arguments are really little more than shams.

All that said, there are good reasons to prefer that laws be made, in general, by people who have a vested interest in conforming those laws to the desires of the people who are governed by them. See Jeremy Waldron, *The Dignity of Legislation* (Cambridge University Press, 1999).

person with authority to create law is generally free to choose how a law should be drafted for use in the archive, and what expectations there should be of it, bound only by the problems of small-group dynamics in ensuring the eventual enactment of the law according to the rules governing its creation.

As to adjudication and administration, this discretion is owing to the indeterminacy of rules as they exist in the archive, in which certain details of the application of a rule in the archive demand interpretation according to the patterns of legal culture – the techniques, tropes, even rituals that other members of the culture expect to be followed.[27] The culture then guides applications according to the expectations of officials as to the proper result.[28] In some instances, there are many, equally acceptable, decisions that an official might make, and the selection among them is, by definition, left to the official.

OFFICIALS ARE NOT EXEMPT FROM GENERAL OBLIGATIONS

Natural Law as a Critique of Officials

One of the most important legal theorists at the dawn of the modern state was Christian Thomasius, considered the founder of the Enlightenment in Germany. Thomasius was well aware of the obligations of magistrates under the law but argued powerfully that these obligations must be considered subordinate to a sphere of right action.[29] Applying that theory, Thomasius condemned, and successfully halted, the trials for witchcraft then still prevalent in Germany.[30] It was a triumph of what is often called the criticism of law by what is often called natural law.

The argument sometimes raised by traditional naturalists (though more often raised by their critics) is that the law of the state includes natural law. This argument is based on a reading of Thomist and scholastic authors, in which natural law is integral to understanding civil law.[31] There is ambiguity in what people mean when they invoke natural law, whether it is nothing more

---

[27] See H. L. A. Hart, *The Concept of Law* 128–36 (2d ed.) (Oxford University Press, 1994).

[28] The culture in this model is a culture of legal officials, and not the culture of society as a whole, so culture does not imply that a result reached according to the patterns of culture ought to conform always to a particular outcome that promotes the good or the right, but it does imply what is usually a messy affair of a variety of choices among culturally acceptable tools. See Chapter 1.

[29] Christian Thomasius, *Fundamenta Juris Naturae et Gentium* (1705) (Scientia Verlag Aalen, 1979), reprinted as *Fundamentos de Derecho Natural y de Gentes* (Salvador Rus Rufina & Asunción Sánches Manzano) (Tecnos, 1994).

[30] There is still very little of Thomasius's work that has been translated into English, and still less scholarship on him. The best appreciation in this language is probably still Andrew Dickson White, *Seven Great Statesmen in the Warfare of Humanity with Unreason* (Garden City Publishing, 1926).

[31] It is probably a misreading of Aquinas to take literally his idea that a law of man that is contrary to natural law is not law at all. See John Finnis, *Aquinas: Moral, Political, and Legal Theory* (Oxford University Press, 1998).

than a sense of inevitable conduct,[32] or whether it is a sense of what is always moral,[33] or whether it is a sense of justice from which arguments about the state can be derived.[34] The sum of these arguments is that there is a sense in which an idea of what a good person does, or what a rational person does, is an appropriate basis for assessing the substance of the law: the law should promote virtues, the good, or reason, and it should discourage vices and the harmful in people's lives.

The usual forms of natural law have been well developed elsewhere and need not be described at length here.[35] These arguments are bases for the criticism of the content of the archive, arguments that are to be employed for reform in institutional settings. Yet implied within them are inherent claims upon the individual official. The good official is one whose actions promote the naturally understood virtues, good, or reason in the polity.

Moral Assessment of Official Acts

All legal officials are subject to the assessment of other people in their conduct, just as they would be judged if they were not officials. There is no reason why that assessment should not be an argument of what would be morally right to be done, as opposed to any other grounds. The fact that an official's discretion

---

[32] This is the sense in which Hart uses it, to represent a reason why the law ought to reflect an understanding of mankind, in which individuals will be physically vulnerable, are of rough equality among one another, have limited altruism and limited strength and will, and always have scarcity of resources. See H. L. A. Hart, *The Concept of Law* 193–200 (2d ed.) (Oxford University Press, 1994).

[33] Here Thomas Hobbes has a list of nine principles of natural law. The basis of *Leviathan* is that every person ought to (1) seek peace but have a right to war when peace is impossible, (2) when possible, surrender his liberty and defense to a common purpose, (3) perform his contracts, (4) receive benefits from others without remorse, (5) be sociable, (6) pardon those who seek it, (7) base revenge on future peril not past acts, (8) avoid hatred, (9) recognize equality among all persons. See Thomas Hobbes, *Leviathan: or the Matter, Forme & Power of a Commonwealth, Ecclesiasticall and Civill*, Chapters 14–15 (C. B. MacPherson, ed.) (Penguin Classics, 1982).

[34] This is the basis for modern natural law theory. See, for example, Robert P. George, *In Defense of Natural Law* (Oxford University Press, 2001). The flourishing of the theory of natural law at the dawn of the modern state is captured nicely in the landmark series of books brought back to life in Knud Haakonssen's series for Liberty Fund, *Natural Law and Enlightenment Classics*, now in forty-four titles.

[35] Two of the most prominent modern arguments are by George and Finnis. See Robert P. George, *Making Men Moral: Civil Liberties and Public Morality* (Oxford University Press, 1995); John Finnis, *Natural Law and Natural Rights* (Oxford University Press, 1980). Both of these authors promote a Thomistic approach, which is not the only means of natural criticism of the law. A more process-oriented approach along the lines of Grotius and Thomasius has not been strongly defended of late, although greater understanding of these theories in their own time has been encouraged, particularly by Knud Haakonssen and Richard Tuck. See, for example, Richard Tuck, "Introduction," in Hugo Grotius, *The Rights of War and Peace* (Richard Tuck, ed.) (Liberty Fund, 2005).

is often limited by rules as understood from the archive of laws or by its culture does not forbid a judgment that what the official does is good or evil. A harsh or a praising judgment might be moderated by the knowledge that the officials felt that the assessed conduct was circumscribed by laws, but there is no reason for that moderation to be complete, or even significant.[36]

The most fundamental touchstone for such assessment is complex and controversial: it is the deep sense of what is right and what is wrong in the treatment of others by any person. Although there are reasons to beware the word, and to prefer "natural law," or "virtues" or "values," one might as well call this source of these obligations "morality."[37]

Consider this hypothetical: a convict sentenced to death petitions a judge for a hearing to determine whether there are grounds to allow a second hearing to determine whether to set a new trial based on compelling evidence of the convict's actual innocence, which was discovered after the convict's trial. Whether or not permitted under the rules of law, the judge might feel strongly that the moral argument requires the hearing. Under this view it would be morally right to allow the first hearing, and it would be morally wrong to deny it. One could posit that there are specific reasons why this is the morally correct conclusion, but these reasons need not be apparent to the judge. The judge will rule, expressing reasons derived from the archive and culture of the law.[38] If the

---

[36] This is Heidi Hurd's main reason for rejecting a role-based conception of official morality. See Heidi Hurd, *Moral Combat* (Cambridge University Press, 1999).

[37] I chose "morality" here thinking it is the least distracting collective noun for these forms of nonlegal obligations of the official, though some readers will be distracted anyway. There are alternative terms, chiefly "ethics" and "conscience." I prefer "morality" over "ethics" mainly to avoid the nuance of "ethics" as the study of certain ideas within morality. See Robert Audi, *The Cambridge Dictionary of Philosophy* 244 (Cambridge University Press, 1995). I use "morality" here in a way resonant with "conscience" in the essays in Philip Cowley's *Conscience and Parliament* (Frank Cass, 1998), at least as it refers to the "sense of right and wrong that governs a person's thoughts and actions." Stephen Perry nicely spins three views of morality as attempts to best answer three questions: "Which human beings ought we to care about? What is truly good for those we should care about – and what is bad for them? And how should we resolve conflicts between goods – in particular, between what is good for some we should care about and what is good for others we should care about?" Stephen J. Perry, "What Is "Morality" Anyway?" 45 Villanova Law Review 69, 100 (2000). To this I'd add some ideas of the right manner of answering such questions and of pursuing such cares.

As I warned in the preface, I will not defend "morality" as a term in itself or in a given origin. I just don't think such debates answer much for the purposes here. For instance, Richard Joyce has argued that morality, actually moral realism, rests on foolish ideas with little meaning for us at all, but he falls back on a Pascalian solution, which is to act as if morality were real, because of the benefits we receive in well-regulated lives. Richard Joyce, *The Myth of Morality* (Cambridge University Press, 2001).

[38] There is no federal ground for judicial review of a state court's refusal to consider evidence of actual innocence first acquired by the defense after a verdict. Only if a prisoner can allege that there was a constitutional violation during the trial will such evidence be heard in a federal challenge to state confinement. It is up to the state's officials to decide to hear or not to hear such evidence. See *Herrera v. Collins*, 506 U.S. 390 (1993).

judge believes that the archive and culture unequivocally require denial, then the judge will likely deny the hearing, reaching the morally wrong answer.[39] Although observers might understand why the judge committed a morally wrong act, and although the judge's belief that the law gave no discretion to do otherwise might diminish somewhat the observers' perception of the judge's moral responsibility, there is no reason to extinguish that blame entirely.[40]

There are those who might persist in the view that there can be no wrong in denying a hearing that the archive of the law does not allow. For these people, the written law is the sole source of right, by definition, at least in such matters as whether a person deserves a legal hearing. These people must reject the idea that the judge has any legitimate moral status or agency other than that invested in the judicial office by the law.[41] Such an impersonal rejection of moral agency in the legal action echoes the words of Angelo, Shakespeare's hypocritical judge in *Measure for Measure*, who reassures Isabella, the sister of Claudio, whom he has just condemned to death for fornication. "Be you content, fair maid, It is the law, not I, condemn your brother."[42] Yet it is still the act of Angelo and one that he has chosen. The audience knows that Angelo has chosen to enforce strictly the long-neglected sex laws.[43]

Yet even if Angelo were acting as judges before him had, he could not be free from responsibility for his act, claiming that the law alone is held to

[39] See Chapter 5. For now, let us at least consider that the judge in fact has many options other than denial, although perceiving such options may require courage and imagination. See, for example, Robert M. Cover, *Justice Accused: Antislavery and the Judicial Process* (Yale University Press, 1975).

[40] Some argue that moral responsibility demands an alternative reasonably be available, and that the official be morally blameless if the law clearly and undeniably bars any but a repugnant choice. See Harry Frankfurt, "Alternative Possibilities and Moral Responsibility," in *Moral Responsibility and Alternative Possibilities* (David Widerker & Michael McKenna, eds.) (Ashgate, 2003). There are two problems in this argument, that as a matter of fact, it is really quite amazingly rare that there truly is no alternative. Yet assuming that it is sometimes true that the law gives no alternative, the official has still chosen to be in the circumstance in general, and this gives alternatives. This problem is explored in Chapter 5.

[41] True beliefs can be lost in stentorian public announcements, but I can find no historical figure whom I am willing to lumber with such a wretched view. Despite his pronouncements in some death-sentence cases, I doubt even Justice Scalia believes the view above. See *Schlup v. Delo*, 513 U.S. 298, 350 (1995) (Scalia, J. dissenting) (claim of actual innocence in a second petition for habeas corpus should be rejected).

[42] William Shakespeare, *Measure for Measure*, Act 2, Scene 2, Line 80, in *The Riverside Shakespeare* 594 (2d ed.) (Riverside Press, 1997). This pious assurance only sets the stage for Angelo's offer to Isabella to free her brother Claudio from his execution, at the price of Isabella's sexual favors. See *id.*, Act 2, Scene 4. Granted, one might defend Angelo's sentiment above by asserting its plausibility when made in the strictest good faith. In Angelo's case, this would still leave substantial room to demur, given that Angelo has convicted Claudio for fornication under a law that has been unenforced for centuries, even though Claudio slept with his *fiancée* only a short time before their intended wedding.

[43] *Id.*, Lines 42–116, pp. 586–7. Angelo's great line is, "The law hath not been dead, though it hath slept." *Id.*, line 90.

account. This becomes clearer once the law is seen as an archive and a culture. Within the scope of the play, some Viennese judge or legislator, long before, had decreed that fornication was an act punishable by death. Presumably, for a time, officials enforced the law, and it was then the culture of the law to do so. Then, enforcement became rare and the culture shifted, although the archive remained unchanged. Angelo's act is, in its way, made as an agent of the unknown drafter of this portion of the archive. Angelo's choice is essential. Without his decision to enforce the law, Claudio would not be imprisoned awaiting death. At best, Angelo could truly say only that he is merely an agent or collaborator of other officials.

Subjects, other officials, anyone is free to assess the morality of the acts of the official. We in the audience are meant to condemn Angelo.[44] It is appropriate that we should.

One word more might be warranted in considering the idea that legal officials are not exempt from moral assessment. It is sometimes suggested that a strict definition of law, identified with legal positivism, requires the rejection of moral agency in determining the sum of the obligations of lawmakers.[45] This complaint was powerfully raised by the German legal scholar Gustav Radbruch, who heard statements such as Angelo's pave the way to the Nazi regime and the Holocaust.[46] And yet, positivism's definitions of law do not exclude the use of moral ideals from the legal framing of rules, and more importantly, do not require the law to be the sole source of obligation. As the twentieth-century legal positivist Herbert Hart put it, "Surely the truly liberal answer to any sinister use of the slogan 'law is law' or of the distinction between law and morals is, 'Very well, but that does not conclude the question. Law is not morality; do not let it supplant morality.'"[47]

---

[44] Angelo's sovereign does condemn him, as does initially Isabella. Yet, Angelo reforms and regrets the prosecution, and Isabella comes to accept its justice at least in that he had done what he was accused of doing. Through a procedural error, however, Claudio survives and is pardoned. *Id.*, Lines 445–90, pp. 617–18.

[45] This view, at its extreme, is known by the bulky term "legal autopoieticism," which stresses law's autonomy, its normative closure, its structural determination, its reflexive identity, and its potential fitness for computer modeling. See Gunther Teubner, *Autopoietic Law: A New Approach to Law and Society* (Walter de Gruyter, 1987). Gunther Teubner, "The King's Many Bodies: The Self-Deconstruction of Law's Hierarchy," 31 Law & Society Review 763, 764 (1997). This view is sometimes ascribed to legal positivism, but positivism does not prohibit moral norms as the inspiration for primary rules; positivism requires only that the moral norm be reflected in a law created according to the laws.

[46] See H. L. A. Hart, "Positivism and the Separation of Law and Morals," 71 Harvard Law Review 593 (1955), discussing the work of Gustav Radbruch ("Gesetzliches Unrecht und übergesetzliches Recht," 1 Suddetsche Juristen-Zeitung 105 (Germany, 1946)). See also *The Legal Philosophies of Lask, Radbruch, and Dabin* (Kurt Wilk, trans.) (Harvard University Press, 1950).

[47] H. L. A. Hart, "Positivism and the Separation of Law and Morals," reprinted in –, *Essays in Jurisprudence and Philosophy* 49, 75 (Oxford University Press, 1983). Hart's argument was

Indeed, Hart was later quite clear that moral norms play important roles in the legal system. The obvious point is that the law mirrors moral obligations in myriad legal obligations, providing primary laws for citizens that reflect their moral obligations. But he also recognized the importance of moral ideals in interpreting the open texture of laws, in ascertaining the nature of justice, in criticizing law – even to the point of demonstrating the legitimacy of resistance and rebellion against laws and the legal system.[48] "The further ways in which law mirrors morality," he said, "are myriad, and still insufficiently studied."[49] The positivist notion of law does coexist with moral obligations, and legal officials ignore the effect of these obligations at the expense of the law itself.[50]

THE STAKES AND THE SPECIAL TEMPTATIONS OF POWER

The arguments considered so far in this chapter have been based on general propositions concerning the substance of law, as those propositions apply to individuals, as well as general propositions for moral assessment concerning all individuals. This is to say, thinking back to the actions of Stoughton in the witchcraft court at Salem, that there are bases for assessing him as violating an oath or being an architect of bad law, and these are different from assessing him as a bad man *per se*.

There are additional bases for considering that officials accept a particular obligation to carry out their duties according to right and good principles, considerations arising because of the peculiar nature of their role. We have reasons for assessing whether Stoughton is a bad judge that arise from Stoughton's having accepted the judgeship and that transcend his oath of office and the general obligations of morality. First, officials have accepted an office in which they must understand that their actions affect the stakes others have in the law. Indeed, in the light of the stakes as considered in Chapter 1, the actions

---

not dependent upon liberal theory but was part of his definition of law. In his discussion of the positivist description of law, even if one rejected the noncognitive view, the distinction between what law is and what law ought to be, Hart maintained that the division of law from morality was maintained, and because of this he viewed morality as a viable source by which to evaluate the law. See *id.* 84.

[48]   H. L. A. Hart, *The Concept of Law*, 200–12 (2d ed., 1994) (this section is the revised form of *Positivism and the Separation of Law and Morals*).

[49]   *Id.* 204.

[50]   Even the autopoietic notion of law, noted earlier, recognizes the continuing influence of morality on law. "Politics, morality, and many other nonlegal forces certainly affect law in autopoietic legal systems – how could they not? – but they do not determine the validity of legal acts and communications." Arthur J. Jacobson, "Survey of Books Relating to the Law; VII: Legal Theory and Philosophy: Autopoietic Law: The New Science of Niklas Luhmann. *Autopoietic Law: A New Approach to Law and Society.* Edited by Gunther Teubner," 87 Michigan Law Review 1647, 1648 (1989).

of officials affect the lives of stakeholders dramatically and thoroughly, and the stakeholders are, by and large, without any power to control the particular instances of these influences. Second, the very nature of office – just the social fact of authority over others – in itself means unusual risk that the individual in office will behave badly.

The Official Accepts Responsibility for the Stakes

The stakes for citizens in the sword, the shield, the coin, the commons, the balance, the guide, and the mirror are tremendous. An official whose action affects the law in any way will have, to the degree of the effect, an effect on the potential for at least some subject to have these stakes altered. The sword creates for some subjects a great burden and for all subjects some fear. The monopoly inherent in the shield makes citizens dependent upon it, whether it is provided when needed or not. The balance provides resolution, order, and peace among citizens. The guide commands the citizen to act or refrain from conduct in nearly every aspect of life; the coin and the commons are essential to personal survival and economic success; and the mirror establishes a significant aspect of the citizen's moral reasoning and personal identity. Yet, owing to the vagaries of the seal and of the veil, the citizen remains dependent on others, anonymous as they usually are, to see that all of these forces of the law are carried out.

This dependence is involuntary for the subject, but voluntary for each official, with the exception of jurors. The official freely and willfully accepts the role on which others depend. By doing so, the official unequivocally accepts a series of affirmative moral duties that might be more doubtful otherwise.

The easy example is the chestnut question of whether there is a moral duty to rescue someone in distress, when the possible rescuer could do so without danger.[51] This idea is the basis for much of the literature of Christian duty to others, as well as the general moral sense of what is owed between strangers.[52] It is particularly compelling when there is a relationship of proximity between the victim and the potential rescuer.[53]

In the case of the official's relationship to the subject, the choice of the individual to assume office not only places the official in a particular relationship

---

[51] This is not the same question as whether the law ought to enforce such a duty, which is likely in civilian states and unlikely in common-law states. See Martin Vranken, "Duty to Rescue in Civil Law and Common Law," 47 International and Comparative Law Quarterly 934, 938–9 (1998); *The Duty to Rescue: The Jurisprudence of Aid* 93 (Michael A. Menlowe & Alexander McCall Smith, eds.) (Dartmouth Publishing, 1993).

[52] For the history of the duty in law, see Kathleen M. Ridolfi, "Law, Ethics, and the Good Samaritan: Should There Be a Duty to Rescue?" 40 Santa Clara Law Review 957 (2000).

[53] See Jeremy Waldron, *On the Road: Good Samaritans and Compelling Duties*, 40 Santa Clara Law Review 1053 (2000).

of power over the subject; by entering into the office, the individual denies that office to someone else.

So the official has become more than just a passing stranger when a struggling swimmer calls for help. The official is like the lifeguard. Not only has the lifeguard promised to act – a promise on which the swimmer is entitled to rely – but also other observers will expect the lifeguard to act and, believing the guard will do so, are less likely to aid the swimmer themselves.

In such a relationship as the official's to the subjects, however, the relationship is far more comprehensive. The lifeguard here can harm as well as help, instruct and represent, and alter the nature of personal identity. In such a relationship, every aspect of the manner in which an official commits an act of office is properly subject to scrutiny: the motives for actions, the preparations for or failure to prepare before acting, the actions themselves, the consequences of actions, the apparent significance of actions. All of these are fair grounds for the official to be assessed by others. The bases of their assessment will vary, but they are not tied to rules found in the archive or practices in the culture of the law. Subjects, and other officials, are justified in forming an opinion of an official's actions, basing those opinions on notions of the good or the right. Such an opinion could be based on an undifferentiated and unarticulated idea of whether the act is one that a person of good conscience or morals would make. An opinion formed by comparison to any of these standards of judgment is likely to be fair and sufficient as a basis for praise or condemnation of the official for that act, all the more so if the opinion is formed by someone who is disinterested in the official's act. It would be hoped that the official, given the stake the official has in the seal, would perceive this form of judgment as proper owing to the nature of the office. As the judge and philosopher Gottfried Leibniz said, better judges, those with "larger and finer views, would not wish that anyone complain in their lack of goodness."[54]

The idea that a moral obligation is best assessed by the opinion of disinterested observers is a powerful notion, both in the literature and in popular culture. In the movie script of Tom Wolfe's *Bonfire of the Vanities*, Morgan Freeman plays the role of Judge Leonard White, attempting to explain to an unruly courtroom the basis for right and wrong in judging official misconduct:

> "You dare call me a racist? Well I say unto you, what does it matter the color of a man's skin when witnesses perjure themselves and prosecutors enlist the perjury; when a district attorney throws a man to the mob for political gain and men of the cloth, men of God, take the prime cut? Is that justice? Let me tell you what justice is. Justice is the law. And the law is man's feeble attempt to lay down the principles of decency. Decency! And decency isn't a

---

[54] Gottfried Leibniz, *The Common Concept of Justice* (c. 1702–03), quoted in *Political Writings* 54 (Patrick Riley, ed.) (Cambridge University Press, 1988). Leibniz's ideas are considered in Chapter 4.

deal, it's not a contract or a hustle or an angle! Decency . . . decency is what your grandmother taught you. It's in your bones! You go home now. Go home and be decent people. Be decent!"[55]

At this focus, the particular reasons for the immorality in the actions of those he described were irrelevant. What mattered was that an unbiased observer in whose sense of decency others should trust would condemn these things. That is, sometimes, enough.

The Nature of Office Encourages Bad Behavior

A social fact about official conduct gives rise to an unfortunate reason for both subjects and officials to expect officials to act in their powers according to the good and the right. The fact is that the nature of office makes it more, not less likely that officials will act in immoral ways. Certain aspects of the role of a legal official make good behavior harder in itself. These aspects of legal office tempt the officeholder to bad conduct, luring the individual toward deviance from what the individual knows to be right. This is, again, what Lord Acton meant when he said that "power corrupts."[56] Thanks to social science, we know a bit more about how this corruption occurs than we did in Acton's day.

Tribalism

The very fact of group identity affects moral beliefs. The pursuit of goals in a group allows a privilege for one idea over others because it arises in the group. Ideas and attitudes resonant with those in the group are more valued than all others. The group closes ranks, and those who are with the group are instinctively preferred.[57] Thus, the official is placed in a community in which the perspective is already distinct from that of the subject whose interest the official is obliged to protect, and the subject's perspective is categorically less acceptable than the perspective of other officials.

---

[55] Michael Cristofer, *Bonfire of the Vanities* 288 (Warner Bothers, 1990) (Brian DePalma, director, 1990). The lines above are as they were delivered. In the third draft of the screenplay, the line was "Decency is what your mother taught you!" The further remove of a grandmother creates a powerful effect.

[56] When penning his famous aphorism Acton was talking of standards of moral judgment for popes, kings, and other absolute rulers and whose actions must be judged by other people, and indeed they should be judged by a higher standard than would apply to ordinary subjects. John Emerich Edward Dalberg-Acton, *Essays on Freedom and Power* 364 (Beacon Press, 1948).

[57] The research of Gerd Gigerenzer, of the Max Planck Institute for Human Development in Berlin, merits close examination on this point, which supports the instinctive point about morality among police comrades. Why would police do something that they would otherwise see as immoral? "Don't break ranks." Gerd Gigerenzer, *Gut Feelings, The Intelligence of the Unconscious* 181 (Viking Press, 2007).

Conformity

The nature of group decision-making, particularly when the decision-makers have long-term commitments to a cohesive group (such as an appellate court, an administrative agency, or a legislative committee), is to minimize conflict and reach consensus within the group. Group conformity through the evolution of the decision becomes more important than an accurate decision, because the decision becomes unlikely to be subjected to critical testing, analysis, or comparison to competing ideas. This phenomenon is known to social scientists as "groupthink." Among other effects, groupthink gives rise to baroque rationalizations for mistakes, continued commitments to failing or foolish projects that can turn mistakes into fiascoes, and an attraction to secrecy.[58] Most importantly, groupthink destroys independence; by accepting certain commitments either by the group as a whole or by a leader of the group, the other members of the group either do not or cannot assert an independent judgment. This process of entrapment can occur indirectly, through accepting certain commitments that entail others in a sequence of interrelated decisions.[59] Thus, an official is placed in circumstances in which acceptance of the decisions of others is more likely, not less likely, to be based on an independent decision.

Office, with a few exceptions, places the official in a hierarchical structure, making the official not only a part of a group but subject to the authority of other officials and keen to assert authority over others. The natural instincts to conform – to obey authority, even malevolent authority – will (for most individuals) diminish independent moral judgment. This problem was famously illustrated by Stanley Milgram's experiments, in which two-thirds of his test subjects were willing to administer lethal electrical shocks to volunteers, merely because they were told to do so by authority figures.[60] To accept such a role is to reject responsibility for one's own moral choices and become merely the agent of the authority.[61] Thus, the authority of hierarchy risks moral agency rather than moral independence, for precisely the individuals whose independence is most needed for a legal system that reflects the rule of law.

---

[58] See Irving L. Janis, *Groupthink: Psychological Studies of Policy Decisions and Fiascoes* (2d ed.) (Houghton Mifflin, 1982); –, *Victims of Groupthink: A Psychological Study of Foreign-Policy Decisions and Fiascoes* (Houghton Mifflin, 1972).

[59] See Paul 't Hart, *Groupthink in Government: A Study of Small Groups and Policy Failure* 96–7 (Johns Hopkins University Press, 1990).

[60] Stanley Milgram, *Obedience to Authority; An Experimental View* (Harper & Row, 1974).

[61] Milgram describes his "agentic" interpretation of the experiment at *id.* 132–4. This is not unlike more classical explanations of the acceptance of authority. See Étienne de la Boétie, *The Politics of Obedience: The Discourse of Voluntary Servitude* (1550) (Kessinger Publishing, 2004).

Hubris

Officials are vulnerable to false confidence, especially to a misplaced sense of technical expertise. Placed in a position of responsibility, officials are likely to engage in specialized training that reinforces groupthink, and they are likely to have an exaggerated sense of technical competence. This type of assumed expertise takes many forms, and most people are familiar with the problem of a person thinking that an office equates to a skill related to the office, with unfortunate results. For our purposes, a single example will serve to illustrate the point. Police officers in the United States are given specialized training in interrogation, with the particular object of recognizing falsehoods. Study after study suggests that completing such training does not make trained officers substantially better at spotting liars than anyone else; but it does raise their confidence in their opinions.[62]

Immunity

The nature of the bureaucracy allows decisions to be made anonymously, incrementally, and with a minimum of responsibility. This is the problem described earlier in the veil, but it is a particular aspect of the definition of office. It is the banality that Hannah Arendt described when dissecting the moral failures of the Nazi German government.[63]

The nature of the anonymous act in bureaucracy, coupled with the status of an official, also leads to a sense of immunity from judgment. This idea of immunity, being subject to none, is the basis of the absolute corruption that Acton had in mind.

Domination

Last, and most significant, is the fact that officials see themselves as different from subjects, that there is a divide between the guardians and the guarded. This sense of difference, the division between us and them, is the basis for a competitive, tribal behavior in which officers see themselves apart, subject to different rules and different obligations. The special character of the office among officers allows the officer to distort observations of the other group, rationalizing behavior by members of the official group as good and that by the subject group as bad. It allows emotional distance between the groups, in which, given any power relationship, a cycle of domination, resistance, and reprisal further divides those who identify with the two groups.

---

[62] See Ray Bull, "Training to Detect Deception from Behavioral Cues," in *The Detection of Deception in Forensic Contexts* 251 (Pär-Anders Granhag and Lief A. Strömwall, eds.) (Cambridge University Press, 2004).

[63] Hannah Arendt, *Eichmann in Jerusalem: A Report on the Banality of Evil* (Viking Press, 1963).

The classic illustration of this form of behavior was the lesson Jane Elliott gave her third-grade class in Riceville, Iowa, after listening to broadcasters speaking in the us-and-them language of race relations in the week following the murder of Dr. Martin Luther King, Jr. In a two-day experiment that would be unlikely to be permitted under later standards of instruction, she divided her all-white class of students between those with blue eyes and those with brown eyes, telling them that each was the more important group on one of the two days. The students descended quickly into shocking mistreatment of one another.[64] As she described it in an interview soon after, the mere suggestion from authority that one group of children defined by a trivial difference was better and more deserving than the other was enough. "I watched what had been marvelous, cooperative, wonderful, thoughtful children turn into nasty vicious, discriminating little third graders in the space of fifteen minutes."[65]

When this tribal instinct is coupled with a sense of authority, it led nice Stanford students to brutality and violence when acting the role of prison guards, and in this form it is the same instinct that led upstanding soldiers to commit the same forms of brutality at Abu Ghraib.[66] The lurid elements of these illustrations cannot blind us to the risk that all officials face, that the sense of difference between the official and the subject can allow the official moral latitude to except official actions from the usual limits of morality. This, too, was an essential step in allowing the German legal system to descend into terror, and it is just not as hard to imagine in other countries as modern observers would hope.[67]

The Challenge of Office to Morality

These five aspects of modern legal office – tribalism and its resulting conformity, false confidence, a sense of anonymous immunity from reprisal, and the will to dominate others – challenge our ordinary commitments to morality in profound and varied ways. This particular allure has been with us always: it is the seduction of power.

At the very moments when the subject – and indeed the success of the legal system – most require a morally independent agent, and indeed when the stakes of the subject are most at risk, the nature of office diminishes the incentives for independence of action and for the moral assessment of official conduct. The nature of office itself endangers the stakes that the citizen must have in it. The official, having accepted responsibility for the office and thus for

---

[64] See William Peters, *A Class Divided: Now and Then* (Yale University Press, 1987).
[65] *Frontline: A Class Divided* (William Peters, dir.) (Yale University Films, 1985).
[66] See Philip Zimbardo, *The Lucifer Effect: Understanding How Good People Turn Evil* (Random House, 2007).
[67] See, for example, Richard L. Rubenstein, *The Cunning of History: The Holocaust and the American Future* (Harper Perennial, 1987).

the stakes that others have in it, has also accepted a heightened risk of betraying the trust that the responsibility for those stakes entails.

SYNTHESIZING MORAL OBLIGATIONS FROM DIFFERENT SOURCES

We have considered obligations upon officials to act on bases other than the strict rules in the legal archive that arise both from the law itself and from sources outside the law. The sources in the law – oaths and commitments to the integrity of the law and the rule of law – and the sources outside the law – general obligations of moral conduct and the peculiar risks of abuse of the trust of office – may differ somewhat in the scope of the obligations each entails. In any event, it appears that the natures of these sources are complementary, and the obligations that arise from each would reinforce or supplement the obligations that arise from the others.

One might be able to parse these sources and then to delineate elements of duty that arise from one and not another. Yet, these various bases of obligations seem more similar than different in what they might require. To create a model of obligations that reflect each and all of these sources will inevitably yield some obligations whose basis in a given obligation is a bit tenuous. Yet the pragmatic benefits of considering what obligations appear congruent with all of these sources is to reduce the complexity of the whole project.

The risk would be to a reader who accepts some sources of obligation but not the others. Say, for instance, you might agree that oaths give rise to obligations to the institution and perhaps to those subject to law, but you do not agree that officials are bound in their office by general principles of moral conduct. You might wish to reject any moral obligations that seem to arise from general obligations but accept such obligations that seem required by an oath of office. To help a reader like you, the obligations that have been explored in the next chapter are organized, very roughly, into categories that might ease such distinctions.

4

The Moral Obligations of Legal Officials

The first office of justice is to keep one man from doing harm to another, unless provoked by wrong; and the next is to lead men to use common possessions for the common interests, private property for their own....

The foundation of justice, moreover, is good faith; – that is, truth and fidelity to promises and agreements.... There are, on the other hand, two kinds of injustice – the one, on the part of those who inflict wrong, the other on the part of those who, when they can, do not shield from wrong those upon whom it is being inflicted.

Cicero, *On Duties*, Book I, Chapter VII.[1]

If one accepts that officials have obligations to use their discretion according to principles that arise from anything other than the law, then the content of those principles must be quite important. Indeed, you might accept the idea that there are principles that a legal official must follow, even if you rejected all of the arguments to this point in this book.

Attempting to sort out such principles is complicated. It is hard sometimes to know which among the voices clamoring for influence that one must hear. And, even when an individual has a fairly clear view of what must be done, if the individual also has a healthy sense of skepticism, there is the nagging concern that such seemingly clear views might yet be wrong.

This chapter considers both the problems of assessing arguments for a moral obligation and a catalogue of basic forms that such obligations must take. To consider assessment we look to the source of perspectives that are likely to help in making a good decision, as well as those that are likely to distract from one. Recognizing the dangers of organizing lists, the chapter proceeds to outline a list of obligations by form and content. Moral obligations as presented here are divided among four rough groups: personal, institutional, procedural, and substantive obligations. Most of these are not fully explored in

---

[1] Marcus Tullius Cicero, *De Officiis* 25 (Walter Miller, trans.) (Loeb edn.) (Cambridge: Harvard University Press, 1913).

this summary text, although the most obvious of the personal obligations are considered – charity, knowledge, and personal virtues – and the most central of these is treated with a bit more detail, the obligation of charity. Institutional obligations of fairness and substantive obligations of promoting just laws are considered only briefly, because there are already many other books that deal well with these topics.

INITIAL PROBLEMS

Each official must decide, personally, what is right in office, and although we all must judge such decisions, nothing can meaningfully substitute for the official's personal responsibility for the decision. The poet Václav Havel, the dissident who became president of Czechoslovakia and the first president of the Czech Republic, described this responsibility to a joint session of the U.S. Congress:

> From time to time we say that the anonymous megamachinery we have created has enslaved us, yet we fail to do anything about it.
>
> In other words, we still don't know how to put morality ahead of politics, science, and economics. We are still incapable of understanding that the only genuine core of all our actions – if they are said to be moral – is responsibility. Responsibility to something higher than my family, my country, my firm, my success. Responsibility to the order of Being, where all our actions are indelibly recorded and where, and only where, they will be properly judged.
>
> The interpreter or mediator between us and this higher authority is what is traditionally referred to as human conscience.
>
> If I subordinate my political behavior to this imperative, I can't go far wrong. If, on the contrary, I am not guided by this voice, not even ten presidential schools with two thousand of the best political scientists in the world can help me.[2]

Havel's sense of responsibility is wonderfully balanced between the moral action that is required and the tugs of interest that it must transcend. It is personal, a matter of private conscience, and yet it is universal, a matter of human conscience as well. Without this moral sense of responsibility, no formula for action can guide an official. It is the unique task for each official to determine its requirements, and yet the decisions that are made by the official affect others, guide others, and so must be accessible to the judgment of others.

It is not enough to suggest that there are moral obligations in how officials carry out their duties. Officials and subjects are both capable of assessing

[2] Václav Havel, "A Joint Session of the U.S. Congress, February 21, 1991," in *The Art of the Impossible: Politics as Morality in Practice* 10, 19 (Paul Wilson, trans.) (Fromm, 1997).

those obligations, and they are both fit to judge each official on how the office is performed. The questions for each is, what are the bases of assessment? Knowing what is right or good, and how to do the right thing in a particular instance, is not easy, and indeed it tends to be controversial. Fair-minded, thoughtful people can disagree on moral obligations, because there are so many ways to think about them.

All this difficulty and such disagreement do not suggest either that there is no core basis for describing moral obligations, either in general or for legal officials. The fact that one might argue about whose sports club is best doesn't suggest that there aren't better and worse teams in the game. The most important problem is how to know what criteria matter for evaluation.

Moral Knowledge and Moral Error

As noted in the caveat in the introduction, this book accepts the existence of morality as a given, and it does not seek to argue for one or another source of what is good or right or proof of how we would know what is good or right. (There are plenty of books that do this sort of thing already that the reader can choose.[3]) In the particular context of legal office, however, there are tools that we can add to the usual range of reason, observation, instinct, passion, and history that we might otherwise have available to consider moral questions.

Listening to the Right Voices

Foremost, it is well to remember that each official bears an independent responsibility in the exercise of every office. Like soldiers in an army unit, even those officials who are subject to hierarchy cannot escape the unique moral responsibility each official retains, whether ordered to act in a given way or given leave from above to do so.[4] Yet independence of action and judgment is not

---

[3] A few choices: For those who like the idea that morals are innate in the human being, see Marc Hauser, *Moral Minds: How Nature Designed Our Universal Sense of Right and Wrong* (Ecco, 2006), or John Finnis, *Natural Law and Natural Rights* (Oxford University Press, 1981). For those who like the idea that morals result from human society through a social contract, see J. L. Mackie, *Ethics: Inventing Right and Wrong* (Penguin, 1991) or David Gauthier, *Morals by Agreement* (Oxford University Press, 1986). For those who think that trying to prove the origin of morals is as nonsensical as proving the origin of mathematics, see Hilary Putnam, *Ethics without Ontology* (Harvard University Press, 2004). For the idea that subjectivism and controversy are inherent parts but not all of moral thinking, see Bernard Williams, *Morality, An Introduction to Ethics* (Cambridge University Press, 1993), and for the idea that the substantive moral arguments that specifically relate to the law are always going to be controversial, see Stuart Hampshire, *Justice Is Conflict* (Princeton University Press, 2000).

[4] The defense of superior orders cannot, under international law, exonerate a soldier accused of a crime under the laws of war, though it might mitigate a sentence for a soldier found guilty. See, for example, Lt. Col. Michael Davidson, "Staff Officer Responsibility for War Crimes," 81 Military Review 2 (March–April, 2001).

isolation from advice and consultation. Thus, while each official must consider each question in the quiet realms of personal conscience, there are tools that an official might well consider in doing so, and indeed recognizing these tools is essential to performing a moral duty. The most essential is learning the nature of moral duty in itself.

Regardless of what idea one has about the nature of morality, the problem of learning to apply morals in specific circumstances gives rise to difficulty. In determining both the source and the application of morals, we are influenced by some ideas, some people, some arguments, and in all of them by some more than others. Whom we choose to listen to will inevitably affect what arguments we find persuasive, just as they will inform our instincts by making us more sensitive or more callous to various stories and ideas.

Those Who Fear the Stakes: The subjects, who depend on the shield and the balance, the coin and the commons; who fear the sword and accept the mirror and guide – their view of what the law ought to do must deserve the first rank of concern for the official. This is the basis of democracy and the implicit promise of freedom, that the desires of the people shall guide the formation of government and the application of law. This is what it means to speak of "government of the people, by the people, and for the people." Indeed, some argue that it is the essential promise not only of the American revolution but also the Constitution of 1789.[5]

Officials must heed the views of subjects, not their presumed views, as to what they need, fear, hope for, depend on. In this sense, it was quite right of the colonial judges to worry about the people's fear of witches in seventeenth-century New England. Their beliefs that witches walked the earth and hurt people, regardless of what one might now think of them, mattered in the balance and in the shield of the law. The law's acceptance of that belief reinforced it, affecting the guide and the mirror, and it drove the sword.

The law, however, is not the same as democracy, and the balance cannot be swayed by popular opinion. When in Massachusetts the balance was poorly used, the power of the sword was too great, and when, as in Connecticut, it was carefully used, the sword could be sheathed with little harm.

Those who fear the stakes of a given legal system, those who fear the sword particularly, include an important group beyond the subjects and the officials

---

[5] See Larry D. Kramer, *The People Themselves: Popular Constitutionalism and Judicial Review* (Oxford University Press, 2004). This view of democracy in the Constitution is not universally accepted. See, for example, Terry Bouton, *Taming Democracy: "The People," the Founders, and the Troubled Ending of the American Revolution* (Oxford University Press, 2007). Even so, one need not go as far as Prof. Kramer to find a role for the people as a necessary influence on officials in the American constitutional structure. See, for example, Max M. Edling, *A Revolution in Favor of Government: Origins of the U.S. Constitution and the Making of the American State* 115–28 (Oxford University Press, 2007).

of the stakes, whose claims upon officials of a state are weak but still evident – the officials and subjects of other states. Describing and rationalizing the implications of the stakes among peoples of different states are tasks generally beyond the scope of the present book, but there is an important argument here, especially in shield against illegal action by officials but also and perhaps most enduringly in the nature of the mirror and the guide. The views of those who fear the stakes of a given state cannot artificially or arbitrarily end because of the extent of a border or the definitions of citizenship.

Those Whose Ox Is to Be Gored: What is the view of the person who will be hurt by the law? How can this view not be considered in the making and enforcement of laws? If African Americans had been heard when Jim Crow laws were passed, generations of injustice would have been avoided. The idea that those who would be harmed must be accounted in considering how officials should act has several distinct manifestations.

First, whereas one of the benefits of genuine democracy is that those whose interests are at stake cannot be excluded from the discussion, one of the benefits of law is this insurance for democracy. A central idea of due process of law demands that no one's interests should be harmed through the law without adequate prior notice of the risk, and an opportunity to appear and be heard by the officials responsible.[6]

This argument might suggest that the reason to listen to the potential victim is merely owed to the victim. Leaving aside the ever-present chance that we each can be victims of the law, there are still compelling reasons for officials to consider the view of the victim of the law, even if one takes the tribal approach of governors to the governed, treating the people subject to law as enemies. As in the declarations of the "War on Crime" or "Public Enemy Number One," there is a danger in failing to think genuinely about "the enemy's" view. Looking back over his controversial years in government, including his tenure as Secretary of Defense during the Vietnam War, Robert McNamara declared that his most valuable lesson was empathy for his enemy, which required one to "put yourself in their skin and look at us through their eyes, just to understand the thoughts that lie behind their decisions and their actions."[7]

---

[6]   In Justice Pitney's famous phrase, "The fundamental requisite of due process of law is the opportunity to be heard." *Grannis v. Ordean*, 234 U.S. 385, 394 (1914).

[7]   James G. Blight & Janet M. Lang, *The Fog of War: Lessons from the Life of Robert S. McNamara* (Rowman & Littlefield, 2005), quoting Robert S. McNamara in the documentary *The Fog of War*. McNamara's illustrations are more subtle than mere application of the ancient military truth that one must know one's enemy. His most stark illustration is that the best advice John F. Kennedy received during the Cuban missile crisis came not from him or Curtis LeMay, who sought to attack, but from ambassador Llewellyn Thompson, whose genuine empathy for Nikita Krushchev allowed an accurate understanding of Krushchev's motives, averting the war that McNamara's advice might likely have wrought.

Voices from Past Injustice: The history of the law is also a history of injustice. American law has sanctioned and defended slavery, treatment of women as near chattel, dispossession of the Indian tribes, lynchings and mob violence, exclusion of the Chinese, disenfranchisement of the poor, physical abuse of laborers, protection of corrosive trusts and monopolies, *de jure* racial segregation, and discrimination in commerce and society against nearly everybody but healthy, rich, conformist, unindicted white male Protestant citizens between the ages of twenty-one and fifty-five.

These experiences have all been understood by officials as good reasons to change the law itself, most famously when recognition of horrible treatment in the past gives rise to changes in the law that forbid such treatment in the future, as when rights are created to prevent past wrongs.[8] Officials in these circumstances understood that what had been done in the name of the law in the past was wrong, and the officials altered the law to end the wrongdoing.[9]

In considering the risks and harms raised in every action under the law – every law, arrest, tax, verdict award, punishment, indeed every action by an official – officials must consider parallels to the cases of other times and places in which similar questions arose. In many instances, these actions led to great and unnecessary hardship for the subject.

It is not enough to have a superficial understanding of the officials of other times, a superficiality that allows their mistakes to be distinguished and dismissed.[10] What would keep a legislator, or a judge today from acting more like Phips or Stoughton, rather than Jones or Sewall? Conscience informed by the cases of history is likely to be the only answer. Thus William Shirer prefaced *Rise and Fall of the Third Reich* by juxtaposing the statement of a Nazi war criminal with George Santayana's great aphorism. General Frank's "A thousand years will pass and the guilt of Germany will not be erased"[11]

---

[8]   This is Professor Dershowitz's fundamental argument for the existence and protection of rights against officials. See Alan M. Dershowitz, *Rights from Wrongs: A Secular Theory of the Origin of Rights* (Basic Books, 2004). On a broader scale, the development of rights probably reflected a change of attitude that first made clear the actions of the officials were wrong and then argued for an ethical standard to prevent them. See Lynn Hunt, *Inventing Human Rights: A History* (W. W. Norton, 2007).

[9]   The problem of whether an official has the power to change the law utterly or whether the official has within the discretion of office only the power to mitigate a harm is considered in greater detail in Chapter 5.

[10] This is the complaint that journalist David Halberstam raised against officials of the second Bush administration, deriding their opportunistic use of the rhetoric of the judgment of history not only as a tool to avoid the judgment of the present but also as a chronic inhibition from learning history well enough to actually learn anything from it. See David Halberstam, "The History Boys," Vanity Fair (Sept. 2007) (available at www.vanityfair.com/politics/features/2007/08/halberstam200708).

[11] William L. Shirer, *Rise and Fall of the Third Reich*, unpaginated front leaf (Touchstone, 1990), quoting Hans Frank, governor general of Poland, before his hanging at Nuremburg.

takes on a particular focus for us through Santayana's lens, "Those who do not remember the past are condemned to relive it."[12]

Voices from Reason and Instinct: Each official must ultimately judge each case alone, just as each observer will judge the official's act alone. Even so, we all may inform our judgment through discourse and conversation with others. To consult with people whose judgment one respects, even to follow advice, is not the same as abdicating responsibility, as the choice to follow the advice and the responsibility for action based on it remain with the advisee.

But the consultation need not be only with contemporaries. The study not only of history but also of analytic tools can enhance our analytic ability, or sense of morality, and our instincts of right and wrong. Whether morality is inherent or learned, there is no question that its application can be refined through reflection and study, particularly in the examination of cases in which the decisions of officials have been greeted over time with respect or condemnation. Officials and citizens alike can learn tools, such as the mechanisms of assessing the greatest good for the greatest number or the ideas of Kant's moral imperatives, Hume's moral agent, or Rawls's two principles of justice, all of which give perspective on individual questions of moral judgment. These tools conflict, and of course they can be badly chosen or poorly applied; yet they do inform our judgment, particularly in times when our moral instincts are either weak, owing to the novelty of a situation, or troubled, owing to competing claims for moral action or doubts about what our lessons should be from past cases.

Listening to the Wrong Voices

There is a risk of error in every action. Officials confronted by a decision might well believe that there is a strong moral argument to enforce a law or to abolish it, yet many others would reject what the official supposed to be the moral position. There have been, after all, plenty of passionate and seemingly reasoned defenders of slavery, inequality, and tyranny. There are tools that can diminish the likelihood that one would take such a position, but there is no perfect insurance against it.

Experience teaches us that it can be quite dangerous for officials to rely on certain perspectives, which run unusual risks of action in violation of the official's obligations. Listening to voices from these perspectives is likely to

---

12   *Id.* quoting George Santayana. Santayana's line, which was slightly altered by Shirer, deserves quotation in full:

> Progress, far from consisting in change, depends on retentiveness. When change is absolute there remains no being to improve and no direction is set for possible improvement: and when experience is not retained, as among savages, infancy is perpetual. Those who cannot remember the past are condemned to repeat it.

George Santayana, 1 *The Life of Reason: Reason in Common Sense* 82 (1905) (Prometheus Books, 1998). His theory of historical repetition is at p. 408.

diminish not just a sense for the moral obligations in an office but also a recognition of the legal obligations binding the official as well. These voices cannot be ignored by officials. Indeed, officials run great risks by prejudging an idea by its source or by neglecting a source of ideas without knowing what ideas might arise from it. The risks from such voices must be balanced against the obligations in a democracy of allowing all to participate meaningfully in the civic arena and in a just legal system for allowing all to be heard. Our experience, in the light of our values, does not suggest an official can – or should – be deaf to such voices. Rather it suggests reservation when such voices seek authority in the legal system. Thus, in such settings, history requires not ignorance but skepticism.

Partisan Voices: It is an awful truth that politics and law are nearly indistinguishable to many people in the United States, and so to them, to win political power is to win power over the law to benefit oneself and one's cronies. This is not new, and indeed the spoils system once ensured that loyalty in legal offices was first to one's party above all else.[13] Even so, the effects of partisanship on the law in the United States remain real and corrosive.

In legislation, the very ideas of party discipline and opposition place loyalty to party ahead of the best interests of the subjects in each specific enactment.[14] Nowhere is the idea of party discipline more contrary to the office of the legislator than in the very notion of the party whip, the person in a legislative chamber whose job is to ensure that legislators do not vote their conscience but vote according to party instructions. This is an outrageous intrusion on the obligation of the individual legislator's will. When the legislature acts as a court to punish or condemn, the intrusion is all the greater.[15] To the degree that a senator, representative, council member, or any other official votes the party line, or relies upon party dictate rather than informed personal judgment, the legislator violates the obligations of office.

In administration, partisanship often takes the role of supporting the policies of agency superiors. Officials tasked with developing a factual or scientific

---

[13] Perhaps the greatest failing of the early American constitutions was in failing to predict and curb the power of political parties. On their origin, see Richard Hofstadter, *The Idea of a Party System: The Rise of Legitimate Opposition in the United States, 1780–1840* (University of California Press, 1970).

[14] Edward Stanley, Earl of Derby, is said to have observed, "The duty of an Opposition [party is] very simple . . . to oppose everything and to propose nothing." Antony Jay, *The Oxford Dictionary of Political Quotations* (Oxford University Press, 1996) (quoting a Mr. Tierney, a great Whig authority in 1841).

[15] The problem of usurpation in an impeachment is considered in greater detail in the section entitled "Humility." See also Richard K. Neumann, Jr., "The Revival of Impeachment as a Partisan Political Weapon," 34 Hastings Constitutional Law Quarterly 161 (2007). Similar concerns might attend the process of legislative approval to office, yet there are many differences, not the least being that the deliberate selection of provocative and partisan candidates for office presents different choices in approval than they might in impeachment.

understanding of the law, or the environment or business or human activity regulated by the law, are expected to alter reports, omit or add information, or even change the emphasis in a study so that the data conform to executive preference. Such partisanship impugns the office of both the superior and the cooperating subordinate, and in 2007, it appeared that the U.S. Department of Justice had demanded that prosecutors bring politically motivated indictments, indeed removing those few who would not.[16] To the degree that an official describes a fact or event with an interpretation intended to please or serve a superior, or to the degree that an executive exercises the powers of office based only on a superior's preference rather than independent judgment – to that degree, the official is morally corrupting the performance of the office.[17]

Conformist Voices: The pressure to conform, to abide by the expectations of one's tribe or peers, is a never-ending burden of office. One of our most fundamental instincts is to not break ranks.[18] This instinct leads to at least two distinct forms of erroneous moral consideration. The first is a generalized tribalism, in which conformity with the group's view is a value unto itself and informs individual ideas of what is right and wrong. This conformity could be limited to a small group, such as those working in a prosecutor's office, or to a whole culture.[19] These are the problems of groupthink, discussed earlier in Chapter 3.[20]

The second risk of conformity to moral independence is to build an argument of tradition and identity, as in, "Good Americans have always believed

---

[16] It is too early to judge the accuracy of these allegations. One of the most significant is that U.S. Attorney David Iglesias was fired in part by a Republican attorney general for not indicting Democratic officials, even when Iglesias thought there was no case against them. For a summary of the dispute, see "Fired U.S. Attorneys," Washington Post (March 6, 2007) (available at http://www.washingtonpost.com/wp-dyn/content/graphic/2007/03/06/GR2007030600062.html) (last visited September 6, 2007).

[17] That legal officials serve the law more than their supervisors is a romantic notion, one nicely caught by the genre-defying novelist Terry Pratchett, whose policeman Vimes refused to return to his job after being fired by an administrator for failing to toe the party line: "You can't give me my job back. It was never yours to take away. I was never an officer of the city, or an officer of the king, or an officer of the Patrician. I was an officer of the law." Terry Pratchett, *Guards! Guards!* 274 (HarperCollins, 2001).

[18] See, for example, Gerd Gigerenzer, *Gut Feelings, The Intelligence of the Unconscious* 181 (Viking Press, 2007). Gigerenzer, the director of the Max Planck Institute for Human Development in Berlin, argues for an instinctive basis for moral behavior, which is strongly informed by the groups one joins. As used here, this would be instinct informed by moral ecology.

[19] Even the more atomized world of judges is sufficiently encultured to encourage parallel actions in response to a variety of common stimuli. A classic discussion of this process is in Karl N. Llewellyn, *The Case Law System in America* (Paul Gewirtz, ed.) (Michael Ansaldi, trans.) (University of Chicago Press, 1989).

[20] See Chapter 3, the section entitled "The Stakes and the Special Temptations of Power."

thus." Yet, arguments for this form of conformity not only diminish the potential for progress,[21] they interfere with the individual official's obligation of independent assessment and personal moral choice. To the degree an official relies on either cultural expectation or tradition to determine the moral obligations of the office – to that degree the official is likely to be violating the fundamental obligations of the office.

A third risk of conformity is special to the hierarchy that distinguishes bureaucracy: the special problem of flattery. When an official gives advice to a superior, there is an inherent risk that the advice is colored by the dependence of the official on the superior's favor. Independence in office, especially executive office, depends either on a genuine sense in which the official's future career and opportunities are free from the influence of the superior or on a real independence through an ease by which the official can resign. This effect is hardly different when the superior is an individual or the electorate.[22]

Voices of Lucre: Money influences the law. This is the lesson of Anatole France's line against false claims to equality, by which the law "prohibits the wealthy as well as the poor from sleeping under the bridges, from begging in the streets, and from stealing bread."[23] The influence of wealth in official calculations takes many forms, some quite constructive and essential, as in the promotion of the coin and the protection of the commons, such as by investments and subsidies that benefit the wealthy in order to provide benefits to all.

Still, in at least two distinct forms, money corrodes legal office. First, clearly, is when an act of office is made because of a gift, whether already made or hoped for in the future, whether in the form of money or objects or a promise of employment or favors. In most instances this is simple bribery, as demonstrated by the pricing menu for influence offered in 2006 by a member of Congress.[24] Yet American legal officials have long pretended that the same activity is not bribery when done in the guise of election campaign fundraising. Indeed, the ability to offer such funds is even cloaked in constitutional protection under the freedom of speech. Yet the stink of the law for sale hovers over all of this

---

[21] The problems of past injustice, such as the legal support of slavery, were suggested already in this section. Probably all types of change are inhibited by the invocation of tradition. See, for example, Iain Gately, *Tobacco: A Cultural History of How an Exotic Plant Seduced Civilization* (Grove Press, 2003).

[22] Von Mises sees the adulation of the common man as a form of traditional flattery, nicely conflating two forms of conformity. Ludwig von Mises, *Bureaucracy* 105–8 (Center for Futures Education, 1969).

[23] Anatole France, *The Red Lily*, Chapter VII (available at www.online-literature.com/view.php/red-lily/8?term=bridge).

[24] In 2006, U.S. Congressman Randall Cunningham, known as Duke, was sentenced to eight years in prison for selling votes and other privileges of his office. See Tony Perry, "Cunningham Receives Eight-Year Sentence," Los Angeles Times, A1 (March 3, 2006). For the general history and significance of bribery, see John T. Noonan, Jr., *Bribes* (Macmillan, 1984).

artifice.[25] As George Washington said, "Few men have virtue to withstand the highest bidder."[26] To the degree that an official acts, fails to act, or casts a vote that is in any way based on a gift or hope for a gift, the official cannot be basing the decision on a moral ground.

The second form is the more indirect and in some regard the more invidious. One need not be a Marxist to observe that some officials bring a form of economic class bias to office, in which the effect of money on a decision creates a likelihood of prejudgment.[27] Although this bias might work both ways, the nature of office being an effect of power and wealth suggests that it is more likely to occur among wealthy officials protecting capital from the predations of the poor. To the degree that an official bases a judgment on a preference for or against wealth or poverty, corporations or claimants, to that degree the official is likely not to be acting within the moral obligations of office.

Voices Others Cannot Hear: Some officials believe it is appropriate to rest decisions of law on the dictates of revealed religion.[28] The idea that one can discern one's moral obligations from religion is indeed the source of many of the great reforms of western law, not the least being abolition and the civil rights movement in America.[29] Even so, advocates who believed they listened to God informed both sides of these debates, defending slavery and inequality as divinely ordained.[30] Religion as a source of moral thinking is different from other sources of moral ideas, in part because it is so often tied to a group membership that it encourages another form of rivalry among the adherents of different religions. For this reason among others, early American colonists and constitutional framers – themselves aware of the religious aspect of the recent

---

[25] This is, of course, an international problem, not merely an American one. See, for example, Michael Johnston, *Syndromes of Corruption: Wealth, Power, and Democracy* (Cambridge University Press, 2006).

[26] George Washington, Letter to Robert Howe, August 17, 1779 (George Washington Papers at the Library of Congress, 1741–1799: Series 3b Varick Transcripts) (available at http://memory.loc.gov/cgi-bin/query/P?mgw:2:./temp/~ammem_msNV::).

[27] See Donald C. Nugent, "Judicial Bias," 42 Cleveland State Law Review 1, 42–5 (1994).

[28] See, for example, Roy Moore & John Perry, *So Help Me God: The Ten Commandments, Judicial Tyranny, and the Battle for Religious Freedom* (B&H Publishing Group, 2005).

[29] The origins of the abolition movements in Great Britain and the United States in the protestant church is well known. See, for example, Robert H. Abzug, *Cosmos Crumbling: American Reform and the Religious Imagination* (Oxford University Press, 1994). As for the role of churches in the twentieth-century civil rights movement, see David L. Chappell, *A Stone of Hope: Prophetic Religion and the Death of Jim Crow* (University of North Carolina Press, 2005).

[30] See, for example, John Patrick Daly, *When Slavery Was Called Freedom: Evangelicalism, Proslavery, and the Causes of the Civil War* (University Press of Kentucky, 2004); Mitchell Snay, *Gospel of Disunion: Religion and Separatism in the Antebellum South* (Cambridge University Press, 1993). For its twentieth-century analog, see Carey L. Daniel, *God the Original Segregationist, and Seven Other Sermons on Segregation* (Carey Daniel, 1954).

civil war in England and the effects of religious discrimination by law – limited the role of religious reasons in the entry of office as well as in the substance of laws.[31] The question remains, though it will be only briefly examined here: to what extent may an official properly rely on revealed religious doctrine to inform the moral obligations of office,[32] or, as Kent Greenawalt has argued, to what extent must an official practice self-restraint in relying on comprehensive ideas of the good life that are not accessible to everyone?[33]

The most useful device for distinguishing a moral obligation from an exclusively religious obligation is whether the religion gives rise to obligations that do not rely on the authority of God or of a church to persuade others. These arguments are cosmopolitan, capable of argument "in a world of strangers."[34] Such arguments are appropriate in the civic sphere, and the fact that they reinforce (and are reinforced by) religious arguments does not detract from their civic validity. A correlative application of this rule would be that officials cannot properly rely on a religious claim for a moral obligation by either officials or subjects that requires or encourages someone to accept the truth of a religious doctrine or practice. In general, officials must be skeptical of the validity of revelation as the basis of civic argument, owing to the danger of offering shambolic rationales cloaking asserted dogma.

---

[31] British law had required officeholders to swear to particular doctrines, mainly to limit Catholics and Nonconformists from office. Following the 1678 revision of earlier test acts, 30 Car. II. st. 2 (repealed by the Roman Catholic Relief Act of 1829, 10 Geo. IV. c. 7), officeholders had to take this oath:

> I, N, do solemnly and sincerely in the presence of God profess, testify, and declare, that I do believe that in the Sacrament of the Lord's Supper there is not any Transubstantiation of the elements of bread and wine into the Body and Blood of Christ at or after the consecration thereof by any person whatsoever: and that the invocation or adoration of the Virgin Mary or any other Saint, and the Sacrifice of the Mass, as they are now used in the Church of Rome, are superstitious and idolatrous. . . .

> Such tests for office are barred by the U.S. Constitution, Article VI, which provides that "no religious Test shall ever be required as a Qualification to any Office or public Trust under the United States." The First Amendment provides "Congress shall make no law respecting an establishment of religion, or prohibiting the free exercise thereof. . . . " For more on oath-taking as a predicate to office, see Chapter 3, the section entitled "Oaths of Office."

[32] There are great complexities to this question, which range far beyond the scope of this book, which is here presenting ideas strongly influenced by the much more nuanced arguments in Kent Greenawalt, *Religious Convictions and Political Choice* (Oxford University Press, 1991). In general, a terse, historically rooted introduction of the problem is provided by Mark Lilla, "The Politics of God," New York Times Magazine 28 (August 19, 2007).

[33] See Kent Greenawalt, *Private Consciences and Public Reasons* (Oxford University Press, 1995).

[34] This wonderful phrase comes from Kwame Anthony Appiah, *Cosmopolitanism: Ethics in a World of Strangers* (Norton, 2006). The content of Appiah's ethics has much in common with the later argument for charity. See the section entitled "Personal Obligations."

Developing a Coherent View of Duties from Sources and Cases

How can we refine a sense of the obligations arising from the various sources discussed in Chapter 3? Those arguments included some principles that are general to all people and so apply regardless of role, as well as some that are specially explicit in the role through oaths and implicit in the role, arising from the stakes others have in the office that are voluntarily accepted and from the special risks of the power relationships of legal office.

The obligations that are special to a given role, such as the particular covenants or terms of general moral obligation in an oath of a given office, could give rise to a scheme of obligations, by which the various oaths are surveyed, and from which a genealogy of obligations based on them is developed with particularity for the offices from which oaths are derived. In some cases, a useful picture of obligations would emerge.

It would, however, be incomplete. A genealogy based on oaths alone would lack the ancillary obligations that are only implied in specific expressions of the oaths, as well as all of the obligations that arise by implication from the nature of the office itself. Most importantly, it would fail to account for the general obligations, for any reason, we might believe apply to all human conduct, that are not relieved merely because of the role an individual happens to occupy. The better means would be to consider the variety of sources of obligations that affect officials and develop a theory or organization that appears significant owing to the official's role. Six sources were suggested in Chapters 2 and 3, though each suggests a different basis for nonlegal obligations and a varying array of duties:

- Oaths bind each holder of these offices, and these oaths demand commitments to morality beyond the legal definitions of the role.
- Obligations arise as an aspect of office, defined by the role the official occupies rather than by the laws alone creating it.
- The rule of law and other ideas of the proper substance of law imply compelling arguments for officials to ensure that the law reflects these ideas.
- There are general ideas of morality that people accept, at least broadly, as the bases for identifying good people or people who act morally or rightly.
- Each official accepts office, knowing that both subjects and other officials have grave stakes in how that office is performed.
- Each official takes a position of trust, yet the very nature of the position is unusually prone to abuse and bad conduct.

A comprehensive theory of moral obligations accounting for these sources of obligation is possible, if it accounts for the particular obligations that arise from roles, both expressed and implied by that role, as well as the general obligations that describe moral life as applied to that role. Such a theory of moral obligations is likely to focus on particular forms of conduct related to the many forms of office.

The most recurrent and influential models of obligation based on particularized conduct have been based on specific virtues. These models emphasize particular motives, conditions, or outcomes in action, rather than universal claims. This is not to say that there have been no comprehensive theories of moral conduct-based universal claims, or that an interesting model of official obligations cannot be based on them. Immanuel Kant's categorical imperative is a powerful model from which, he believed, all moral obligations could be derived. Jeremy Bentham's model of utility, developed from quite different predicates, was asserted as a basis for universal measurement of moral conduct. Both authors created detailed theories of an ideal legal system built on their models. The scope of conflicts among these varying schools of morality is rich and is beyond the scope of this book.

Instead, we can begin with cases arising in history, considering them both as normative approaches and as narratives. The first is to consider historically important arguments for the obligations of officials. Religion, law, and theory have all yielded arguments of what is to be done by the good official, and there seems to be no particular reason not to consider such points of reference. In particular, these references can then be illuminated by cases to better assess the strength of the initial arguments.

By considering the examples of officials to consider what personal strengths led to official acts that have been widely accepted as just, or what personal failings contributed to injustice, a rough inventory of such strengths and failings can be assembled. This case approach is the basic tool for many models of official obligation, from the many stories Marcus Tullius Cicero used to instruct his son on the nature of office to Alan Dershowitz's construction of a model of rights from the examples of past injustice.[35]

It is probably important here to distinguish this approach from the method criticized by the great philosopher David Hume, who argued that it is never possible to deduce judgments of value from matters of fact.[36] This is sometimes known as the "is versus ought" maxim, that one cannot know what ought to be the case from what is the case. It would seem that this is what we're doing, attempting to deduce obligations from observations, but that isn't exactly the problem that Hume has in mind. He was concerned with looking at facts and

[35] Compare Cicero, *On Duties* (M. T. Griffin & E. M. Atkins, eds.) (Cambridge University Press, 1991), with Alan M. Dershowitz, *Rights from Wrongs: A Secular Theory of the Origin of Rights* (Basic Books, 2004).

[36] David Hume, *Enquiries Concerning Human Understanding and Concerning the Principles of Morals* (L. A. Selby-Bigge & P. H. Nidditch, eds.) (Oxford University Press, 1975).

supposing that how things are is how they ought to be; he had no problems with considering the way we value what we observe could give rise to our values. That is, there is no problem, at least according to David Hume, with evaluating a story and then building our ideas about obligations on our evaluations.

So what stories should we use? A variety of techniques should be used to identify cases. Some cases are famous as great successes or (more often) failures by officials, which have been recurrently seen as having great moral implications. Solon's moderation of the Draconian laws of Athens and the legal allowance of the German policy toward the Jews in the 1930s need no additional reasons for their selection. Other cases arise from fictional narratives that have captured the public imagination as firmly as the data of history, such as the crisis of conscience suffered by Captain Vere as he judged the case of Billy Budd. Still others, as suggested earlier, may be selected to illustrate putative arguments for morals in general or the claims made by observers of the legal system as to what the moral limits of officials may be. From all of these cases, the grist of a theory can be milled.

The mill comes in the form of reflective equilibrium, the tool John Rawls employed in testing his theory of justice. Rawls argued that the best way to develop a theory about the just organization of society was to start from specific cases and then to posit and refine ideas about the implications of the cases for a theory, then to model the theory against applications in more cases, rejecting or accepting aspects of the theory, then refining the theory until it satisfies our "considered judgments" of a just outcome at all levels of generality or specificity.[37] This approach is quite attractive, in part as it reflects the most significant contemporary narrative for the development of truth in theories: the scientific method.[38]

---

[37] See John Rawls, *A Theory of Justice* 20, 48 (Harvard University Press, 1971). There are several forms of reflective equilibrium. Narrow reflection considers only a single case and the principles that might apply to it from a single perspective. Wide reflection considers many cases and assesses them from competing perspectives. Rawls attempts an exercise in wide equilibrium by testing his hypothetical theory of justice as fairness against competing theories, namely utility and perfectionism. That he loaded the dice when doing so does not change the use one can make of his system. See Steve Sheppard, "The Perfectionisms of John Rawls," 11 Canadian Journal of Law & Jurisprudence 383 (1998).

  As used here, I intend to consider something more like narrow reflection in each case offered and wide reflection toward the sum of the cases. Space is too limited in this book, and in any event it would be quite boring to detail all of the consideration that has been needed to develop and refine this game through iteration after iteration of lists and examples.

[38] There are countless variations on the scientific method, but at its core, it provides the recognition and refinement of a question, the development of a testable hypothesis, the collection of data and comparison of the data to the hypothesis, the acceptance or rejection of the hypothesis, and, if need be, a refinement of the hypothesis for new comparison against appropriate data. See Enoch I. Sawin, "The Scientific Method and Other Bases for Evaluation Procedures," 62 ETC.: A Review of General Semantics 683 (2005). On the genealogy of reflective equilibrium and its relationship to the scientific method, see, for

The test of reflective equilibrium will be to examine a particular obligation in the light of cases and then compare the result to the stakes of the subjects in the law. Does the theory, both generally and in its particulars, satisfy the interests represented in the stakes others have in officials' conduct? Does the theory respond adequately both as a general proposition and in specific applications to the difficulties for the subjects and the officials posed by the problems represented by the sword, the shield, the balance, the guide, the mirror, the commons, the coin, the seal, and the veil? This is the goal.

The Dangers of Taxonomy and the Catalogues of Virtues

Cases tend to be most easily understood in a list, and lists pose problems. Organizing human endeavor into categories is as potentially distracting as it is helpful. In some manner, this distraction is roughly the same as the dangers of metaphors.[39] There is a tug toward a seemingly exhaustive catalogue that can mask duplication and omission or add unnecessary confusion through overfine definition and categorization. Moreover, the industry of inventory can distract us from the function of the items; or, worrying too much about the identity of one or another specific obligation can distract us from the whole enterprise of obligations.[40]

Western thought has a fascination with ordering the universe into categories. Linnaeus believed that he could understand the nature of all of God's creation, if only he could sufficiently inventory it.[41] From this belief came the useful binomial system of naming the species of animals and plants, an advance at the time but an increasing source of confusion and misdirection to botanists and biologists, and maybe one that distracts from biology after the discovery of genetic mapping.[42]

example, Robert Hockett, "The Deep Grammar of Distribution: A Meta-Theory of Justice," 26 Cardozo Law Review 1179, 1191 (2005).

[39] See Chapter 1, the section entitled "Discretion and the Definition of the Legal Office."

[40] Most writers fight this impulse by establishing ideas about what virtues are in general. Aristotle, for instance, described all virtues of character as *hexeis*, which in places seems to be an effect on the feelings and in others seems to have an objective characteristic. See D. S. Hutchinson, *The Virtues of Aristotle* (Routledge & Keegan Paul, 1986). But here, I think the idea of obligation is larger than the idea of virtue, and I am content to leave the boundaries pretty well confused, assuming most readers can work something out for themselves.

[41] See Carl von Linne, *Linnaeus' Philosophia Botanica* [The Philosophy of Plants] (Stephen Freer, trans.) (1751) (Oxford University Press, 2005).

[42] See, for example, David N. Stamos, *The Species Problem, Biological Species, Ontology, and the Metaphysics of Biology* (Lexington Books, 2004). Recent arguments over the use of the degree of dissimilarities of DNA to identify species, as opposed to differences in reproductive technique or body parts, have led to great controversy as to the meaning of "species." This debate has profound implications for the future of the laws governing biodiversity. See, for example, Brian Czech & Paul R. Krausman, *The Endangered Species Act: History, Conservation Biology, and Public Policy* (Johns Hopkins University Press, 2001).

History presents us with many catalogues of obligations, especially when the obligations are labeled virtues. Perhaps the most well-known today in the United States are the seven heavenly virtues of the traditional Roman church, which are divided into two classes. The four cardinal virtues are prudence, temperance, fortitude, and justice.[43] The three theological virtues are faith, hope, and charity.[44] Then there are the capital virtues: humility, liberality, brotherly love, meekness, chastity, temperance, and diligence, which are the converse of the capital or deadly sins: pride, avarice, envy, wrath, lust, gluttony, and sloth.[45] As noted in Chapter 1, John Finnis articulated seven basic goods, which are quite like virtues.[46] These catalogues are not, of course, the only lists of virtues in even just the Christian tradition; Thomas Traherne's once well-known *Christian Ethicks* of 1675 listed eighteen, twenty if one distinguishes (as Traherne does) between charity toward God and charity toward one's neighbor and temperance in matters of Art from temperance toward God.[47] Then, of course, there are the numerous catalogues of moral obligations beyond the virtues, such as Adam Smith's division of morals into those defined by their nature – namely propriety, prudence, and benevolence – and those defined by human motive – namely self-love, reason, and sentiment.[48] In his recent essay, French philosopher André Comte-Sponville illuminates eighteen virtues.[49]

---

43 Aquinas presents them in *Summa Theologica* II(I), qq. 61–68, though even here there are choices, as seen in John Oesterle's commencement of his lovely translated edition, *Treatise on the Virtues*, at question 64. St. Thomas Aquinas, *Treatise on the Virtues* (John A. Oesterle, trans.) (Notre Dame Press, 1984). Aquinas echoes Ambrose and Augustine, who apparently took them from Plato, although Plato added holiness, or piety, to his list in the Protagoras. "Then no other part of virtue resembles knowledge or justice or courage or temperance or holiness." Plato, *Protagoras* 330b, in *Protagoras and Meno* 62 (W. K. C. Guthrie, trans.) (Penguin Books, 1956). Peter Geach offers a very nice and beautifully readable modern defense of the cardinal virtues in *The Virtues* (Cambridge University Press, 1977).

44 1 Corinthians 13. These are discussed further in the consideration of charity in the section entitled "Charity: The Fundamental Obligation."

45 These apparently are derived from the *Psychomachia* of the late Latin poet Aurelius Clemens Prudentius, after which they influenced Aquinas in the *Summa* as well, of course, as Milton. See *Prudentius Psychomachia: Commentary and Text* (Rosemary Burton, ed.) (Bryn Mawr College, 1989). For the development of the labels and variations on their meaning, see *New Catholic Encyclopedia* 704 (Catholic University of America, 1967).

46 See Chapter 1, the section entitled "Discretion and the Definition of the Legal Office."

47 Traherne's strongly Thomistic list includes knowledge, love, eternal love, truth, wisdom, righteousness, goodness, holiness, justice, mercy, faith, hope, repentance, charity toward God, charity to our neighbor, prudence, courage, temperance in matters of art, temperance in matters of God, patience, meekness, humility, contentment, magnanimity, modesty, liberality, magnificence, and gratitude. Thomas Traherne, *Christian Ethicks* (Carol Marks, & George Guffey, eds.) (Cornell University Press, 1968).

48 Adam Smith, *The Theory of Moral Sentiments* (Knud Haakonssen, ed.) (Cambridge University Press, 2002).

49 André Comte-Sponville, *A Small Treatise on the Great Virtues: The Uses of Philosophy in Everyday Life* (Owl Books, 2002). Comte-Sponville selects politeness, fidelity, prudence, temperance, courage, justice, generosity, compassion, mercy, gratitude, humility, simplicity, tolerance, purity, gentleness, good faith, humor, and love.

Comprehensive and useful as all these lists are, they remain vulnerable to the criticisms that they either do too little or too much. In 2007, the entry for "virtue" in the online, open-source encyclopedia Wikipedia lists 106 virtues, most, but not all, of which arise from one or another ecclesiastic tradition.[50]

In the light of this multiplicity of approaches to cataloguing virtues and obligations, the attempt here is to organize the obligations derived from the stories, and then to place the stories within that organization, with an eye toward the significance of the stories to the law and to the stakes that people have in the law. The organization is therefore based somewhat on the functions of the law and somewhat on the patterns in the stories that equate them with functions of obligations.

FOUR TYPES OF MORAL OBLIGATION: PERSONAL, INSTITUTIONAL, PROCEDURAL, AND SUBSTANTIVE

Personal Obligations

The obligations grouped into this category are selected general obligations that apply to everyone, but that acquire a particular significance to those in the role of a legal official. The isolation of these general notions of obligations might be justified by a variety of ideas. Each of the obligations described in this section has some basis in religious tradition, in reason as developed by past writers or as hypothesized from cases, in moral sentiment (at least as considered by some observers), or in the expositions of legal theory.

Charity: The Fundamental Obligation

The most essential personal obligation toward others, and one that is historically most linked with the obligations of officials, is charity.[51] It is the broadest in scope of all of the duties considered here. As many writers have considered duty, charity is integral to all other obligations anyone has toward other people.[52] Its very breadth makes it sometimes difficult to assess and to apply

---

[50] http://en.wikipedia.org/wiki/Virtues (last visited September 7, 2007).

[51] Of course, some writers believe there are more fundamental duties, not the least those, like Bentham, who have argued for utility as the ur-duty officials. Perhaps the most compelling argument of late is David Beatty's argument for proportionality as the "ultimate" rule of law; yet the arguments he presents for its central role as well as its application in practice fit nicely as defenses of charity, and there would actually be few places where a genuinely charitable evaluation of a question would not lead to a proportionate outcome. See David S. Beatty, *The Ultimate Rule of Law* (Oxford University Press, 2004).

[52] Leibniz, whose work on charity has long been neglected, is discussed later. A more modern argument for charity as the basic obligation inseparable from life, power, and justice is given in Paul Tillich's wonderful lectures, *Love, Power, and Justice* (Oxford University Press, 1960).

in specific circumstances. We will consider its history and some of the various descriptions in a bit of detail here, both because of its relationships to other duties and because of its difficulties in application.

The Persistence of Charity as the Foundation of Duty to Others: Today, "charity" is sometimes just a synonym for generosity, but this is a shallow understanding that disregards the broad responsibility that charity implies. In the language of the United States, its sense is probably more often captured in the word "kindness," with its connotation of continuous obligations toward all.[53] Charity, or benevolence, is the obligation of each person to treat every other person with care, offering dignity, respect, fairness, and honesty. It is the moral duty to act toward others with the love of mankind.

In religious discourse around the globe, charity is central to all conceptions of right conduct to other people. *Caritas* is the core of the obligation, indeed the form of the word "love" used in the command to love others as one loves oneself, and it is from this source that charity entered the English language.[54]

Although Christian doctrine has been particularly important to European writers, the concept of charity is older and more dispersed than the Christian tradition. Ancient obligations to provide hospitality to travelers and care for others recur in Norse myth, Greek tales, and Jewish gospels.[55] Charity is as central to other religious structures of obligations on Earth, in the Jewish obligations of *Tikkun olam, mitzvahs,* and *tzedakah,*[56] as it is to the Hindu requirement

---

[53] The nineteenth-century American schoolbook concept of charity was based on the word "kindness." See, for example, Austin Bierbower, *The Virtues and Their Reasons* 26 (Geo. Sherwood & Co., 1888).

[54] In English, the earliest usages of "charity" are religious, translated from *caritas* in the Vulgate to depict the love of God toward mankind. The OED notes its relationship to Christ-like love, as the manner of fulfilling the commandment to love others as oneself. *Oxford English Dictionary, New Edition,* q.v., def. 1 (Oxford University Press, 1999). In a secular sense, it suggests a lenity of judgment, owing to an allowance for an individual's faults and shortcomings, but at its barest, charity is fair-mindedness even toward people disapproved of or disliked. *Id.,* def. 3a.

[55] For a nice comparison of ancient Norse and modern American ideas of hospitality, see Jeremy Waldron, "On Humiliation," 93 Michigan Law Review 1787, 1799–1802 (1995) (reviewing William Ian Miller, *Humiliation and Other Essays on Honor, Social Discomfort, and Violence* (1993)).

[56] *Tikkun olam* is the obligation to spiritually repair the world, and it has been argued by some rabbis as the basis for the pursuit of justice for all. *Mitzvah,* or the using of one's talents to improve the world, is the basic requirement of good works, one of the most basic aspects of which is *tzedakah* (derived from *Tzade-Dalet-Qof,* the obligation of righteousness, justice, or fairness), which requires not only giving a tenth portion of one's property to the poor but also enabling others to live independently. See Rabbi Maurice Lamm, Day to Day Judaism: Charity (available at http://www.aish.com/literacy/mitzvahs/Day_to_Day_Judaism_Charity. asp).

of *dharma*,[57] the Buddhist *karma*,[58] and the Islamic idea of *sadaqah*.[59] Indeed, it may well be that Hindi obligation of acts of *dharma* and the earlier Jainist concepts of respect for all forms of life as an aspect of *karma* reflect a widespread understanding that a central obligation of religion is to treat others with care.[60] It is reflected in Confucian altruism, considered in the hierarchy of Chinese culture, by which one ought to render perfect service to one's superiors but to forgive lapses by one's subordinates.[61]

[57] *Dharma*, the central obligation of Hindu law, is centered on a selflessness that obliges each person to cherish others above the self. It has not always been seen as an obligation for acts beyond one's station, but it persists as a basis for a social law within which each person is bound to others. See Anthony Sudil, "Establishing *Dharma* as Process of Liberation," 9 Integral Liberation 171 (2005).

[58] Buddha taught King Bimbisara the triple doctrine of charity, precepts, and good works, for which the king created a monastery. All are related, and the doctrines of *dharma* and *kharma* influence one another. A significant strain of Buddhism conceives of charity as an aspect of all living things. See Richard Riley, *Rationalizing the Golden Rule: A Buddhist Perspective*, 2003 Hawaii International Conference on Arts and Humanities (January 12–15, 2003), at http://www.hichumanities.org/AHproceedings/Richard%20Reilly.pdf.

[59] There are many references to charity in the *Qur'an*, particularly, "O ye who believe! cancel not your charity (*sadaqat*) by reminders of your generosity or by injury, – like those who spend their substance to be seen of men, but believe neither in Allah nor in the Last Day. . . . Give in charity of the good things you have (honorably) earned and of what We have brought forth for you from the earth, and do not choose for charity the bad quality which you will not accept for yourselves except with closed eyes." *The Holy Qur'an: Text, Translation & Commentary*, Al Baqarah (Cow)/ 2:264-66 (Abdullah Yusuf Ali, ed.) (Tahrike Tarsile Qur'an, Inc., 2004). *Sadaqat* is one element of *zakah*, payment of the divine tax, which is one of the five great duties of the devout Muslim (the others being testimony of faith, prayer, fasting, and pilgrimage). *Zakah* is similar to the Christian notion of the tithe, but its justification is based upon the purification of the remaining property as well as bringing the giver closer to Allah.

The Christian notion of *caritas* includes an obligation of conduct beyond the giving of wealth and property, which parallels the distinct Islamic obligation of good works on Earth. The Prophet says, "Lo! Those who believe and do good deeds and establish *salah* and pay *zakah*, their reward is with their Lord; and no fear shall come upon them, nor shall they grieve." *Id.* (Baqarah (Cow)/2:277). Indeed, the Prophet considered the obligation to do good works an essential parallel between Islam, Judaism, and Christianity. See *id.* (Family of 'Imran/3:113–15).

[60] Jainism, one of the oldest religions still observed, is based on the eleven Angas, often attributed in part to the prophet Mahavira (599–527 B.C.), which describe the three jewels of religion – right faith, right knowledge, and right conduct, the chief obligation of right conduct being the obligation to preserve all life. See Jyotiprasāda Jaina, *Jainism, the Oldest Living Religion* (Jain Cultural Research Society, 1951).

The influential fourth-century logician Vatsyayana divided *dharma* into a framework of liberation from *adharma*, or ego, of which *dana* (charity) is first. See "Dharma and Moksha," in *Studies in Indian Literature and Philosophy* 115 (Rocher Ludo, ed.) (Motilal Banarasidass, 1988).

[61] The Confucian idea of considerability is a part of The Way, derived from *chung* (loyalty), which is governed by *shu* (empathy) and *li* (propriety), but results in *jen* (humanity). The result is to require "the utmost mindfulness of what propriety strictly requires" toward superiors, measured by how one "would wish inferiors to act toward oneself." One must place

The obligation to love all others as one loves oneself is the central teaching of the Christian Gospel.[62] Indeed, the relationship between "love" and "charity" is so great that the terms serve as substitutes for one another in the famous passage regarding the idea of *agape* in Paul's letters. In his first letters to the Corinthians, rendered by James I's translators as, "And now abideth faith, hope, charitie, these three, but the greatest of these is charitie."[63]

Yet, Paul's epistle remains instructive on the duty and nature of charity. Knowledge, acts, or words have no intrinsic value unless they result from a

oneself in the positions of one's inferiors, and understand the stresses and issues they face, not demanding from them "perfect compliance or loyalty to li." See Richard Riley, *Rationalizing the Golden Rule: A Buddhist Perspective*, 2003 Hawaii International Conference on Arts and Humanities (January 12–15, 2003), at http://www.hichumanities.org/AHproceedings /Richard%20Reilly.pdf, quoting David S. Nivison, "Golden Rule Arguments in Chinese Moral Philosophy," in *In the Ways of Confucianism: Investigations in Chinese Philosophy* 59–76 (David S. Nivison & Bryan W. Van Norben, eds.) (Open Court Press, 1996); Philip J. Ivanhoe, "Reweaving the "One Thread" of the *Analects*," 40 Philosophy East & West 17, 33 (1980). On the similarity to Christian *caritas*, see Jeffrey Wattles, *The Golden Rule* 9 (Oxford University Press, 1996).

62   Perhaps the central lines of Christian faith are these, prompted by questions from a Pharisee lawyer. "Thou shalt love the Lord thy God with all thy heart, and with all thy soul, and with all thy mind. This is the first and great commandment. And the second is like unto it, Thou shalt love thy neighbour as thyself. On these two commandments hang all the law and the prophets." Matthew 22:32–5 (KJV). Similarly, see Mark 12:28 and Luke 10:25, the Sermon on the Plain, in Luke 6:31, and the Sermon on the Mount, in Matthew 5:20–4 and 6:12–14. In all this, Jesus quotes the law in Leviticus 19, in verse 18, in which God speaks to Moses, "Love your fellow as yourself: I am the LORD," and, in verse 34, "The stranger who resides with you shall be to you as one of your citizens; you shall love him as yourself, for you were strangers in the land of Egypt." *Tanakh: The Holy Scriptures: The New JPS Translation* 185–6 (Jewish Publication Society, 1985).

63   1 Corinthians 13:13, in *The Holy Bible* (Robert Barker, 1611). The editors of the 1611 authorized version apparently adopted John Wycliffe's translation, which was unchanged by Purvey in 1688 and persisted in various editions through the edition under James. See, for example, *The Holy Bible* (The Bishops' Bible) (Christopher Barker, 1584). Tellingly, Noah Webster kept the translation as "charity" in his new American translation in 1833. See *The Holy Bible* (Noah Webster, ed.) (Durrie and Peck, 1833) (Baker Book House, 1987).

Nineteenth-century Biblical editors substituted "love" for "charity," owing to charity's association in the nineteenth century with alms alone rather than with the wider duties of charitable acts and benevolence. The first influential translation to employ "love" in this passage appears to be the 1881 translation resulting in the English Revised Version and the American Standard Version. See *The New Testament* (C. J. Ellicott et al., eds.) (Oxford University Press, 1881); *The Holy Bible* (Philip Schaff et al., eds.) (Thomas Nelson & Sons, 1901). "Love" might have grown preferred owing to the nineteenth-century vogue of "charity" as the label for relief of the poor in England and the United States, which led to its strong identification with workhouses, orphanages, and other Dickensian institutions. See Robert H. Bremmer, *Giving: Charity and Philanthropy in History* 85–169 (Transaction Press, 2000). In the Revised Standard Version it is, "So now faith, hope, and love abide, these three; but the greatest of these is love." The RSV is available online, at http://etext.lib.virginia.edu/rsv.browse.html.

spirit of charity.[64] Faith without charity is nothing,[65] and good works toward others are empty without charity.[66] An act of charity is good in itself, and not for its appearance to the actor or observer; if it is born in love, it is inherently good and incorruptible, true and unending in its nature.[67] Charity is not the self-regarding thought of a child, but the difficult task of understanding others that comes when adults attempt to understand one another.[68]

In that light, it is unsurprising that charity was an essential aspect of Christian duty for early Christian ethicists. Augustine considered the command to love one's neighbor as a requirement of a proper motive in action, according to which acts of kindness must be motivated by a universal sense of Christian care, not only for Christians but for all people.[69] This idea of charity forms the theme for Augustine's central distinction between the Earthly city and the Heavenly city. "These two cities were made by two loves: the earthly city by the love of self unto the contempt of God, and the heavenly city by the love of God unto the contempt of self."[70] (This last phrase ought not to be overemphasized; neither Augustine nor most other Christian ethicists would forbid constructive forms of self-love, because such a prohibition would contradict the command to love others as oneself).[71] Centuries later, Abelard would emphasize the motive implied in Augustine's *summa*: "The Law commands nothing but charity and forbids nothing but greed."[72] Comparing the similarity of God's offering the

---

64 "Though I speak with the tongues of men and of angels, and have not charity, I am become as sounding brass, or a tinkling cymbal." 1 Corinthians 13:1 (KJV) (spelling modernized). (Sounding brasses were natural amplifiers in a theater, seemingly implying that a voice without charity is a mere echo.)

65 "And though I have the gift of prophecy, and understand all mysteries, and all knowledge; and though I have all faith, so that I could remove mountains, and have not charity, I am nothing." *Id.*, verse 2.

66 "And though I bestow all my goods to feed the poor, and though I give my body to be burned, and have not charity, it profiteth me nothing." *Id.*, verse 3.

67 "Charity suffereth long, and is kind; charity envieth not; charity vaunteth not itself, is not puffed up, Doth not behave itself unseemly, seeketh not her own, is not easily provoked, thinketh no evil; Rejoiceth not in iniquity, but rejoiceth in the truth; beareth all things, believeth all things, hopeth all things, endureth all things. Charity never faileth: but whether there be prophecies, they shall fail; whether there be tongues, they shall cease; whether there be knowledge, it shall vanish away." *Id.* verses 4–8.

68 "When I was a child, I spake as a child, I understood as a child, I thought as a child: but when I became a man, I put away childish things. For now we see through a glass, darkly; but then face to face: now I know in part; but then shall I know even as also I am known." *Id.* verses 11–12.

69 St. Augustine, *City of God* (Book 21, Chapter 27) 805. (Marcus D. D. Dods, trans.) (Modern Library, 1950).

70 *City of God* 477 (Book 14, Chapter 28.).

71 See Darlene Fozard Weaver, *Self Love and Christian Ethics* (Cambridge University Press, 2002).

72 Peter Abelard, *Ethics*, Book 1, Paragraph 55, in –, *Ethical Writings* 12 (Paul Spade, trans.) (Hackett, 1995).

death of Christ as an act of sacrifice with Judas Iscariot's offering of him as an act of betrayal, both Augustine and Abelard see the difference in motive alone. The charity of an act is not to be judged by the result but by the intention that underlies it.

From the general framework as developed by Paul, Augustine, and Abelard, Thomas Aquinas developed from a detailed argument for a Christian duty the virtue of charity. Aquinas, typically, integrated his argument for charity into his fuller framework of divine, natural, and human laws and an array of virtues. Among these, he located charity as a theological virtue, which (along with faith and hope) was constituted by God, as opposed to the cardinal virtues of prudence, justice, temperance, and fortitude, which could be exercised by human will alone and without divine intervention.[73] Aquinas is quick to point out, though, that charity is still the result of the human will, divinely infused with love for God and humankind.[74]

Aquinas divided his study into the nature of charity, the objects of charity, and the effects of charity. Although it is potentially misleading to consider one aspect of this scheme without the contexts either of Thomas's wider project of the virtues or of his more specific plan for charity, for our purposes, it is probably enough to recognize that Thomas's view of charity is a kind of friendship with particular obligations and limits within which the will of the individual is required to pursue the increase of charity. Among these obligations is the requirement to love other persons, as well as to love ourselves. This obligation extends to loving every person as our neighbor, including the guilty and sinful.[75] We must love our enemies, although in this, Thomas is careful to distinguish the demand to love the humanity in one's enemies from any requirement to show love to each enemy individually.[76] This distinction comports with Aquinas's division among the natural objects of charity. One should love all of one's neighbors more than oneself, but it is still appropriate to love those closest more than others.[77]

To understand Aquinas's notion of charity, it might help most to consider the vices he considered directly opposed to it: hatred, sloth, envy, schism, war,

[73] On Thomas's virtues generally, John Finnis, *Aquinas: Moral, Political, and Legal Theory* (Oxford University Press, 1998); for Aquinas's exposition on charity, see *Saint Thomas Aquinas on Charity (De Caritate)* (Lottie Kendzierski, trans.) (Marquette University Press, 1993); Thomas Aquinas, 3 *Summa Theologica* 1263–1379 (II-II, qq. 24–46) (Fathers of the English Dominican Province, trans.) (Christian Classics, 1981).

[74] For his argument of the divine infusion of charity in man, see *id.* at 3 *Summa Theologica* 1270–1 (II-II, q. 24, arts. 1–3). See also Michael S. Sherwin, *By Knowledge & by Love: Charity and Knowledge in the Moral Theology of St. Thomas Aquinas* (Catholic University of America Press, 2005).

[75] On this particularly, see 3 *Summa Theologica* 1282–3 (II-II, q. 25, art. 6).

[76] *Id.* 1285–7 (II-II, q. 25, arts. 8–9).

[77] *Id.* 1291–9 (II-II, q. 26, arts. 3–13). The measure of moral distance remains a critical question, necessary to determine the strength of moral obligations.

strife, and scandal. It is then Aquinas explores wisdom, which "corresponds" to charity and which is opposed by vice.[78] Aquinas then provides a notion of charity as essential to the manifestation of many other virtues.

Particularly, Thomas grounds the obligation of justice on charity, even in the strictest sense of the duty of a judge to render to others what is due to them. "Just as love of God includes love of our neighbor, ... so too the service of God includes rendering to each one his due."[79] This notion of charity was profoundly influential in the Middle Ages, and church art and sculpture frequently presented an anthropomorphized representation of charity, which in many ways prefigured later representations of justice in statues.[80]

The idea of charity as essential to other virtues is most fully explored by Gottfried Leibniz, who defined justice as the "charity of the wise."[81] In doing so, Leibniz deliberately invoked a sense of the divine command in his claims to earthly justice, as a part of his effort to construct from Roman law and the law of contemporary states a universal jurisprudence that could reunite the increasingly factious states of Europe. Any attempt to understand Leibniz's claim must consider it as much a religious duty as an ethical duty, and yet he saw it as a duty nonetheless that both could give practical guidance to state officials and would be recognized as a compelling obligation by states, princes, and officials across the range of religious commitments of seventeenth-century Europe.[82]

---

[78]   *Id.* 1335–79 (II-II, qq. 34–46).

[79]   *Id.* 1429 (II-II, q. 58, art. 1, obj. 6). For the purposes of reaching a final conclusion as to immoral or moral conduct, one must also account for Aquinas's double effects test, by which an immoral act made to achieve a moral end is justified under some circumstances, particularly for self-defense and for action in a just war. *Id.* (II-II, q. 64, art. 7). It might be applied in wider contexts, although this is less clear. See, for example, John Finnis, *Aquinas: Moral, Political, and Legal Theory* 190–1 (Oxford University Press, 1998).

[80]   See R. Freyhan, "The Evolution of the *Caritas* Figure in the Thirteenth and Fourteenth Century," 11 Journal of the Warburg and Courtauld Institutes 68 (1948).

[81]   This idea of justice was integral in his great argument for the relationship among faith, reason, and freedom. G. W. Leibniz, *Theodicy: Essays on the Goodness of God, the Freedom of Man and the Origin of Evil* (1710) (E. M. Huggard, trans.) (Open Court Press, 1998). Leibniz's most concise single exploration of justice, and its relationship to charity and to wisdom, is his *Meditation on The Common Concept of Justice*, written in 1702, but the idea is integral to most of his writings on morals, law, and the state. The best introduction in English is Patrick Riley, *Leibniz' Universal Jurisprudence: Justice as Charity of the Wise* (Harvard University Press, 1996).

[82]   His practical and cosmopolitan ambitions reflect the breadth of Leibniz's own experience as judge, legislator, political advisor to heads of state, and ambassador, moving through his professional life among both Protestant and Catholic states. Gottfried Leibniz lived from 1646 to 1716, serving as adviser to the Electors of Mainz and of Hanover, and he traveled extensively. The only real biography of him in English is Eric J. Aiton, *Leibniz: A Biography* (Hilger, 1985), although there is a fine biographical introduction in Patrick Riley's books and in the general introductions to his work, such as the very nice new book by Nicholas Jolley, *Leibniz* (Routledge, 2005).

Integral to this model of the law, which was built on models of reason, was its moderation by a separate notion of justice that looked to ideas of proportion and harmony that reflect the structure of the creation. This is his idea of charity of the wise:

> Justice is charity or a habit of loving conformed to wisdom. Thus when one is included to justice, one tries to procure the good for everybody, so far as one can, reasonably, but in proportion to the needs and merits of each; and even if one is obliged sometimes to punish evil persons, it is for the general good.[83]

To determine the "proportion to the needs and merits of each," Leibniz looked to the three great maxims of Roman law, reduced in the *Institutes* of Justinian, to do no one harm, give each his due, and live rightly.[84] These duties he analyzed so that the lower forms of justice were not to harm and to give each their due, assigning the highest value to living honestly, or with probity.[85]

One of the most important aspects of Leibniz's thought is that, having given proofs of a negative duty of charity, in doing wrong to no one, he argued that such a negative duty can have no real significance without a positive duty to prevent harm and bring felicity to everyone. "Whether one does evil or refuses to do good is a matter of degree, but that does not change the species and the nature of the thing."[86] In this, he contrasts judges who seek only to cause no harm with those of "larger and finer views, [who] would not wish that anyone complain in their lack of goodness."[87]

Leibniz has a fair claim to be at once both the last scholastic and the first rationalist. Although a theology of charity persists, since Leibniz, most philosophers arguing for an obligation of or like charity have done so without predicating their arguments on a divine creation or a divine love.

Arguments for charity do not depend on a religious foundation, however. Cicero had argued that the goal of an individual engaged in civil society was to promote the common interests, not merely individual interests.[88] Hobbes

---

[83] Gottfried Leibniz, *Notes on Felicity* (c1694–98), quoted in Gottfried Leibniz, *Political Writings* 18 (Patrick Riley, ed.) (Cambridge University Press, 1988).

[84] Institutes, I.1.3. *Honestus*, which I presented as "rightly" earlier, is a word rich in meaning. Although it is usually translated into English as "honestly," it invoked a broader sense of honor and integrity in classical Latin than the word "honesty" now means in English, and it surely had this broader connotation to Leibniz. See M. S. Kempshall, *The Common Good in Late Medieval Political Thought* (Oxford University Press, 1999).

[85] See, for example, Gottfried Leibniz, *Codex Juris Gentium* (c1693), quoted in Leibniz, *Political Writings* 165, 174–8.

[86] Gottfried Leibniz, *The Common Concept of Justice* (c1702–03), quoted in Leibniz, *Political Writings* 45, 55.

[87] *Id.* 54.

[88] There are passages throughout Cicero's works in this regard. See, for example, Cicero, *De Officiis* I.10.31, I.19.62 (Walter Miller, trans.) (Heinemann, 1921).

had claimed the reciprocity of the Golden Rule as his foundation for natural law.[89] One of the most influential of these rational constructions of charity is that of Immanuel Kant to develop an ethics based on duty arising from reason alone, the centerpiece of which is his categorical imperative.[90] Of the various statements Kant makes of it, the most fundamental is, "Act only on that maxim whereby thou canst at the same time will that it should become a universal law."[91] To act in such a way is to ensure that the action is based on appropriate reason, which for Kant ensures that it will be moral. One result of this morality, however, is an element of reciprocity, akin to Christian charity. It also ensures that the manner of deciding a course of conduct toward another is more important than the outcome itself: a rational person must "so act as to treat humanity, whether in thine own person or in that of any other, in every case as an end withal, never as means only."[92] Thus we find Kant's ultimate nature of human charity, in that all ends-oriented thinking must promote the humanity of each person. No person may be used as a means to achieve another end.[93] Treatment of each person must be according to that person's acts and thoughts, not for some other enterprise.

Jeremy Bentham altered the equation of charity in fundamental ways. What he believed was the essential aspect of moral thought – judging every action by the degree to which it promoted human happiness or diminished pain – is a notion like charity, at least insofar as it demands each actor to seek the good

---

[89] See Thomas Hobbes, *Leviathan: Or, the Matter, Forme & Power of a Commonwealth, Ecclesiasticall and Civill* (Book 1, Section 15) 97–114 (A. R. Waller, ed.) (1651) (Cambridge University Press, 1904).

[90] On the relationship of Kant's moral theory to his legal theory, see George P. Fletcher, "Law and Morality: A Kantian Perspective," 87 Columbia Law Review 533 (1987).

[91] Immanuel Kant, *Foundations of the Metaphysics of Morals* 38 (Thomas K. Abbott, trans.) (Library of Liberal Arts, 1969). The "maxim" is a Kantian term or art, similar but still quite different from "motive" in the modern common law. Identifying accurately a Kantian maxim can be a difficult enterprise, in part because Kant appears to believe that only one true maxim applies to justify any action.

[92] *Id*. 46.

[93] Kant was convinced that this formulation was a better foundation for moral duty than the principles of reciprocity associated with Christian charity.

> [The common *quod tibi non vis fieri, etc.*,] it cannot be a universal law, for it does not contain the principle of duties to oneself, nor of the duties of benevolence to others (for many a one would gladly consent that others should not benefit him, provided only that he might be excused from showing benevolence to them), nor finally that of duties of strict obligation to one another, for on this principle the criminal might argue against the judge who punishes him, and so on.

> *Id*. 47, n.14. This line is common not only because it is in Matthew but also as it is the maxim of equity in the Rule of Benedict, *Quod tibi non vis fieri, alteri ne feceris* [What you would not have done to yourself that do not you to another?] *The Rule of St. Benedict* 97, 104 (M. L. Del Mastro & Anthony C. Meisel, trans.) (Image Books, 1975).

of others in deciding what to do.[94] To act to achieve the greatest good for the greatest number is to encourage something like the felicity sought by Leibniz, though it lacks (until corrected by John Stuart Mill) the particularity of giving to each his due, which is another way of considering Kant's obligation to treat each person as an end and not as a means. The effect, however, of Bentham's approach is usually to aggregate happiness, leading to situations in which it can become appropriate to act toward one person in a manner that seems lacking in charity, because that is required to maximize utility for the whole of a population.[95]

Western understanding of charity in the twentieth century advanced the Christian and Kantian notions of duty, building more robust ideas of reason and scope into the moral calculus. One question that persisted was how to treat someone who would treat themselves badly; to treat them as they would treat themselves is to miss the point. Thus Richard Hare developed a complex means of making universal a moral judgment, by using imagination to place oneself in the position of the person one is judging.[96] He thus argued that for a Nazi to kill a Jew would require that the Nazi accept that he, too, would have to die if he were in fact Jewish. [97] New views of charity have also followed the charge made by Peter Singer that charity cannot meaningfully extend only to human beings, but it must consider all beings with an interest in avoiding suffering, regardless of species.[98] Singer's argument, though it has attracted increasingly serious attention, has not yet gained wide acceptance.

This brief history cannot support the idea of a universal acceptance of an idea of charity, much less charity as an aspect of official life. Charity has come to be less a matter of the treatment of individuals by individuals, and certainly less of a direct action of a particular official to a particular subject. Rather, it has become synonymous with private or public acts or welfare, or financial support by wealthier people to poorer people, and generally in acts through

---

[94] Jeremy Bentham, *An Introduction to the Principles of Morals and Legislation* (J. H. Burns & H. L. A. Hart, eds.) (1789) (Athlone Press, 1970). Bentham actually equates charity with a narrow idea of public utility, although quite rarely and generally in his efforts to show that all motives to which his readers would be sympathetic could be better explained as acts of utility. See *id.* 103–12.

[95] This result is, of course, very controversial, and there are rich debates between different branches of the utilitarian family. Utility measured by the preference stated by those in the calculus probably most limits the treatment of individuals as means. See, for example, R. M. Hare, "A Kantian Utilitarian Approach," in *Moral Rights in the Workplace* 184 (Gertrude Ezorsky & James W. Nickel, eds.) (State University of New York Press, 1987).

[96] See R. M. Hare, *Freedom and Reason* (Oxford University Press, 1977); *Moral Thinking* (Oxford University Press, 1981).

[97] Responding differently to the same flaw, Alan Gewirth argued that only rational desires could be the basis for charity, and so among other outcomes argued that charity could support the recognition of rights in other people. See Alan Gewirth, *The Community of Rights* (University of Chicago Press, 1996).

[98] Peter Singer, *Practical Ethics* (2d ed.) (Cambridge University Press, 1993).

the state or private agencies that aggregate the collection and distribution of aid. In that sense, charity remains a strongly accepted notion in the popular culture, although it is often, wrongly, seen as a strictly voluntary duty.[99]

Some modern theories of the state from both ends of the political spectrum would reject charity as a general duty. Libertarians and others with a robust sense of individualism reject any duty that is not voluntarily created by the person who would act according to it.[100]

On the other hand, modern liberals, at least those following John Rawls, would reject a notion of charity by public officials, if that notion went further than accepting a state in which all are treated with fairly strict equality. The notion that an agent of the state would extend care specifically toward some not sought by all does not sit easily in the just legal system mapped by Rawls. Indeed, to Rawls, private charity is possible, but only as a supererogatory duty, and public acts of charity through the state are possible only through a system of unanimous approval.[101]

Still, even though most people would find a general duty of charity a compelling idea, this is in part owing to the difficulty with which its limits can be defined. We say with ease that we have a duty of charity to those we want to help but no duty to those we do not want to help, but this is to misunderstand the nature of the duty, at least in part. Charity is an obligation with particular beneficiaries, people to whom it is owed, particularly individuals who are either affected or may be affected directly by one's actions. Identifying these beneficiaries can be messy, although charity, at least in the Thomist tradition that Leibniz has presented, is not specific toward one or another person but is an obligation toward each and all to do well by them. The best model of who these people are does not create a concrete set of people to whom one owes charity but understands that the beneficiaries are circumstantial. They are the people whose need is most proximate to the person who can satisfy it.[102]

---

[99] The modern exponent of the positive duty of charity is Jeremy Waldron. See Jeremy Waldron, "Welfare and the Images of Charity," 36 Philosophical Quarterly 463 (1986); taking a similar view but in a broader framework, see Alan Buchanan, "Justice and Charity," 97 Ethics 558 (1987).

[100] See, for example, Ayn Rand, *The Virtue of Selfishness* (Penguin, 1961); Robert Nozick, *Anarchy, State and Utopia* (Basic Books, 1977).

[101] John Rawls, *A Theory of Justice: Original Edition* (Harvard University Press, 2005).

[102] One of the traditional questions of moral distance leads to recurrent arguments that were defining of who are, or are not, the beneficiaries of a person's duty. In the terms of the parable of the Samaritan, who is one's neighbor? Jeremy Waldron's analysis of this question is a great improvement on the quest to put a Samaritan in or out of the set of neighbors. By considering the question one of proximity, by looking, as Jesus and Kant did, at who is thrown together by chance, and finding that a duty arose thanks to the chance of nearness and the potential benefits of action, Waldron has done two things. First, he demonstrated the basis of care, but, second, and more fundamentally, he demonstrated this with a test that is a matter not of a rigid category but of degree. People are not perfectly proximate or

So although charity does not always require the satisfaction of claims made by supplicants, it requires the best conduct toward those whom one is capable of helping. This might lead to conflicting obligations, but the nature of the conflict is not merely between two different people who each may prefer different treatment; it is within a more limited range of the best outcome for the person helped. Charity thus incorporates important general obligations to respect the dignity of others, treating them, as Kant would say, as ends and not as means. It incorporates obligations more particular to the role, such as fairness, equality of treatment, and a hearing of each person's claim on the official without prejudgment. *Caritas* may be seen in the materials of law as the highest possible standard of care, a concept somewhat incorporated into the notion of the fiduciary: one who acts with fidelity toward another, such as a trustee or guardian toward a beneficiary or ward.

A Summary of Official Charity: From this narrative, we can discern a view of charity as it has been occasionally developed, and we can then consider its value in the light of cases. Charity is personal: it is a relationship between individuals, perhaps most importantly between the official and every subject whose life is affected by a particular act or omission within the scope of office. Even though some decisions by an official might affect only one person, and another decision might affect hundreds of millions, in both instances the obligation is personal as to each and every one. Bentham's aggregations notwithstanding, the stronger tradition, running from Christ to Kant, requires that charity be direct. In that tradition, an official may not trade off the harm done to one subject by considering the benefit to another; the benefit to the other does not diminish the direct relationship and obligation of charity to the first subject.

A charitable official treats others as the official would not irrationally desire to be treated if their positions were reversed. This reversal is rather important, and as we learned from Hare, it usually isn't enough unless we remember that the bad man cannot presume that in the shoes of a victim he would somehow deserve to be victimized. It rarely can be rational to desire to be a victim.[103] On the other hand, it is rational to expect to be punished when one knows one has voluntarily done something wrong or harmful, so the requirement of a not irrational desire would allow a full understanding of the reasons why the subject would expect to be treated well or poorly.

distant. The more proximate, and the more likely I am to be able to help someone in distress, the greater my duty. This is quite sensible. See Jeremy Waldron, "Who Is My Neighbor?: Humanity and Proximity," 86 The Monist 333 (2003).

[103]   There are cases of civil disobedience and other rare cases when it is rational to be a victim. Hare does not actually use doubly negative formulae for rationality, and yet there are dangers that come of not doing so, explored in the following paragraph.

A charitable official treats each person as a real individual with particular desires and not hypothetical interests. In considering reciprocity as a measure for treatment, it is more important that the subject's desires be real, or at least likely, rather than rationalized or hypothesized. The official does not acquire additional power over the subject through charity, such that the official can stifle the subject's actual desires or hopes and substitute what the official would claim is rational. Limiting desires by limiting those that are not irrational is only a tool for avoiding the irrational, not for demanding one choice among rational choices.

A charitable official does not favor one subject over another, unless it is rational to do so. Thus, one subject can be disfavored for the benefit of another if it would be rational for the loser to prefer the winner to receive the benefit.[104]

A charitable official treats a person as an end and not as a means. In other words, officials must treat each individual as the reason for the laws, not the other way around.

A charitable official treats each person as an individual and not as a demographic unit. If the official treats a subject according to membership or identity in a group, it must be rational to do so, and it would be rational for a member of that group to desire to be treated that way.

A charitable official is most interested in, and owes the greatest degrees of duty toward, the individuals who will be most immediately affected by a given act or omission by the official.

A charitable official does not become a chump through charity. Charity requires respect and dignity, but it does not require the unquestioned acceptance of the statements of others, or their preferences. Rather, it demands such statements and preferences be given the same weight that the official would expect to be given to similar statements or preferences if others heard the official express them. Neither does charity generally require mercy, unless mercy is appropriate for particular reasons. Charity demands respect, love, and care, but none of these prevents punishment.

Narratives and Cases: The regrettable history of western law can ascribe most of its greatest injustices to failures of charity by officials. Many of the most horrific cases, ranging from pogroms and mass death on the basis of class or religion, to slavery by race and disenfranchisement by gender, suggest that a

---

[104] Although this notion here comes from the Leibnizian construct of giving each person his due, it is quite near to Rawls's later idea of the difference principle. What I take is Leibniz's notion of fairness, unlike Rawls's, is not based on self-interest but on a rational conception of fairness, or what is due. I might receive less than another and not be made better off by the other's receiving more, yet I can still imagine scenarios in which I would consider it fair that the other receive more than I do.

legal system that fails to accord equal charity to all persons within its domain runs a great risk of injustice.

This knowledge, however well known it is to the contemporary world, appears to have been insufficient to prevent atrocities under the law in the past. To understand the nature of charity, and how it can be manifest or denied to the members of a whole group, requires understanding its failure at the level of the individual. Here again, examples are legion, but in the American experience, among the worst have been the experiences of lynching and violence sparked by racism.

We see it, and yet we don't see it. As a teacher in twenty-first-century America, at a university in the South, I am often surprised to hear from my students in class discussions of segregation as if it happened only to a distant people, rather than in their own culture only a generation before. In its way, this egalitarian confusion by the young over how anyone could be so mistaken is a cause for celebration; and yet the dangers inherent in such a divorce from the dangers in one's own culture are real, too.

After trial and error, the best illustration I have found yet of how such a failure of charity happens is in screening two scenes from the movie of Harper Lee's *To Kill A Mockingbird*,[105] the scenes in which Brock Peters plays Tom Robinson, the black man accused of raping a white woman. Peters's performance is utterly compelling as the testimony of a good man, wrongly accused by the person whose own conduct harmed him. As difficult as this scene is to watch, the greater horror comes in watching the jury of twelve white men bring in a verdict of guilt. Watching students in the classroom watch the jury on the screen, it becomes clear that they see how this injustice could happen, how people who were probably otherwise morally upstanding could reach such a wrong conclusion, with such unjust results. Indeed, the results lead to a final insult when Tom is killed attempting to escape from such a system. Seeing how easily it happened makes the injustice become more real to them.

The failures of human decency in this scene occur at many levels, and to isolate one cause is a mistake if it would seem to deny other causes. Yet the overwhelming cause, at least as I read the book or watch the movie – and regardless of the history it represents or with that history firmly in mind – is the failure of charity by the white men of that jury, and indeed the accusers, toward the black man, Tom Robinson.

A charitable juror would not have given less credence to his testimony than he would have given to his own. First, he could not have discounted what Tom said owing to race, nor would he have given credit to his accusers on account of theirs. The obligation of charity to act toward others as you would have them act would forbid it; the juror would expect then to be thought to lie on account

---

[105] Robert Mulligan, director, 1962.

of his race as well, which is a conclusion he would reject. But second, and more fundamentally, the jurors each suffered a failure of empathy, a failure to treat the defendant as a full human being entitled to the same dignity as themselves. Nothing else can explain the difference between the evidence and the result.

This narrative cannot be dismissed as art. The unfortunate truth is that white people in the United States were guilty of such horrible and uncharitable conduct on a wholesale basis, and it happened – it still happens – all too often in courts of law.

The same form of failure of charity must explain the trial in Mississippi of Roy Bryant and J. W. Milan, the killers of Emmett Louis Till in 1955. Despite overwhelming evidence that these two men beat the fourteen-year-old black visitor to their Mississippi town to death, because he whistled at a white woman, the jury brought in a quick verdict of not guilty.[106]

Despite the compelling nature of failures of charity in such dramatic cases, failures of charity happen on a recurring and nearly constant basis in the legal system. Charity requires effort, usually persistent and uncelebrated effort – not the stuff of gala dinner speeches but the recurrent slog, like the generally unsung service of Jonathan Jones in the colonial Connecticut trials. In the pursuit of one goal or another, officials frequently fail in such efforts toward the people through whom these goals are pursued.

For example, the testimony of victims has become an important aspect of criminal trials, particularly the guilt phase of capital cases. This is often presented as a means of providing closure to the victims or their survivors. It should be a clear illustration of charity toward the victims or survivors to present their stories. Yet this is rarely the case. Prosecutors do not present such evidence for the benefit of the witness but for the purpose of securing their preferred verdict in the trial. Indeed, prosecutors have notoriously barred survivors whose testimony did not fit their case. An example is the trial of Timothy McVeigh for the murders resulting from the bomb he set in Oklahoma City in 1995. Joseph Hartzler, the Clinton administration's prosecutor, selected only those survivors who would argue that McVeigh should die. Other survivors, such as Bud Welch, whose daughter had died in the bombing but who did not want to see a retributive death, were barred from testifying.[107] Hartzler's treatment – not only of the witnesses he barred but also of those he presented – was

---

[106] See Steven J. Whitfield, *A Death in the Delta: The Story of Emmett Till* (Johns Hopkins University Press, 1991). A new documentary on Emmett's murder and trial has led, at last, to a reopening of the case. See *The Untold Story of Emmett Till* (Keith Beaucham, director) (2005) (see http://www. emmetttillstory.com/) (last visited February 12, 2006).

[107] See Bruce Shapiro, *Victims' Rights – and Wrongs: Why Didn't We Hear from the Relatives of the Dead Who Don't Want Timothy McVeigh to Die?* Salon.com (last visited June 13, 1997) (available at http://archive.salon.com/june97/news/news970613.html). See also David Hoffman, *The Oklahoma City Bombing and the Politics of Terror* (Feral House, 1998).

uncharitable, in that it treated all of the witnesses as a means of presenting the case he personally believed best. Hartzler did not treat the witnesses as humans in themselves, each entitled to personal dignity, but as a means to make his case.

This illustration demonstrates the wrong that may be done in the pursuit of an end that at least some would consider to be right. Even if we agreed with Hartzler that the execution of McVeigh was right, we can still judge his conduct toward the witnesses as wrong, both on the basis of his conduct toward them and for the resulting failure of the jury to hear a complete story from the victims.[108] Defense attorneys usually cannot call victim evidence in criminal trials.[109]

Knowledge

The idea that one should have knowledge is ancient and persistent in western culture. Aristotle, for example, considered knowledge to be essential to all moral action.[110] Knowledge is more, however, than the acquisition of facts; it is the product both of inclination to learn what one practically will need to know, and of sufficient education in the data available.[111] Because we can never know everything, acquiring knowledge is a process, and knowledge itself is a matter of degree, of sufficiency.[112]

---

[108] This skew is not uncommon. See Susan Bandes, "When Victims Seek Closure: Forgiveness, Vengeance, and the Role of the Government," 27 Fordham Urban Law Journal 1599 (2000).

[109] See Susan Bandes, "Empathy, Narrative, and Victim Impact Statements," 63 University of Chicago Law Review 361 (1996).

[110] "In order for an act to be virtuous, it needs first of all to be done knowingly... What is done through ignorance is involuntary." Aristotle *Ethics*, Book 3, Chapter 1, Book 2, Chapter 4, in *Complete Works of Aristotle* 2152, 2205–6 (W. D. Ross, trans.) (Jonathan Barnes, ed.) (Princeton University Press, 1984).

[111] Aristotle considered knowledge to be the result of both aptitude and study. Neither alone was sufficient.

> Now each man judges well the things he knows, and of these he is a good judge. And so the man who has been educated in a subject is a good judge of that subject, and the man who has received an all-round education is a good judge in general. Hence a young man is not a proper hearer of lectures on political science; for he is inexperienced in the actions that occur in life, but its discussions start from these and are about these; and, further, since he tends to follow his passions, his study will be vain and unprofitable, because the end aimed at is not knowledge but action. And it makes no difference whether he is young in years or youthful in character; the defect does not depend on time, but on his living, and pursuing each successive object, as passion directs. For to such persons, as to the incontinent, knowledge brings no profit; but to those who desire and act in accordance with a rational principle knowledge about such matters will be of great benefit.

> Aristotle, *Nicomachean Ethics*, Book 1, Chapters 3 and 4 (W. D. Ross, trans.) in *Complete Works of Aristotle* (Jonathan Barnes, ed.) (Princeton University Press, 1984).

[112] The literature on knowledge is vast, but in these ideas, I rely particularly on Charles Van Doren, *A History of Knowledge: Past, Present, and Future* (Ballantine Books, 1992);

An official must have the knowledge necessary to carry out the office, as well as sufficient skill in assessing and using that information. This knowledge is both general and particular. General information requires education of the official, not only into the nature of laws but also into the nature of the human activities that are regulated by the office. It cannot be enough to rely on guesswork, instinct, or luck in fashioning the legal duties of other people. Specific information relates to the affairs of citizens who are affected by a given act by the official. To craft legislation, a lawmaker ought to know enough about the affairs to be regulated to assess the value of the new requirement, as well as enough about them to tailor a rule to alter human behavior to achieve the required result and no more. In other words, a lawmaker ought not to write a law that would regulate ships at sea without knowing a great deal about ships and what happens to them at sea.[113] That is a considerable knowledge of human affairs. To it must be added knowledge of how officials and citizens employ laws. To judge some conduct, as in determining the guilt of a criminal defendant or the liability of a civil defendant, the trier must have considerable knowledge of the events in issue as well as of the law that governs the issue.

Questions and learning are essential to knowledge. An official is unlikely to know all one can ever know about a situation or idea. Within the time and means available, no official can be content with the level of knowledge had at the start.

Official action without such knowledge of facts and the operation of laws is all too common, as action contrary to what the official knows. Officials who fail to seek knowledge sufficient for their actions, or who fail to act on knowledge once it is acquired, are the cause of poor legislation, wrongful arrests, detentions, and punishments, as well as failures to act in numerous cases when peril could have been averted.[114] Among the most difficult failures of knowledge to countenance are efforts by prosecutors to hide exculpatory evidence from courts and juries, even when such evidence would free the innocent.[115]

John Locke, *An Essay on Human Understanding* (1689) (Peter H. Nidditch, ed.) (Oxford University Press, 1989), and works discussed in Steve Sheppard, "The Metamorphoses of Reasonable Doubt: How Changes in the Burden of Proof Have Weakened the Presumption of Innocence," 78 Notre Dame Law Review 1165 (2003).

[113]   The temptation here to consider the acts of officials that are less legal in substance and more commitments of government policy in war is too strong to overcome. The decisions to commence wars by the United States against Spain, Vietnam, and Iraq were all based on poor knowledge, respectively, of the cause of the destruction of the U.S.S. *Maine*, whether U.S. vessels were attacked in the Gulf of Tonkin, and whether Iraq possessed weapons of mass destruction in violation of commitments to the United Nations.

[114]   See, for example, the papers in the symposium introduced by Ellen Yankiver Suni, "Introduction to the Symposium on Wrongful Convictions: Issues of Science, Evidence, and Innocence," 70 UMKC Law Review 797 (2002).

[115]   Compare U.S. Department of Justice, *Convicted by Juries, Exonerated by Science: Case Studies in the Use of DNA Evidence to Establish Innocence after Trial* (1996), with Jim Dwyer, Peter

A narrative of great power in the illustration of obligation to act from knowledge is the fictionalization of the Scopes trial, when the character Matthew Brady, played by Frederic March, admits that he has never read the works of Darwin, though he has – at length – condemned them in his argument. Such a failure of knowledge is the ultimate evidence to the audience of the injustice of Brady's case.[116] Official condemnations of acts and individuals based on questionable or unreviewed or nonexistent evidence happens recurrently.

Lack of knowledge by officials is important in more than merely the laws applied in the courtroom. Lack of knowledge, for instance, exemplified by the failure of any official to investigate even the simplest aspects of the Johnstown dam was integral to the disaster, which could have been averted without the loss of the dam and the deaths of thousands.[117]

Admittedly, certain roles in the law have acquired a license for a limited ignorance, as when a lawyer willfully remains unaware of some facts of a client's case.[118] Yet such compartmentalization of one's moral life are not without cost, and the fact remains that when an official acts on such ignorance, such behavior is to that extent immoral.

Personal Virtues

Charity, to Leibniz and others, was understood as a sufficiently broad obligation as to encompass all that an official needed to do toward others. Knowledge, according to Aristotle, is essential to all moral action.

There are, however, other strains in the literature that consider a host of virtues that are distinct from one another, and that a good person would manifest in action toward others. These are no less significant for officials, for the reasons considered in Chapter 3. Thus, a brief inventory of those virtues with particular application to the roles of officials can be helpful, at least as a starting point, for considering more fully the whole of the official's obligations. This initial inventory here includes prudence, truth, humility, action, and courage.[119]

Neufeld, & Barry Scheck, *Actual Innocence: Five Days to Execution, and Other Dispatches from the Wrongly Convicted* (Doubleday, 2000).

[116] See *Inherit the Wind* (Billy Wilder, director, 1960). The lines are in the play, Jerome Lawrence & Robert E. Lee, *Inherit the Wind* 76–7 (Ballantine Books, 2003). The show trial of John Scopes is more accurately detailed in Edward J. Larson, *Summer for the Gods: The Scopes Trial and America's Continuing Debate over Science and Religion* (Harvard University Press, 1998).

[117] See David McCullough, *Johnstown Flood* (Peter Smith Publisher, 1987).

[118] David Luban, "Contrived Ignorance," 87 Georgetown Law Journal 957 (1999).

[119] For another list, nicely assembled, see Chenise S. Kanemoto, "Bushido in the Courtroom: A Case for Virtue-Oriented Lawyering," 57 University of South Carolina Law Review 357 (2005).

Prudence: As it is usually understood, knowledge alone is insufficient to determine the best course of action to reach the best outcome by the best means. The application of knowledge to a specific circumstance to select the best result and achieve it is prudence.[120] The prudent course is often one of moderation among competing values and demands. Prudence is not the same as expediency. To fail in a duty because it is difficult, costly, or dangerous is hardly prudent.[121] Rather, it is to do what thoughtful parents do when raising children: to pick the important battles, rather than fighting them all and losing the war.[122] Prudence keeps the good person from zealotry, as it keeps the law from the pursuit of moral purity, particularly by requiring respect for the private lives of citizens.[123]

An official must exercise prudence, that form of practical wisdom that includes determining the best results in human affairs, the forecast of events by understanding the results in human affairs of certain causes in the law; it is the basis for conduct likely to bring that about. It takes many forms in the role of the official, not the least being care to create and enforce laws that promote the conduct or circumstances intended. In that sense, prudence demands a special form of knowledge, as discussed earlier.[124] But prudence is also the basis for action derived from that knowledge, as well as (perhaps even more importantly) the recognition of the forms of action that would impede the conduct or circumstances sought.

Illustrations of prudence are difficult, owing to the relatively inscrutable basis of judgments based on prudence. Still there are many. One illustration of prudence is the decision of Chief Justice Marshall in *Marbury v. Madison*,[125] one of the greatest of all judicial opinions.[126] The dispute before the Court was over a delicate question of politics: should the Court order the secretary of state to deliver a judicial commission to an appointee who was a political opponent of the secretary? The Court would have had a difficult time enforcing such

---

[120]   See Josef Pieper, *The Four Cardinal Virtues* (Richard Winston et al., trans.) (University of Notre Dame Press, 1966).

[121]   Cicero, *On Duties* (M. T. Griffin & E. M. Atkins, eds.) (*De Officiis*, Book III, v. 8) (Cambridge University Press, 1996).

[122]   As to tantrums by a two-year-old child: "You'll have to pick your battles." Winning every argument over a child's behavior and ability to control herself is self-defeating, leading the child "only to explode later." T. Berry Brazelton, M.D., and Joshua D. Sparrow, *Mastering Anger and Aggression: The Brazelton Way* 45 (Da Capo Press, 2005).

[123]   Illustrations of the dangers of imprudent law abound. See, for example, Barrington Moore, Jr., *Moral Purity and Persecution in History* (Princeton University Press, 2000).

[124]   Ignorance is an important basis for laws failing to achieve their ends, although it is by no means the only one. See Steven M. Gillon, *That's Not What We Meant to Do: Reform and Its Unintended Consequences in the Twentieth Century* (W. W. Norton & Company, 2000).

[125]   5 U.S. (1 Cranch) 137 (1803).

[126]   See Chapter 6 in George P. Fletcher and Steve Sheppard, *American Law in a Global Context: The Basics* (Oxford University Press, 2005).

a decree, but failing to rule on the questions alleged by the appointee would surrender much of the power of the Court to enforce the laws. Chief Justice Marshall's opinion, finding the ability of the Court to rule on the matter in general but not in this case owing to a defect in the statute granting jurisdiction, was a masterpiece of prudence.[127] On the one hand, it protected the Court's authority under the Constitution, yet on the other hand, it avoided a collision with an opposing executive that might have been disastrous.[128]

Prudence is not, however, merely good political skill by officials, and it is as easily seen in the successes of carefully drawn legislation, which produce the intended results. A superb example in that regard has been the success of the environmental statutes passed in the early 1970s, which were based on carefully examined science, with carefully set goals and finely tuned rules to pursue that balanced the protection of the environment with reasonable limits on business and private actions that harmed it.[129]

Truth: Truth is a commodity that is surprisingly hard for many people to agree upon, in part owing to the many ways in which the word is now employed. As an aspect of personal obligation, it is not the same as establishing the ultimate truth or falsity of a proposition, or even whether something is so well proved as to be able to be treated as true.[130] Rather, the personal nature of truth is that an individual should not act falsely. Truth is the presentation of information with authenticity and with a minimum of alteration of the data.

This form of personal obligation is one of the most telling in the law. It is the source of authenticity in judgments in disputes before the court. It is the basis for legislation, and perhaps most importantly, it is the basis for accurate political communication among officials and between officials and subjects. In this sense of truth, the official must act with candor and honesty, regarding both what is done in office and why.

A truthful official presents evidence without altering it for a preferred interpretation or result, letting the interpretations follow from the evidence and working as diligently as possible to interpret it in a manner that most establishes the historical, social, or scientific facts as they are in the world, not

---

[127] There are reasons to believe that, prudent as it may have been, Marshall saw the opinion as the correct application of the law. See *id.* 148–9. Yet the prudential view of the case remains seen as a deliberate goal. See, for example, Christopher L. Eisgruber, "Marbury, Marshall, and the Politics of Constitutional Judgment," 89 Virginia Law Review 1203 (2003).

[128] Granted, this result meant somewhat less to William Marbury, and in the name of prudence, Marshall might not be seen entirely to have managed a great degree of charity toward him. Yet, in some regard, Marbury reaped what he had sown, as he had the ability to pursue his claims in other courts but had not.

[129] See Richard J. Lazarus, *The Making of Environmental Law* (University of Chicago Press, 2004).

[130] For questions of truth in that regard, see Dennis Patterson, *Law and Truth* (Oxford University Press, 1996).

as they would be conveniently or politically established.[131] And, a truth-seeking official expects other officials to do likewise.

One of the most compelling narratives in this regard comes at the end of Abby Mann's play *Judgment at Nuremburg*, when the character of Judge Haywood, the American judge of a war crimes tribunal, meets the character Ernst Janning, the German judge who has confessed to his complicity in the legal atrocities of the Third Reich and been sentenced by Haywood. Janning seeks to exonerate himself for the false convictions he oversaw by depicting his efforts to ameliorate the worst excesses of the regime and by suggesting that the collapse of justice was unforeseeable when he began. Haywood stops him, noting that, "It came to that the first time you sentenced to death a man you knew to be innocent."[132]

Humility: Humility is understanding one's true limitations, whether in the person as a whole or in one's beliefs, actions, or knowledge. It is a rejection of arrogance and certitude, a particular willingness to question oneself and one's beliefs. "When men are most sure and arrogant they are commonly most mistaken, giving views to passion without that proper deliberation which alone can secure them from the grossest absurdities."[133] It is the corollary to equality and closely related to charity. It is more than avoiding the limelight or fame. To exercise humility is not to debase oneself toward others but to keep a respectful relationship toward all, and not to seek more than one is due. It is the essence of civility and of good manners.[134] It is the basis for understanding the limits of our knowledge.[135]

Humility is the hallmark of a good official.[136] In an official it is the constant reminder that the office exists to serve others. Officials do not own their offices, but exercise them on behalf of the whole legal system. Both as to citizens and as to other officials, the particular holder of an office is constantly limited by the obligation to respect others, and quite often to charitably privilege

---

[131] The dangers of our inclination to falsify facts and abandon principles to avoid the belief that we are doing wrong is explored in David Luban, "Integrity in the Practice of Law: Integrity: Its Causes and Cures," 72 Fordham Law Review 279, 309 (2003).

[132] Abby Mann, *Judgment at Nuremburg* 110 (New Directions, 2002). The convictions of countless innocents in German courts during this period are chronicled in Ingo Müller, *Hitler's Justice: The Courts of the Third Reich* (Deborah Schneider, trans.) (Harvard University Press, 1991); see also the invaluable work in Michael Stolleis, *The Law under the Swastika: Studies on Legal History in Nazi Germany* (Thomas Dunlap, trans.) (University of Chicago Press, 1998).

[133] David Hume, *Enquiry into the Principles of Morals* 78 (Chapter 9) (J. B. Schneewind, ed.) (Hackett Publishing, 1983).

[134] See, for example P. M. Forni, *Choosing Civility: The Twenty-Five Rules of Considerate Conduct* (St. Martin's Press, 2003); Stephen L. Carter, *Civility* (Harper Perennial, 1999).

[135] David Cooper, *The Measure of Things: Humanism, Humility, and Mystery* (Oxford University Press, 2002).

[136] See Suzanna Sherry, "Judges of Character," 38 Wake Forest Law Review 793 (2003).

their interests or actions above the official's. In particular, humility in this context requires an awareness of the limits of the official's role, the limits of discretion, when that role intrudes into others. Most of all, officials must be aware of themselves as beholden to the subjects of the law, the stakeholders of the law.

The humble official recognizes that she or he is as likely to be wrong as anyone else, no matter how confident the official is in an opinion or belief. A humble official therefore questions beliefs and knowledge, no matter how certain. Good officials act with skepticism toward every belief of metaphysical truth, or of historical practical events, even if these claims are made by the official or other officials. This sense of humility must extend beyond the individual to the institution. No official can be certain that both that official and other officials have accurately assessed any situation, whether it is of fact or metaphysics, and so every effort must be made to increase the likelihood of an accurate assessment, including the consultation with others in decision-making. Most importantly for decisions that must be made concerning an historical fact, humility requires a great resistance to implying knowledge from incomplete evidence, as well as a requirement to investigate all possible evidence from which a factual inquiry might proceed.

The humble official will not usurp the authority of other officials, particularly when such a usurpation is for the usurper's personal benefit or the benefit of a group of allies such as a political party. Humility requires respect for other roles of officials in the legal system. There may, however, be authentic demands of action and courage requiring an enlargement of authority beyond the limits of office, and this might not be a question of humility. The fact of an arrogation of power raises concerns that can only be resolved for each of us by our approval or disapproval of the risk that is taken.

The most important question when an official enlarges the role of an office is what ends are to be promoted by the increase in the role of the office. What is the purpose of the adventure beyond the role's prior boundaries? If it is for an improper purpose, such as to benefit the officeholder, or to embarrass a political rival, or to promote the private benefit of some at the expense of others, or if it is to limit the access of some citizen to justice, the impropriety is compounded. If it is to protect some fundamental value of the law, such as fairness or equality of treatment, or the prevention of an unwarranted harm to a citizen, then the protection can validate the official's extension of the role of the office.

There are all too many illustrations of officials acting without humility, but two here will suffice to illustrate different aspects of the problem. First, as to the humility requiring truth in motives.

In the 1880s, the white members of the San Francisco Board of Supervisors adopted an ordinance regulating laundries, one of the few businesses in the city that were open to Chinese laborers.[137] The law prohibited laundries located in wooden buildings without the consent of the Board, but laundries in brick or stone buildings needed no approval. The Board presented a law that on its face appeared intended to combat fires, yet the real purpose was to limit Chinese competition with Anglo-run laundries. The Supreme Court overturned the ordinance based on the real motive and not on its facial purpose.[138] While this is an illustration of the value of truth, it is also an illustration of the value of humility. Had the San Francisco Board members been humble toward their own subjects, they would have admitted what they were doing, and they would have said why. If they were unwilling to do so, they ought not to have presented false evidence to others of what they had done.

Another example is one of usurpation. Although officials may alter their discretion from time to time, it is incumbent on each to respect the authority of others. In 1999, when the question of impeachment of President Clinton came before the House and later the Senate, party leaders attempted to influence the vote on impeachment along partisan lines. No one appears to have been more forceful in attempting to persuade Republican members of the House to send articles of impeachment than the majority whip, Representative Tom DeLay. His persistent lobby, apparently based as often on claims to party loyalty as on any other ground, was influential in delivering a party-line vote to commence impeachment.[139]

Such actions by a party whip had long been accepted in matters of party-line voting on legislation, yet this was different. In lobbying his colleagues to find cause to impeach the president for high crimes and misdemeanors, DeLay was doing what, in another context, would amount to importuning a grand juror.[140] The constitutional framework of impeachment leaves to members of

---

[137] Owing to labor restrictions, Chinese immigrants tended to concentrate in certain businesses. Chinese labor was 97 percent of the cigar-makers in San Francisco, 84 percent of the boot- and shoemakers, 88 percent of garment-makers, and 89 percent of laundry workers. See Sarah H. Cleveland, "Powers Inherent in Sovereignty: Indians, Aliens, Territories, and the Nineteenth Century Origins of Plenary Power over Foreign Affairs," 81 Texas Law Review 1 (2002).

[138] *Yick Wo v. Hopkins*, 118 U.S. 356 (1886).

[139] See, for example, Peter Baker, *The Breach: Inside the Impeachment and Trial of William Jefferson Clinton* (Scribner, 2000); Gebe Martinez & Jackie Koszcuk, "Tom DeLay: 'The Hammer' That Drives the House GOP," Congressional Quarterly (June 5, 1999); Nicol C. Rae & Colton C. Campbell, *Impeaching Clinton: Partisan Strife on Capitol Hill* (University of Kansas Press, 2004); Frank Sesno & Jeanne Meserve, "Just in Time: The Big Push to Impeach," CNN Newsday, December 7, 1998, Transcript 98120702V11.

[140] "Whoever . . . by any threatening letter or communication, endeavors to influence, intimidate, or impede any grand or petit juror . . . , or by any threatening letter or communication, influences, obstructs, or impedes, or endeavors to influence, obstruct, or impede, the due administration of justice, shall be [imprisoned for not less than ten years]." 18 U.S.C. § 1503 (2007). Threatening a grand juror has been an offense for a very long time. See *U.S. v. Caton*, 1 Cranch C.C. 150, 25 F.Cas. 350 (C.D.C. 1803).

the houses of Congress the obligation to determine to impeach, and no other official should have attempted to intrude on that obligation. This is not to say that discussion and persuasion of views regarding the sufficiency of the charges, the meaning of Article I or the nature of the evidence was not in order, but lobbying according to partisan identity is to intrude too far upon another office and amount to a breach of humility.

Action: Action is the basis of human conduct, and it is integral to the judgment of others. To understand that there is a duty can alone never determine whether it is fulfilled.[141] Whether we act or fail to act when action is required is the fundamental basis for judgment of the performance of any moral duty. Action requires persistence and commitment to complete the action once commenced, although this aspect of action may lead to conflict with prudence.[142]

The official is uniquely charged with action. The moral standard of care in determining whether an official has performed the duties given is not what the official has done but what the official has allowed to occur.[143]

In some ways, the obligation of action is the corollary to the obligation of humility. Decisions must be made, even in the absence of sufficient evidence to confidently make one, and those cases when we know information is incomplete may remind us of the false appearance of knowledge in the others. Action must be taken at times without sufficient knowledge, or preparation, to avert worsening circumstances. Delay may well cheat justice as much as any other cause.[144]

The active official determines when a decision is needed and is prepared to make it when necessary. The active official performs the duty that is expected in office, not shunning this responsibility for others. The active official does not allow procedure to overwhelm substance, so that activity takes the place of action.

There are countless narratives by which action, or its opposite, can be assessed. One of the greatest failure of action in any time was the near-abdication of action by members of the German parliament during Adolf Hitler's leadership of Germany. The Reichstag simply passed an Enabling Act,

[141] See, for example, Benedetto Croce, *Philosophy of the Practical: Economic and Ethic* (Douglas Ainslie, trans.) (Biblo and Tannen, 1969).
[142] The classic figure of Inspector Javert demonstrates the danger of excessive zeal in action. See Victor Hugo, *Les Misérables* (1862) (Signet, 1987).
[143] This standard, which used to be common in military courts martial for dereliction of duty, is now still found in administrative reviews of failures of policing. See, for example, Norma Jean Almodovar, "For Their Own Good: The Results of the Prostitution Laws as Enforced by Cops, Politicians and Judges," 11 George Mason Law Review 609 (2003).
[144] "To no one will we delay right and justice." Magna Carta, from paragraph 39.

delegating its powers to the executive, approving such measures as were brought to it.[145] Likewise, one of the great failures to act in judgment was narrated in the decision by Pontius Pilate to render Jesus, then a criminal defendant charged with sedition, for punishment. Although Pilate, believing there was no proof against Jesus, could have freed him and barred further trial, he chose the apparently politic route of transferring the prisoner to a more aggressive court, which convicted him.[146] After doing so, according to Matthew, Pilate declared, "I am innocent of this man's blood; you will see."[147] And yet, he was not. He could have acted to save the life of the innocent under his jurisdiction, and because he failed to do so, Pilate remains one of the hated figures of history.[148]

Laws can provide sham bases for inaction when there is an inescapable moral demand for action. For instance, in some of the signal events of the American civil rights movement, a failure of action by officials led to horrible failures to shield those in grave need of protection. In 1957, for example, Dwight Eisenhower ordered soldiers to enforce the federal integration orders for Little Rock, Arkansas, during the integration of Central High School. But he would not extend the soldiers' protection to the individuals whose lives

---

[145]   The Ermächtigungsgesetz of March 23, 1933, was entitled the "Law to Remove the Distress of People and State." As signed by von Hindenberg, it provided:

> Article 1. National laws can be enacted by the National Cabinet [Reich Cabinet] as well as in accordance with the procedure established in the Constitution. . . .
>
> Article 2. The national laws enacted by the National Cabinet may deviate from the Constitution so far as they do not affect the position of the Reichstag and the National Council. The powers of the President remain undisturbed. . . .
>
> Article 4. Treaties of the Reich with foreign states which concern matters of national legislation do not require the consent of the bodies participating in legislation. The National Cabinet is empowered to issue the necessary provisions for the execution of these treaties.

> Law to Remove the Distress of People and Reich (Enabling Act); reprinted in U.S. Department of State, Division of European Affairs, *National Socialism. Basic Principles, Their Application by the Nazi Party's Foreign Organizations, and the Use of Germans Abroad for Nazi Aims.* Washington, D.C.: U.S. Government Printing Office, 1943, Appendix, Document 11, pp. 217–18. This simple delegation of legislative authority to the executive was similar to other statutes passed in the development of twentieth-century fascism. See, for example, Peter L. Lindseth, "The Paradox of Parliamentary Supremacy: Delegation, Democracy, and Dictatorship in Germany and France, 1920s–1950s," 113 Yale Law Journal 1341 (2004).

[146]   The trials of Jesus in the Gospels are well known. See particularly Luke 23, Mark 27, and John 19.

[147]   Mathew 27:24.

[148]   Perhaps unjustly. See Ann Wroe, *Pontius Pilate: The Biography of an Invented Man* (Modern Library, 2001).

were under constant threat in the same town, while the police stayed idle despite beatings, bombings, and daily assaults. Taking refuge behind a claim of federalism, he ignored pleas for help from civil rights workers and allowed the terrorism, backed by local police and officials, to continue. Despite the impressive array of executive authority to enforce judicial orders and federal statutes ensuring civil rights and public order, the president's assistant merely stated, "The matter seems to be one within the exclusive jurisdiction of local authorities."[149]

Other examples are more mundane, though in their very ordinariness they demonstrate the persistent need for careful and deliberate but speedy and resolute action in everyday action throughout the legal system.[150] The narrative of the horrible case of *Jarndyce v. Jarndyce* in Charles Dickens's *Bleak House*,

---

[149] Following the arrest on trumped-up charges by the Arkansas state police of all of Daisy Bates's bodyguards, she wired President Eisenhower:

> Dear Mr. President, Despite repeated bombings, attacks by gunfire, and rocks, and other assaults on our home – attacks provoked by the fact that we have stood steadfast for this community's compliance with the federal law – both local and federal authorities have declined to provide protection that we have requested. Now state police have begun to arrest and harass the upstanding citizens who have provided us with volunteer protection, leaving us defenseless before those who constantly threaten our lives. I appeal to you, Mr. President, to provide the basic protection that will give us the freedom from fear to which citizens of our free American society are entitled.

The response from Gerald D. Morgan, deputy assistant to the president, was:

> Your telegram of August thirteenth to the President is acknowledged. Although matters seems to be one within the exclusive jurisdiction of local authorities the president has referred your telegram to the Department of Justice from which I am sure it will receive prompt and appropriate action.

No action or further communication ever followed. Daisy Bates, *The Long Shadow of Little Rock* 179 (University of Arkansas Press, 1987).

[150] The classic administrative position is to avoid action. The narrative below is between the characters of Sir Humphrey Appleby and Sir Richard Wharton, describing the four stages of avoiding action employed historically by the British Foreign Office.

Stage One
We say that nothing is going to happen.

Stage Two
We say that something may be going to happen but we should do nothing about it.

Stage Three
We say that maybe we should do something about it, but there's nothing we can do.

Stage Four
We say that maybe there was something we could have done but it's too late now.

Jonathan Lynn & Anthony Jay (eds.), *Yes Prime Minister: The Diaries of the Right Hon. James Hacker* 160 (Salem House Publishers, 1988).

perhaps too typical of the Chancery Court of the nineteenth century, stands still as a reminder of the danger that procedure poses to resolution.[151]

Courage: Courage is in some regard an aspect of action. It is the ability to act despite fear of the consequences of the action. It is often thought to be a physical as much as mental virtue.[152] Yet the fundamental questions of moral courage are measured by whether a person fulfills a moral duty when there is a price to pay in doing so, whether the price is in physical pain or in political opportunity, social prestige, or other lost opportunity.

In popular narratives, official courage is often seen in the form of the official who acts even at the risk of unpopularity, loss of office, or even personal harm. The archetype is the heroic official facing down the lynch mob.[153]

The realities of courage in more mundane circumstances are, thankfully, at hand as examples. One of the most significant was the willingness of officials who were not personally overly sympathetic to the plaintiffs of civil rights cases, but whose duty and courage were essential to the success of those cases. Richard Taylor Rives, Elbert P. Tuttle, John R. Brown, and John Minor Wisdom, judges sitting on the Fifth Circuit Court of Appeals, which had jurisdiction then over the entire deep South, ruled consistently in accord with the Supreme Court's precedent, opening lunch counters, public schools and pools, and countless other facilities, despite great hostility from their neighbors, friends, and families.[154] That type of courage is essential to every official.

Personal Virtue and Personal Morality: Personal virtues as discussed earlier – prudence, truth, knowledge, action, and courage – differ from the more commonly encountered ideas of personal morality, which in the United States seem largely to be matters related to sex, drugs and alcohol, and the use of other people's money. The question is sometimes a dubious game of politics in which a private weakness is exploited for the political gain of others, but there may be underlying questions of whether the personal immorality affects personal virtues, or otherwise an unethical act unrelated to office can influence an aspect of a moral obligation related to the office, rather than to the private life of the individual alone.

---

[151] Charles Dickens, *Bleak House: An Authoritative and Annotated Text, Illustrations, A Note on the Text, Genesis and Composition, Backgrounds, Criticism* (Norton, 1977). See also G. K. Chesterton, *Charles Dickens* (Strauss, 2001).

[152] See William Ian Miller, *The Mystery of Courage* (Harvard University Press, 2002).

[153] For this, see *To Kill a Mockingbird* (Robert Mulligan, director) (1962).

[154] Jack Bass, "John Minor Wisdom and the Impact of Law," 69 Mississippi Law Journal 25 (1999); Jack Bass, *Unlikely Heroes: The Dramatic Story of the Southern Judges of the Fifth Circuit Who Translated the Supreme Court's Brown Decision into a Revolution for Equality* (University of Alabama Press, 1990).

There is no exact answer to this question, no boundary between what is truly private and what is truly a matter of office. Some aspects are obviously immoral acts of office that also violate the law, such as the violation of law in office or the use of one's office to further immoral private conduct or to hide it from others.[155] More often, the question is one of conduct that does not directly involve the office or its duties, but is conduct that might be the basis of offense or of moral judgment, such as a case of adultery, or the use of illegal drugs, or participating in an abortion. Some people find such actions proof of immorality and would condemn the participant, office notwithstanding. Others see no immorality here at all. Others yet see these acts as the basis for disqualification from office.

From the perspective here developed, no one answer among these is required, but each case must be considered as one of degree, and the responses to immoral actions assessed primarily because of their damage to the law as an institution and to the individuals who must be governed by law, and on the degree to which the action harms the trust people must have in their officials as a whole. These may vary according to differing values in the culture, but at some level they may reveal a degree of hypocrisy, untrustworthiness, or unreliability that cannot but damage these institutional goals.

Institutional Obligations

As well as personal obligations, the official has institutional obligations, which arise as a result of the role occupied in the legal system. Institutional obligations arise both from express oaths and from the implied moral expectation that one who accepts a role within an institution will exercise that role with loyalty to the institution and fidelity to its purposes. These ideas, particularly those of implication, have attracted much debate in the literature recently, notably the discussions based on Dworkin's arguments of fidelity and Fletcher's arguments of loyalty.[156] There are, however, much older arguments than these recent debates, and some consideration of the problem of loyalty by Royce and Lieber and of fidelity in the arguments arising from the higher law tradition also inform this discussion.

Carrying Out the Duties of Office

At a minimum, moral obligations within the legal system require a duty to carry out one's defined legal obligations in the office one holds. This is, after all, the duty most central to the acceptance of the role and the oath with which

---

[155] See the section entitled "Obedience to the Law as a Citizen."
[156] See Ronald Dworkin, *Freedom's Law: The Moral Reading of the American Constitution* (Harvard University Press, 1996); George Fletcher, *Loyalty: An Essay on the Morality of Relationships* (Oxford University Press, 1995).

it is entered. Within that obligation is an obligation to use one's best efforts to carry out one's duties, even if such an obligation might meet the resistance of bureaucratic inertia. Such an obligation of best efforts does not mean that the official must carry out every possible duty in the manner of the popular television icon of the overzealous policeman, but it does mean that each official has a duty to initiate official conduct within the scope of that official's discretion when that conduct will further the purposes of the law.

The scope of this duty ought to be defined in a manner that justifies the respect of other officials for its performance. In other words, each official ought to act so as to justify the humility of the other officials. This leads to a fundamental requirement of each official to carry out their duties well, with respect for the rule of law. It is seen in an obligation of best efforts to perform the jobs assigned by the rules of law, in the light of the needs of the subjects and officials brought with one's jurisdiction. It is the sense in which public office is a public trust.[157]

Obedience to the Law as a Citizen

Officials cannot be, or be seen to be, above the law. It is essential that the same standards that govern the citizen govern the official, and that the official be held to task for them. As Theodore Roosevelt wrote, in a note about the regulation of monopolies and trusts, but that he would have considered unquestionably applicable to officials as well:

> No man is above the law and no man is below it; nor do we ask any man's permission when we require him to obey it. Obedience to the law is demanded as a right; not asked as a favor.[158]

Nor could it be otherwise. If the officials disregard the law, why should the people obey it? The obligation to obey the law represents a moral commitment to the institution that one has chosen to serve and to its claims that its rules bind everyone.

There are, to be certain, a wide range of violations of this obligation. We do not imagine that an official commits the same level of moral breach by, say, speeding on the highway, or even breaking laws regarding adultery, that we would if the official used the powers of office to avoid punishment or

---

[157] This was a campaign slogan of Grover Cleveland in 1884, and he wove it into the opening of his first inaugural address. "In the exercise of their power and right of self-government they have committed to one of their fellow-citizens a supreme and sacred trust, and he here consecrates himself to their service." U.S. Congressional Budget Office, *Inaugural Addresses of the Presidents of the United States* (1989).

[158] Theodore Roosevelt, "Message to Congress, December 7, 1903," reprinted in Joseph Bishop, 1 *Theodore Roosevelt and His Time Shown in His Own Letters* 258 (Charles Scribner's Sons, 1920).

committed crimes that directly affected the office the official holds. Even this sense of relationship can be a matter of nuance and proportion.

An official who commits the conduct that official was sworn to prevent diminishes the confidence that others would have in the justness of the prohibition and in the fairness of its prosecution. For instance, whereas the use of prostitutes might be thought to be a generally private matter, even when committed by a state official, it amounts to official hypocrisy when the official, Eliot Spitzer, had been a prosecutor who had charged prostitutes and their clients.[159] Such a direct relationship between official duty and private offense is hardly required for the citizen to perceive contempt for the law.

Rather famously, an official might lie about committing adultery, and both the infidelity to the official's marriage and the private lie would be considered generally immoral, yet of a rather minor sort of immorality and only marginally related to the obligations of office. Yet the moral stakes increased dramatically when the official, Bill Clinton, repeated the lie in a court proceeding under oath.[160]

We cannot expect legal officials to be saints. There are many trivial private acts, even some that violate the laws, that fall into the realm of minor immorality. Yet there is a considerably greater immorality in an official's conduct that violates the law and demonstrates contempt for law itself, a willingness to use one's office for personal advantage under the law, or that demonstrates a willingness to hold citizens to a standard that the official will not abide personally.

Promoting Truth and Law over Officials and Superiors

The official has a duty to the long-term success of the institutions of the law. Actions that diminish the habits of obedience to the rules of those institutions by citizens or officials are wrong for this reason. Such loyalty sometimes appears to conflict with a duty of honesty, but only in the short term. The official must place commitment to the institution's long-term success above other commitments, including the political success of incumbent officials. The long-term success of the institution is invariably served by the truth. It was the failure to distinguish the loyalty to the institution from the much lesser duty

---

[159] See Michael Powell and Nicholas Confessore, "4 Arrests, Then 6 Days to a Resignation," New York Times (March 13, 2008). Mr. Spitzer was active in prosecuting prostitution rings as New York Attorney General. See Jake Mooney, "A 2004 Prostitution Case, Viewed in a New Light," New York Times (City Room) (March 14, 2008), particularly increasing penalties for clients. See Nina Bernstein, "Foes of Sex Trade Are Stung by the Fall of an Ally," New York Times (March 12, 2008).

[160] See *Jones v. Clinton*, 36 F.Supp. 2d 1118 (E.D. Ark.,1999) (Wright, J). Judge Wright properly found that the president's false statements under oath were distinct in their contempt of court, and the remedy for contempt was for different reasons, from the proceedings based on perjury of which he was acquitted in impeachment. *Id.* 1124.

of loyalty to superiors that led to the case of Albert Dreyfus, one of the great examples of modern injustice, even in military law.

In Dreyfus's case, a court-martial was quick to convict a French intelligence officer of espionage, based on little evidence beyond his Jewish identity, leaving a spy among the French general staff. Rather than admit the truth of Dreyfus's innocence, of which there was much evidence, French army lawyers kept him on Devil's Island for twelve years. The scandal over the cover-up was, perhaps, greater than the outrage at the injustice or the reaction to the army's preference to continue harboring a spy, a major named Esterhazy who was only caught two years after Dreyfus's court-martial.[161] That the Dreyfus affair nearly brought down the government of France might have been a warning to White House officials who covered up their subordinate's illegal acts in the Watergate Hotel,[162] but the lessons from both events remain: officials have a moral obligation to the institution of the law to disclose and repudiate official misconduct.

Fidelity to the Purposes of Law

Other aspects of a duty arising from office are more contested. One of the most important but most argued is fidelity to the basic principles of the legal system. The first requirement of fulfilling such a role requires a prudent evaluation of what ought to be the law's fundamental values about the human in society that are promoted by law. Although it would be convenient to assume that these are obvious, or logical, or fixed, that does not appear to be true. At one time, it would have been law's fundamental value to protect the monarchy, at another to protect the church, at another to uphold slavery, or at least an oligarchic sense underlying both imperialism abroad and manifest destiny at home. Nor is it enough to look to progress or the improvement of the human being or even the human condition, for that way once held the promise of sterilization for eugenics.[163] The answer is not to be had through faith in either progress or tradition. It is the object of genuine controversy. That is as it must be, and

---

[161] See Alfred Dreyfus, *The Dreyfus Case* (Yale University Press, 1937); Jean-Denis Bredin, *The Affair: The Case of Alfred Dreyfus* (Braziller, 1986). The heroes of the case, military prosecutor Lt. Col Picquart and Emile Zola, whose article challenged the high command, were unaware that the evidence fabricated against Dreyfus may have been an absurd military intelligence plan. See Gen. Andre Bach, *L'armée de Dreyfus. Une Histoire Politique de L'armée Française de Charles X a L'Affaire* (Tallandire, 2004). A surprisingly good movie, *Prisoner of Honor* (Ken Russell, director, 1991), seems to have relied a bit on David Levering Lewis's excellent *Prisoners of Honor: The Dreyfus Affair* (William Morrow, 1974).

[162] See Carl Bernstein & Bob Woodward, *All the President's Men* (Simon & Schuster, 1974); –, *The Final Days* (2d ed.) (Simon & Schuster; 1994); Fred Emery, *Watergate* (Touchstone, 1995).

[163] See Edwin Black, *War against the Weak: Eugenics and America's Campaign to Create a Master Race* (Four Walls, Eight Windows, 2003).

perhaps as it should be.[164] From such controversy has emerged a commitment to the recognition of equal human dignity. From it has emerged the balances among equality and freedom, peace and security, wealth and welfare.[165]

Fidelity in the Practice of Law

One group of legal officials in the United States has a unique division of responsibility, both to serve as officers of the courts and to serve as representatives of their clients. Lawyers have a moral obligation of fidelity to the institutions of the law, both in their dealings with their clients and in their dealings with others on their clients' behalf.

Faith in law requires the lawyer to be honest in describing the law and what it requires and in ensuring that the client acts lawfully not only toward the courts and the institutions of the state, but also toward rivals and those whom the client might disadvantage in violation of the law. This form of fidelity is described in many forms, not the least as civility among lawyers. It does not conflict with zealous advocacy of a client's interests, because zealousness cannot exceed the bounds of legal obligation.

There are many – too many – illustrations of lawyers who fail the institutions of law by breaching this moral obligation. Lawyers who file lawsuits or who file their defenses without knowing or caring whether the facts they've asserted or rejected are true or false. Lawyers who permit material evidence to be hidden from the courts and from their opponents. Lawyers who use delay to frustrate the settlement of lawful debts and claims. Lawyers who lie or promote the lies of their clients to save their client's money. Lawyers who give their clients bad advice, because they fail to learn the facts of the client's situation or the law that would apply to it. Lawyers who just do not do the work required to know enough or act skillfully enough to represent their clients and do right by the other litigants and the court. None of these is uncommon. None of these should be tolerated, either as violations of law or, more fundamentally, as violations of the lawyer's moral obligations to the institutions of the law.[166]

---

[164] See Stuart Hampshire, *Justice Is Conflict* (Princeton University Press, 2001).

[165] See George P. Fletcher, *Our Secret Constitution: How Lincoln Redefined American Democracy* (Oxford University Press, 2003).

[166] An early draft of this section had nine fat notes, each with two or three examples for the statements in the text. I've removed them because I wish to avoid the impression they give that Hell is other people, that somehow lawyers elsewhere, punished and lost on appeal, have done these things. The reader should have a greater sense of immediacy than that. If you need examples, see Howard Brill, *Arkansas Professional and Judicial Ethics* (7th ed.) (M&M Press, 2006), or Deborah L. Rhode and David Luban, *Legal Ethics* (4th ed.) (Foundation Press, 2004). I doubt you will need examples. I gave a CLE talk on this section to a hundred or so members of a local bar recently, and all of them were looking at their shoes pretty quickly when I worked through a similar list.

Procedural Obligations: Fairness in Creation, Application, Change, and Practice

There is a particular type of role obligation that applies to officials whose duties give them special responsibilities over procedures in the law. These obligations relate to the means by which officials carry out the law. According to these obligations, officials must exercise the care necessary to ensure that the rules are made and enforced fairly. These obligations of officials to ensure procedural fairness require many of the aspects of the exercise of law made famous by Lon Fuller in his debate with H. L. A. Hart.[167] Fuller's arguments for inner morality are not here presented as arguments defining law but as obligations of legal officials.[168] This is expressly a manner in which he sought not to present his theory, and yet, as suggested to Fuller by Leo Strauss, these arguments make strong claims to bind officials as a moral proposition.[169] One can describe these duties as obligations of fairness in the creation and application of the law.

From that perspective, officials have an obligation to ensure that the law is universal – that it is not a private matter favoring or hindering one person alone, but the burdens fall upon all in the state. Officials must ensure that law is fair among citizens in its creation and in its application. Officials must ensure that legal obligations for citizens are established with certainty, with as little ambiguity as possible, and with as much consistency over time as practicable. Officials must ensure that citizens can follow a legal obligation without undue hardship. And the official must ensure that they can do so without contradiction by other laws. Officials cannot act in secret. The law must be established with public notice, to apply prospectively, in a comprehensible manner. It is wrong of officials to create secret laws, unintelligible laws, or unpredictable laws. Officials must ensure that the laws do not change so often as to confuse the subject or so quickly that the subject is taken by surprise. To these, we might add an obligation of equity. Officials must at times relax procedures and must create new rules when necessary to prevent or right

---

[167] See H. L. A. Hart, "Positivism and the Separation of Law and Morals," 71 Harvard Law Review 593 (1958); Lon L. Fuller, "Positivism and Fidelity to Law – A Reply to Professor Hart," 71 Harvard Law Review 630 (1958).

[168] See Lon L. Fuller, *The Morality of Law* (Yale University Press, 1964). For a later attempt to present a similar position against positivism, see Robert Alexy, *The Argument from Injustice: A Reply to Legal Positivism* (Stanley L. Paulson & Bonnie L. Paulson, trans.) (Oxford University Press, 2002). Alexy argues that legal systems always reflect morality as a social fact, in an argument not unlike Dworkin's. See Ronald Dworkin, *Law's Empire* (Duckworth, 1977). But Fuller, despite the seeming failure of his argument to overcome Hart's objection, gives us more satisfying fare with his eight specific claims he believes morals must make on the law.

[169] Letter of Leo Strauss to Lon L. Fuller (Harvard University Library, Fuller Papers, Red Set).

a wrong. This is not to suggest that equity is without procedures or that it encourages new rules, but that the nature of equity is to moderate the injustice that is created by the unforeseen application of law to a new circumstance or to an unusual case.

Substantive Obligations

All the theories of justice are far beyond the scope of this paper, and yet it is clear, in the light of the idea of moral obligations that have been developed thus far, that the arguments as to what is just are, by definition, arguments about what officials ought to make law. The nature of the law, as guarantor of the shield, arm of the sword, and frame of the balance, guide, and mirror, requires that all arguments about how these effects will be carried out in people's lives, or altered, are in fact arguments about how officials define and perform their duties. Who among legal officials responds to one or another form of argument is often an important question given the structure of a legal system, and yet that someone must act is still essential for any meaningful argument for justice to be reflected in law. Thus, arguments from the right and the good, for liberty and equality, for safety and order, for prosperity and opportunity, for tradition and custom, all are brought to legal officials in one form or another as claims that they are obligated to fulfill. The sword, shield, balance, mirror, and guide can only be morally justified if certain conditions of justice are pursued. For instance, the shield's monopoly of force cannot be justified unless subjects are protected from violence at the hands of other subjects.

Evolving Obligations

One of the great achievements of the modern state is to enshrine in the law protections not just of the rulers from the subjects, and of the subjects from one another, but of the subjects from the rulers. Indeed these protections have grown truly universal, moving to erase millennial barriers and stigma that have deprived individuals of freedom and dignity for no reason other than race, caste, gender, color, or religion.

The justifications for law must respect the stakes of all of those subject to the law. They balance the need for the shield and the sword among subjects of the law, they ensure fair use of the balance and reflect a high ideal in the mirror and the guide. These justifications are that the law's purposes are to ensure freedom of the subject, equality of treatment among subjects, and official obedience to the procedures of law as well as to freedom and equality. Such once-novel propositions are now enshrined in the Constitution of the United

States, the Charter of Fundamental Rights of the European Union, and other basic laws of modern states, as well as charters and treaties that bind states themselves, such as the Charters of the International Military Tribunals, the Geneva Conventions, the Convention against Torture, and the Rome Treaty establishing the International Criminal Court.

There are those who argue whether the states enshrined a further set of justifications that ensure the safety of the human environment and an economic subsistence for all subjects. Such propositions are enshrined in most countries' domestic laws and are recognized in more contentious international agreements, such as the Rio Framework Convention on Climate Change.

The United States has taken pride since before its founding in its special place in human history as a refuge for the individual and as a bastion for the protection of human dignity. Here, we believe that the people's will should flourish, instituted by the people's servants through laws that protect the equal dignity of all. Recognizing our errors in the disenfranchisement of people by race and gender, we understand that our view of the more perfect union has evolved and will continue to evolve; indeed it must change to ensure the participation of all in the legal system.[170]

The quest, then, is to ensure that the U.S. legal system protects its most valued traditions of freedom and due process, while incorporating evolving standards of decency.[171] It is hardly easy to identify or apply a standard as it changes, but it is essential for the law to do more than just keep pace with the moral expectations of the subjects whose stakes are invested in the legal system. Officials must guide those standards, protecting the freedoms and dignity of the individual that ultimately justify the law, indeed the entire democratic exercise.[172] This is what Abraham Lincoln meant when he hoped that the government would be protected by "the better angels of our nature."[173]

The framers of the Constitution well understood that the better angels of our nature could not in fact be trusted to prevent a tyrant from arising

---

[170]   This idea is beautifully captured in Stephen Breyer, *Active Liberty: Interpreting Our Democratic Constitution* (Vintage, 2005).

[171]   In *Stanford v. Kentucky*, 492 U.S. 361, 369 (1988), the Court held that a national consensus on the use of the death penalty could be found by analyzing patterns of legislation among the states to ascertain evolving standards of decency.

[172]   See Nigel Simmonds, *Law as a Moral Idea* (Oxford University Press, 2007), advancing the neo-Lockean idea, though drawn from Hobbes and Kant, that the only meaningful justification for laws is to promote the freedom from the will of others. As for equal dignity, justice, and freedom as the justification of democracy, see Bill Moyers, *Moyers on Democracy* (Doubleday, 2008); Paul Fairfield, *Why Democracy?* (SUNY Press, 2008). For the idea that democracy is much more based upon networks of trust, which themselves depend on equality, see Charles Tilly, *Democracy* (Cambridge University Press, 2007).

[173]   Abraham Lincoln, "First Inaugural Address, March 4, 1861," 4 *Collected Works of Abraham Lincoln* 271 (Roy P. Basler, ed.) (Rutgers University Press, 1953).

from among our officials, unless the government was so crafted that other officials held tools with which to prevent such a tyrant from emerging. These tools included the power of democratic election, a tool that then became both assurance and assured as an aspect of government, that is a tool assured by other tools dividing the powers of government so that no usurper of the authority of other officials should go long without being checked by both the limits of office and the powers of others.

The Special Obligations of the People as Sovereign

In a nation such as the United States, which claims a democratic sovereign, justice is the responsibility of its citizenry. When officials cannot or will not pursue their moral obligations, at some point it becomes the obligation of each citizen to demand such justice from the officials. From this obligation can come not only a right but also an obligation to reject the individual officials who will not provide moral action through law and to refuse to elect or reelect them. In extreme cases, this obligation requires a rejection of the authority of the government. This is precisely what led the founders of the United States to rebel against the British state, a rebellion whose cause American legal officials forget to the peril not only of themselves but also of their subjects, that cause being first the actual representation of the will of the people in laws, to ensure that the private lives of the common people are not destroyed by the privileges of aristocracy. Ultimately, this cause, which was expressed in the bill of particulars of the Declaration of Independence, was to be protected by constitutional laws dividing the interests of the powerful officials for the protection of the citizenry, who held one collective power through suffrage, a power that has been extended through moves of successively inclusive and egalitarian definitions of citizenship.

The whole point of democracy as a source and assurance of the laws must be that the people have a duty to ensure the morality of their officials. Each voter has a duty to use the power of appointment to demand that elected officials behave morally, and each must see that their officials are not only moral in their own actions but also vigilant in ensuring the morality of the actions of their appointees. Otherwise, democracy itself is immoral.

The voters have their powers because they have the most to lose by allowing the officials to act immorally. The people fear the power of the sword abused or the shield denied; they need the balance, the coin, and the commons; they are shaped by the mirror and the staff; and they recognize the dangers and deceit that are posed by the veil. Yet Aristotle and many since have seen the risk of democracy losing its commitment to the law and becoming no more than a mob, a tyranny of many heads.

Daniel Defoe, the English novelist and pamphleteer, understood this well when he wrote:

> That all Men wou'd be Tyrants if they could.
> Not Kings alone, not Ecclesiastick pride,
> But *Parliaments* and all Mankind beside;
> All men, like Phaeton, would command the Reins,
> 'Tis only want of Power that restrains.[174]

From this perspective, it is senseless to expect moral restraint among power-mongers. Yet, Defoe did not expect this satirical conclusion to be the order of the day; both he and his successor, the author in the next generation of *Cato's Letters*, accepted that moral obligations have some influence against such impulses, and both recognized the moral necessity of a legal system that could indeed restrain by creating a want of power.[175] This recognition was well known in the founding generation.[176]

So it behooves us to consider what forms of restraint were embedded in the American legal order, and what result came from this recognition that the demands of the power-hungry require restraint. There are two basic forms of restraint, both political opportunities that are enshrined in legal obligations: election or appointment of officials, and division of labor.

The mob can demand power for itself as easily as a president can. The people can trade ease for justice as easily as a senator or a judge. Only a permanent commitment to law and to justice and to a constitutional order ensures the

---

[174] Daniel Defoe, *History of the Kentish Petition* (August 1701), reprinted in *The Shortest Way with the Dissenters and Other Pamphlets by Daniel Defoe* (Basil Blackwell, 1927). Defoe seems to have had the idea from a satire by Rochester, but in Defoe's setting, the line influenced the authors of *Cato's Letters* and remained current from Defoe's own writings for the revolutionary generation in North America.

[175] "I readily own what I have been proving, that Men are very bad where they dare, and that all Men would be Tyrants, and do what they please. But still let us preserve Justice and Equality in the world." 2 John Trenchard & Thomas Gordon, *Cato's Letters: Or Essays on Liberty, Civil and Religious and Other Important Subjects, Considerations on the Restless and Selfish Spirit of Man* (August 5, 1721) (No. 40) 55 (Liberty Fund, 1995).

[176] See, for instance the recognition expected of John Adams by Abigail.

> I long to hear that you have declared an independancy – and by the way in the new Code of Laws which I suppose it will be necessary for you to make I desire you would Remember the Ladies, and be more generous and favourable to them than your ancestors. Do not put such unlimited power into the hands of the Husbands. Remember all Men would be tyrants if they could. If perticuliar care and attention is not paid to the Laidies we are determined to foment a Rebelion, and will not hold ourselves bound by any Laws in which we have no voice, or Representation.

Letter, Abigail Adams to John Adams, March 31, 1776, 1 *Adams Family Correspondence* 370 (L. H. Butterfield, Wendell D. Garrett, & Marjorie E. Sprague, eds.) (Harvard University Press, 1963).

divisions of authority that can keep the will of a president in check, the powers of a judge or a bureaucrat focused on their jobs, and the will of the people dedicated to the common good. This is the justification not just of democracy but for governance, that through the security of good laws well administered, the people will secure for themselves and their posterity the blessings of liberty.

GOOD FAITH

This daunting list of obligations, already jostling one another for primacy, must all be understood through the lens of good faith: each official must have a bona fide sense that the goals they say they pursue – indeed the goals they believe they pursue – are the fundamental goals they actually pursue. It is all too easy to cloak a grasp for personal power in a seemingly charitable act, to claim the protection of a client's interests in order to drive up a client's fees.

Good faith is an ancient concept by which the conduct of those who would make obligations for themselves and for others must be judged.[177] It is an irreducible element of each and all of the moral obligations upon a legal official.

---

[177] See, for example, David J. Bederman, *International Law in Antiquity* (Cambridge University Press, 2001).

5

Patterns of Relationship between Legal and Moral Obligations

Thus it is the error of men who are not strictly upright to seize upon something that seems to be expedient and straightway to dissociate that from the question of moral right. To this error the assassin's dagger, the poisoned cup, the forged wills owe their origin; this gives rise to theft, embezzlement of public funds, exploitation and plundering of provincials and citizens; this engenders also the lust for excessive wealth, for despotic power, and finally for making oneself king even in the midst of a free people; and anything more atrocious or repulsive than such a passion cannot be conceived. For with a false perspective they see the material rewards but not the punishment – I do not mean the penalty of the law, which they often escape, but the heaviest penalty of all, their own demoralization.

Cicero, *On Duties*, Book III, Chapter VII[1]

If the obligations for an official to act are derived from both legal and nonlegal sources, then there will be at least some recurring patterns of interaction among the resulting obligations. This interaction sometimes presents an official with choices, particularly when different obligations would require inconsistent conduct. Any given choice can be quite complex, resulting from a variety of reasons or instincts that apply in varying degrees. The interplay among these obligations could be so diverse that a complete analysis of any given action might not be meaningful, but the interplay may still be examined, to some extent, by considering the relationships among obligations for an official to act, when some of those reasons arise from law and some from morality.

The patterns that are created from these relationships can be understood first by seeing how citizens cope with varying sources of obligations. We are familiar with the legal claim that citizens must obey the laws as well as with the argument over whether or under what circumstances citizens have a moral duty to do so. Most observers accept that there are some justified occasions for civil disobedience or even for revolution when the legal system becomes unjust

---

[1] Marcus Tullius Cicero, *De Officiis* 303–4 (Walter Miller, trans.) (Loeb edn.) (Harvard University Press, 1913).

or corrupt. Yet, in the main, citizens find that moral and legal obligations are compatible, with only some dissonance.

In the case of officials, the obligations to the legal system are more significant, and yet the interrelationship between legal and moral obligations is similar. Most of the time, the moral and legal obligations are compatible. When they are not, the official may attempt to change the law or to alter the moral significance or content of the obligation. The official may attempt to alter the official's role to mitigate or end the conflict. The official may break the law or act immorally, or the official may resign, which may be just as immoral.

THE COMPLEX RELATIONSHIP BETWEEN LAW AND MORALS: THE EXAMPLE OF CITIZENS

We are familiar with complex patterns between the moral and legal obligations of citizens, and many nuanced theories seek to describe this relationship. Some of these theories emphasize the frequent arenas of agreement between the moral duties of citizens and legal duties of citizens.[2] Some theories articulate grounds for disobedience to immoral laws.[3] The interplay between such theories suggests a range of relationships between the moral and legal duties of citizens, which may resolve into a particular pattern of relationships between moral and legal duties.

The Law's Claim to Obedience, Again

The law claims an obligation on every citizen to obey the law, to uphold order through its dictates. For many people, though not for all, these legal claims that everyone must obey appear to be morally compelling.

Further, the law gives reasons for people to act in accord with other moral reasons when the law requires conduct that is morally sound. When a particular law conflicts with moral duties, the citizen might still have a superior obligation to obey the laws of a legal system that generally promotes morally sound

---

[2]   See, for example, Richard Hooker, *Of the Lawes of Ecclesiastical Politie: Eight Bookes* (Andrew Crooke, 1666); Roscoe Pound, *Law and Morals: The McNair Lectures, 1924* (University of North Carolina Press, 1924); Arthur L. Goodhart, *English Law and the Moral Law* (Stevens, 1953).

[3]   A nation founded in acts of civil disobedience has, perhaps, a greater tolerance for such acts, which are a recurrent and lightly punished phenomenon in the United States. Mark Edward DeForrest, "Comment: Civil Disobedience: Its Nature and Role in the American Legal Landscape," 33 Gonzaga Law Review 653 (1997). The most important modern defense of the practice, however, requires not only that any legitimate claim for disobedience to law be based on a moral argument that is of great stringency, but also that a conflict be inescapable according to the structure of the law. See Kent Greenawalt, *Conflicts of Law and Morality* (Clarendon Press, 1989).

conduct.[4] Superiority in this sense can be quite controversial; it usually requires that the system provide a sufficient moral ecology for the citizen and that it do so through means that are generally moral in themselves. Such requirements are open to debate, not only as to whether they are sufficient requirements themselves but also as to whether they are met by a given system at a given time.

The Problem of Civil Disobedience

The theories of a citizen's obligation to obey the law become even more intricate, however, when there is a conflict for the citizen between the demands of the law and the demands of conscience. At the heart of American culture, a strong belief persists that moral grounds sometimes exist to justify the disobedience of an unjust law. On a collective basis, this independence is the central argument of the Declaration of Independence. On an individual basis, it is the central argument of the civil rights movements of the 1950s and 1960s.[5]

In recent years, many legal philosophers have agreed with these arguments. The once-reigning proposition was that there is a prima facie moral obligation to obey the laws of a legal system that is generally just. That is to say, we presume a moral obligation of obedience to the law, but this presumption can be rebutted if the laws prove to be unjust or unjustly enforced.[6] There are a variety of justifications for this presumptive moral claim of law. Some are rooted in mythic notions of the social contract,[7] but the strongest reason is probably that there is a moral duty of fair play.[8] All of us benefit from the obedience to

---

[4]   *Id.*

[5]   See Declaration of Independence; Martin Luther King, "Letter from Birmingham Jail" (1963) in S. Jonathan Bass, *Blessed Are the Peacemakers: Martin Luther King, Jr., Eight White Religious Leaders, and the "Letter from Birmingham Jail"* (Louisiana State University Press, 2001).

[6]   W. D. Ross, *The Right and the Good* 26–8 (Clarendon Press, 1930). Ross based his argument on somewhat overlapping factors, including gratitude for benefits received, expectations created by remaining in a state in which obedience is expected, enjoyment of protections of law deliberately invoked, and potential for laws to improve the general good. *Id.* 27.

[7]   Of the many contractarian claims to a moral obligation to obey the law, the most outrageous to an American sensibility is probably that of Hobbes. See Thomas Hobbes, *Behemoth, or the Long Parliament* (1668) (Cass, 1969). David Hume put much of this argument in perspective with the observation that no one really ever consented to such contracts. David Hume, "Of the Original Contract," in *Essays, Moral, Political and Literary* (1777) (Liberty Classics, 1985). Jeremy Waldron offers a rehabilitation of the contractarian impulse by demonstrating its reliance on consent, which is more akin to the arguments for fair play, described later. See Jeremy Waldron, "Theoretical Foundations of Liberalism," in *Liberal Rights, Collected Papers 1981–1991* 35 (Cambridge University Press, 1993).

[8]   C. D. Broad, "On the Function of False Hypotheses in Ethics," 26 International Journal of Ethics 377 (1916). Significant exposition of this justification seems to begin with Hart. See H. L. A. Hart, "Are There Any Natural Rights?" 64 Philosophical Review 175, 185 (1955). Its most prominent defense and careful exposition is in Greenawalt. See Kent Greenawalt, *Conflicts of Law and Morality*, 121–58 (Oxford University Press, 1989).

law of everyone else, whether we intend to benefit or not, and it is unfair to the other citizens for us not to go along.[9] But although this and other reasons, such as the nature of people in community, somewhat support this position, none of them do a very good job of articulating when the moral claims of disobedience are so strong that the presumption that it is morally right to obey the law is rebutted.[10] The presumptive approach cannot tell us when obedience is no longer morally required, or at what stage disobedience is allowed, or at what stage disobedience is morally demanded.

Obedience to the Law or to Officials

Instead, some legal philosophers have turned their attention from the citizen's obligations to the official's actions. Officials exercise authority through laws over citizens, and so long as this authority is legitimate, there is a legitimate moral claim of the officials on the citizens to obey: officials may require citizens to assist them in carrying out their duties.[11] Legitimacy is the result of a complex amalgam of good ends and right means. This amalgam varies somewhat among observers, but it could be reduced to a scheme of law by which not only are officials fair and respectful in the manner they treat all citizens, but also the rules of law are designed to increase the conditions of moral conduct, freedom, and happiness.[12] Ronald Dworkin has added to this amalgam an obligation that the laws have integrity, which is a requirement that the laws be morally coherent.[13] To the extent that laws promote such ends and means or are necessary in one

[9] Philip Soper has suggested that this duty of fair play is owed not to other citizens but to officials. P. Soper, *A Theory of Law* 75–90 (Harvard University Press, 1984). Kent Greenawalt has illustrated Soper's approach with a nice metaphor, in which a fellow reluctantly allows himself to be recruited to coach a basketball team: disobedience to the fellow's reasonable instructions would be unfair to the fellow and so be immoral. Greenawalt's metaphor seems fairly to encompass Soper's concerns, but it also demonstrates the limits of Soper's suggestion: legal officials (with the exception of jurors) are genuinely volunteers, and anyway the citizens' relationship to officials is different. Acts of disobedience to an official's edict might anger the official, but anger alone is no proof that the disobedient citizen is being unfair to the official. See Greenawalt, *Conflicts* 148–9. The real answer probably depends on whether the disobedient act is contrary to a reasonable instruction, and if so how compellingly so.

[10] *See* M. B. E. Smith, "Is There a *Prima Facie* Obligation to Obey the Law?" 82 Yale Law Journal 950 (1973); "The Duty to Obey the Law," in *A Companion to Philosophy of Law and Legal Theory* 465 (Dennis Patterson, ed.) (Blackwell Publishers, 1996).

[11] See Greenawalt, *Conflicts* 47–61.

[12] See, for example, Glenn Negley, *Political Authority and Moral Judgment* (Duke University Press, 1965); John Finnis, *Natural Law and Natural Right* (Oxford University Press, 1970); Rolph Sartorious, *Individual Conduct and Social Norms: A Utilitarian Account of Social Union and the Rule of Law* (Dickenson, 1975); Joseph Raz, *The Morality of Freedom* (Oxford University Press, 1986).

[13] Ronald Dworkin, *Law's Empire* (Harvard University Press, 1986).

manner or another to such ends and means,[14] officials have a moral claim to citizens' obedience, and the citizens have a moral duty to obey.

Even if officials support laws that promote such ends, a gap remains between the idea that we might not be morally bound to obey a law and the idea that we might be morally justified in disobeying it. Merely to say that an official, or all officials, has no moral claim upon us for our obedience is not necessarily the same thing as saying that we have a moral ability, much less a moral duty, to disobey. That moral basis of disobedience will still depend on the nature of the claims the officials make.

This gap can exist when any person claims authority over another: even if that claim of authority is not based on a sufficient reason to create a moral obligation to follow it, it does not follow that the command does not reflect what the putative follower ought to do anyway. We see this all the time. If Maggie says to her little brother William, "Be nice to your sister Katie, because I told you to," her authority as older sister might not be sufficient as a sole basis for William to act on her statement. But the statement, for reasons other than Maggie's claim to authority, reflects a moral obligation that William has anyway. William might have no obligation to do what Maggie tells him, but he still has no basis for not doing what she has said.

There remains no clear certainty of what form or extent of illegitimacy is sufficient to justify disobedience by a citizen. What difference does it make if the sense of injustice is based on a religious impulse? Is there a difference between laws that are illegitimate in their requirements or burdens and laws that are illegitimate in their procedures of adoption or enforcement? Can laws be unjust solely because they affect finance, or must they more directly affect liberty or personal dignity? What of laws pursing a legitimate end in a generally illegitimate system? Is disobedience more or less justified if committed in protest of another's burden under the unjust law? The answers to such questions are unlikely to be immutable.

The Problem of Viewpoint

One reason for the uncertain extent to which a person is bound to obey an unjust law is the complexity of views regarding what justice and legitimacy are. If we consider legitimate laws to be those that require obligations of citizens that are morally sound, we beg the question of whose view of moral soundness matters. The citizen who must obey? The richest citizens? The poorest? The majority of the citizenry? The particular officials who adopt the law? The officials who must enforce it?

---

[14]   See Tony Honore, "Must We Obey? Necessity as a Ground of Obedience," 76 Virginia Law Review 39 (1981).

The problem of whose viewpoint is sufficient to determine the content of the just is seen by some as no problem at all.[15] Moral realism, like earlier views of natural law and divine law, is based on a premise that certain notions of morality are knowable and immutable.[16] There may be widespread agreement in favor of certain core beliefs of such systems, such as that just laws ought to be clearly based on the Ten Commandments, or on the Holy Qur'an, or on the Golden Rule, or to protect a short list of fundamental goods.[17]

Yet, even such agreement gives way easily to differing conceptions of interpretation, and the problem of viewpoint is not always resolved even when there is widespread acceptance of a single premise of justice.[18] This may seem a recent problem, but in European history it was as much the case during the Reformation, when the divine right of kings to rule was asserted against papal authority, and the Protestant right of personal inspiration was asserted against royal power. All of the authorities in these struggles asserted their claims to interpret for the whole what a Christian understanding of God's justice demands.[19]

Justice Ascertained by Overlapping Consensus

An influential model for the sources of justice is that John Rawls has asserted, which pursues a definition of justice through overlapping consensus. In this model, he seeks to find nearly universal views of the just by accepting only

---

[15]   Kant, for instance, believed that no one's point of view was necessary, because a logical operation of duty from the categorical imperative is the only way in which legislators can realize the well-being of the legislature as an autonomous agency of the just state. The just state is, by this method, based on right and not on the good of the citizens. See George P. Fletcher, "Symposium on Kantian Legal Theory: Law and Morality: A Kantian Perspective," 87 Columbia Law Review 533, 552 (1987), quoting Immanuel Kant, *The Metaphysical Elements of Justice* *318 (J. Ladd, trans.) (Bobbs-Merrill, 1965). Of course, Kant was convinced that, reasoning from the categorical imperative, one right answer could solve any problem.

[16]   See Jeremy Waldron, "Moral Truth and Judicial Review," 43 American Journal of Jurisprudence 75 (1998), commenting on Michael Moore's criticism's of Waldron's rejection of moral realism, and distinguishing Waldron's arguments against judicial review from that debate. Discussing Michael S. Moore, *Law as a Functional Kind*, in *Natural Law Theory: Contemporary Essays* 188–242, 227 (Robert George, ed.) (Oxford University Press, 1992), and Jeremy Waldron, *The Irrelevance of Moral Objectivity*, in *id.* 158.

[17]   For the modern natural law approach, see John Finnis, *Natural Law and Natural Rights* (Oxford University Press, 1981).

[18]   A wonderful example of the problem is in Professor Levinson's example of the church and the pseudo-adulterers. See Sanford Levinson, "The Adultery Clause of the Ten Commandments," 58 Southern California Law Review 719 (1985).

[19]   In many ways, the idea of a divine right of kings was a theory of liberation, at least from papal domination of national laws. The idea of local governmental interpretation of divine law, freed from papal decree, did not depend on a monarch, however. See Paolo Sarpi, *Historie of the Counsel of Trent in Eight Books* (Robert Young & John Ravvorth) (Whittaker, 1640).

such views of justice as are compatible with everyone's comprehensive moral and religious views of the just.[20] This idea of justice, fleshed out, might lead to a resurgence of the dictates of modern natural law, in an ideal of justice based on the pursuit of universally accepted goods.

Among all of these views, however, the viewpoint remains either abstract and ideal or institutional and professional. The pope, priest, or king determined what God demanded of law in most early modern views. The philosopher or cultural anthropologist is necessary to later views. The citizen can hardly employ any of these theoretical approaches in measuring the claim that a law is unjust.

Injustice as a Measure of Justice

One view of justice that is more accessible for citizens' use is their private sense of the moral exerted to the extreme. A useful example of this view is that developed by Edmund Cahn, who argued that it is usually much easier to agree on what is truly unjust than to agree on what is truly just. His sense of injustice is a concept in which most people find a result that comports with Rawls's overlapping consensus. This concept, though, turns on two conditions that are sometimes hard to satisfy. The label "injustice" must be reserved for truly serious institutional acts violating nearly every scheme of morality, and those who observe the institution must not somehow become inured to injustice.[21]

From this viewpoint, one can ignore the usual effort to resolve the problem of when a citizen must obey an unjust law by measuring it against what is just. Rather, each citizen can determine whether it violates a sense of injustice. If the citizen is truly convinced that a law is unjust, this belief may be sufficient for the citizen to conclude that there is a moral ground to disobey. There are, of course, gradations of such convictions. A critical line might be drawn between a conviction that a law is unjust within a generally just system and a conviction that a law is unjust and either is so unjust as to corrupt the whole legal system or is otherwise symptomatic of a generally unjust legal system. The citizen's case for disobedience to the laws that cross such a line is correspondingly greater.

None of this means that the citizen who disobeys a law that the citizen believes is unjust will be free from legal enforcement. Indeed, in the twentieth century, the lawyer Mohandas K. Gandhi refined the use of the enforcement

---

[20] John Rawls, "The Idea of an Overlapping Consensus," 7 Oxford Journal of Legal Studies 1 (1987), revised in John Rawls, *Political Liberalism* 133 (Columbia University Press, 1993).

[21] Edmond N. Cahn, *The Sense of Injustice: An Anthropocentric View of Law* (New York University Press, 1949). This idea was developed further in Chapter 4. For the legal system's contribution to a lost sense of justice, see Negley, *Political Authority*; Richard Rubenstein, *The Cunning of History: Mass Death and the American Future* (Harper & Row, 1975).

of unjust laws as the tool for demonstrating the moral imperative to disobey them, a lesson brought strongly to bear in the American civil rights movement, particularly through the leadership of Martin Luther King, Jr.

Moreover, the citizen will not be free from moral condemnation by others who do not share that citizen's belief. Many, many people – even many among the oppressed – disagreed with the actions of Gandhi and of King as immoral, not only because their actions were illegal, but because the system they attacked was seen by these people not as immoral at all but as salutary in one manner or another. Although the lessons of history have strongly shown that imperial Britain and the Jim Crow South were unjust, at its core the notion of injustice can be as controversial as the notion of justice. Still, the sense of injustice does provide a powerful tool for describing when citizens believe they have moral freedom, indeed a moral duty, to disobey the law.

Consonance and Conflict for the Citizen

In considering the whole of the legal obligations and moral obligations that apply to a citizen, patterns emerge. There are significant areas of consonance between the two sets of obligations, areas of potential conflict, and potential areas of unavoidable conflict. The nature of these patterns is dependent upon the nature of each set of obligations at any one time. So it is clear that, because each set of obligations changes with time, the specific pattern of relationships between legal and moral obligations also changes over time.

Conflict between moral obligations and legal obligations for citizens is still profoundly different from the conflict between moral and legal obligations for officials. The citizen has a different stake in it. The citizen has an outsider's relationship to the legal system. The official has chosen a deliberate commitment to act within a system, and this choice may well alter the nature of the official's freedom to act from a sense of injustice.

PATTERNS OF LEGAL AND MORAL OBLIGATION:
THE PROBLEM OF OFFICIALS

The interplay of obligations that arise for an official from the law and from morality is even more intricate than this interplay for citizens. Given the complexity of laws and the complexity of morals, the relationship between laws and morals is also complex. It is unlikely that we could ever perfectly describe, much less compare, the final balance of legal obligations weighed against moral obligations in any given act by an official. Compound this incapacity in sorting out the obligations that might relate to a single act by multiplying the sorting over the vast enterprise of a legal system, and the task of description obviously cannot be an empirical enterprise. Some observations can be made, and from these a certain incomplete logic can emerge, a logic from which patterns can be discerned.

The law provides officials both with the power of office to act, which we can call their role, and with reasons to act, which are the substantive rules of law that might apply in a given situation presented to them related to that role. Moral reasoning may provide an independent source of reasons for the official to act or not to act to exercise that power.[22]

There is no symmetry between the moral and legal sources. Only the law gives power, but both give reasons. Regardless of this asymmetry, there is a likely interplay of reasons from sources in the legal material and moral understanding. This interplay is repeated for every action of every legal official. For any given decision to act, the official might be more or less aware of the reasons available, or even of the reasons upon which an action is based; the fact remains that both as a moral agent and as a legal agent, two sets of reasons are available as bases for action.[23]

We should dispose of one fallacy here. The relationship between morals and law as bases for official action is not a case for "either/or" binary results. In most instances, the notion that officials would follow either the law or their conscience is not a terribly accurate understanding of the options the officials have as a practical matter. Further, such a dichotomy ignores the additional patterns within the amalgam of moral obligations created by moral obligations of loyalty toward the institutions of law.[24]

Consider a metaphor from the sea: A series of waves moves across the sea and encounters a second series of waves coming from a different direction, at

---

[22] Indeed, Weber believed that the particular way officials applied moral notions – a "sense of proportion" and "inner concentration and calmness" – was the only way to ensure that the apparatus of the state is used with justice. Max Weber, "Politics as a Vocation," in –, *From Max Weber*, 125 (H. H. Gerth & C. Wright Mills, eds.) (Oxford University Press, 1958).

[23] It might be worthwhile to point out that no one is very pleased with any models for legal reasoning that dictate particularly what the reasons are for an act by a legal official. Even when the inquiry is pared down to the seemingly simplified question of what legal sources provide a rationale for a decision, arguments abound over the limits of reasons, whether legal sources alone can answer legal questions, and whether legal sources include social information. Ronald Dworkin has been the lightning rod for many of these questions as his fictional judge Hercules has moved from job description to job description over the years. Compare Ronald Dworkin, "Hard Cases," in –, *Taking Rights Seriously* 105–30 (Duckworth, 1977), to Ronald Dworkin, *Law's Empire* 393–7 (Harvard University Press, 1986).

This book proceeds upon the following assumptions: (1) For legal reasons, as for moral reasons, there is a nearly infinite number of potential reasons for any given act. (2) Those reasons that matter are those with a higher degree of salience, or significance in the context of the decision to be made. (3) Salience may be but need not be based on historical provenance, institutional significance, actual reliance by an actor, believed reliance by an actor, or stated reliance by an actor. (4) The employment of one reason does not exclude the potential to employ other reasons, even if one reason is logically exclusive of the other reasons.

[24] See the institutional obligations described in Chapter 4.

different frequencies. Depending upon the strength, frequency, and angles of the wave, an interference pattern results. At times, the waves will become stronger in one direction than either wave set alone could have been. At other times, the waves may cancel one another out, leaving the water still. Sometimes a whole new set of wave patterns might be set off, a rip tide moving at a tangent to either of the originals. If we imagine that obligations are somewhat like the waves in affecting the people they encounter, we could imagine that moral obligations sometimes cause people to act in a given way, and that legal obligations cause similar but different actions. The interference patterns resulting from the interaction between moral and legal obligations might be similar to the interference patterns caused in the sea. Patterns emerge, sometimes reinforcing, sometimes neutralizing or angling, and sometimes reversing the patterns from their sources.[25]

Generally, the patterns of reasons formed by these two sets of reasons fall into three bands. First, moral obligations may provide an independent, additional, and reinforcing reason for an official to act according to legal obligations. They may provide a compelling reason for an official to exercise power that otherwise might not be employed because its employment is, according to legal rules, a matter of the official's substantive discretion. Moreover, they may provide a compelling reason for the official to exercise discretion by not employing such discretionary power. Second, moral obligations may provide compelling reasons for the official to attempt to alter the scope of legal power or discretion, and moral obligations may provide a rationale for not making such changes. Third, moral considerations may provide grounds for rejecting the use of a given legal power, even to the point of official disobedience to a legal command.

These bands are not sequential but complex, varied, and often muddled. They are the types of patterns that result from the interference, and like the waves at sea, their sequence is dependent on their sources. The resulting patterns of obligations can be just as confusing to an official at any moment as the waves might be to a mariner in a storm.

Agreement between Legal and Moral Obligations

One ideal for the law is that there is constant agreement between the dictates of legal rules and moral reasoning, that the law never requires a citizen or an official to act in an immoral manner.[26] Although such constant agreement

---

[25] For the physics maven, this metaphor can obviously be recast in any wave matrix, from electric signals in a wire or radio waves in space to sand dunes in the desert. Ship-at-sea metaphors have a long tradition in the law, *pace* Plato's *Republic*, and I have chosen the waves of the sea to play with this. My thanks to Jeremy Waldron and Bill Sheppard for their conversations fleshing this idea out.

[26] This ideal is the central conception of the just state as a matter of natural law. See Thomas Aquinas, *Summa Theologica*, qq. 95–6; Finnis, *Natural Law*, 353–66. It is not, however,

between moral reasoning and legal rules is impossible, not least for the reasons considered so far in this chapter, we are more likely to consider this agreement as an obligation to be satisfied not in every law, but in each law. More often than some critics might believe, this ideal is realized in most legal obligations.

Moral Obligations Reinforce Legal Reasons to Act

When a particular rule of the law dictates that an official should act, this provides a presumptively sufficient reason for the official to do so. Although at first blush it might seem that there is no need for any further reasons for the official to act, as demonstrated earlier, this is not necessarily so.

The sword of the law is a terrible thing, and the acts of officials often work considerable hardship in the world of citizens. Citizens subject to such acts may be spied upon, searched, detained, imprisoned, and killed. They might lose their fortunes, their children, their opportunities. They might lose the right to immigrate, or to engage in some industry cheaply enough to compete.

Further, the law may give an official specific reasons not to act, but this too may well be an insufficient reason for inaction. The shield of law, when denied, can expose citizens to the violence of others and to the hardships of the citizens' own mistakes. The educative powers of the state in the guide of the law may also be terrible, particularly when its powers are directed to promote wicked ends throughout the state, as the object of the citizens' moral views. And the identity of the citizen that is affected by the state as the moral agent of all of the citizenry is diminished when officials fail to pursue good and noble ends through the power of the law.

These unfortunate results follow, at times, from the reliance by legal obligations on the law alone as a basis for action and inaction. In such cases, there is no reason to suppose that legal officials lack compassion for the people whom they are called upon to govern through law. In at least some of these cases, the official's belief in the necessity of the hardships created or required by the law will be insufficient to compel the official to act to inflict such hardship. Rather, the official may act in reliance both on the law as a reason for action and on independent moral grounds that it is right that such actions take place. If the law requires what morality requires, there is a greater basis for action. Indeed, when the official is empowered to act as morality requires, and the official is the sole person with the discretion or opportunity and discretion to act, moral reasoning creates an independent obligation for the official to act according to law. The mere fact that the moral consideration requires the official to do what the law demands does not in any way diminish the real consequences of either

a strictly religious view. See 1 William Blackstone, *Commentaries on the Laws of England* (Clarendon Press, 1765); Plato, *The Statesman* (J. B. Skemp, trans.) (Routledge & K. Paul, 1952); Niccolò Machiavelli, *Discourses on Livy* (Harvey Masfield, trans.) (University of Chicago Press, 1998).

the moral reasoning or its resultant sense of obligation in serving as a practical reason for the official to act. The moral and legal obligations reinforce one another.

Moral Obligations Reinforce Legal Reasons Not to Act

The law also provides curbs on official conduct, curbs that accord with moral principles. Such curbs may be the result of affirmative limits or injunctions, such as the famous provisions of the Fourteenth Amendment that no person shall be denied due process of law or equal protections of the laws.[27] They may also result from the limits of a particular role as defined by law.

When the law provides that an official may not use power in a particular manner, an official who seeks to enlarge the powers and discretion of the official's office might well seek to overcome that provision. If, however, the act the official would perform is itself morally wrong, moral reasoning independently provides a reason for the official not to attempt to violate or alter that limit on the office.

Legal Obligations Reinforce Moral Reasons to Act

The law may be seen as encouraging moral action. This result is the opposite of the ideal in which moral obligations reinforce legal reasons for action. Its difference is in the priority of causation. In this instance, an official does what is moral *because* it is a legal obligation. This idea is more common for most of us in the context of citizen obligations, in which many legal obligations enforce moral obligations as a matter of state police powers.[28]

There are, however, specific moral obligations that arise from the stakes that others have in the office they have voluntarily accepted. These reinforce legal duties that are consonant with them. Moral obligations, such as that officials must see that disputes are judged, the dangerous are quelled, the weak are shielded, and citizens are treated with dignity by the state, all parallel legal obligations.[29]

Moral Obligations Provide Reasons to Act within Legal Discretion

As well as the cases when the law demands that an official act, or curbs an official from a particular action, there remain many cases in which the reasons from the legal materials are neither compelling reasons to act nor compelling

---

[27] U.S. Constitution, Amendment XIV, Section 1.

[28] For more on this Millian notion of the law as a force of moral education, see Steve Sheppard, "The State Interest in the Good Citizen: Constitutional Balance between the Citizen and the Perfectionist State," 45 Hastings Law Journal 969 (1994). The manner in which moral arguments are framed in the creation of legal obligations is discussed in *The Concept of Legal Perfectionism* (M.Litt. Thesis, Oxford University, 1999).

[29] See Chapters 1 and 3.

curbs from acting. These cases are the domain of discretion, in the senses of substantive discretion.

Moral considerations may influence actions within an official's substantive discretion. If there is a range of actions in which an official can satisfy the requirements of law, then moral reasoning can provide reasons for action in selecting among that range. Such reasons can be positive, in which one or several courses clearly would lead to a morally sound act or result, or they can be negative, in which one or several courses clearly would lead to a morally rotten act or result.

Of course, there is no assurance that moral reasoning can dictate all actions, whether for officials or for anyone else. There is often a range of conduct that is morally indistinguishable in a given situation. Yet, when the range of available action is much wider than this range of morally similar conduct, moral reasoning provides a foundation for narrowing the range. Thus, even when moral reasons do not provide a sufficient reason for an official to act in only one manner in a case within the official's discretion, moral reasons might well provide reasons to reject certain actions or to commit certain actions.

Reconcilable Conflict between Legal and Moral Obligations

When possible, officials are likely to find mechanisms to reduce the degree of conflict between their bases for reasoned action. As Professor Cover observed in his study of abolitionist judges who enforced the Fugitive Slave Act, the judges acted whenever possible to lessen the cognitive dissonance between what they believed the law required and what they believed their consciences demanded. The strategies they developed allowed them to diminish the dissonance, although not to extinguish it, by altering the significance of one or the other of the claims upon them.[30]

Officials Alter Their Legal Obligations

Moral considerations may require officials to alter their legal obligations. The idea of alteration is one that suggests a continuum of practice. The result in some cases may be subtle changes of legal obligations, in others a vast re-creation of laws. This response to interference between moral and legal reasons remains within the preexisting scheme of legal obligations.

What is important in this approach is that officials alter the law only to the degree that the conflict is resolved. A complete reversal of legal norms may not be necessary. A recasting of a dispute, or an issue, or a problem may allow a

---

[30] See Robert Cover, *Justice Accused: Anti-Slavery and the Judicial Process* 226–7 (Yale University Press, 1975).

compromise so that the moral aim is accomplished, or the immoral aim is not furthered.

In some cases, the official has sufficient authority to be capable of successfully reversing a legal obligation that conflicts with a moral obligation. When such a decision is made effectively, it is not actually a breach of the obligation but an obliteration of the obligation. At this extreme, this response is by far the most dramatic consequence of the relationships for officials between law and morality.

Probably the most discussed example of this forum of change in the American system is the rejection of precedent by an appellate judge.[31] In these instances, we can discern the variable perceptions of official strategies for resolving conflicts between moral and legal reasons.

One might see such an action in several lights. In one, because of the inherent limits of *stare decisis*, the judge was legally empowered to take such an action before the decision. The decision changes only the future legal obligations of a judge while changing the present obligations of legal officials. In this sense, the decision to reject a precedent is really just an exercise of substantive discretion and not the generation of a new obligation. In another view, though, the binding effects of precedent as a legal reason for action are so compelling that the rejection of a precedent amounts to a breaking of a legal obligation, a condition described later. In the third view, the forms of legal reasons for action are, at least in part, dependent on the rationale supporting each reason, and a new rationale offered to create an alternative approach to the precedent alters the legal obligations of the judge, by forming a new reason for acting to grant the mandate of the court to one or another litigant. None of these views is clearly right or wrong. Each depends on the view one takes of the legal doctrines of *stare decisis*, about which there is little consensus. In at least one sense, though, the rejection of precedent forms the basis of new legal obligations.

Despite the attention lavished on judicial change of their legal obligations, the more central, and more common, examples occur when officials alter legal rules in a legislative manner, through constitutional and statutory change, through rule-making, and through executive management. Although some lawyers might dismiss such changes as administration or politics rather than law,[32] such discrimination misses the point that changes of law occur as a result of officials employing administration and politics.

---

[31] The traditional legal conception of *stare decisis* and the use of its doctrinal limits for legal reform are discussed in Albert Kocourek & Harold Koven, "Renovation of the Common Law through *Stare Decisis*," 29 Illinois Law Review 971, 973 (1935).

[32] The archetypical argument that law is made on the bench alone is in John Chipman Gray, *Nature and Sources of the Law* (1909) (Gaunt, 1999).

Moreover, administrative and legislative officials are just as prone to conflicts of law and morality as are judicial officials. The primary difference is not that judges are somehow closer to the law but that judges are more insulated from public and bureaucratic backlash.

Officials Alter Their Moral Obligations

Legal considerations may require officials to alter their moral obligations. This might seem impossible: as we usually think of it, morality cannot be changed by individual fiat. Although an official, or an official body such as a legislature, can declare some act, say drinking alcohol, to be legal or illegal, it would seem that neither can declare drinking spirits to be moral or immoral in any effective way.[33]

This judgment could be a bit hasty. While officials might not be able to affect the moral connotations of some acts through law, and while they might not be able to make immoral any act by fiat, it does not follow that officials cannot change the moral connotation of an act. In particular, officials can indeed change the moral connotations of an act in the future.

The legal acts of officials can change their future moral obligations in two ways. In the first, the change of legal rules obviously alters the legal duties of officials, and so any moral obligations that arise from acting according to legal duties are likewise changed. In the second, the effect of the altered legal obligations leads over time to a new understanding of the moral stakes at issue in the obligations, and a changed perception of the moral obligation follows.

Consider the problem of a judge's application of *stare decisis*, a doctrine that has both a moral and a legal dimension for official conduct. Not only is it a legal custom that requires judges to act in later cases according to the actions of judges in earlier similar cases, but also it is a moral constraint to treat citizens in equal circumstances with equality. A judge might believe in a strong moral obligation to oppose a particular ruling on an issue and so dissent from that ruling. But when the same issue is presented, the judge might consider the legal effects of the precedent already established, over that judge's veto but established nonetheless, to create a new legal obligation. This new legal obligation might have concomitant moral obligations both in the duties toward the institution and in the duty to treat equally placed citizens equally.[34]

---

[33]   See, on this point, H. L. A. Hart, *The Concept of Law* 175–7 (2d ed.) (Oxford University Press, 1994). Compare to the movie line given to Al Capone, "People are gonna drink. You know that. I know that. We all know that. All I do is act on that." *The Untouchables* (1987) (Brian DePalma, dir.).

[34]   This approach roughly describes the position taken by O'Connor, Kennedy, and Souter in *Casey*, that whatever the stakes for constitutional protection of a mother's right to abortion before *Roe v. Wade*, the stakes were fundamentally changed in favor of Roe's outcome afterward. See *Planned Parenthood v. Casey*, 505 U.S. 833, 845–6 (1992). For a criticism of

The most profound manner in which officials change their moral obligations is by acting to change them in the future. If we accept the notion that an important source of moral obligations is that reflected in the community's normative structure, then a change in that structure will change the nature of moral obligations.[35] It is fair to observe that such changes happen constantly on a small level, but that even on a grand scale, actions of officials alter the moral ecology of the society and alter, sometimes quite dramatically, the moral obligations relative to the original action. The legal decisions ending *de jure* racial segregation in the United States surely presaged a sea change in social understanding of moral obligations to treat each person with equal dignity.[36]

Last, it should also be noted that officials can sometimes change the relative significance of a moral obligation by altering their perceptions of the conflict between the legal and moral obligations in issue. By enhancing the apparent significance of the legal obligation, or by diminishing the apparent significance of the moral obligation, the official is able to recast the seeming conflict until it is nearly or completely reconciled.[37]

Officials Alter Their Role Discretion

Moral considerations may require officials to diminish their discretion or to enlarge it, by which they might personally escape a conflict of competing obligations. Moral considerations might also require officials to enlarge their discretion in order to act with powers that might not otherwise be within their roles in order to resolve a conflict. Sometimes these changes in role may be accomplished by informal means of changing the perception of the office, particularly the institutional loyalties owed by the officeholder. Sometimes, these changes may happen more formally through alteration or reinterpretation of the legal materials according to which the role is defined, so that the role allows an act in a situation that the official, before that change, would not have been allowed.

the equality argument for *stare decisis*, see Christopher J. Peters, "Foolish Consistency: On Equality, Integrity, and Justice in *Stare Decisis*," 105 Yale Law Journal 2031 (1996).

[35] Although communitarianism gained considerable attention in the later twentieth century, there have been numerous earlier approaches to the same idea. Compare F. S. C. Northrop's argument for the living law in Filmer S. C. Northrop, *The Complexity of Legal and Ethical Experience* (Little, Brown 1959), with Philip Selznick, "The Idea of a Communitarian Morality," 75 California Law Review 445 (1987).

[36] See, for example, David Luban "Legal Storytelling: Difference Made Legal: The Court and Dr. King," 87 Michigan Law Review (1989). The struggle between legal and moral obligation for judges on the Fifth Circuit Court of Appeals during this period is well captured in Jack Bass, *Unlikely Heroes: The Dramatic Story of the Southern Judges of the Fifth Circuit Who Translated the Supreme Court's Brown Decision into a Revolution for Equality* (Simon and Schuster, 1981).

[37] Professor Cover suggests that this method was often used by abolitionist judges, who raised the stakes in defending the system of law as a means of lowering the stakes in abolition. Cover, *Justice Accused* 199.

Changing the role of an official has profound implications for the rest of the legal system as a whole. The legal system depends on the division of labor among officials, which requires a general respect for the limits of office in order for others to have a sufficient scope of office. Further, the legal system as a whole has boundaries, arenas of human conduct beyond which citizens are free to act without interference. Alterations of role may jeopardize either or both of these aspects of the legal system.

Among the many ways in which an official may change the perception of one office's role discretion is the process of defining, or redefining, a duty of loyalty within the legal bureaucracy. There are both legal and moral obligations of loyalty. The legal duty might be based on an administrative hierarchy, as when a lawyer in a government agency is given the task of carrying forward policies set by an agency head. Or there may be legal duties that arise from a tradition or culture of performance for a particular role, as when judges accept a duty not to discuss their conversations with other judges in preparing a decision. The legal nature of the loyalty in these instances is toward a particular group within the legal system, and there are moral obligations that follow from these legal definitions.[38] When a legal duty is asserted within one of these groups, and the legal duty is opposed to a moral obligation, the official subject to the dueling obligations might reconcile them by successfully arguing a loyalty to a differently defined group.

One example of this redefinition of loyalty occurred in 1969, when lawyers in the U.S. Department of Justice found themselves in a conflict caused by Attorney General John Mitchell's instruction to delay enforcing school desegregation orders. Their legal obligation of loyalty to the attorney general by carrying out his policies was in conflict with their moral obligation to pursue equal treatment of citizens. Their obligation to the attorney general was also at odds with their obligation to the U.S. Constitution, as construed by the U.S. Supreme Court. They wrote a letter of protest, arguing that their loyalties were to the larger cause, not to the smaller team. The protest was ineffectual in changing the department's (ultimately unsuccessful) policy in that case, but it may have influenced later departmental policy.[39]

More enduring, perhaps, are the mechanisms by which an official or group of officials can alter their role discretion. The most famous of the mechanisms is probably the 1803 declaration by Justice John Marshall that the U.S. Supreme Court held the power of judicial review over federal statutes.[40] Such redefinitions of role have occurred in both the legislative and executive branches

---

[38] For the moral duty of loyalty arising from legal and other formal duties, see George P. Fletcher, *Loyalty: An Essay on the Morality of Relationships* (Oxford University Press, 1993).

[39] Gary Greenberg, "Revolt at Justice," in *Inside the System: A Washington Monthly Reader* (Charles Peters & Timothy Adams, eds.) (Praeger, 1970).

[40] *Marbury v. Madison*, 5 U.S. 137 (1803).

in the federal government, particularly in the massive realignments of role that accompanied the New Deal.[41] Similar actions, however, occur often in all branches and levels of the legal bureaucracy.

A further alteration of the official's role is accomplished through the devices of delay and avoidance. These may be effected sufficiently subtly or according to such usual bureaucratic activity that no one other than the official is aware that these nonactions *are* mechanisms of conflict avoidance. The obvious difficulty with such a redefinition of role in this manner is that it is often a violation of obligations (legal, moral, or both) but done through omission rather than commission.

It should be noted that such redefinitions of role come often with a great moral cost in diminishing an official's obligations to the institution. Not only can these redefinitions lead to institutional conflict over the ability to control the institution, but such conflicts can detract from the capacity of all of the affected officials to objectively weigh the moral obligations they would otherwise weigh in their actions. Thus, when one arm of the legal system creates a power that is redundant of another arm's, each is less responsible for the use of that power. Moreover, when responsibility is vested by rules in one office and assumed through action by another, the appearance of legitimacy of both offices as bound by legal rules is weakened, thus weakening the appearance of legitimacy of the system as a whole.[42] These harms to the system can be severe but still not well accounted for in the calculus of acting to satisfy a strong moral obligation outside the institutional framework.

Irreconcilable Conflict between Legal and Moral Obligations

There are many instances in which a legal official may breach a moral obligation. As described in Chapter 4, a comprehensive understanding of the problems created by conflicting moral obligations suggests the problem of "dirty hands": the inevitability that officials will engage in certain types of moral wrong, strictly as a result of competing moral reasons without regard to the dictates of legal obligation.[43] There remain, however, cases in which there is an unambiguous moral obligation that inescapably conflicts with an unambiguous legal obligation.

The examples of conflict between moral and legal obligations that have been discussed so far can each be reconciled without the official's violation

---

[41]   See Steve Sheppard, "The Second New Deal," in *Encyclopedia of the Great Depression and the New Deal* (James Ciment, ed.) (Sharpe Reference, 2001).

[42]   These are component arguments of Waldron's criticism of judicial review. See Jeremy Waldron, *The Dignity of Legislation* (Cambridge University Press, 1999); *Law and Disagreement* (Oxford University Press, 1999).

[43]   See Chapter 4.

of an unambiguous legal obligation. The independence of legal from moral obligations, as well as the examples of history, ensures that such a reconciliation is not always possible. The irreconcilability of such a conflict might be the result of choice by an official or officials to eschew any form of reconciliation. It might also be the result of an absolute failure of options by which to reconcile. In either case, the effects will be the same. There are three courses available that can reconcile the official's competing obligations: the official may breach the moral obligation, the official may breach the legal obligation, or the official may resign.

Officials Breach Their Moral Obligations

In an irreconcilable conflict between a moral obligation and a legal obligation, it is probably correct to observe that most officials adhere to the legal obligation at the expense of the moral. In his study of antebellum judges who resisted slavery, Professor Robert Cover recognized that in many instances antebellum judges avoided conflict between the law and good conscience by altering technical aspects of the law to avoid its substance. He still concluded, "Whenever judges confronted the moral-formal dilemma, they almost uniformly applied the legal rules."[44] This is not an isolated conclusion; judges and legal officials supported the most famously unjust regimes of the twentieth century, in Nazi Germany and in apartheid South Africa.[45]

There are numerous views of why this is so. The first, which must be considered with some care, is that violating moral obligations is an inevitable consequence of the role. In some regards, this is certainly true, and yet it is important that one not take such conclusions too far. There are two distinct senses of this problem of the "inevitably dirty hands" of officials.

The first sense includes the problem of mortals in an ideal role. As developed in Chapter 4, in the section entitled "Good Faith," the sum of moral obligations that attach to the role of the legal officials is an unattainable ideal. The conflict among duties, for instance to act with deliberation but efficacy, or with knowledge but speed, dooms an official never to be able to satisfy all obligations. Yet,

---

[44] Cover, *Justice Accused*, 199. Cover's path-breaking conclusions, however, are based almost entirely on studies of famous appellate judges, particularly John McLean, Joseph Story, and Lemuel Shaw. Later study focusing in part on McLean, who rode the federal circuit in Ohio and Michigan, but considering more fully the cases in state courts leads to more nuanced conclusions, particularly that judges found more opportunities for reconciliation than Cover noted. See Stephen Middleton, *The Black Laws: Race and the Legal Process in Early Ohio* (Ohio University Press, 2005).

[45] See, for example, Norman L. Greene, Herbert S. Okun, Fritz Stern, Jack B. Weinstein, Richard H. Weisberg, David Luban, & Ruti G. Teitel, "Symposium: Nazis in the Courtroom: Lessons from the Conduct of Lawyers and Judges under the Laws of the Third Reich and Vichy, France," 61 Brooklyn Law Review 1121 (1995); Stephen Ellmann, "Executioners, Jailers, Slave-Trappers and the Law: What Role Should Morality Play in Judging? To Resign or Not to Resign," 19 Cardozo Law Review 1047 (1997).

these obligations are not in opposition to legal obligations, and the choices among legal obligations are mirrored in the choices among moral obligations. The sum of these conflicting obligations is a complex alloy of duties, which can be satisfied only incompletely, at a standard of best efforts.[46]

The second sense includes the broader problems of devil's bargains and unintended consequences. In the same manner, moral philosophers are fond of debating (usually the utilitarians versus the deontologists) whether it is right to deliberately sacrifice one person to save the life of two, or whether the torture of a terrorist may be justified to save the life of the terrorist's innocent victim. These are the traditional problems of "dirty hands" when considered by philosophers.[47] These problems have no good answer, only right answers. Someone always dies, or gets hurt, or gets blown up, even if the officials do the best that can be done, because those are the circumstances. It simply is not possible for officials charged with resolving a situation like Nozick's example, of an innocent victim strapped to a tank that is attacking an innocent third party, to do so without hurting someone or allowing someone to be hurt.[48] This is similar to the problem of the unintended consequence, in which officials make the best decision with the data available, which produces regrettable knock-on effects.[49] The best that legal officials can do is to choose the least evil.

Although the results of actions made in such circumstances might be horrific, no action based on such circumstances is truly immoral. The cause for violating moral obligations is not a rejection of moral bases for action in preference to legal bases for action.

An official who honors a legal obligation at the expense of a conflicting moral obligation is acting immorally, at least at some level of moral reasoning. Whether the reason for the immoral act is to serve a greater morality, or the result of an erroneous understanding of moral obligation, or just carelessness clearly affects what judgments the official (or others) might make of such a decision, but they do not alter the result as to that action: it remains immoral.

---

[46] See Chapter 4.

[47] See, for example, Max Weber, "Politics as a Vocation"; Michael Walzer, "Political Action: The Problem of Dirty Hands," 2 Philosophy & Public Affairs 160, 164–72 (1973); Stuart Hampshire, *Innocence and Experience* (Harvard University Press, 1989).

[48] Robert Nozick, *Anarchy, State, and Utopia* 35 (Harper and Row, 1975).

[49] See Philippa Foot, "The Problem of Abortion and the Doctrine of Double Effect," in *Virtues and Vices* 19, 21 (James D. Wallace, ed.) (Cornell University Press, 1978), reprinted in Philippa Foot, *Virtues and Vices and Other Essays in Moral Philosophy* (Oxford University Press, 2002). Foot's illustration, the famous one with the fat man blown up in the mouth of the cave not with an intent to hurt him but intending only to make him smaller, is an example with quite foreseeable consequences, but the problem is only slightly mitigated when the consequences are unforeseeable. See Steven M. Gillon, *"That's Not What We Meant to Do": Reform and Its Unintended Consequences in Twentieth-Century America* (W. W. Norton, 2000).

One of the classic narratives of this choice is in Herman Melville's *Billy Budd, Foretopman*, long a favorite of law professors examining the choice between moral and legal duty.[50] The story is well known: On board H.M.S. *Indomitable* in 1797, Billy is the handsome and perfect sailor, of whom Claggart, the master-at-arms, is insanely jealous. When Claggart lies to Captain Vere and accuses Billy of mutiny, Billy, shocked and tongue-tied, strikes the lying Claggart and kills him. Vere is bound by the Articles of War to try Billy and hang him for striking a superior. Vere knows that Claggart and not Billy was the author of his fate, and probably loves Billy, but he still convenes the court-martial, argues against clemency for fear that the crew might see it as weakness, and in great but quiet torment, has Billy hanged.[51] One can easily see a moral argument for mitigation of Billy's punishment, contrasted with a legal argument for strict enforcement. Vere chose the legal argument as his duty and stuck by it. Billy, fundamentally lacking a guilty mind, was hanged so as to maintain fleet discipline.

Officials Breach Their Legal Obligations

Moral obligations may require officials to breach their legal obligations, to exercise power contrary to their legal obligations. Although such an action might have significant effect upon the official or the institution, there are many means by which this can be accomplished without institutional repercussions, not the least through stealth. When officials act in secrecy, it can be very difficult for other officials, much less for the citizenry, to know either the nature of an action taken or the manner in which actions are taken.[52]

---

[50] Herman Melville, "Billy Budd, Foretopman," in *Selected Writings of Herman Melville: Complete Short Stories, Typee [and] Billy Budd, Foretopman* 803 (Modern Library, 1952). See also Philip C. Kissam, "Disruptions of Literature: Disturbing Images: Literature in a Jurisprudence Course," 22 Legal Studies Forum 329 (1998) (considered as pedagogy); Kevin W. Saunders, "Billy Budd and the Federal Sentencing Mandates," 22 Oklahoma City University Law Review 211 (1997) (considered as critique of the law). The chance that Melville's Captain Edward Fairfax Vere is a metaphorical depiction of his father-in-law, Chief Justice Lemuel Shaw, as he grappled with fugitive slave cases is considered in Robert Cover, *Justice Accused: Antislavery and the Judicial Process* 1–7 (Yale University Press, 1975), an argument extended in Steven L. Winter, "Melville, Slavery, and the Failure of the Judicial Process," 26 Cardozo Law Review 2471 (2005).

[51] It might be well to remember that by keeping control of Billy's punishment, Melville's Captain Vere saved him from a worse fate. Had he resigned the judgment and passed Billy on to the fleet for punishment, Billy would certainly have been keelhauled through the fleet, a much more horrible way to die.

[52] The usual emphasis of writers concerned with the use of official secrecy is to demonstrate the dangers of secrecy in promoting right conduct by officials. See Gerald Wetlaufer, "Justifying Secrecy: An Objection to the General Deliberative Privilege," 65 Indiana Law Journal 845 (1990); Sissela Bok, *Secrets: On the Ethics of Concealment and Revelation* (Pantheon Books, 1982). One might conclude from the previous observations, however, that secrecy may indeed make more likely some changes of law in the interests of morality. See *id.* 217.

On the other hand, public violations of the law in order to achieve a moral end are the official's greatest gambles. Such acts may be met with impeachment or dismissal, the reversal of the action taken, or even arrest and punishment.[53] On the other hand, if the act is followed by the general agreement of other officials, the law becomes changed and the act is made legal *ex post*.[54]

At the greatest extreme, revolutions are born in public violations of the law on the basis of conscience or moral obligation. This, indeed, is the very basis of the American Declaration of Independence, a cause that succeeded and whose morality is rarely questioned. It is also the basis for the secession of the states of the Confederacy, a cause that failed and whose morality is now barely countenanced in the popular American culture. The gamble of public violations of law on the basis of moral obligation can often be cashiered only at the bank of history.

A narrative of this type of choice contrasts nicely with the choice made by Captain Vere in *Billy Budd*. In the third volume of C. S. Forester's novels of Horatio Hornblower, Forester presents Hornblower with a dilemma that, though moderated, is similar to that faced by Melville's Vere. In 1803, Hornblower captains H.M.S. *Hotspur*, on which his personal steward is Doughty, who had been steward to the admiral. Doughty was working with a crew to load supplies into the ship when Mayne, a bosun's mate, swung a heavy whip at him for not obeying a foolish order. Doughty punched him, an offence for which death was the only punishment.[55] Hornblower's legal duty was to convene a court, try Doughty, and have him hanged. He was faced with the demand that he order killed not only a good and loyal servant but one who was also not the real cause of his offense. Like Billy Budd, Doughty's putative victim was largely the author of the offense against him. Hornblower followed his conscience rather than his duty, and he allowed Doughty to escape the ship and evade the punishment, although he felt considerable guilt for his breach of duty.[56]

---

[53] See the comparison of stories of Otto Otepka and Daniel Ellsberg, leakers of classified information for the political left and right in the Kennedy/Nixon years in Taylor Branch, "The Odd Couple," Washington Monthly (1971), reprinted in Amy Gutman & Dennis Thomson, *Ethics & Politics: Case and Comments* 90 (3d ed.) (Nelson-Hall Publishers, 1997).

[54] See, for example, the Supreme Court's allowance of congressional authorization of Lincoln's blockade, after the fact. The Prize Cases, 67 U.S. (2 Black) 635 (1863).

[55] C. S. Forester, *Hornblower and the* Hotspur 340 (Little, Brown & Co., 1990).

[56] *Id.* 351–8. One might see this as an instance of altering one's legal duty rather than breaking it. Melville's Vere gave himself only one choice in whether to carry out or not the duty to hang his prisoner. Forester's Hornblower found an artful choice between duties – selecting between the duty to punish a prisoner and the duty to keep a prisoner. Once he breached the duty to keep the prisoner, he was freed from the much more serious duty of carrying punishment decreed by the Articles of War. This is not, however, the type of enlargement of an official's role contemplated earlier, because it is still a breach of the duty, or the legal obligation, in favor of the moral imperative of fair punishment.

Officials Resign from Office

Each official remains ultimately responsible. There are occasions when the conflict between the obligations of law and morality cannot be reconciled, and it is best to breach neither the legal obligation nor the moral obligation but to resign from the legal office. Given the practical obstacles of altering moral and institutional obligations, seen earlier, resignation is sometimes the only morally and institutionally acceptable choice in these situations.[57]

The act of resignation can be one of the most principled decisions an official might take. But it also presents complex moral and practical questions. The most difficult moral question is whether the act of resignation might be merely a selfish attempt by the official to protect the official's own innocence or moral purity at the expense of others. The practical dilemma is formed by the responses that are likely visited upon the resigning official by the official's former colleagues.

There is, of course, the moral dilemma of whether the official is ultimately more capable of serving the common good through resignation or through continued immoral performance of the role. Such a balance is contingent on many circumstances, not the least being the degree to which the official's very existence in the role serves to legitimate injustice by the regime as a whole.[58]

Resignation often requires courage, not only to find alternative means of employment but also to bear the potentially grave burdens that follow an official who leaves in such circumstances.[59]

To begin with, resignation does not always end the conflict, because the obligations may persist in some manner still binding the former official. In one of the most famous of all conflicts between law and conscience, Thomas More's resignation as Chancellor of England failed to end his conflict between a legal obligation to recognize legal officials as heads of the church and a conscientious belief that only the pope could hold such a role. His legal obligation to accept the king's primacy persisted despite his resignation. Even so, the trial that ensued was not technically grounded in his refusal to take the oath, but in

---

[57] See Gutman and Thompson, *Ethics & Politics* 79 (according to a view of legal officials that lacks discretion and is based on consent to accept the office and accountability for its performance, "The moral responsibilities of the nonelected public official are completely captured by the injunction, 'obey or resign'").

[58] See, for example, Norman L. Greene, Herbert S. Okun, Fritz Stern, Jack B. Weinstein, Richard H. Weisberg, David Luban, and Ruti G. Teitel, "Symposium: Nazis in the Courtroom: Lessons from the Conduct of Lawyers and Judges under the Laws of the Third Reich and Vichy, France," 61 Brooklyn Law Review 1121 (1995); Stephen Ellmann, "Executioners, Jailers, Slave-Trappers and the Law: What Role Should Morality Play in Judging?: To Resign or Not to Resign," 19 Cardozo Law Review 1047 (1997).

[59] Most officials who resign in protest over a principle of conscience seem to face considerable bureaucratic backlash. See Edward Weisband & Thomas M. Franck, *Resignation in Protest: Political and Ethical Choices between Loyalty to Team and Loyalty to Conscience in American Public Life* (Grossman Publishers, 1975).

perjured testimony of other treason, and his beheading is regarded by many as a vindication of moral obligation.[60]

In less dramatic fashion, resignation is capable of reconciling conflicts of moral and legal obligation only at an institutional level, when the conflict can be ended by a failure of the official to act. Even though resignation saves the resigning official from the task of decision, a conflict that can be reconciled only through action is rarely ended by the departure of one official. A resignation in that circumstance is likely merely to shift the burden to another official, albeit one who potentially is less troubled by the conflict or the moral obligations that give it rise.

---

[60] More's life has given rise to many biographies, most recently John Guy, *Thomas More* (Oxford University Press, 2000) (with pith); Peter Ackroyd, *The Life of Thomas More* (Nan A. Talese, 1998) (without pith). On his life as an official, see J. A. Guy, *The Public Career of Sir Thomas More* (Yale University Press, 1980).

6

Breaching Obligations

"But stay," someone will object, "when the prize is very great, there is excuse for doing wrong." . . .

Work out your own ideas and sift your thoughts so as to see what conception and idea of a good man they contain. Pray, tell me, does it coincide with the character of your good man to lie for his own profit, to slander, to overreach, to deceive? . . . What is there that your so-called expediency can bring to you that will compensate for what it can take away, if it steals from you the name of a "good man" and causes you to lose your sense of honour and justice? For what difference does it make whether a man is actually transformed into a beast or whether, keeping the outward appearance of a man, he has the savage nature of a beast within?

Cicero, *On Duties*, Book III, Chapter XX[1]

Legal officials will breach their duties. The duties are too many, too conflicting, and too hard. What matters is how the individual official decides what to do and what not to do in an imperfect world in which some measure of failure is certain.

Dirty hands, the longstanding label for the impossibility of an official's satisfying all obligations of office, cannot, however, excuse the official from the duties themselves, nor can it justify failures of morality or illegality. The official is required, dirty hands notwithstanding, to do the best one can do to act legally and morally, which is (as with citizens) often best assessed by making the least unjust choice. The moral significance of the legal system in the lives of the citizens depends on every official doing their best. Most importantly, the breach of one official cannot, ever, excuse the breach of the next.

The problem of remedy for a breach seems vexing, primarily because the answers are so simple. The law might or might not provide remedies for breaches of legal obligations. Whether the archive allows a remedy, the use of

---

[1]   Marcus Tullius Cicero, *De Officiis* 351, 355 (Walter Miller, trans.) (Loeb edn.) (Cambridge: Harvard University Press, 1913).

remedy will depend on the will of officials in the contemporary and successive legal culture, but such remedies are quite rare in practice.

When an official violates a moral obligation with no correlative legal obligation, in extreme circumstances, the law is altered so as to create a legal remedy for such immorality, but usually the remedy is not legal. Rather the remedy is personal and social, in that the individual's reputation is damaged and, in many cases, the individual's public and self-image are damaged. Citizens and other officials may judge the official harshly, may hold the individual as an object lesson for others, and may disparage the official, or interfere with professional advancement or retention in office. This limited response is unsatisfying for many people, but morality not incorporated as law has no other responses.

THE IMPOSSIBILITY OF PERFECT PERFORMANCE, AND THE PROBLEM OF DIRTY HANDS

Humans are not perfect, and we do not live in a world in which perfection is attainable in human affairs. We cannot meaningfully judge ourselves or others by whether we meet a standard of perfection, because we never do. We can only measure ourselves by degrees against ideals, hoping we are better or, at least, not too much worse than our predecessors.

In pursuing this ideal, officials will invariably find themselves faced with choices between a bad and a worse situation. All offices include a range of tasks ranging from the possible to the impossible.[2] At times, the best that can be done is to pick the bad over the worse. At others, luck or imagination will allow the official to see new alternatives, new choices, that avoid or mitigate the worst elements of the choice to be made.

Whether "Ought" Implies "Can"

We have long believed that in order to have a moral obligation, it must be possible to fulfill that obligation. This requirement of obligations, that "ought implies can," suggests that in a very real sense, any meaningful idea of a moral obligation requires that it can be achieved, that the person with the obligation can carry it out.[3] This is no less true if the obligation binds a legal official than it

---

[2] See Erwin C. Hargrove & John C. Glidewell, *Impossible Jobs in Public Management* (University of Kansas Press, 1990).

[3] *See* Immanuel Kant, *Critique of Judgment* 345 n.48 (Werner S. Pluhar, trans.) (Hackett, 1987). "[W]e ought to conform . . . consequently we must be able to do so." For implications of the ought-implies-can principle as a limit on obligations, see Derek Parfit, *Reasons and Persons* 15–16, 506–9, n.14 (Oxford University Press, 1984). Recent determinist attacks on the maxim "ought implies can" are considered and criticized in Ishtiyaque Haji, *Deontic Morality and Control* 78–84 (Cambridge University Press, 2002).

would be if the obligation bound anyone else. To put it another way, saying that there is an obligation appears to require that the person with the obligation be able to realize it. Thus, according to this belief, a full discussion of such types of duty must consider practical obstacles to a person's performance of it. The extent of the duty is the extent to which it can be achieved, and indeed usually we mean the extent by which it can be achieved within a reasonable expectation of skill, effort, and the circumstances of fortune.

Yet that is only one approach to morality. The other is to recognize that ideals can exist in our moral imaginations, even if they cannot be fully realized. An obligation is an obligation to reach as closely as one can to the ideal, to fulfill as much of the obligation as possible.

It may be that the very nature of morality is this way: we do our best, but we are not perfect. Thus, we often fail to fully manifest our moral duties, and we judge our morality as a matter of degree. The more we fulfill our moral obligations – or the less we fail in them – the better. This possibility is a bit abstract even in this discussion, and there is no reason to explore it further in general. The point for now is to what degree legal officials can achieve their competing moral and legal obligations.

Dirty Hands

The moral obligations described of legal officials are impossible to perform fully. In many instances, they are impossible to perform individually. From this impossibility we arrive at the one doctrine that has been somewhat explored in the literature, the problem, first identified in Max Weber's famous essay, of dirty hands:[4] certain choices must be made from options that are all tragic. This is the result of conflict among obligations.

The obligations of personal moral obligation are, by themselves, rife with inherent conflict. The conflict, for instance, between the obligation to act and the obligation to investigate every matter fully before action as matters of knowledge and humility. No one can ever know all of the facts and conditions necessary to establish a full investigation, and yet an action based on such an investigation must be made.

Of course, Kant did not invent the doctrine of impossibility. What makes his formulation of such interest to philosophers is it reverses our intuitions about impossibility. Kant commences with a proven obligation, then he derives the possibility of its performance from existence of the obligation. Intuitively, we might see it otherwise: first determining the range of what we can do, then selecting from that range what we are obligated to do. In a practical sense, the benefit of the Kantian approach might be to demand a fuller appraisal of what can be done than might have been clear to us otherwise.

[4]   Max Weber, "The Profession and Vocation of Politics," in *Political Writings* 309 (Peter Lassman & Donald Speirs, eds.) (Cambridge University Press, 1994).

Conflicts are likely among moral obligations of every type. Obligations of procedural and of substantive justice have both internal conflict and conflicts between one another, and a few illustrations will suffice in this regard, as the reader is bound to be familiar with many already. The protection of certain values of justice often requires the sacrifice of others, such as the conflict between the protection of individual privacy and the need to investigate potentially criminal behavior.

Because these obligations are impossible to perfectly fulfill, and some on occasion must be utterly breached in order to satisfy others, we have become familiar with the doctrine of dirty hands. As developed by Max Weber and Stuart Hampshire, the doctrine considers the irreconcilable conflicts between moral and legal obligations, as a result of which officials are, as a condition of office, morally compromised.[5]

What has not been considered adequately is what follows from the doctrine of dirty hands. It cannot be sufficient to write off the moral loss as inevitable.

One possibility in reconciling conflicting moral obligations would be to attempt to establish an order or hierarchy among them all. This red herring, however, is subject to very little in the way of logical comparisons among very different types of obligations and would be unlikely to give rise to consensus. In any event, any series of rules would be subject to such a raft of exceptions that the rules would be less significant than the exceptions to them.

A more useful approach is a requirement of best efforts by the official to satisfy all of the relevant obligations that ought to be apparent in making every single decision, carrying out every action, or failing to carry out an action that might be within the official's discretion. The idea of best efforts is both subjective and objective; it is based on the understanding and talents of each particular official, but it is subject to the evaluation of observers.

Although no absolute hierarchy is possible among obligations in general, several methods may be useful for preferring one obligation over another in a specific circumstance. Among them are a rebuttable presumption of those obligations that comport with legal obligations, the principle of selection by salience, and, most important, the ranking of obligations that most respond to the greatest injustices.

Three Forms of Dirty Hands

Therefore, the doctrine of dirty hands persists as an accurate description of many choices and actions in an official role, in that officials are indeed subject to moral obligations that cannot be perfectly satisfied. This is true in three senses.

---

[5] See *id.*, and Stuart Hampshire, *Innocence and Experience* (Harvard University Press, 1989).

Two of these senses are general, applying by implication to every official action. The first is abstract; the nature of the conflicts among personal, institutional, procedural, and substantive obligations is unlikely to allow any action to manifest all of these duties with perfection. The second is more realized in the world of legal institutions: background injustices that are implicated by every action; and lack of resources in time, money, and personnel to ensure that the predicates to just actions are satisfied throughout the legal system. These two background senses of dirty hands are rarely the senses in which it is most obvious.

The more likely form dirty hands takes is in a choice between two practical alternatives, neither of which appears morally satisfying. These are practical in the sense of one excluding the other, as in having enough money to build a bridge over one river but not the other (no matter how hard one tries to raise more money in the time available); if there is a need for both bridges, one need will be unsatisfied. If a lawmaker had promised the villagers near both rivers a bridge, one promise must be breached to fulfill the other. These are almost always presented as binary choices – either build one bridge or the other – rather than as two priorities among thousands, such as build the bridge or pay more for salaries for civil servants.

The Occasional Ruse of Dirty Hands

Such apparent practical choices, sometimes called "tragic choices," are typified by justifications for the use of pain in interrogation. These choices are often pictured as a choice between an abstract threat to law or rights versus a concrete harm to the public, such as Judge Richard Posner's illustration in which he can allow torture, when it is the balance between a hypothetical terrorist with certain knowledge of an accomplice's impending smallpox attack and the open-ended euphemism of using as "much pressure as it takes."[6]

Such choices are given popular credence by movies such as *Guarding Tess*, in which Nicholas Cage plays the role of a Secret Service agent who shoots a toe off the foot of a kidnapper to save a former first lady from suffocation, and shows such as the Fox Television drama *24*, in which weekly villains are stopped from awful actions thanks to carefully measured pain.[7] In all these fictions, the choice is between the gain of real information that the police know a detainee is withholding, which could thwart a horrible crime about to occur.

[6] Richard A. Posner, "Torture, Terrorism, and Interrogation," in *Torture, A Collection* 289, 291 (Sanford Levinson, ed.) (Oxford University Press, 2004).
[7] See Bill Keveney, "Fictional '24' Brings Real Issue of Torture Home," USA Today TV-1 (March 13, 2005). As for the movies, see Jonah Goldberg, "Harrison Ford & the Ticking Time Bomb," National Review On-Line (December 9, 2005), at www.nationalreview.com/goldberg/goldberg200512090853.asp.

Yet despite Judge Posner's certainty, these stories are fictions, every one of them. There are simply no true stories like them.[8] Television and movie scripts notwithstanding, it is rare to find an accomplice just before the crime, about which the police can know such details but not know the final missing link. Although one member of a conspiracy might be found before the event, the dramatic timing and recalcitrance of the conspirator required to justify these stories are each more improbable facets of the story. Indeed, a team of experts in military interrogation tried but failed to explain to the producers of *24* not only that their stories were implausible but that other, less dramatic techniques were more effective.[9]

Not that it matters: the whole reason for such stories as Judge Posner's is not that they are likely but that they create sympathy for the mundane torture of detainees who might, or might not, have any knowledge of a crime or an enemy unknown. That sort of torture yields not only false and potentially misleading information,[10] at best it provides no more information than better interrogation techniques, the type of trust-based interrogation used by more mature and well-trained intelligence services. After years of experience in the administration of intelligence and counterintelligence, including the supervision of British intelligence throughout the Troubles in Ireland, Lord Robin Butler of Brockwell summarized the whole business of torture in interrogation by saying, "It just doesn't work."[11] Similar conclusions by Alberto Mora, the chief lawyer for the U.S. Navy, whose oversight included Naval Intelligence for several years in the second Bush administration, should not be lightly dismissed.[12]

The idea of dirty hands cannot serve in many instances when officials will snatch for it as a fig leaf. Most of the time, it covers only a bare act of immoral

---

[8] Legal ethicist David Luban has called the ticking bomb scenario a form of intellectual fraud, a jejune example that has become the "alpha and omega of our thinking about torture." David Luban, "Liberalism, Torture, and the Ticking Bomb," in *The Torture Debate in America* 35, 44 (Karen J. Greenberg, ed.) (Cambridge University Press, 2005).

[9] The story of a visit by the Dean of the Academic Board of the U.S. Military Academy at West Point, Brigadier General Patrick Finnegan, and his team, with a group of producers of the television show is described in Jane Mayer, "Whatever It Takes: The Politics of the Man behind '24,'" The New Yorker (Feb. 19, 2007).

[10] See, for example, the attempt by Attorney General Alberto Gonzales to rely on the false confession of Khalid Sheikh Mohammed for the killing of Daniel Perle. Jane Mayer, "The Black Sites: A Rare Look Inside the C.I.A.'s Secret Interrogation Program," The New Yorker (August 13, 2007), available at www.newyorker.com/reporting/2007/08/13 /070813fa_fact_mayer?currentPage=1.

[11] Lord Robin Butler of Brockwell, remarks at *Law, Intelligence, and Democracy*, University of Arkansas School of Law, Fayetteville, Arkansas, April 2007. See 40 Arkansas Law Review 809, 848 (2008). Lord Butler, as head of the Home Civil Service of the United Kingdom under Prime Ministers Thatcher, Major, and Blair, had unusual oversight roles in intelligence throughout the U.K., including Northern Ireland.

[12] Alberto Mora, remarks at *Law, Intelligence, and Democracy*, University of Arkansas School of Law, Fayetteville, Arkansas, April 2007. See 40 Arkansas Law Review 809 (2008).

expedience. As Cicero argued, most arguments for immoral expedience aren't really what they seem to be, because the moral course is – in fact – expedient; it just isn't what the official wants to do.[13] Instead, dirty hands is offered to excuse errors, especially a lack of skill, imagination, effort, independence, or preparation by the official.

The fact of dirty hands, even when it is unavoidable, can neither absolve officials from the performance of conflicting duties nor excuse them from the judgment of others for failing to satisfy them. Even in an emergency – especially in an emergency – officials are required to exercise their best efforts to satisfy their institutional, personal, procedural, and substantive moral obligations while carrying out their offices, the most important aspect of this requirement being to carry out their lawful obligations in the manner that is the least tolerant of injustice.[14]

BREACHING OBLIGATIONS

As we have seen, officials are usually immune from legal liability for failing in their legal duties,[15] although there are occasional legal repercussions for officials who violate their legal obligations. In the least degrees of response, an official's decisions may be reversed on appeal or by the intervention of other officials. More significant responses are institutional: an official's budget may be cut or the powers of office diminished. More seriously for the individual, officials may be publicly embarrassed or censured; they may be demoted, suspended, or fired; they may even be fined or imprisoned, although, again, it is quite rare for officials to punish other officials using the tools of the law.[16]

---

[13] Marcus Tullius Cicero, *De Officiis*, Book III, Chapters VII–XIII 303–35 (Walter Miller, trans.) (Loeb edn.) (Harvard University Press, 1913) (a portion of which is quoted in the epigraph to this chapter).

[14] A fine summary of these notions comes from an observer of the law in the nineteenth century. In an emergency, the law, said Peleg Chandler, depends on its experts from quieter times: "[W]ithout the assistance of those who have made its principles the study of their lives, and its practice their daily occupation, its energies are powerless; or it may become, in the hands of ignorant and designing men, the most powerful engine of oppression which human ingenuity can invent." Peleg W. Chandler, 1 *American Criminal Trials* 138 (Little and Brown, 1844).

[15] See Chapter 1.

[16] Presidents, governors, legislators, and judges are rarely punished with removal. No U.S. president has yet been convicted following impeachment. In two centuries, there have only been three close calls: Richard Nixon's resignation avoided impeachment by a whisker, and Andrew Johnson avoided conviction by a single vote in 1868. Bill Clinton avoided conviction in 1999 by a vote of 45 to 55, with a requirement of 67 votes to convict.

There are roughly 30,000 full- and part-time judges on the state and federal benches of the United States. From 1990 to 2001, an average of ten judges per year were removed from

The moral significance of official conduct is distinct from any sanctions or support for the actions of an official in the law itself. A person's official behavior – as the holder of a specific office, as an official *per se*, and as a person – is subject to scrutiny by both officials and by citizens for its moral content, not only for its legal sufficiency. Though someone observing official behavior must recognize the difficulty of performing fully all of the obligations of the office, both officials and the subjects have strong reasons to judge officials, and to praise and condemn them according to the degree to which they have met the legal and the moral obligations of their positions.

Breaching Legal Obligations

Chapter 5 explored the relationship between legal and nonlegal obligations. The consideration there was limited to the problem of coordination among obligations. As a practical matter, though, we must accept the notion that officials breach legal duties for many reasons, and only rarely do they do so owing to a commitment to a moral obligation. Usually, the breach is much more self-serving.

Oversight and the Legal System

The bureaucratic nature of the modern legal system depends on a complex web of offices, in which there is always oversight. Indeed, the oversight takes two forms, one of which is the more famous – the contemporaneous division of labor. The other is less obvious but as essential – the possibility of correction over time.

the bench in all of the U.S. state courts, which have roughly 10,000 full-time judges. See Cynthia Gray, *A Study of State Judicial Discipline Sanctions* (American Judicature Society, 2002). Of the roughly 2,000 federal judges, none were impeached during that period. The last impeachment of a federal judge was of Walter Nixon. See *Nixon v. United States*, 506 U.S. 224 (1993). The process of federal impeachment is particularly well described in Charles L. Black, *Impeachment: A Handbook* (Yale University Press, 1998).

Discipline of attorneys is barely more frequent. In the ABA's 2004 survey, out of 1.3 million lawyers, 127,000 complaints were filed with state disciplinary bodies, leading to the charging of lawyers with offenses in only 3,500 cases. Of those 5,600 cases in the survey, which included cases pending from prior years, in which some form of sanction was imposed, only one out of ten were disbarred, and nearly half, 2,300, were only privately reprimanded. ABA 2004 Survey on Lawyer Discipline Systems (available at http://www.abanet.org/cpr/discipline/sold/04-ch1.pdf).

At the other end of the spectrum, in 2002, of the roughly 300,000 police officers in the United States, in one year there were 26,000 complaints against police officers, just for the use of excessive force. Of these, 97 percent received some form of investigation, and 9 percent were sustained by some review process. Matthew J. Hickman, *Citizen Complaints about Police Use of Force* (Bureau of Justice Statistics, 2002); see also Samuel Walker, *The New World of Police Accountability* (Sage, 2005).

Division of labor is inherent in many aspects of the modern legal system. The doctrines of separation of powers and bicameral legislation, the structure of federalism, the right to legal and administrative appeals, the interposition of congressional and legislative inquiry, and countless other tools provide the potential for the scrutiny of every action of every official in the legal system. Such oversight both allows the participation of a variety of officials in any given decision and encourages correction of errors in any given case or situation. The law allocated offices widely, for instance, in the criminal justice system, which requires dozens of different offices in two branches of government as well as laypeople to agree that a citizen is to be punished, not even counting the hundred or so legislators who must agree that conduct like the citizen's conduct should be punishable.[17] This allocation of authority depends on the independence of each official to personally examine the case for guilt and to personally act in creating the criminal law or punishing someone for it. The complexity allows each to correct an error in the law made by the others. It allows mistakes of legal and factual judgment to be reversed. It allows the breach of duty by one official to be corrected by the next before the burdens of the mistake grow larger. That is, the legal system *can* correct such breaches, if and only if each official takes seriously the independence and responsibility of the office, rather than following others blindly in carrying out their duties.

The other form of oversight is less apparent to an observer of the legal system at any given moment. It is the process of a legal system over time. Mistakes that are not remedied when they are made can be corrected later. Congresses can repeal bad statutes; courts can overturn opinions that are found to be counter to the altered culture or to the newer archive of the law. Former officials (and

---

[17] For instance, when the system of criminal law is not short-circuited by a plea bargain, several hundred officials must coordinate their actions to convict someone of a crime. For a person to be sentenced to prison for a serious crime in Arkansas, for example, at least a majority of 35 senators and 100 legislators must agree, usually with the assent of the governor, that some conduct is to be made a crime. Officers of a police or sheriff's department (usually two) must then find evidence that a specific person has committed an act, that a prosecutor (or two) believe amounts to the punishable conduct. The prosecutor then takes the evidence to the sixteen members of the grand jury, who must agree there is probable cause that the person committed the crime, after which a judge must issue an arrest warrant or summons. In most cases, a police officer (usually more, especially if there is an investigation, but we'll say one) arrests the now-defendant, after which a judge must arraign the defendant. A prosecutor must continue to assert the charges against the defendant, which the judge does not dismiss, and twelve jurors must unanimously agree that the evidence proves that the defendant committed the acts and that the acts amount to the criminal conduct prohibited by the legislature. The judge must agree (usually again) that the trial was fair and the evidence supports a verdict, a judgment that is usually reviewed and assented to by three judges on appeal. Not counting witnesses, clerks, and others, this tallies up to 136 people required to declare some conduct criminal, and at least 37 more to declare that a defendant is to be punished for that conduct. For the process of a criminal trial generally, see George P. Fletcher & Steve Sheppard, *American Law in Global Perspective: The Basics*, Chapters 27 and 28. See also Arkansas Rules of Criminal Procedure (2007).

their former allies) who once escaped censure for their breaches of the law can be tried by new generations of prosecutors and jurors. The legal system is as eternal as the states the people support; bad decisions once accepted can be rejected, and the officials who once accepted them corrected, later. (Although there is, of course, no assurance that such corrections will occur.)

Oversight over time is, of course, usually unhelpful to those who bear the burdens of a bad act by an official at the time, but it does serve some purposes. It is the engine of legal progress and change, allowing the abolition of slavery, universal suffrage, and all of the other advances of a morally progressive society governed by laws. It is the means by which the mirror of the law is refocused when specific views of the person subject to law or of the role of law become obsolete. It is the means by which failures of the shield, abuses of the sword, and failures to conserve the coin and commons are remedied.

The fact that there is oversight, both in bureaucratic diversity and in changes over time, does not ensure that the legal system will enshrine laws that comport with moral obligations, but it does create the opportunity to do so. The oversight, like all acts of officials, cannot ensure a moral outcome. Indeed, although the fundamental purpose of most aspects of this oversight is to ensure a moral aspect of the laws – that they are accurately and fairly applied – the purpose of much of the oversight is to ensure compliance with legal obligations. Even so, the nature of the oversight is such that every official still has the power to alter the outcome of a given case, to demand the fundamental reassessment of the legal obligations involved and their applications and burdens on a given subject. The oversight authorizes officials to act, and it gives to each a discretion to act according to law for the good of the legal system and of the people.

The general structure of the legal system provides a particular stream of authority in every case, in every cause of a citizen whether it is brought or not brought into a court. There are officials responsible for legislation, administration, and adjudication of every facet of the stakes of a citizen's life – shield, coin, commons, guide, and mirror. Each official is responsible for an aspect of these stakes, usually in review of coordinate or previous officials' exercise of the same responsibility. That is how the bureaucracy works. It is also how moral and legal errors are both corrected (or perpetuated) throughout the legal system. They are caused, cured, or continued by individual officials.

Acts and Omissions

How should we consider whether individual officials have performed their legal obligations? The traditional analysis of the common law turns on whether harm is caused by another's action or through their inaction. This difference arises in part from the old writ system of pleadings, in which certain types of harm caused by someone's actions were pled in trespass and in which certain harms caused by someone's unfulfilled promises were pled in debt. The idea of act or omission was, for a time, captured in the legal terms of malfeasance, distinguishing misfeasance from nonfeasance in examining unmet obligations.[18] Although the distinction between act and omission has become a dead letter for many proceedings in law,[19] it has continued in some senses for the evaluation of officials charged with dereliction of office. Most discipline for officials is for conduct that violates the criminal law or that amounts to actual corruption, or for demonstrable abuses of office. Little enforcement occurs for failing to carry out an office, or for carrying out an office poorly, or with poor judgment, or according to the dictates of others rather than through personal commitment and decision.

In a sense, it seems quite natural to judge someone's action more harshly than someone's inaction. When there is action, a specific event, there is less chance of error in the judgment regarding the person's motives or knowledge than when there is a failure of action. Also, actions take place at a particular time, and inaction usually must continue for some time. An action is more specific than mere inaction, and it can be compared to other actions in greater detail. There is more commitment in an action and a greater sense in which reliance by others is more justified. Thus, the Good Samaritan law in many jurisdictions attaches no liability for citizens who fail to offer aid in a roadside accident,[20] but it will make someone offering aid liable if they give it negligently.[21]

Legal Obligations and the Scope of Office

The Good Samaritan laws illustrate the complexity of ascertaining the legal obligations of an official. Unlike the motorist passing an accident, the official has already made the choice to engage. The official will perform the task either well or not, but having entered office, there is no more sense in asking whether or not the official should be judged by actions alone. The official should be judged by whether the official has carried out the tasks of the law in that office. Like the trustee of an active trust, an official should be judged not by whether the acts that are made are adequate but by whether the trustee acted with sufficient judgment and prudence in caring for the beneficiaries.

---

[18] On the general parallel of misfeasance with trespass and nonfeasance with debt, a distinction eventually merged into assumpsit; see J. H. Baker, *An Introduction to English Legal History* 374–86, 468 (Butterworths, 1990).

[19] Jean Elting Rowe and Theodore Silver, "The Jurisprudence of Action and Inaction in the Law of Tort: Solving the Puzzle of Nonfeasance and Misfeasance from the Fifteenth through the Twentieth Centuries," 33 Duquesne Law Review 807 (1995).

[20] Eugene Volokh, "Duties to Rescue and the Anticooperative Effects of Law," 88 Georgetown Law Journal 105 (1999). Immanuel Kant opposed a state-enforced obligation of a citizen to rescue another citizen, as the legal obligation would negate the moral performance of the duty. See George Fletcher, "Law and Morality: A Kantian Perspective," 87 Columbia Law Review 533, 548 (1987).

[21] See, for example, Joshua Dressler, "Some Brief Thoughts (Mostly Negative) about 'Bad Samaritan' Laws," 40 Santa Clara Law Review 971 (2000).

The scope of legal obligations for an official is the same as the scope of discretion in the office. What an official is required to do, or given the power to do, is what the official should do. At this definition of legal obligation, the legal system has few formal means by which to enforce the legal obligations of individual officials. Once in office, the individual tends to stay. There is the possibility of throwing rascals out for those officials who are elected, yet political success might be quite independent of legal performance in office.

The Breach of Legal Obligations and the Culture of Law

In most cases, the only systemic response for a legal official who fails in legal obligations is through informal means. If the failures of legal duty are beyond the pale – that is, if the errors or omissions are sufficiently greater than a range of performance that other officials customarily accept – the other officials mindful of the culture of law create dissonances: reputation among officials declines, opportunities for promotion or preferment among officials diminish.

This dissonant response from the legal culture is not assured, and there is actually a danger that the opposite result will follow. The immoral conduct will alter the equilibrium of the moral ecology of the officials. Failures will first alter the legal culture and ultimately be enshrined in the archive of the law. Particularly if the failing aspect of the relevant legal obligations is not great, or the moral losses are not at least much beyond the range of what is considered acceptable by other officials, the failures alter the legal culture, which comes to accept the poor performance of officials as the cultural standard. This sort of race to the bottom happens in many professional subcultures,[22] and it is hardly uncommon among officials.[23]

In the end, the standards of law are unlikely to be sufficient to ensure that officials carry out their office with independence and commitment. The only too that actually can ensure that officials will perform their offices well, including their oversight of other officials, is a moral commitment by officials to do so. That moral commitment is defined, at least in this context, by the commitment to the particular office.

Breaching Moral Obligations

Each official is personally responsible for carrying out the moral duties of office, balancing competing moral demands to fulfill the greatest demands and to promote the least unjust result. What is the result when officials do not?

---

[22]   See, for example, David Callahan, *The Cheating Culture: Why More Americans Are Doing Wrong to Get Ahead* (Harcourt, 2004).
[23]   See, for example, Michael W. Quinn, *Walking with the Devil: The Police Code of Silence* (Quinn and Associates, 2004).

And, at the end of the day, what is the response available to others when an official breaches these duties?

Western philosophy has usually believed that moral obligations such as charity are incapable of enforcement, either by those who might benefit from the duty directly or by a superior such as the law or the state. So charity, and other duties that cannot be temporally enforced, have been called imperfect or supererogatory duties.[24] They have been informally relegated to a minor league, in which they have been considered less significant and have been less studied: perceived as less of a basis for public criticism or action by one who violates such a duty. Indeed, one might suppose that in a legal world in which every duty by Tom implies a right in Dick or a claim by Harry, the absence of such rights and claims means that there is no duty.[25] That would be a mistake.

Historically, Christian, western philosophy covered the gap in imperfect duties by expecting the judgment of God to make up the difference. A person who lacked charity would be judged the more harshly, or at least not be given the blessings of the almighty.[26] In a more secular age, a duty with no apparent enforcement agent lacks this significance.

Even so, it is a mistake to assume that there is no enforcement of moral obligations. Although this sort of enforcement usually lacks the worldly effect of legal enforcement, it does not always do so, and there are at least five significant forms that the responses to a breach of moral obligations might take.

1. Moral obligations are reflected in legal obligations.
2. Moral obligations are matters of individual conscience and private image.
3. Moral obligations are matters of public image.
4. Moral obligations are the special province of shame, a matter of private conscience and public image.
5. Moral obligations are enforced through the power of appointment, which is the basis of politics.

Before considering problems arising from these responses, one abiding concern must be considered, which is how to assess the moral significance of personal conduct as an aspect of systemic or group action.

---

[24] As to imperfect duties, see, for example, Samuel von Puffendorf, *The Whole Duty of Man, According to the Law of Nature* 50n (1691) (Ian Hunter and David Saunders, eds.) (Liberty Fund, 2003). As to supererogation, see Gregory Mellema, *Beyond the Call of Duty: Supererogation, Obligation, and Offence* (SUNY Press, 1991).

[25] See Wesley Hohfeld, *Fundamental Legal Conceptions as Applied to Judicial Reasoning* (W. W. Cook, ed.) (Yale University Press, 1964).

[26] See, for example, Jonathan Edwards, *Christian Charity, or the Duty of Charity to the Poor, Explained and Enforced* (1732), an exegesis of Deuteronomy 15:7–11.

Systemic Moral Failures and Individual Responsibility

The most difficult question arising from the intersection of law and morality is what to make of an official who encounters a question in which any answer seems to result in a conflict between a moral obligation and a legal obligation. Chapter 5 considered the logical possibilities of such a conflict, in which the official reconciles the duties, breaches the legal obligation, or breaches the moral obligation. When the choice is to breach the moral duty, how is the official to be judged?

When, for instance, the nineteenth-century judge enforced the Fugitive Slave Act and returned an escaped slave, how should we assess the judge? (Or how should we have assessed the judge then?)[27] Clearly, not all of the judges who enforced the law would be equally at fault. After all, there is a difference, at least of intent, between the judge who enforced the law happily and the judge who enforced it under duress from a court of appeals. Yet such a difference was no solace to the person returned by the law to a life of miserable bondage.

The moral failure of the Fugitive Slave Act was systemic, and yet its effect on those subject to the law was the product of countless individual actions, actions by the constitutional framers, the statutory drafters, the slave hunters, the prosecutors, the judges, and (in a few cases) the juries. Did each of these people have the same moral burden, or should it be seen to vary according to the degree of discretion the law allowed for them to alter the application of the act or to repeal the act itself?

From the seventeenth century, the barbarity of slavery was not universally appreciated throughout American or European culture. Indeed the ideas of abolition grew more known throughout the eighteenth and early nineteenth century, a growth of influence affected not only by changes in technology and economy but also by threats the powerful citizens perceived that slavery posed to their cultural status and personal security. Would an official have the same moral burden in 1750 as in 1850?[28] Would the burden be the same in New York, which abandoned slave labor early as less economical for its mills, or in Virginia, which suppressed slave revolts as it relied on slavery all the more heavily while it industrialized textile production?[29] To what extent should we

---

[27] See the brief discussion in Chapter 5.

[28] The literature on the evolution of antislavery thought and politics is considerable, but it has been redefined in recent decades, particularly following the careful studies of Davis and Foner. See, for example, Christopher Leslie Brown, *Moral Capital: Foundations of British Abolitionism* (University of North Carolina Press, 2006); David Brion Davis, *The Problem of Slavery in Western Culture* (Oxford University Press, 1988); *The Problem of Slavery in the Age of Revolution, 1770–1823* (Oxford University Press, 1999); Eric Foner, *Forever Free: The Story of Emancipation and Reconstruction* (Vintage, 2006).

[29] Compare David Nathaniel Gellman, *Emancipating New York: The Politics of Slavery and Freedom, 1777–1827* (Louisiana State University Press, 2006), with Eva Sheppard Wolf, *Race*

consider officials guilty merely by association with a system of slaveholding that demanded the assistance of free citizens in the return of slaves attempting to reach their freedom? Indeed, are we even capable, much less right, to judge officials from such a distance, in times so clearly different, with countless pressures upon them of which we know next to nothing?[30] And, what do we make of the contrast between such officials and others, who despite such pressures or reservations, chose to promote freedom and human dignity?[31]

The answer to these questions must depend on the basis for the moral obligations at issue. Obligations arise from the oath of office, from the basic values of humanity that apply to all people (even officials), from the acceptance of responsibility for the stakes others have in the system, and from a recognition of the great dangers of office in failing to protect those stakes. These varied origins give rise to moral obligations in different degree, and to varying degrees of public awareness and acceptance.

Some such judgments are very likely to be controversial, but many will be widely accepted by both officials and citizens. Some obligations, rooted in morals as well as or in lieu of law, are so essential to success of the legal system that an official's failure would amount to an implied failure of legal obligations. These are at least prone to knowledge by an official.

An official who does not learn the scope of office, who does not assess the moral significance of official actions, or who does not realize the effects of his or her orders on particular subjects breaches a moral obligation. Although there might not be an express legal obligation of competence, the moral obligation of knowledge can hardly conflict with legal obligations that otherwise define or bind the office. In other words, a sincere effort to ascertain the moral stakes in the decision, the competing values, and the loss to the law by any choice, particularly the immoral choice, is a less immoral method of official action.

Similarly, obligations of fairness, of justice, of right procedure are unlikely to be foreclosed to a given official by other legal obligations. Careful application of the rules of the law through all of its applications to a given case, most notoriously the use of procedural devices to avoid the morally wrong

---

and Liberty in the New Nation: Emancipation in Virginia from the Revolution to Nat Turner's Rebellion (Louisiana State University Press, 2006).

[30] The poster child for the conflicted official must be Thomas Jefferson, whose egalitarian sentiments are forever contrasted to his keeping slaves, including Sally Hemings. See Shannon Lanier, *Jefferson's Children: The Story of One American Family* (Random House, 2002).

[31] Washington, for instance, had all or more of the pressures of Jefferson, yet took the high road. See Henry Wiencek, *An Imperfect God: George Washington, His Slaves, and the Creation of America* (Farrar, Straus, and Giroux, 2004). John Adams had many reasons not to appear in slave cases at the end of his career but argued for the *Amistad* slaves in an attempt to correct what he saw was a dreadful wrong in American law from the *Antelope* decision. See Iyunolu Folayan Osagie, *The Amistad Revolt: Memory, Slavery, and the Politics of Identity in the United States and Sierra Leone* 11 (University of Georgia Press, 2000).

but substantively required result, quite often allows a compromise between seemingly opposed moral and legal obligations.[32]

And yet, knowing better how immoral an act is, and attempted but failed efforts to avoid it, may still provide an official no apparent means to avoid acting according to law in an immoral way. At that point, there is a moral obligation upon an official to signal the moral error being made. Public statements of the error of the law can be made by sheriffs, judges, policemen, legislators, governors, even executioners. An official's statements of moral qualms have significance for other officials and may have influence over time. Even if the statement alone is insufficient to prevent a miscarriage of justice, such statements may encourage officials to alter the law so that there will be justice in similar circumstances in the future.

Such statements are, of course, rare. Although supervisors might not like such statements and even punish their utterance in some cases, the tribal fear of breaking ranks is usually a greater restraint than a fear of actual retaliation from above. Thus, when these statements are made, they must be seen as a significant mitigation of the moral wrong committed by the official who unwittingly acts unjustly.[33]

When the official acts so as to honor a legal obligation and so breach a moral obligation, it is perfectly appropriate to believe that the official's act is immoral. That the action is required by law does not prevent such a belief.

Yet such a judgment cannot be fairly made monochromatically. Some officials bear more responsibility than others. There are great differences between actions in which the official is particularly responsible for an act that is squarely within the official's discretion, such as a legislator voting for the passage of an unjust law or a president authorizing the cover-up of illegal activity, or those in which an official has no apparent legal discretion, such as a jailor ordered to lock down a prisoner. The greater the degree to which the official might have altered the situation for a person harmed by an unjust action, the greater the responsibility, and the harsher the moral judgment for failure to do so must be.

On the other hand, acts of the official may be immoral, but our judgment of their immorality might be mitigated by a variety of circumstances. Two have been discussed already: the degree to which the official sought to understand

---

[32] This is what, in fact, many judges did under the Fugitive Slave Act. See Cover, *Justice Accused.*

[33] The ability of officials to speak out regarding their own actions and to provoke legal reform might well require legal officials to engage in speech relating to the law outside of their official acts of office. In this light, attempts to silence officials with unpopular views – even to squelch the extrajudicial speeches of the likes of Roy Moore – are not in the interest of the legal system, whatever effects such speeches might have on the trust of the people in the legal system. See, for instance, efforts to silence Judge Wendell Griffen in his speeches. *Griffen v. Arkansas Judicial Discipline & Disability Commission*, 355 Ark. 38; 130 S.W.3d 524 (2003).

and avoid the immorality, and the amount of effort with which the official voiced disapproval of the official's own action.

One seeming mitigation that must not diminish an official's moral culpability is the use of agents to carry out an immoral or illegal act. This is the case whether an official orders another to act in a manner that would be immoral for the official or knowingly allows such an act to occur. In this sense, officials who employed foreign agents to engage in torture they would not commit were morally responsible for the torture, from some perspectives all the more so than if they had accepted the responsibility for the actions they brought about.[34]

All these considerations – the degree to which an official may influence a decision, the degree to which the official acts to comprehend its significance, and the degree to which the official acts to end an immoral practice – still do not resolve certain questions of responsibility for overwhelmingly systemic immorality. To what extent is an official responsible through distant complicity for the immoral conduct of all officials?

There is a sense that all officials were tainted by a system that allowed radical acts of evil. The history of nearly every state has episodes of tremendous wrongdoing under the aegis of the law. Whether it is evil on a grand scale – American slavery and racial segregation, Spanish expulsion of the Moors, French abuse of the Huguenots, most European treatment of the Jews, or the universal western disenfranchisement of women – or on a more individual level such as a false criminal conviction or an unfair statute, there is a sense that all who participate in the system are guilty of its wrongs through association.

There are those who believe there is no justification for guilt by association. By this view, collective guilt is impossible, and the only moral judgment possible is of a person's own actions or, at most, the person's inaction when a reasonably effective act was available and neglected.[35] Yet such a position neglects a variety of senses in which individuals feel shame for the actions of members of their

---

[34] On the use by Americans of foreign agents to engage in torture forbidden under international and American law, see Richard Clarke, *Against All Enemies: Inside America's War on Terror* 143–4 (Free Press, 2004). On its expansion, see Benjamin Wittes, *Law and the Long War: The Future of Justice in the Age of Terror* 27–30 and 206–8 (Penguin, 2008). Morally and practically unfit as this practice is, it is hardly new to the Bush II administration; there are direct antecedents in the Cold War, when American agents sent suspected double agents to the German police for interrogation with similar expectations. See interview of Randall Woods with William Egan Colby, U.S. CIA agent in Stockholm, 1951–1954 (on file with the author).

[35] The idea of guilt by association, in which an individual is a member of a group and the group commits wrongdoing, is only one sense of guilt by association. The logical fallacy of association is one in which a person is a member of a category or shares an attribute with another person, thereby bearing the responsibility for what that person is or does. See T. Edward Damer, *Attacking Faulty Reasoning: A Practical Guide to Fallacy-Free Arguments* 54–6 (Wadsworth, 1995).

groups, as well as the many instances in which outsiders ascribe responsibility to a group for its members' conduct, even when the membership involved is a small sample of the whole.[36] More specifically, each member of such a group participates in a Moral Ecology that – directly or indirectly – supports the misconduct of leaders of the group. Even when such leaders maintain their power over the group by force and fear, they acquire it and maintain it through an acquiescence that requires complicity from the group as a whole.[37] In some circumstances, the immoral acts of some officials cannot be committed but for a breadth of acquiescence that amounts to a form of indirect complicity.

Again, such judgments may not be made easily. Among other influences in such a judgment, a view that one official's inaction in the face of another's wrongdoing amounts to systemic complicity might be mitigated, and our sense of outrage or sorrow at the immorality of the inactive individual should be diminished or increased, by the amount of knowledge the inactive official had, by the opportunity the inactive official might have had to intervene, by the relative importance of the official, and by the degree to which the immoral act was consonant with existing official moral ecology. The more in keeping with prior official expectations is a given official's action, the more we observers must accept a sense that the moral guilt of the act is at least somewhat mitigated. We cannot expect people, even officials, to be that much better than those around them.[38]

Thus we find that there is a difference between individual forms of judgment and social forms of judgment. An individual's judgment of the immorality of an official's act may have great or little significance to the official, depending more on who the person in judgment is, how the judgment becomes known to the official, and how the official perceives the basis and source of the judgment. As to the rest of society, however, such judgments communicated among other citizens may form the basis of discourse that leads to consensus, and social judgment and shame become possible.

In the absence of such a consensus, particularly once a conflict in the culture arises, once the culture is itself set against others in, say, the defense of slavery or of the Nazi doctrine of territorial expansion for *Lebensraum*, the mitigation of moral ecology must diminish. Each person becomes more responsible only for making a personal choice on one side or another of the controversy.

---

[36]   See the approaches from both internal and external perspectives in *Collective Guilt: International Perspectives* (Nyla R. Branscombe & Bertjan Doosje, eds.) (Cambridge University Press, 2004).

[37]   See Etienne de la Boétie, *The Politics of Obedience: The Discourse of Voluntary Servitude* (Harry Kurz, trans.) (Black Rose, 1998).

[38]   This idea is developed a bit more in Steve Sheppard, "Passion and Nation: War, Crime, and Guilt in the Individual and the Collective," 78 Notre Dame Law Review 751 (2003).

The effect of such a failure of a consensus must be significant for the official. In the absence of a consensus, the moral judgment of the official by others must accept the failure of moral ecology.[39] This failure can be seen as a condition that mitigates the sense that the official is fully responsible for immoral conduct. That mitigation cannot be sufficient to find the conduct not immoral, particularly if the conduct clearly harms individuals or allows harm to individuals without a powerful argument that the harm is just, or at minimum, the least unjust outcome possible in the circumstance.

Legal Sanctions for Moral Breach

As already discussed in the section entitled "Breaching Legal Duties," moral obligations may be, and often are, reflected in legal obligations upon the official. Though there is a wide range of discretion that the official may exercise without any fear of legal repercussions, outright corruption and abuse of the office may result in legal sanctions for which the office grants no immunity. Thus, many wrongful acts by an official also amount to crimes committed through the use of an office, and these may be prosecuted by other officials.[40] This possibility exists both in personal actions, such as criminal indictments, and in official actions, such as impeachments.[41]

Private Image: Regret and Guilt

The self-image of the official may be affected by the wrongful act, although this requires either a high degree of self-awareness or a means of personal guilt arising through the condemnation of others. As we saw in Chapter 3, in the section entitled "The Stakes and the Special Temptations of Power," self-awareness is difficult to achieve when one exercises power, but it remains possible for officials to act with knowledge and regrets, as we saw in the story of Samuel Sewall.

A breach of the official's obligations may be severe, but there may be no public outcry, no shaming statements: the act may be unknown in the great mass of the legal machinery, or those affected may have no voice to respond. Even so, the official may have a sense of guilt or regret, what in a more naive era one could call a guilty conscience.[42]

---

[39] On the failure of a public moral consensus as thwarting moral expectations for officials, in this case for spies, see Lance Liebman, "Legislating Morality in the Proposed CIA Charter," in *Public Duties: The Moral Obligations of Government Officials* (Joel Fleischman, Lance Liebman, & Mark H. Moore, eds.) (Harvard University Press, 1981).

[40] The conviction of Congressman Cunningham and the problem of corruption are considered quite briefly in Chapter 7.

[41] The U.S. Constitution expressly bars the president from pardon in cases of impeachment. U.S. Constitution, Article II, Section 2.

[42] Rousseau's praise of conscience would embarrass most hearers today. "Thou infallible judge of good and evil, who maketh man to resemble the Deity." Jean-Jacques Rousseau,

The sense of guilt, categorized and tested by modern psychologists, is a strong negative emotion, sometimes accompanied by physical symptoms of illness. It is usually retrospective: the guilt arises following a breach of responsibility. Yet for the official with an ongoing responsibility, guilt from past breaches of moral obligations may spur a desire for more noble performance in the future as a means of avoiding it.[43]

Public Image: Reputation and Shame

Moral condemnation or recognition, the stuff of reputation, might seem to some observers to be of little value, and perhaps in the modern world its cost has diminished. The time may have nearly passed when judges like Samuel Sewall would reflect and regret on their errors in public. If so, this also is a question of moral ecology, and the means to change it are threefold. Both officials and subjects must rebuild their confidence in the ability to make meaningful moral judgments, employing a vocabulary suited to such assessment. Officials must respect this discourse and incorporate it into the culture of the law. It must have occasional influence on both the preferment and the selection of officials.[44] Such pragmatic steps have not always been needed. In an age when reputation mattered more, and perhaps in an age when officials were more conscious of the fragility of their office and the legal system with which they were entrusted, moral judgment alone carried greater weight. Thus, in Philadelphia in 1793,

---

1 *Profession of Faith of a Savoyard Vicar* 64 (New York, 1889), quoted in Theodor Reik, *Myth and Guilt: The Crime and Punishment of Mankind* 15 (George Braziller, 1957).

[43] The magnitude of guilt a person will experience after exposure to a negative event is posited to be a function of the presence and magnitude of a combination of five factors . . . distress (about a negative outcome) and four interrelated beliefs about one's role in the event: (a) perceived responsibility for causing a negative outcome, (b) perceived insufficient justification for actions taken, (c) perceived violation of values, and (d) beliefs about foreseeability and preventability – the degree to which a person thinks he or she knew (in advance) that a negative outcome was going to occur and could have prevented its occurrence.
  Edward S. Kubany and Susan B. Watson, "Guilt: Elaboration of a Multidimensional Model," 53 Psychological Record 51 (2003).

[44] There will always be officials with a robust power of self-deception or self-confidence, whose belief in the righteousness of their actions or in the sanctity of their actions places them above the petty judgment of others. There are others whose desire to abuse their office is sought by those who would put them there. This, indeed, was the populist cause of segregationist politicians, some of whom compromised their earlier moral stance to achieve power for such ends. See, for example, Roy Reed, *Faubus: The Life and Times of an American Prodigal* (University of Arkansas Press, 1997).
  There is a strong case that individuals who are so committed to an inappropriate ethic are simply unfit and should never be allowed to hold office; they are just not right for the job. "An agency's culture of integrity, as defined by clearly understood and implemented policies and rules, may be more important in shaping the ethics of police officers than hiring the 'right' people." Carl B. Klockars, Sanja Kutnjak Ivkovich, & Maria R. Haberfeld, *Enhancing Police Integrity*, NCJ 209269 (National Institute of Justice, 2005).

George Washington accepted his second inauguration as president, and fully half of his address was this:

> Previous to the execution of any official act of the President the Constitution requires an oath of office. This oath I am now about to take, and in your presence: That if it shall be found during my administration of the Government I have in any instance violated willingly or knowingly the injunctions thereof, I may (besides incurring constitutional punishment) be subject to the upbraidings of all who are now witnesses of the present solemn ceremony.[45]

It is accepted by some that shame is an outmoded concept, that the public condemnation of immoral behavior no longer matters or represents a pathological mistake.[46] Shame has been supplanted by offense, in which the observer of the immoral act seeks not a shared public regard for a broken duty, but a sense of reprisal against some conduct that offends the observers or ought to offend others. The differences are profound. Offense is more of an effect within the observer; it is about the righteousness of the offended person and that person's claim for remedy. Shame is more of an effect within the actor; it is about the failing of the immoral person and that person's need for atonement. More, shame is empathetic, and observers sharing shame feel a form of empathy with the actor. That one purpose of some expressions of offense is to shame does not alter their fundamental difference.[47]

Despite this concern for the demise of shame, or at least shamefulness, shame may yet remain an important tool in discouraging moral misconduct. Especially when shame is coupled with an effect that diminishes public image, shame retains the potential to influence behavior. Shame remains controversial as a tool in regulation of citizens by the law, mainly because of a conflation

---

[45] George Washington, Second Inauguration, March 4, 1793. The original transcript, in the hand of Washington's secretary, is available at http://memory.loc.gov/ammem/pihtml/pi002.html.

[46] See, for example, John Bradshaw, *Bradshaw on the Family: A Revolutionary Way of Self-Discovery* 2-4 (HCI, 1988). Bradshaw, a popular psychologist, distinguishes guilt from shame in that shame is criticism of the self, whereas guilt is criticism for an act.

[47] A good model of shame is that felt by Jim for his failure to save his passengers and the shame mixed with offense in the officers of the inquiry in Joseph Conrad's *Lord Jim* (Blackwood, 1900). A useful guide to offense is in Christian Lander, *Stuff White People Like: A Definitive Guide to the Unique Taste of Millions* (#101 Being Offended) (Random House, 2008). That there is a continuing reservation about shaming as a punishment, see James Q. Whitman, "What Is Wrong with Inflicting Shame Sanctions?" 107 Yale Law Journal 1055 (1998). The shaming punishment now growing more common is the shaming aspect of some notice requirements for sexual offender notice laws, which copy an older form of shaming sentence. See Courtney Guyton Persons, "Sex in the Sunlight: The Effectiveness, Efficiency, Constitutionality, and Advisability of Publishing Names and Pictures of Prostitutes' Patrons," 49 Vanderbilt Law Review 1525 (1997).

of shaming exercises, such as the pillory on the colonial village green, with generating a sense of shamefulness.[48]

Shamefulness is not really a legal remedy at all, but an aspect of culture and behavior. In this sense shame is probably so deep-seated an aspect of human behavior that its genuine capacity to alter behavior can survive the trends and fads of culture.[49] Although in times when shame is out of favor it might seem to be an inadequate response for grave immoralities by officials, it may still serve its purpose when it is the focus of the opinion leaders of the legal culture or of the general culture of the nation. It is, of course, also effective when – like Judge Sewall – the malefactor accepts the shame within.[50]

Law, Image, and Politics: The Limited Remedies for Moral Breach

It is frustrating to our sense of justice, but there is no legal remedy for the breach of a moral obligation that is not also a legal obligation. The law always has a possibility to change to create such a remedy, by creating a legal liability that mirrors the moral obligation, though such changes in the United States would be inherently prospective in their reach. Even so, history suggests that the promise of such changes cannot reconcile us to the bane of unpunishable immorality by officials.

Shame and guilt are the responses for moral breach that arise from moral understanding alone. They are not, however, the extent of all moral responses or remedies. More valuable is the role that morality may play as an influence in a given culture to encourage moral practice and discourage its breach. In other words, the most important remedy may be to learn from the breach and to prevent its repetition, to incorporate a strong resistance to immoral actions into the moral ecology of the legal culture. This amounts to a moral basis for the change of legal culture that reflects the concern to correct errors of law, though in this case it is errors of moral obligation.

Such a change to the legal culture does not depend upon changing the archive of the law. New statutes and indictments are not needed. These changes arise more subtly, in preferments, in giving the benefit of the doubt, in subtle but widely understood changes in reputation – in the countless ways in which moral condemnation occurs in a community.

---

[48] See Toni M. Massaro, "The Meanings of Shame: Implications for Legal Reform," 3 Psychology, Public Policy, and Law (1997).

[49] The moral philosopher Bernard Williams argued that shame, an essential basis for ethical enforcement in ancient Greece, retains this influence in modern life. See Bernard Williams, *Shame and Necessity* (University of California Press, 1993). Although his argument was based on Greek drama and history, there is a nice parallel in comparisons to Athenian law. See S. C. Todd, "The Language of Law in Classical Athens," in *The Moral World of the Law* (Peter Cross, ed.) (Cambridge University Press, 2000).

[50] See Chapter 2, the section entitled "A Second Case Study from Colonial Massachusetts."

Beyond this, however, a more powerful opportunity for change in the moral ecology of the officials exists, in the change of personnel. In the many instances, this occurs by the use of the power of officials to appoint other officials. That power can be used in a moral fashion only by appointing officials who are the best qualified and who are considered in good faith by the appointing official to act with the greatest moral sense in office, as opposed to acting for the benefit of the appointing official or the official's allies. Thus neither patronage nor tribalism, whether in the corrupt days of the Tammany Machine or through the recent ideological litmus tests, can be morally justified uses of the power of appointment to legal office.[51]

The ballot is one of the very few ways in which the citizens directly influence the official view of the law. Citizens in a democracy may use their suffrage, their powers to elect the legal officials to punish immoral officials and to prefer those in whom they have confidence or moral action.

As a practical matter, the idea that democracy will be exercised on strictly moral grounds is, at best, idealistic. Yet it is an important justification for a democratic government. There is no moral justification for electing a legal official on grounds of greed or partisanship alone. To have the power to elect a pandering shill does not make it right to do so. In a legal system that is ultimately responsible to the people, it is the people who must ultimately act to punish immoral officials, either directly by voting those out who act badly, or indirectly by voting out those who appoint immoral officials. Thus, although officials may act as a scapegoat for the people when the citizenry blames them for their misdeeds, in a democracy, this shift of the blame can never be complete. As the French lawyer le Comte de Maistre observed, every country has the government it deserves.[52]

---

[51]   As to Tammany Hall, see Theodore J. Lowi, *At the Pleasure of the Mayor: Patronage and Power in New York City, 1898–1958* (Free Press, 1964). It appears that the sense of patronage in legal appointments has been alive and well in the White House lately. See John Solomon & Dan Eggen, "White House Backed U.S. Attorney Firings, Officials Say," Washington Post A1 (March 3, 2007). As to the litmus tests of ideology, see Statement of Glenn A. Fine, Inspector General, U.S. Department of Justice before the Senate Committee on the Judiciary Hearing concerning "Politicized Hiring at the Department of Justice," July 30, 2008, at www.usdoj.gov/oig/new.htm (August 29, 2008).

[52]   Joseph Marie de Maistre, Letter to M. le Chevalier de . . . , August 15, 1811, in 1 *Lettres et Opuscules Inédits du Comte J. de Maistre* 264 (5th ed.) (Vaton, 1869).

7

Tools for the Trade: Maxims and Fallacies

Indeed it is not an easy matter to be really concerned with other people's affairs. . . . Nevertheless, when things turn out for our own good or ill, we realize it more fully and feel it more deeply than when the same things happen to others and we see them only, as it were, in the far distance; and for this reason we judge their case differently from our own. It is, therefore, an excellent rule that they give who bid us not to do a thing, when there is a doubt whether it be right or wrong; for righteousness shines with a brilliance of its own, but doubt is a sign that we are thinking of a possible wrong.

Cicero, *On Duties*, Book I, Chapter IX[1]

How should officials use their instincts for right and wrong, their understandings of their moral obligations? Throughout this book, in which we have asked who are officials, what are the stakes of others in their acts, what obligations are required other than law, what moral obligations relate to legal office, how do obligations affect one another, and what is the meaning of breach, the problem of how do it has lurked just beneath the surface. There is, to be sure, a gap between describing duties and applying them. The law must be seen by the people to be fair, and the officials must work to achieve fairness for those who hold the stakes, if they are to retain the trust of the people subject to the law or to achieve the official aims of the law itself.[2] At the same time, though, no statement or manual of obligations can abridge the fundamental obligations of each official to assess independently what ought to be done and to take personal responsibility for what is done or not done. No formulae can ensure that officials do the right thing.

---

[1]   Marcus Tullius Cicero, *De Officiis* 31 (Walter Miller, trans.) (Loeb edn.) (Harvard University Press, 1913).

[2]   Public perceptions of fairness, a respect for the individual, and engagement with communities and individuals to share understandings of motives and purpose are essential for trust in law enforcement. See Tom R. Tyler & Yuen J. Huo, *Trust in the Law: Encouraging Public Cooperation with the Police and Courts* (Russell Sage, 2002).

Even so, we can synthesize our experiences, cumulating the lessons from the cases we know or find in the archive, not only of the law but of the interplay between the legal culture and the broader culture of citizens over time. We can consider cases analogous to our own at a moment, and we can seek a moral precept from them that, as Cicero suggests, appears to shine with a brilliance of its own or to raise doubts we ignore at our peril.[3] The result of such a synthesis is a rough, initial catalogue of rules of thumb that are more likely than not to assist in reaching a moral decision, or at least a less immoral decision.

This chapter, then, presents some rules of thumb, in both positive and negative forms, as maxims and fallacies. Maxims, general principles of conduct, pose their own risks in application, but they have proved useful in the law for millennia. Fallacies, statements of error for one or another reason, serve as a warning, a lesson learned from mistakes that ought not to be made again. Both will be occasionally illustrated by the types of official depicted in Chapter 1 – Phips's politician, Stoughton's true believer, Sewall's accommodating penitent, and Jones's committed skeptic – with some illustrations that are a bit more contemporary.[4] This effort cannot be the end of the matter, but it might spur debate that could improve our understanding of what the legal official ought to do.

THE NATURE OF MAXIMS

A maxim is a general statement of behavior. Maxims are often written so as to serve as a guide to conduct as well as to provide its own rationale. Often, the rationale is implied or self-evident, as in George Washington's statement, "I have all along laid it down as a maxim, to represent facts freely and impartially."[5]

Maxims have an ancient place in law. Lawyers and judges have coined and applied thousands of maxims.[6] The maxims in law are the bases of decision, an authority on which a case can be decided on broad principle rather than on a narrow and specific rule. In the words of Sir Edward Coke, a maxim is "a sure foundation or ground of art, and a conclusion of reason, because a maxim is of the same worthiness and most certain authority as something which is

---

[3] See epigraph in this chapter.

[4] The four officials as types are summarized in Chapter 2, in the section entitled "Four Models of Legal Official."

[5] John Marshall, *Life of George Washington, Special Edition for Schools* ¶ 94 (Robert Faulkner and Paul Carrese, eds.) (Liberty Fund, 2000).

[6] Bryan Garner has collected well over two thousand maxims in his eighth edition of *Black's Law Dictionary*. His sources include Blackstone's *Commentaries*, Bracton, Coke's *Reports* and *Institutes*, and Justinian's *Digest* and *Institutes*. (Bryan Garner, ed.) *Black's Law Dictionary* 1765 (Thompson West, 1999).

completely proved to everyone, so sure and uncontrollable as that they ought not to be questioned."[7]

The law has a special place for maxims, especially in the pleading and resolution of cases in equity, where ancient maxims of equity still hold sway as principled bases of decision in American courts.[8]

Maxims are also fundamental to American constitutional law, because the text of the Constitution, particularly the articles written in the eighteenth and nineteenth centuries, employs so many standards written in the style of maxims rather than in the style of rules. Broad principles such as "No person shall . . . be deprived of life, liberty, or property, without due process of law" in the Fifth Amendment[9] or "All legislative Powers herein granted shall be vested in a Congress of the United States, which shall consist of a Senate and House of Representatives" in Article I[10] are much more in the form of maxims than rules, a point made clearer when these are compared to the rules of the Imposts and Exposts Clause.[11]

To an extent, reliance on maxims became less central to the law in the twentieth century, as the study of equity declined, as the volume and role of legislation increased, and as the nuances of traditional maxims became less known to the bench and the bar. Even so, new maxims are still coined with surprising frequency, and American case reports are awash with maxims asserted because their self-evident arguments buttress the points the judges and lawyers either seek or enshrine in the law.[12]

---

[7] Sir Edward Coke, *First Institute* 11a, in 2 *Selected Writings of Sir Edward Coke* 646. The opening lines are a quote from Plowden's *Commentaries* 27b, rendered from the original Law French by Coke into English here.

[8] See Steve Sheppard, *Equity and the Law* (Subject Article 6.31.4.1), in *UNESCO Encyclopedia of Life Support Systems* (available at www.eolss.net). Maxims were used in ancient Rome, where they were collected by jurists into handbooks.

[9] U.S. Constitution, Amendment V.

[10] U.S. Constitution, Article I, Section 1.

[11] "No State shall, without the Consent of the Congress, lay any Imposts or Duties on Imports or Exports, except what may be absolutely necessary for executing its inspection Laws: and the net Produce of all Duties and Imposts, laid by any State on Imports or Exports, shall be for the Use of the Treasury of the United States; and all such Laws shall be subject to the Revision and Controul of the Congress."

U.S. Constitution, Article I, Section 10, Clause 2.

[12] In just one summer week in 2007, from August 13 to 17, the Westlaw database of opinions recorded ten opinions naming maxims as a point of argument or decision. These included two quite traditional uses of the maxim *expressio unius exlusio alterius* (the expression of one thing excludes another). See *Ultrasound Imaging Corp. v. Hyatt Corp.* WL 2345256 (N.D. Ga., Aug. 13, 2007), quoting *Rogers v. Frito-Lay, Inc.,* 611 F.2d 1074, 1084 (5th Cir. 1980); *Wells v. Tennessee Bd. of Regents,* 2007 WL 2332962 (Tenn., August 17, 2007). One maxim shown through the double lens of law and general culture was the "street maxim: 'Don't do the crime if you can't do the time.'" *Cook v. U.S.,* 2007 WL 2323487 (D.C., August 16, 2007). Others cited included the "fundamental maxim that the public has a right to every man's evidence." *Hatfill v. Gonzales,* 2007 WL 2296767

Maxims exist in a creative tension, particularly maxims applied in the jurisdiction of equity. Different maxims support different outcomes in general, as in the difference between "equity loves equality" and "where rights are equal, the first in time prevails." Yet a careful application of the facts, coupled with a knowledge of the customs of usage of the various maxims, usually allows one or another of the competing maxims more clearly to apply. This is not always true, and there are maxims at odds with one another, though not so fully opposed as some critics have claimed.[13]

Some readers might need to know that the technical sense in which lawyers use maxims in pleadings and arguments differs from their popular use. Commonly, a maxim is a general guide for behavior, like a moral or a proverb, such as those we associate with Benjamin Franklin or, perhaps, la Rochefoucauld.[14] The main difference between a maxim in the law and a more general, practical maxim is that legal maxims are rules of law and sources in themselves of legal obligations. Lawyers think of them as principles that a judge uses to determine the merits of the actions of litigants before the bench. Maxims have arcane uses besides those of law, particularly as philosophers use them, sometimes following Immanuel Kant's maxims. Kant described subjective reason for any action as a maxim, testing his maxims with logic to determine whether they reflect objective duties. Kant's type of maxim is more akin to what lawyers would know as a motive; lawyers would have said a maxim describes the duty, not the motive.[15] Some philosophers argue that a maxim has no

(D.D.C., August 13, 2007). My favorite is a maxim against maxims, which is very popular with courts these days. "If the text and context are unambiguous, our inquiry ends and we need not resort to legislative history or maxims of statutory construction." *Sedgwick Claims Management Services v. G. Jones*, 2007 WL 2318687 (Or. App., August 15, 2007).

[13] The greatest complaint against the balance of maxims was raised by Karl Llewellyn, who argued that the number of opposing maxims of statutory construction gave too much latitude to interpretation by judges. See Karl N. Llewellyn, "Remarks on the Theory of Appellate Decision and the Rules or Canons about How Statutes Are to Be Construed," 3 Vanderbilt Law Review 395 (1950); *The Common Law Tradition: Deciding Appeals* (Little, Brown, 1960). Despite the enjoyment Professor Llewellyn's article can provide, it is not that difficult to refute, especially in the light of hierarchies of maxims. See the response from the bench by Judge Sills in *Halbert's Lumber, Inc. v. Lucky Stores, Inc.*, 6 Cal. App. 4th 1233, 8 Cal. Rptr. 2d 298 (Cal. App. 4, 1992).

[14] See François duc de la Rochefoucauld, *Collected Maxims and Other Reflections* (E. H. Blackmore, A. M. Blackmore, & Francine Giguere, trans.) (Oxford University Press, 2007). Many of Rochefoucauld's maxims are to us aphorisms, not reaching the fundamental notion of an idea. Franklin's Poor Richard, however, gets to the heart of the maxim with his pithy settings of basic advice. See Benjamin Franklin, *Poor Richard's Almanac* (Peter Pauper Press, 1980). The most massive collection of commonsensical maxims is surely the nearly three thousand pages of Burton Stevenson, ed., *The Macmillan Book of Proverbs, Maxims, and Famous Phrases* (Macmillan, 1987).

[15] See Immanuel Kant, *Groundwork of the Metaphysic of Morals* (1785) (Thomas Kingsmill Abbott, trans.) (Bobbs-Merrill, 1949).

exceptions,[16] whereas for the lawyer maxims are contextual and subject to a body of interpretation built up over time. It would be unusual for a legal maxim to have no exceptions, and exceptions to maxims are often expressed as other maxims. Last, though legal maxims may be often aphoristic in their pith and clarity, they are not aphorisms in the philosophical or literary sense.[17]

Maxims, whether popular or legal, tend to be painted in shades of grey, not in black and white, yet they have solid core values that cannot be ignored or excused when applied with anything near to good faith. They are written in general and universal language but apply to specific cases. They often rely on matters of degree, they incorporate exceptions and balances, and, in the legal sense, they often depend on their application to be made by arbiters acting in good faith. They are tools of legal argument with inherent moral balance.

For instance, the most fundamental legal principle, indeed the most fundamental principle of equity and of all the law, is "there is no wrong without a remedy." A powerful idea, and essential to understanding how law works, it is a nuanced idea full of qualifications and exceptions, some expressed and some implied. Maxims in the legal tradition arise and are tested through their applications in specific cases.[18] There is an inherent balance of interests and of commitments built into the equation and its dependent conditions, not only because the only wrongs that count are those that the law recognizes as sufficiently wrong to justify a remedy but also because those who would take refuge from this maxim may not have done wrong themselves.[19] Maxims therefore are a traditional means of stating legal obligations, in which case most of them

---

[16]   There are some who believe that a maxim cannot be true if there are exceptions to it. Professor Raz disagrees with Professor Finnis over Socrates's maxim that it is better to suffer wrong than to do it, Finnis arguing for it and Raz against it. Joseph Raz, "On the Socratic Maxim," 75 Notre Dame Law Review 1797 (2000). Yet Raz's objection boils down to his belief that there could be trivial exceptions to it. This sort of argument is fun to make (and enjoyable to read) but is not to be taken too seriously.

[17]   See James Geary, *The World in a Phrase: A Brief History of the Aphorism* (Bloomsbury, 2005).

[18]   Well, most maxims arose from cases. There are a few instances when lawyers have tried it from scratch, with varying degrees of success. The most well known met with mixed reviews. See Francis Bacon, *The Elements of the Common Lavves of England Branched into a Double Tract: the One Containing a Collection of Some Principall Rules and Maximes of the Common Law, with Their Latitude and Extent. . . . According to the lawes and customes of this land* (R. Young, 1639). Even Bacon carefully tied his maxims generally to prior legal usage, but for the nonlegal origins and justifications of Bacon's maxims, see Barbara Shapiro, "Sir Francis Bacon and the Mid-Seventeenth Century Movement for Law Reform," 24 American Journal of Legal History, 331 (1980).

[19]   See Herbert Broom, *A Selection of Legal Maxims, Classified and Illustrated* 153–67 (*146– *166) (4th ed.) (T. Johnson & J. W. Johnson, 1854), discussing both *Ubi jus ibi Remedium* (there is no wrong without a remedy) and *Quod Remedio Destituitur ipsa Re valet si Culpa Absit* (that which is without remedy avails itself if there be no fault in the party seeking to enforce it).

have had a dual nature in the tradition. By dictating the obligations of litigants, legal maxims have directed the judgment of judges.

The next section offers maxims with a similar pair of roles, but reversed. Here the maxims dictate the obligations of officials and direct the judgment of subjects (and other officials) who would assess them.

MAXIMS FOR LEGAL OFFICE

Reconsidering the stakes of the law, we might imagine what would have better affected the work of legal officials in all cases. In the opening chapter, the case studies from New England in 1692 offered brief views of four officials – three colonial Massachusetts judges: the self-certain Stoughton, the politically sensitive Phips, and the thoughtful and sympathetic Sewall; and the Connecticut judge: the careful and hard-working Jones. There is much that we can learn from the stakes, from Jones, from the lives of the other three, and from the reflected judgments of history that might give rise to general principles that all four ought to have reflected in their investigation and prosecution of the accused witches. If these principles are well drawn, they will then be as apparent in later cases, both for good and for ill.

The maxims here presented are a means of stating and organizing moral obligations (or at least some of the nonlegal obligations) suggested by the arguments in Chapter 5, with an additional focus from the preliminary questions about the stakes in Chapter 1. There are a few maxims from the law, but these are not legal maxims in the traditional sense, though they could be. This is a sketch, an incomplete list, meant to catalyze discussion. No doubt many more maxims can be added, and surely all of these can be refined. It is only a start.

As with the maxims of equity discussed earlier, there is some overlap, even some contradiction, among these maxims. In that, the maxims reflect somewhat (if only slightly) the competing moral values catalogued in Chapter 4. All of these maxims are subordinate to the most general maxim of the legal official, which must be this: The law must be always created and carried out by officials acting in good faith for the benefit of each and all of the people governed by the law.

Some Maxims from the Nature of Legal Obligations

Follow the Law, Both in Its Spirit and to Its Letter

The sword must be used from time to time, but it must only be used according to the rules and limits of the law itself. The law represents the resolutions and techniques tested through experience, and an official who believes that the law is insufficient for the task and that new tools are required would do well to consider Stoughton's reliance on new forms of evidence, which led to so many false convictions. Plodding like Jones's, if done carefully, thoughtfully, creatively, in the paths laid down by law, is likely to succeed.

Certainly, the law is imperfect, yet it has evolved in response to past mistakes as well as to past successes. The law's procedures, its rules of evidence, its division of labor, all are intended to diminish mistakes, but they will only work when they are followed. When officials attempt to evade the law, particularly when they attempt to deceive other officials or to evade their oversight, the danger of mistake rises quickly. Put another way, this maxim might be, *Don't cheat the law.* An illustration of this idea is the incredible argument made by government lawyers David Addington, William Haynes, Jay Bybee, and John Yoo to distort the spirit, and in the opinion of almost everyone else, the letter of the law when arguing that the United States could torture prisoners and otherwise hold them without regard to the Geneva Conventions.[20] Lesser illustrations happen daily, as when lawyers fail to disclose evidence they should know their clients hold and have been asked to give to their opponents.[21]

Follow the Law, Both as an Official and as a Citizen

The seal demands integrity.

The success of the legal system depends on people believing that they ought to follow it. If officials do not follow the law, their orders to citizens to follow the law look hypocritical at best. Officials must obey the law in their role as officials, responding, for instance, to subpoenas issued by a court or by the houses of Congress. There is much that officials can learn from such obedience, as when Governor Phips realized that he and his wife might be accused of witchcraft.[22]

As an official, the great problem created by President Clinton's behavior with Monica Lewinski was not his private affair while in public office, but that as a citizen he gave misleading testimony about it, therefore breaking the law.[23] Although many people have argued over the legal severity of his offense, it is beyond argument that the president of the United States would have a very powerful moral obligation to tell the truth under oath, which was breached here. Thus, whatever one thinks of the merits of his impeachment, most accepted as just that Mr. Clinton should be rebuked by his state bar for his testimony.[24]

---

[20] See the later discussion of *ad crumenum*: It is true because the money says so.
[21] See, for example, *Baker v. General Motors Corp.*, 86 F.3d 811 (8th Cir., 1996).
[22] See the discussion of the Salem witch trials in Chapter 2.
[23] See *Jones v. Clinton*, 36 F.Supp. 2d 1118 (E.D.Ark., 1999) (Wright, J.).
[24] See "Notice of Suspension, William Jefferson Clinton," January 19, 2001, 36 Arkansas Lawyer 42 (2001) (the five years of suspension ended in 2006).

The Office Does Not Belong to the Officer, Sponsor, or Party, but to the Law

The nature of the seal requires trust that the office will be used for the subjects, and the citizenry lives in rightful fear that the shield, the commons, indeed all of their stakes will be ransomed by those whom they have no choice but to trust. This is the strength of officials like Sewall and Jones, who saw in their offices a trust to be carried out much more than a means to profit or advancement.[25]

Carry out the duties of office for the people, not for the party or profit. Profit, whether the bribery of Congressman Duke Cunningham, or the election contributions for donor coffees with President Clinton, or the Ranger meetings of President Bush, taints every act of office that benefits such donors.[26] When the party seeks to control a vote or secure a decision, as it surely did when Tom DeLay sought to coerce Republicans to vote to impeach President Clinton, no vote that is cast can be without suspicion.

Even those powers of office that are given the greatest discretion must not be exercised for the benefit of the officer or the officer's friends and allies. The use of one's office to benefit one's allies raises an inherent presumption that the office has been abused. Thus, when President Clinton pardoned accused tax cheat Marc Rich, whose wife had given generously to his library, it was widely believed that he had violated his trust.[27] Similarly, it seemed to many that President Bush violated his trust in commuting the prison sentence of Scooter Libby, a former administration official who was convicted of lying on behalf of other officials.[28] Undeniably, the statements recorded of Illinois Governor Rod Blagojevich attempting to sell President-Elect Barak Obama's vacated seat

---

[25] See the discussions of Sewall and Jones in Chapter 2.

[26] Congressman Cunningham created a price list for his votes and support for bills before his arrest and resignation. See "Brazen Conspiracy," Washington Post A20 (Nov. 29, 2005). The seemingly well-documented fundraising activities of Presidents Clinton and Bush were legal, because only such direct trades of money for influence are illegal. The indirect trade of influence for money is legal. That does not make it right or good.

[27] See, for example, Jessica Reeves, "The Marc Rich Case: A Primer," Time (February 13, 2001) (available at http://www.time.com/time/nation/article/0,8599,99302,00.html). President Clinton's defense of the pardon is at William Jefferson Clinton, "My Reasons for the Pardons," New York Times (February 18, 2001) (available at http://www.nytimes.com/2001/02/18/opinion/18CLIN.html? ex=1188100800&en=1dd2394e0cbc1f9f&ei=5070). Rich paid a fine of $200 million. That Rich had used his influence to game the rules up to the moment of his pardon increased the sense that the pardon was not a just use of the pardon power. A strong model of just use of this authority is in Kathleen Dean Moore, *Pardons: Justice, Mercy, and the Public Interest* (Oxford University Press, 1989). On the foreign-policy implications of the pardon, see Joe Conason, "The Real Reason Bill Clinton Pardoned Marc Rich," www.salon.com (Jan. 16, 2009).

[28] See Amy Goldstein, "Bush Commutes Libby's Prison Sentence," Washington Post A1 (July 3, 2007). Many observers objected that the president's reasons to reduce the relatively light sentence were the same that he had often rejected when opposing appeals or rejecting pardons for other criminals. See Harlan J. Protass, *The Quality of Mercy Is Strained: Bush Commutes Libby's Sentence, While His Lawyers Come Down Hard on Everyone Else*, Slate.com (July 3, 2007). Libby paid a fine of $250,000. Progress has been made since James II's practice of selling pardons for two shillings apiece, but the pardon remains a

in the U.S. Senate cannot be tolerated in a legal system requiring the trust of the governed.[29] Treating the powers of office as a personal gift is an abuse of the office, diminishing trust in the legal system as a whole.

The Law Is Not a Church

The guide and the mirror are envied by many who would seek the glory either of controlling them for their own sake or of dedicating them as an offering to their church. The use of office in the service of a church, at least when the state is not a theocracy, is to subordinate the interests of the law to those of the believer. This can run real risks, particularly when the ineffable and unmeasurable demands of one person's faith become the measure of another's guilt. Religious zeal in an official, especially a prosecutor or judge like Stoughton of Massachusetts, can blind the officer to errors that might be apparent even to co-religionists.[30]

Dogma cannot be the basis for law in the modern world. It can be the basis for private worship, but not public commands of the law. The attempts by evangelists to enforce their revelations of the divine will upon others through the requirements of law are of long standing in American history. The officials of Massachusetts colony used the decalogue for their criminal code. Yet when the judges allowed spectral evidence because it was in keeping with divine command, hundreds of innocent people were arrested and twenty killed. How, after all, should Judge Roy Moore require the veneration of his holy relics but a devout Muslim be denied his in the Alabama courthouse? To allow one and not the other, indeed to allow any, endangers the freedom of the subjects to develop their own conscience, while increasing the stakes of the law as a game of religious winners and losers. To limit the law from enforcing religion does not require law contrary to religion or even in disagreement. The law must be based, rather, on grounds of right and good conduct that are meaningful to all regardless of the view of God each holds or lacks. This limitation is, after all, the basis for religious freedom.[31]

---

personal grant more than a public mercy. See Kathleen Dean Moore, *Pardons: Justice, Mercy, and the Public Interest* (Oxford University Press, 1997).

[29] FBI affidavits filed with the criminal complaint for fraud, in *United States v. Rod R. Blagojevich and John Harris*, allege that the Governor of Illinois, among a host or other forms of fraud and attempts to sell the favors of his office, attempted to trade the Senate seat in his grant for a job for his wife, for a cabinet position for himself, or for cash or take the seat himself, at one point saying "the Senate seat 'is a fucking valuable thing, you don't just give it away for nothing.'" *U.S. v. Blagojevich and Harris*, No. 08-CR1010, Affidavit of FBI Agent Daniel Crain, 56 (N.D. Ill. Dec. 7, 2008).

[30] See the discussion of the Salem Witch trials in Chapter 2.

[31] See the brief discussion in Chapter 4. On the necessity of freedom from civil coercion in order to enjoy religious liberty, see *Dignitatis Humanae: Declaration on Religious Freedom*, promulgated by His Holiness Pope Paul VI, December 7, 1965.

The Law Has No Secrets

The law requires trust, and every office is a trust to the benefit of the people, part of an enterprise shared among all other officials. There simply are no secrets about the office that may legitimately be kept, with the overwhelmingly few genuine exceptions regarding immediate actions to enforce the law or genuine security issues to protect spies and soldiers in the field. This is not to say that officials have nothing to hide, but what they tend to hide is in their interests, not in their offices' interests, to keep hidden. The notion, for instance, of executive privilege to keep information about whom the president or advisers rely upon secret is nearly always to avoid the embarrassment of people who seek favors from the executive. The idea that the president must receive information about, say, energy policy in such secrecy that even its origins cannot be allowed to the Congress or the people is one that might be allowed by law but cannot be anything but self-serving to the president and those self-interested advisers.[32]

Some Maxims from the Nature of Nonlegal Obligations

Protect the Law, and the People Subject to It, from Other Officials

How do officials offer the shield and the sword without risk the sword will become all? Often only an official can bar others from error. Whether the protection comes from someone who has embraced the error and rejects it, like Phips and Sewall, or from someone who avoided it through other commitments like Jones, it is usually the actions of officials that curb abuses by officials like Stoughton.[33]

There are stories beyond number of abuse at the hands of the law. Yet this abuse was not the product of a faceless system; it was committed by the hands of individual officials. It is incumbent on each official who can stop others from their abuses to use their powers of office to do so, every time. Thus, when Adolph Lyons, an African American, was stopped by the Los Angeles police for a broken taillight, he offered no resistance but was still placed in a regulation "choke-hold," causing him to lose consciousness. The only relief he could seek in court was an order forbidding the police from following their rules, which would allow police to choke him again if he was detained; but Justice Byron White wrote that Lyons's claims must be dismissed because he could not prove that he was immediately in danger personally of being choked again.[34] The legal point regarding injunctions was, at best, arguable at the time,[35] but the

---

[32] See *Cheney v. U.S. District Court for the District of Columbia*, 542 U.S. 367 (2004), in which the vice president fought to keep secret who had advised him on energy policy in the United States.

[33] See the section of Chapter 2 entitled "Institutional Obligations."

[34] *City of Los Angeles v. Lyons*, 461 U.S. 95, 105 (1983) (White, J.).

[35] See *City of Los Angeles v. Lyons*, 461 U.S. 113 (1983) (Marshall, J., dissenting).

moral obligation to prevent officials from choking people with bad taillights is beyond argument.

Listen to Those Who Lose by Law

The guide and the mirror demand refinement of the harms the subjects suffer in the name not only of morality but also of administration, policy, and convenience. It would have been better for all if the judges of Massachusetts had truly listened to the impassioned statements of their victims – if they had learned from the quiet courage of Giles Corey, who died rather than falsely confess, or John Willard, the constable who was hanged for refusing to arrest the innocent.[36]

What does the prison guard hear from the prisoner? Trained, professional guards and wardens listen carefully to complaints and suggestions, even from their worst inmates. A failure to hear these voices, a failure of empathy, can lead not only to abuse but also to rebellion.[37]

Sometimes these voices are harder to hear. Officials can only assess the harm of the law when it is known. What is known, for instance, of the harms done by laws against interracial marriage until the voice of those denied is heard?[38] The difficulty of hearing the voices of those whom the law marginalizes is made greater when they cannot speak in the law. Rules of evidence that bar genuine evidence from the courthouse, or rules of procedure that bar claimants from the courthouse door, interfere with these voices and perpetuate wrongs when there is no review for the wronged.[39] The primary lessons of recent years wrought by the study of law from the perspective of women, of races, and of different genders is that the outsider sees the law very differently[40]; it is to see the law from under the bridge.

Pursue the Least Unjust Result

The most important stake in the law is justice, and when justice cannot be had, the next best outcome is to have the least unjust result. Thinking again of the

---

[36] See Chapter 2.

[37] See, for example, Michael Esslinger, *Alcatraz: A Definitive History of the Penitentiary Years* (Ocean View Publishing, 2003) detailing not only warden interviews but the apparent abuse that led to an escape attempt becoming a deadly prison riot in 1946.

[38] See, for example, Charles F. Robinson II, *Dangerous Liaisons: Sex and Love in the Segregated South* (University of Arkansas Press, 2003).

[39] In both 1955 and 1956, the Supreme Court barred claims against Virginia's antimiscegenation laws. See *Naim v. Naim*, 87 S.E.2d 749 (Va. 1955), vacated and remanded on procedural grounds, 350 U.S. 891 (1955) reinstated and aff'd 90 S.E.2d 849 (Va. 1956), appeal dismissed, 350 U.S. 985 (1956). Virginia's laws against interracial marriage were finally dismissed in *Loving v. Virginia*, 388 U.S. 1 (1967). The usual argument on behalf of the *Naim* decision is that the court feared national instability in reaching the question of marriage between races so soon after desegregating schools. See, for example, Cass R. Sunstein, "Timing Controversial Decisions," 35 Hofstra Law Review 1 (2006).

[40] See, for example, Martha Minow, "Justice Engendered," in *Feminist Jurisprudence* 217 (Patricia Smith, ed.) (Oxford University Press, 1992).

Salem trials: what possible injuries could have justified so many executions, so many lost family members, so many deaths? Considering the whole of the enterprise, even the balance of war rhetoric and the religious drama of wickedness and idolatry, the loss of liberty, property, and life for so many could not be just in comparison to all they were said to have done. Sewall's late awakening to this fact, and to the injustice of a process that led to the death of so many innocents, must stand as a testament to the demands of this maxim and the dangers of its rejection.[41]

This is the maxim for the moment of dirty hands: when all the options are genuinely bad, the official is still not free from basic moral responsibilities. The choice must always be for the lesser (or the least) evil choice.[42] Owing to the likelihood in such a circumstance that the agent who must choose will rationalize a poor choice, one benefit of the bureaucratic nature of the legal system is that nearly every decision must be ratified by another official. Thus, for example, during the chaos that followed the 2005 Katrina floods of New Orleans and the failure of officials to evacuate the city, there were great concerns about the effects of displaced persons on public order and about access to scarce commodities, particularly drinking water. Gretna, Louisiana, Police Chief Arthur Lawson, and other officials of Gretna and Jefferson Parish, Louisiana, decided to place an armed blockade of police across the Crescent City Connection bridge over U.S. Highway 90, closing it to all evacuation from the stricken city. Theirs was a choice among evils, yet it was the most evil of choices.[43]

Some Maxims from the Obligations of the Good Person in Office

Act Toward Others as You Would Hope They Would Act Toward You if the Roles Were Reversed

The sword is fearsome, and it can destroy the shield. The best assurance of a balance between them is to imagine the view from those who fear them each, to show true charity to those whom the law would harm by action or inaction. How would the zealous Stoughton have reacted had he been confronted with

---

[41] See the discussion of the three Salem officials in Chapter 2.

[42] This view was best argued in the twentieth-century United States in a wonderful book that has never acquired the wide audience it deserved. See Edmund N. Cahn, *The Sense of Injustice: An Anthropocentric View of Law* (New York University Press, 1949). In general, Cahn argues that justice is the act of remedying what is perceived as injustice, that power must be used to create less injustice. The idea has an allure that has leapt the gap in academic conversation, as seen in Michael Ignatieff, *The Lesser Evil: Political Ethics in an Age of Terror* (Princeton University Press, 2003), though Ignatieff is more concerned with issues of proportionality in the use of force. This approach is related to the idea that law must incorporate morals, at least sufficient to avoid immorality or injustice, as considered in Chapter 4 in the section on procedural obligations, but the approach here turns on a difference between what the law is and what legal officials ought to do.

[43] See, for example, Aaron Sharockman, "Neighboring Town Denied Evacuees," St. Petersburg Times 1A (September 17, 2005).

spectral evidence of his own devil worship, invented by a scared young witness? How, indeed, did the political Phips respond when he was to be treated in the manner he had allowed to his subjects? The asymmetry of such expectations suggests that this application of the Golden Rule remains a powerful tool, particularly in assessing the justice of laws of procedure and evidence.

Charity, treating others as one would be treated, requires each person to be valued by each official. Charity does not require that the guilty go free or that some might not suffer for the good of all, but it does require that the guilty be punished only because of what they have done (not what an official has decided they have done). It requires each person to do what they would hope another would do for them. Charity requires diligent service, particularly the careful performance of one's duties in office. It requires, for instance, the police to prevent crimes as well as to punish the actual wrongdoers. It forbids mistreatment of prisoners and the abuse of witnesses. It forbids underfunded prisons, badly staffed security checks, poorly designed immigration halls, overcrowded jails, and all the other places of involuntary detention in which the subject is treated without dignity, fairness, or even the most minimal competence in the subjects' management.[44]

Charity does not stop at the requests of the subject but goes forward to demand what might have been requested.[45] For instance, charity requires actual corroboration in cases of confession, because every confession is potentially false.[46]

Charity provides the official a nearly constant test of the rightness of action, but the test can be hard to apply when the official is deluded about what the official would really hope if the tables were turned. If one sees oneself as beyond mistake, it is easy to imagine oneself comfortably being held to a standard of judgment against the least error, a standard that realistically would be terrifying. Unfortunately, human beings, including officials, seem to have an innate capacity for self-deception and rationalization.[47] We have an ability to compartmentalize forms of our behavior and our expectations, and this ability allows stunning levels of hypocrisy. It might be one reason why legislators seem so often to argue for strong laws against the precise forms of immoral behavior that they themselves commit. In recent years, a prominent senator, David Vitter, and a powerful congressman, Mark Foley, both of whom built careers on moral legislation under the "family values" rubric or through

---

[44] As if an illustration were needed here, see *Pasha v. Gonzales*, 433 F.3d 530 (7th Cir. 2005) (immigration judge rejected evidence of Albanian persecution of asylum seeker, knowing no Albanian but judging the materials as forged with no basis in fact).

[45] See the brief discussion in Chapter 4, in the subsection entitled "A Summary of Official Charity."

[46] See *An Innocent Texas Inmate Is Freed*, Salon.com, Jan. 17, 2001.

[47] See Carol Tavris and Elliot Aronson, *Mistakes Were Made (but Not by Me): Why We Justify Foolish Beliefs, Bad Decisions, and Hurtful Acts* (Harcourt, 2007).

discrimination against gays, have been found to consort with prostitutes or to procure gay relations with young former staff.[48] Such hypocrisy is hardly new, but it illustrates the requirement of a reasonable hope as part of charity: we must have a clear understanding of what we are doing to someone else, before we could assess by a reasonable hope that we would like to be similarly treated by them if our roles were reversed.

Officials Must Know the Law and the Facts from Every Perspective

Every official must know the law that the office would apply, and although knowing the law is difficult, ignorance of the law is not excused.[49] Mastery of both the archive and the culture to know what is required, forbidden, or possible in a position requires a breadth of knowledge many officials never attain. Yet each official must develop a personal knowledge, for the official who does not will depend on others to the peril of the independence of office. This knowledge cannot be limited either by preference for an outcome or by distaste for a source, but all of its sources must be considered to assess their genuine authenticity and reliability.

This is the problem of the Salem trials in a nutshell. There was no real investigation, no real understanding by the judges of who their defendants were or what was the evidence before them. The rush to judge in the spirit of the moment allowed dodgy evidence to replace the need for genuine knowledge. The contrast between Stoughton and Sewall's reliance on limited and invented testimony and Jones's requirement that the magistrates conduct a thorough review of the facts related to each charge made the difference between life and death to the defendants in each jurisdiction.[50]

The assessment of claims to knowledge is an independent difficulty. Ideas are hard to assess, but the truth or falsity of an idea may grow more obvious the more frames of reference are applied. When, for instance, one thinks of Tituba testifying in Salem in 1692, and one hears in her testimony only the voice of an accused witch, one fails to hear what one could hear in the voice of a scared young Barbadan slave, or what one could hear in the voice of a war refugee.

An official has no moral claim to ignorance. When Attorney General Alberto Gonzales testified to the Congress of the United States that he just wasn't aware

---

48   See, for example, Adam Nossiter, "A Senator's Moral High Ground Gets a Little Shaky," New York Times (July 11, 2007) (Republican Senator David Vitter with a prostitute); Kate Zernike & Abby Goodnough, "Lawmaker Quits over E-Mail Sent to Teenage Pages," New York Times (September 30, 2006) (Republican Congressman Mark Foley with teenaged former congressional pages).

49   Although ignorance of the law might not be a defense for individuals, it is actually an acceptable defense for officials, at least so long as the ignorance was in "good faith," which is to say that a reasonable person would not have known of the law. See, for example, *Hope v. Pelzer*, 536 U.S. 730 (2002).

50   See Chapter 2, the section entitled "A Second Case Study from Colonial Massachusetts."

of any illegal aspect of how his office came to fire U.S. attorneys, he either lied or was willfully ignorant.[51] Either is a breach of faith in his office.

One difficulty in satisfying this obligation is the degree to which officials must depend on other officials for information. This is an obstacle to knowledge, but it is an obstacle that can be diminished by acting without imprudent haste. For instance, Congress has twice passed resolutions allowing the president to use U.S. military force, when the Congress lacked the knowledge to judge that its resolutions were based on false information. In passing both the Gulf of Tonkin Resolution and the Authorization for the Use of Military Force against Iraq, Congress based its hasty decision on information that could have been disproved had it conducted its own investigation before acting.[52]

Officials Ensure the Truth

The shield, the mirror, and the seal – as indeed the coin, commons, and guide – all demand truth. There can be no moral excuse for standing before an innocent person and saying they are guilty of a crime, unless every effort possible has been expended to determine that it is true. This is different from the legal requirement that a case has been made. The moral imperative must be that the statement has been, as far as possible, proved to be true. Thus Sewall, who knew this had not been done, believed that God had punished his children for his error.[53]

The law cannot be applied without facts. Many of the greatest miscarriages of justice occurred because the actual facts, the true events as a matter of history that should have grounded an application of law were either hidden or distorted. There are false convictions, and there are mistaken acquittals, because the story told in court was untrue. Even when a lie is thought by an official to serve a higher goal, it is an abuse of the law to tell it in a legal setting. When, for instance, FBI agents knowingly lied, withheld evidence, and encouraged perjury to protect a Mafia informant, causing Peter Limone, Louis Greco, Henry Tameleo, and Ronald Cassesso to be sentenced to death for a murder that the agents of the government knew they did not commit, they

---

[51] See, for example, Michael Sung, *FBI Director Contradicts Gonzales Testimony on Domestic Spying Program*, Jurist.com (July 27, 2007). Mr. Gonzales had similar problems in 2006 and 2007 with his testimony regarding the firing of U.S. attorneys and with his attempts as White House counsel to goad a hospitalized John Ashcroft into authorizing surveillance activities that Ashcroft believed to be illegal.

[52] On the false report of an attack on U.S. naval vessels in the Gulf of Tonkin on August 4, 1964, see Ezra Y. Siff, *Why the Senate Slept: The Gulf of Tonkin Resolution and the Beginning of America's Vietnam War* (Praeger, 1999); Edwin E. Moïse, *Tonkin Gulf and the Escalation of the Vietnam War* (University of North Carolina Press, 1996). As to the mistakes in Congress's action in Iraq, see the section of this chapter entitled "Some Maxims from Obligations of the Officer to the Institutions of Law." Good officials make their own decisions.

[53] See the discussion of the Salem witch trials in Chapter 2.

violated one of the most fundamental moral obligations to the law: to seek the truth.[54]

Some Maxims from Obligations of the Officer to the Institutions of Law

Officials Must Balance Discretion in Office with Deference to Other Officials

The stakes of the balance, the seal, and the veil demand that every official take responsibility not only for their acts of office but for the potential acts of office and, to some extent, acts of the system as a whole. This demand persists despite the limits of deference, the knowledge that every office is limited by both its own powers and the powers of other offices. Each official must defer to others, while still acting independently within the bounds of discretion. An official can even alter the limits of that discretion when the official believes an injustice has been done or is about to be done that the official has (or might have) the power to correct. This is precisely what Governor Phips did in requesting a special court for the Salem trials, and then in disbanding it.[55] Yet such broad discretion is rare, and the balance between deference and discretion is hard to achieve.

To a degree, balance can be achieved by rules. The standards of review of a jury verdict, of a trial court, give certain powers to an appellate judge, reserving others to the trial judge or to the jury. Yet, in extraordinary instances, the appeals judge (or a majority of the appeals court) may believe that the mistakes made below are too great to allow deference and overturn them.[56] The rules by which courts and the executive defer to Congress, by which the states defer to the federal government, and by which the federal government defers to the states have all been broadly understood by rules refined for two centuries under the doctrines of separation of powers and federalism.[57]

Yet, it can be hard to maintain this balance. In 2005, Terri Schiavo had been in a coma for fifteen years, following a cardiac arrest and collapse that left her brain permanently damaged. Following five years of litigation between Terri's husband and her parents, during which the courts had ordered her examination by five doctors, Florida state judge George Greer granted the husband's motion to allow doctors to remove a feeding tube in her abdomen that had kept her alive. Members of Congress, particularly Senator Bill Frist, a

---

[54] *Limone v. United States*, 497 F.Supp. 2d 143, (D. Mass., 2007) (ordering damages of $1 million per year for false imprisonment).
[55] See Chapter 2, the section entitled "A Second Case Study from Colonial Massachusetts."
[56] See, for example, Steven Alan Childress & Martha S. Davis, *Federal Standards of Review* (Butterworth Legal Publishers, 1992).
[57] See, for example, Tom Campbell, *Separation of Powers in Practice* (Stanford University Press, 2004); Eric N. Waltenburg & Bill Swinford, *Litigating Federalism: The States before the U.S. Supreme Court* (Greenwood Press, 1999).

doctor, decided that Judge Greer's decision was medically and legally wrong, and Congress passed a statute to much public fanfare, ordering federal courts to hear any complaint (in this one case) that the Florida order violated Schiavo's right to life.[58] Despite this act, the federal courts found no violation of federal rights in Judge Greer's order,[59] and at least one judge believed that Congress violated both separation of powers and, probably, federalism and refused to intervene.[60] An autopsy later supported the medical basis of Judge Greer's order.[61] The whole awful story suggests a failure to give deference that was, or should have been, an act of hubris embarrassing to the many legislators involved.

The Schiavo statute failed two basic tests: First, deference to the tasks dedicated to other officials in the legal system should be maintained unless the facts suggest that the officials dedicated to the task have failed in their legal and moral obligations so blatantly that a grave injustice will result. Second, an official's intrusion into the authority of others must be based on general principles that the official will stand by in the future, not on unique, unrepeatable grounds.

The deference in the Schiavo case could not be challenged according to the facts, because Congress never learned the facts but in the most cursory and shallow degree. And, other than disagreeing with a claimed outcome, there is no evidence that the legislators examined the diligence of the judges and lawyers involved. Beyond these failings of the first test, the second ought to have raised some alarm, given that the statute purported to grant the whole jurisdiction of the federal courts to this one matter alone, all others like it being ignored.

The majority opinion in *Bush v. Gore*, the Supreme Court opinion overturning the Florida courts' ordered recount of the election of 2000, appears to have failed this second test, too, by attempting to limit its intrusion into state matters to this one case.[62] That opinion suggests a further test for arguments to change the boundaries of discretion and deference: do the officials whose office is diminished agree that it is in the public interest?

In a legal system divided among branches, deference amounts to a form of respect granted by those who defer (or by their superiors). Deference cannot usually be demanded by officials elsewhere. The independence of different

---

[58] An Act for the Relief of the Parents of Theresa Marie Schiavo, Public Law 109-3 (S 686), March 21, 2005.

[59] *Schiavo ex rel. Schindler v. Schiavo*, 403 F.3d 1289 (11th Cir. 2005).

[60] *Schiavo ex rel. Schindler v. Schiavo*, 404 F.3d 1270, 1271 (11th Cir. 2005) (Birch, J., concurring).

[61] David Brown & Shailagh Murray, "Schiavo Autopsy Released; Brain Damage 'Was Irreversible,'" Washington Post A1 (June 16, 2005).

[62] *Bush v. Gore*, 531 U.S. 98 (2000). The limitation of the precedential value to "the present circumstances" is at *id.* 109.

officials might thwart changes or exceptions to the rules bounding offices. The failure of one official to defer to another official cannot, in itself, prove that either must defer to the other, or that officials in yet third and fourth offices would acquiesce in the deference. Each official up the line must make such a decision.

Yet deference cannot be demanded in a legal system; it must be granted when it is appropriate because the official deferred to has demonstrably performed the obligations of office. Thus, when lawyers for the president told judges that the judiciary might not even inquire into whether executive wiretapping is legal or illegal, the judges rightly and predictably expressed skepticism when told that all such decisions must be deferred to the president.[63]

The government lawyer, a member of the executive branch, is particularly vulnerable to abuse when this form of deference is not accorded by executive officials. This is to say that presidents, governors, and senior administrators have a moral obligation to defer to the opinions of the law given by the lawyers on their staffs. To demand that a lawyer reach a legal conclusion that is politically or personally convenient, or to punish those who reach conclusions under the law that vary from an official's personal philosophy, is to breach one's own moral obligations under the law.[64]

Good Officials Solve Problems

The shield, the coin, and the commons depend on pragmatic and successful management of situations throughout the world of the subject. Crimes against person and property must be few, and they must be resolved in some manner, or the people will become vigilantes. Disputes must be finally resolved by peaceful means, or violence will be preferred. The staples of life must be accessible, or the subjects will revolt to attain them. Either the basic provisions of life, order, and safety must be secured by law, or the officials of law will lose a fundamental basis for the subject to trust them.

Often, the first step is to ascertain the nature of the problem. When the young women of Salem began their accusations, the problem could have been to find witches, or it could have been to counsel and protect these orphans from

---

[63] See Adam Liptak, "U.S. Defends Surveillance before 3 Skeptical Judges," New York Times A13 (August 16, 2007); Dahlia Lithwick, *Lawyers in Wonderland: How Good Lawyers Sprout Whiskers and Top Hats after Drinking Too Much National-Security Punch*, Slate.com, August 16, 2007.

[64] Thus, the apparent decision to remove eleven U.S. Attorneys on political grounds, taken by Justice Department officials in 2005 and 2006, represents a moral breach, regardless of whether it is a legal breach by those who authorized it. See Julie Scelfo, *'Quite Unprecedented': Former U.S. Attorney Mary Jo White Explains Why the Firing of Eight Federal Prosecutors Could Threaten the Historic Independence of Federal Law-Enforcement Officials*, http://www.newsweek.com (March 15, 2007). The shameful treatment of military lawyers who actively represented their clients before U.S. military commissions is discussed later.

war-ravaged towns. Taking the problem as it was first presented, and treating the charges of witchcraft as valid, Governor Phips and the local officials created a circumstance in which the real problems would not be solved.

In the early years of the twenty-first century, the United States saw the idea of solving the problems that genuinely risk order and liberty tested in two dramatic ways – by the attacks of terrorists on September 11, 2001, and by the destruction of New Orleans and the Mississippi coast by Hurricane Katrina four years later. Both catastrophes yielded great hardship for the citizenry and complex problems for the legal system, but the fundamental questions each presented was whether the bureaucracy had been prepared to respond, whether it did respond as well it should have, whether it was diminishing the chances of such disasters in the future, and whether it would be prepared for the next disaster.[65] There was a strong sense of the subjects that, in quite different ways, officials had failed them in each event.[66]

Good Officials Correct Mistakes, Even Old Ones

Mistakes are bound to occur, whether accidental or intentional. Subjects must rely on the balance and the guide, and when they are misused, or even abused, by one official, it is incumbent on all who can to correct the misuse. This requirement is magnificently illustrated in Judge Sewall's apology for his errors in the Salem trials, which not only laid to rest some ongoing questions of law but moved the colony toward mitigating the harms its trials had caused.[67]

An official who can rectify a mistake, even one long past, has an obligation to do so. The official might be so long past a mistake of such wrong that rectification may be impossible, but then at least recognition in itself is a mitigation of the wrongdoing. In this way, official apology for past injustice has its place. More compellingly, officials who have information of a mistake must act to correct it. For instance, in the year 2000, Minnesota state prosecutor Susan Gaertner's office acquired new technology to review evidence in older cases and, following a review of old convictions, learned that David Brian Sutherlin had been convicted following a false confession for a rape he could not have performed. On the state's motion, he was released from his prison

---

[65] In this sense, the distinction that Judith Shklar makes between injustice and misfortune collapses; it is the type of point at which she would say that misfortune becomes injustice. See Judith Shklar, *The Faces of Injustice* (Yale University Press, 1990).

[66] See, for example, National Commission on Terrorist Attacks upon the United States, *9-11 Commission Report* (2004) (available at www.9-11commission.gov/ report/index.htm); Ted Steinberg, *Acts of God: The Unnatural History of Natural Disaster in America* (Oxford University Press, 2006). There are always exceptions, and the performance of the U.S. Coast Guard during Katrina, and the performance of the city fire, police, and emergency services in New York, mitigated the perception of otherwise systemic failure. See, for example, Stephen Barr, "Coast Guard's Response to Katrina a Silver Lining in the Storm," Washington Post B2 (September 6, 2005).

[67] See Chapter 2.

and his sentence of life imprisonment.[68] In contrast, prosecutors and judges have refused to acknowledge other cases, particularly of false confessions, in which DNA evidence patently exonerates a convict.[69] Though the culture of prosecutors and police makes both the investigation of old cases and the admission of error difficult, prosecutors have an obligation to do so.[70] This obligation extends to all aspects of the legal system, which must either act on or refer to others information that suggests error, no matter how jaded the official becomes to such information. For example, in 1998, Achim Josef Marino wrote to Texas Governor George Bush, confessing to the 1988 murder of Nancy DePriest and exonerating Christopher Ochoa and Richard Danziger, who were convicted of that murder and sentenced to life in prison. Governor Bush and his staff were derelict in their office in never turning the letter over to the prosecutor and police.[71]

Mistakes on a grand scale may occur in the law, but even they can be somewhat corrected. The policy of the United States that allows what most observers consider to be unlimited detention and torture is not only immoral in its own sense but also in conflict with international law. To promote such policies makes it very difficult for the United States to argue against other states who might choose to do the same thing. The effects upon international law are likely to be to weaken the protection for America and its citizens, and this is a mistake that ought to be corrected by such officials as have the discretion to do so.[72]

---

[68] Paul Gustafson, "DNA Exonerates Man Convicted of '85 Rape," Star Tribune A1 (November 14, 2002); Jodi Wilgoren, "Prosecutors Use DNA Test to Clear Man in '85 Rape," New York Times A22 (November 14, 2002).

[69] See Alan Berlow, "What Happened in Norfolk?" New York Times Magazine 36 (April 29, 2007).

[70] On the problem generally, with suggestions for administrative reform, see Daniel S. Medwed, "The Zeal Deal: Prosecutorial Resistance to Post-Conviction Claims of Innocence," 84 Boston University Law Review 125 (2004).

[71] See Alan Berlow, Gov. Bush's Office Ignored Murder Confession: Two and a Half Years Later, the Two Men Convicted of the Crime Still Sit in Prison, Salon.com (October 13, 2000).

[72] See Mark Mazzetti, "Rules Lay Out C.I.A.'s Tactics in Questioning," New York Times A1 (July 21, 2007). This is just one problem resulting from recent American policy as it affects international law. Many scholars and jurists believe that the United States violated international law when it invaded Iraq in 2001 in violation of the United Nations Charter. See U.N. Security Council Resolution 1441, Resolution 678. See, for example, Oliver Burkeman and Julian Borger, "War Critics Astonished as U.S. Hawk Admits Invasion Was Illegal," The Guardian (November 20, 2003). Though the effects of that violation were mitigated by later actions of the United Nations, the effects for U.S. officials will continue. The reasons for the invasion offered were thought by many observers to contradict longstanding American expressions of the international law against armed attack. It will be hard for U.S. officials to argue credibly against the precedent it has created by invading, unless that precedent is disavowed. In other words, if another country invades a neighbor claiming to unilaterally enforce a technical U.N. order but without a U.N. sanction to invade, the U.S. officials will have a harder time arguing against the invasion. The most accessible study of these policies

Good Officials Make Their Own Decisions

The nature of the seal is to bear the responsibility. Certain decisions must be delegated; that is the nature of bureaucracy. On the other hand, some decisions are inherent in the nature of office and cannot be delegated to another person in good faith. So when Judge Sewall sat in the early trials of his appointment to the Court of Oyer and Terminer, when he seems largely to have followed the path set by Stoughton as the chair of the court, he apparently failed in this duty, a failure he soon came to regret.[73]

Thus, the Constitution places in Congress alone the power to declare war. When in 2002 the Congress passed the Joint Resolution to Authorize the Use of United States Armed Forces Against Iraq, it neither declared war nor failed to do so.[74] It gave a blank check to the commander in chief to use diplomacy and then "to use the Armed Forces of the United States as he determines to be necessary and appropriate in order to (1) defend the national security of the United States against the continuing threat posed by Iraq; and (2) enforce all relevant United Nations Security Council Resolutions regarding Iraq." It is perfectly appropriate for us to consider whether each of the 374 senators and representatives fulfilled their moral duties in granting the president the power he sought in this bill.[75] In doing so, we might focus on whether these individuals sufficiently exercised their obligations of knowledge in assessing the accuracy of the resolution's assertions regarding "Iraq's ongoing support for international terrorist groups combined with its development of weapons of mass destruction." Yet the more fundamental question is why these individuals would have delegated the power to declare war. The very structure of the resolution leaves it to someone other than the Congress to determine whether war is required. The whole resolution was morally inadequate to the office of the senators and representatives who supported it. In an abdication of authority remarkably similar in the form of its delegation to the conduct of the German Reichstag in the 1930s, this resolution and its much broader predecessor eroded not just the independence of each individual office but the structure of separation of powers, which had protected the independence of the Congress as a whole.[76] Such independence is very hard to regain once it is surrendered.

as this book went to press was the carefully documented PBS program, *Torturing Democracy*, available online at www.torturingdemocracy.org.

73   See Chapter 2, the section entitled "A Second Case Study from Colonial Massachusetts."
74   See Joint Resolution to Authorize the Use of United States Armed Forces against Iraq, P.L. 107-243, 116 Stat. 1498, Oct. 16, 2002.
75   The votes were 296 to 133 in the House and 77 to 23 in the Senate. Roll calls are available at http://thomas.loc.gov/cgi-bin/bdquery/z?d107:HJ00114:@@@R
76   The structure of the Iraq resolution repeated in a narrower form the even more amazing abdication of powers and responsibility in the 2001 Authorization. That resolution allowed the use of the military against any country or person, anywhere in the world, including the United States.

Good Officials Must Act with Courage

The stakes, all of the stakes, require officials to act when their action would be unpopular. It was, for instance, quite unpopular for Deputy-Governor Jones to slow the witch trials of Connecticut with procedures, but that decision saved the lives of innocent people.[77]

It is easy to talk of independence, of action promoting the truth, law, and justice over the interests of oneself, one's superior, or one's party, but it is quite another thing to risk income, preferment, or reputation to do so. In the past five years, an astonishing cadre of officials has, however, done exactly this.

Lawyers and legal officials in the U.S. government and military have been a bulwark against the erosion of legal standards at the behest of politicians. Military lawyers serving as both counsel and commissioners at Guantánamo Bay have required that the prisoners under review there be individually tried according to specific evidence and according to specific allegations and designations under the law, despite the embarrassment and delay such requirements have caused their superiors.[78] Lawyers such as Alberto Mora and William Howard Taft IV doggedly argued the application of international legal standards over detainees, until the policy allowing torture was revoked.[79] When ordered to review the treatment of detainees in Abu Ghraib, General Anthony

That the President is authorized to use all necessary and appropriate force against those nations, organizations, or persons he determines planned, authorized, committed, or aided the terrorist attacks that occurred on September 11, 2001, or harbored such organizations or persons, in order to prevent any future acts of international terrorism against the United States by such nations, organizations or persons.

Joint Resolution to Authorize the Use of United States Armed Forces against Those Responsible for the Recent Attacks Launched against the United States, P.L. 107-40, 115 Stat. 224, Sept. 18, 2001. This resolution and the authority it grants the president remains in force seven years later, and it has had far-reaching consequences for U.S. foreign relations and domestic law, including the president's claim that he was allowed thereby to engage in domestic wiretaps. See *American Civil Liberties Union v. National Security Agency*, 493 F.3d 644 (6th Cir. 2007).

For the text of the Enabling Act of 1933, see Chapter 4.

[77] See Chapter 2, the section entitled "A Second Case Study from Colonial Massachusetts."

[78] See, for example, James Meek, "U.S. Fires Guantanamo Defense Team," *Guardian* (December 3, 2003); Scott Horton, "Colonel with a Conscience," *Harpers* (April 2, 2007) (harpers. com). The first five defense counsel to appear before the commissions were Lieutenant Colonel Mark A. Bridges, Major Michael D. Mori, Lieutenant Colonel Sharon A. Shaffer, Lieutenant Commander Philip Sundel, and Lieutenant Commander Charles D. Swift; all were honored by the American Civil Liberties Union for challenging policies before the commissions. http://www.aclu.org/safefree/detention/24797res20050727.html; Josh White, "Charges against Guantanamo Detainee Set for Trial Dropped over Limit in Law," Washington Post A18 (June 5, 2007). See also the later section of this chapter, "Treason: Questioning Officials Is Disloyal."

[79] Jane Mayer, "The Memo: How an Internal Effort to Ban the Abuse and Torture of Detainees Was Thwarted," New Yorker (February 27, 2006) (newyorker.com).

Taguba chose the truth over promotion,[80] as did Department of Justice lawyers James Comey and Jack Goldsmith, who opposed warrantless spying in the United States.[81]

Courage is required in more mundane realms as well. The lawyer who does the job, regardless of pressure from the client or colleagues not to rock the boat, exercises a particular form of courage. The willingness to take unpopular clients, to admit unpopular truths, to give unwanted but necessary advice – all of these require courage.

Some Maxims from Obligations to the Procedure and Substance of Law

Officials Must Follow the Procedures of Law

The forms the sword can take in an individual's life are varied, and the threat the power of office can pose, coupled with the power of the veil and the immunities of the seal, can be frightening to anyone subject to the law. This fear can be constructive, allowing officials to mildly coerce conformity to the laws, yet it is also the basis for great temptation of the official to abuse the power, even for good ends. Short cuts and mild excesses may ease the accomplishment of an official mission, yet they risk the oversight, accuracy, fairness, and propriety that have been protected by the procedural rules of law. If there is one undeniable difference between the disastrous witch trials of Massachusetts and the successful trials of Connecticut, it was Jones's insistence on following the legal procedures of the Connecticut courts.[82]

Rules such as the prohibitions on torture and involuntary self-incrimination have arisen through regrettable experience, and to evade these bars risks not only mistakes in the present but further erosion of such bars in the future.[83] Similar problems affect every burden on the subject, even in the most humdrum of daily life, such as the collection of assets to secure a debt in dispute.[84] To be sure, some procedures, such as the expensive and dilatory routines of chancery pilloried by Dickens, are unneeded and unjustifiable.[85] Yet reform must be

---

[80] Seymour M. Hersh, "The General's Report: How Antonio Taguba, Who Investigated the Abu Ghraib Scandal, Became One of Its Casualties," New Yorker (June 25, 2007) (newyorker.com).

[81] Daniel Klaidman, Stuart Taylor, Jr., & Evan Thomas, "Palace Revolt: They Were Loyal Conservatives, and Bush Appointees. They Fought a Quiet Battle to Rein In the President's Power in the War on Terror. And They Paid a Price for It," Newsweek 34 (February 6, 2006).

[82] See Chapter 2, the section entitled "A Second Case Study from Colonial Massachusetts."

[83] See Leonard W. Levy, Origins of the Fifth Amendment: The Right Against Self-Incrimination (Ivan R. Dee, 1998).

[84] See, for example, Wyatt v. Cole, 710 F. Supp. 180 (S. D. Miss., 1989 (replevin statute that required judge to issue properly completed application for writ violated due process requirement of independent judicial decision).

[85] See Charles Dickens, Bleak House: An Authoritative and Annotated Text, Illustrations, a Note on the Text, Genesis and Composition, Backgrounds, Criticism (Norton, 1977).

managed with great care. There is a danger that officials will use procedures as a sham obstacle, either to avoid action or to destroy the procedures designed to ensure the values of justice.

Another aspect of this maxim is that officials must act only through the procedures of their office and not through alternative means. The office is abused when officials threaten subjects, just as it is when they use the power of office to spread rumors or scandal.[86]

Officials Must Pursue Justice

This is the ideal that justifies the stakes the subjects allow to the law, to the officials, to the state. What more can one ask of the balance than justice? Of the seal than it should serve justice? Of the mirror than that it should reflect it, that the commons and coin should serve it? That the sword and the guide be bound by it? The idea of justice is the ideal by which all of these stakes, all of these hopes of the subject and of the officials are justified in the actions of officials of the law. We know, from our distance, that justice was had in the witch trials of Connecticut but not in Salem,[87] which is a start. Still, this tells us little of what justice is.

There are many ways to define justice. It might be the protection of rights, or the security of individual freedom, or the provision of equal dignity, or the dedication to truth, or all of these things. Yet the most essential aspect of justice is often the most ignored. Justice is what the legal officials ought to do. Justice is a nice contrast with law, in that law is what the legal officials actually do. Justice, however, can make no sense unless it is formulated as obligations of individual officials, and it makes the most sense in its retail form – granted or not to individuals.

The content of the ideal of justice is, and probably always will be, a matter of great controversy. As Stuart Hampshire says, "Justice is conflict."[88] It is fine to argue whether justice amounts to equality, or to a principle of right, or to the greatest good for the greatest number, or to the instillation of virtue; or whatever mixture of these approaches seems best (for example: which is more fundamental – liberty for all or decency toward all?). But no answer, even

---

[86] The most enduring complaint against Independent Counsel Kenneth Starr may be that his staff in his office employed the press as a tool to harass and pressure potential witnesses and defendants during his investigation of President Clinton. See, for example, James Carville, . . . And the Horse He Rode In On (Simon & Schuster, 1998). Even some of Judge Starr's supporters appear to have had difficulty with the news leaks regarding the investigations. See, for example, I. C. Smith, Inside: A Top G-Man Exposes Spies, Lies and Bureaucratic Bungling in the FBI (Nelson Current, 2004). There is evidence that these leaks were coordinated. See Affidavit of Dan E. Moldea, 24th day of August, 1998, in re Grand Jury Proceedings, Misc. No. 98-55 (NHJ) (D. D.C.) (http://www.moldea.com/aff4.html, last visited August 8, 2007).

[87] See Chapter 2, the section entitled "A Second Case Study from Colonial Massachusetts."

[88] See Stuart Hampshire, Justice Is Conflict (Princeton University Press, 1999).

one that somehow achieved consensus among officials and subjects alike, can have any practical meaning unless there is an obligation upon legal officials to enshrine that answer in the archive and practice it through the culture of the law. That is what justice must be, an obligation of individuals, or there can be no justice in the law.

Thus, the individual legal official is always obligated to decide what justice is, in the midst of controversy and with no assurance of getting it right. As if the job weren't hard enough, the official must not only determine what is just between the state and the citizen (which is to say between other officials and the citizen) but also what is just between two citizens.

Despite the difficulties of this role, officials do have a few guides that are less controversial, not the least being maxims of the substance of justice, which are not unlike those discussed already. The most enduring might be those that introduce the *Institutes*, the great textbook of Roman law authored under Justinian's reign. "The maxims of law are these: to live honestly, to hurt no one, to give every one their due."[89] This benchmark of justice is more than just a trio of glasses into which can be poured all the conflict Hampshire described. They are the ideals that structure arguments about right, equality, and economy, requiring each to be applied into three dimensions, as to the conduct both of officials toward subjects and of subjects toward one another. Each official is a personal guarantor that all of these essential components of justice will somehow be ensured for those subject to the law.

LEGAL OFFICE AND MORAL ERROR

Thinking again of our colonial judicial officers, what gave Stoughton his certainty? Why was Sewall so late to realize the evil of the trials he was hearing? Why did the people take so long to begin to criticize Phips? What false arguments had been accepted, or what bad ideas had been enshrined in legal decisions for two such different people collectively to bring such grief on those subject to their decrees?

One aspect of rhetoric is to recognize that certain arguments are persuasive but false. These arguments, particularly when they follow certain patterns, are fallacies. This section collects certain fallacies related to the stakes and to the obligations considered in Chapter 5. They roughly correspond to the maxims described above, but they here represent not the means to satisfy an official's obligations, but some ideas leading to likely breaches of them.

---

[89] Justinian, *The Institutes of Justinian: With English Introduction, Translation, and Notes*, Book I, Part 1, ¶3. (T. C. Sandars, trans.) (Longmans, Green and Co., 1905).

THE NATURE OF FALLACIES

Some arguments deceive. That fact – the fact of deception – is rather important in attempting to understand something that is already hard, such as how we can know what moral obligations we have. It helps to know that an argument is deceptive, because it cannot deceive unless something about the argument is attractive. As Aristotle said, "There is a certain likeness between the genuine and the sham."[90] Deceptive arguments seduce us into accepting them as true despite their tricks, and they do so regularly. It hardly matters for their falsity whether the speaker knows the argument is false; indeed, a false argument is all the more persuasive to most hearers when the speaker utters it with the full emotional commitment of belief. Still, such commitment does not make the argument true.

An argument based on false reasoning is usually now called a fallacy, though the fallacy has been studied under other names, especially the sophism.[91] To philosophers, there are subtle distinctions among fallacies that render an argument untrue or merely unsound, or that disprove the argument because of failures of descriptions of fact or of reason.[92]

For two millennia, scholars have known that fallacies are common, and indeed they are so common in rhetoric, especially the rhetoric of law, that there are catalogues of them not unlike the catalogues of the virtues. Though writers such as Aristotle, Cicero, and Quintillian listed various fallacies, John Locke put them in the form in which many students still learn them, with a Latin tag to the weakness of the argument. Locke listed three forms of fallacy, which we would today describe as the argument about the speaker (*argumentum ad hominem*), as about a point that has not been defended (*ad ignorantium*), and argument over the authority of a premise or conclusion (*ad verecundiam*).[93] There are nearly unlimited ways to make a false argument,

---

[90] Aristotle, *On Sophistical Refutations* (W. A. Pickard-Cambridge, trans.) (available at http://classics.mit.edu/Aristotle/sophist_refut.1.1.html).

[91] For instance, "sophism" was preferred by the great Isaac Watts in his eighteenth-century logic text, as well the editors of *The Port-Royal Logic*, a popular nineteenth-century textbook translated from the French, *La Logique ou L'Art de Penser*. See Isaac Watts, *Logick, or, the Right Use of Reason* (1796) (Garland, 1984); Antoine Arnauld and Pierre Nicole, *Port-Royal Logic* (T. S. Baynes, trans.) (Oliver and Boyd, 1865) (available at books.google.com). Yet in roughly the same period Richard Whately and John Stuart Mill preferred "fallacy." See Richard Whately, *Elements of Logic* (Harper and Row, 1853); John Stuart Mill, *A System of Logic, Rationative and Inductive* (Routledge and Sons, 1892). The relevant bits of these four basic texts are helpfully collected, with much more, in Hans V. Hansen and Robert C. Pinto, *Fallacies: Classical and Contemporary Readings* (Pennsylvania State University Press, 1995).

[92] John Locke, *Essay on Human Understanding*, Book IV, Chapter XVII, §§ 19–22, quoted in *id.* 55–6.

[93] Fifty fallacies are collected in the wonderfully readable W. Ward Fearnside & William B. Hother, *Fallacy: The Counterfeit of Argument* (Prentice-Hall, 1959).

and there are many ways to organize these ways.[94] The current view of fallacy, carrying about the annoying label of the "pragma-dialectical approach," is to ignore the logical forms of rhetoric and fallacy and to think of fallacies as speech acts, best illustrated by considering the speaker's wrong motives in communication and argument.[95] This approach develops criticism of fallacies based on such popular arguments in law as the slippery slope, shifting burdens of proof, and declaring an argument to be beyond use or criticism.[96]

Despite all of these ways to consider false arguments, there is an important fallacy about fallacies. That an argument is a fallacy does not mean that its conclusion is wrong. To prove an argument is a fallacy only means that the argument, by itself, is no reason to believe the conclusion – but the conclusion of a fallacious argument might still happen to be true.

With that caution in mind, the next section collects a few illustrative fallacies regarding moral obligations and legal office that have arisen from the cases as well as from some of the standard manuals of fallacies. These fallacies cannot, again, disprove a conclusion, and it remains possible that a conclusion argued in this way is sound or advisable or true. But arguments in these forms should alert an official that something deceptive is afoot.

A FEW FALLACIES FOR LEGAL OFFICE

A Fallacy about the Nature of Moral Obligations

Morality Is a Private Indulgence, Not a Public Need

This is a very modern mistake. Indeed the fallacy is a basic idea of modern life, and it is usually coupled to an economic idea that what the public needs are its desires, or to a political idea that what is needed is strength, and in neither case should wealth or power be hamstrung by effete notions of doing the right thing. The fallacy might have been phrased earliest in Henry Adams in his remembrance of his attempts to reject the idea that "Morality is a private

---

[94]   Since Charles Hamblin's work in 1970 seeking a theory of fallacies, writers tend to taxonomy. C. L. Hamblin, *Fallacies* (Vale Press, 2004); see also, for example, Maurice A. Finocchiaro, "Six Types of Fallaciousness: Toward a Realistic Theory of Logical Criticism," in *id.* 120. Finocchiaro would divide the fallacy (apart from mathematical fallacy and a few others) into six types: formal invalidity (the conclusion can be disproved), explanatory (there is another conclusion as easily supported by premises), presuppositional (a premise is false), positive (the premises demand a different conclusion), semantical (the premises are ambiguous), and persuasive (the conclusion is one of the premises).

[95]   See, for example, Frans H. van Eemeren & Rob Grootendorst, *Argumentation, Communication, and Fallacies: A Pragma-Dialectical Perspective* (Lawrence Erlbaum, 1992); Douglas Walton & Erik C. Krabbe, *Commitment in Dialogue: Basic Concepts of Interpersonal Reasoning* (SUNY Press, 1995).

[96]   A particularly useful inventory of these more subtle modern fallacies is in Douglas N. Walton, *Informal Fallacies: Towards a Theory of Argument Criticisms* (John Benjamins, 1987).

and costly luxury," preferring instead the ideals of "George Washington, John Adams, and the rest."[97]

The idea is untrue for several reasons, but essentially it presents a false dichotomy. There is no inherent conflict between the private indulgence of a moral obligation and the public need for it. Although there may be various arguments for what the public need is, one cannot be rejected just because it is the morally sound option, which is what this would imply. Instead, the public need is for officials independently to act according to their obligations, both legal and moral, rather than to fall under the sway of arguments like this one, which is usually encountered when a senior official seeks to knock a naive younger official into compliance with the senior's wishes.[98]

Some Fallacies about the Substance of Moral Obligations

Ipse dixit: *It Is True Because of Who Said It*
Authority is asserting a judgment that others will rely on rather than exercising their own judgment. The whole idea of independent moral judgment forbids reliance on authority as the basis for truth. This is not to say that there are not people whom one can trust to inform, criticize, or validate one's initial beliefs; it is only to say that one is still responsible for actions based on one's belief regardless of their counsel. What one person tells another about moral obligations might be true, but it will not be true just because of who says it.

For instance, when the president says we have the obligation to go to war, that the speaker is the president, or that he is one or another person, cannot in itself prove that we must indeed go to war. That decision as a technical matter is one that must be made not by the president but by a majority of the members of Congress.[99] That decision as a moral matter must be made by every person in the nation, and it must be visited by every official who must carry it out.[100]

Ad hominem: *It Is False Because of Who Said It*
The corollary to *ipse dixit* is to suggest that either the person or something about the person who asserts an argument proves the argument false. This is endemic to a particular type of partisan discourse, and it is always wrong.[101]

---

[97] Henry Adams, *The Education of Henry Adams: An Autobiography* 335 (Houghton & Mifflin Co., 1918).

[98] See the wonderful examples in the interchanges between the two consummate, if fictional, civil servants, Humphrey and Bernard, in Antony Jay & Jonathan Lynn, *The Complete Yes, Minister* (BBC Books, 1989).

[99] This problem is considered further in the later section discussing the maxim "Good officials make their own decisions."

[100] See Mary Wiltenburg, "U.S. Army Struggles with Soldier Who Won't Pull the Trigger: Is the Decision Not to Fight Conscience or Cowardice?" Christian Science Monitor (August 14, 2007).

[101] See, for example, Coulter Anne, *How to Talk to a Liberal (If You Must): The World According to Ann Coulter* (Crown Forum, 2004).

Ad populum: *It Is True Because the People Believe It*

A resort to agreement among the people as a whole is a recipe for cultural prejudgment. Although there are some benefits to allocating a decision among a group, such as a jury or a senate, this is very different from resorting to the idea of popular understanding as a basis for determining what is true. The history of lynching in America is sad testament to popular understanding of guilt and innocence, which often had nothing to do with the actual conduct of the victims.[102]

One of the great moments of the common law was the rejection of this approach, when it was urged on the great English judge Lord Mansfield that the pamphleteer John Wilkes should be acquitted of libel because he was praised by the crowds. "I always minded to regard popularity born of virtue not as a sign of envy but as a sign of glory."[103]

Ad baculum: *It Is True Because There Is Great Danger*

A resort to the stick, or to threats or grave consequences in order to compel agreement, cannot be the basis of truth. One is tempted to see *ad baculum* arguments in every claim to special license in wartime, particularly when an argument is made that a law, or a power, or a judgment is needed, and a failure to grant it will strengthen our enemies. This argument also was raised and rejected in John Wilkes's case, by the claim to Lord Mansfield that the people would riot if Wilkes were not freed, to which he replied:

> Let Justice be done, though the heavens may fall . . . if we do not speak our real opinions, we prevaricate with God and our consciences. No libels, no threats, nothing that has happened, nothing that can happen, will weigh a feather against allowing the defendant, on this and every other question, not only the whole advantage he is intitled to from substantial law and justice; but every benefit from the most critical nicety of form, which any other defendant could claim under the like objection.[104]

His decision to release Wilkes was based on nothing but the legal arguments before the court.

Ad verecundiam: *It is True Because It Was Said by Authority*

This variation on *ipse dixit* is usually employed with the nuance of false authority, or people speaking outside their arenas of genuine expertise. It is usually

---

[102] See, for example, Christopher Waldrep, *The Many Faces of Judge Lynch: Extralegal Violence and Punishment in America* (Palgrave Macmillan, 2002); *Lynching in America: A History in Documents* (NYU Press, 2006).

[103] R. v. Wilkes, 4 Burr 2527, 2563. Originally, *Ego hoc animo semper fui ut invidiam virtute partam, gloriam non invidiam, putarem.*

[104] *R. v. Wilkes* (1770) 4 Burr 2527 at 2561–2562 [98 ER 327 at 346-347]. Originally, *fiat justitia ruat caelem.*

true that people who hold office, however, lack the particular expertise required for decisions by that office. What judge knows about the science underlying patents being adjudged in court? How many appointees to office really know much about the work done by the civil servants in their departments? We might believe that such officials are specially advised by experts and so their authority arises from the advice they receive, but there is no particular reason to believe that this is true. Indeed, there are plenty of illustrations in which officials offer arguments based on the preference of their political masters rather than on any available expertise.[105]

This is not to say that all statements by officials lack expert guidance or authority. Yet such illustrations underscore the fallacy of believing something is true only because it is said by an authority. To rely on authority without developing the tools for independent assessment is to surrender independence to the authority in assessing the truth of the statement. The rules for jury instructions and evidence, for instance, reflect this concern in the limits on the use of expert testimony. Experts may offer opinions that the jurors may assess and choose to employ themselves, but the expert cannot "invade the province of the jury" by offering a definitive answer to questions the jury is to answer for itself.[106]

There are countless ways to err in moral knowledge. The evergreen fallacies just described merely scratch the surface of falsehood in public discourse. There are many obvious variations on these ideas, such pointing to the law itself, or to religion or tradition, or to official actions, commands, or policies as the basis for believing that some idea, policy, or action is moral. None can supplant an independent assessment of the moral obligations implicated in the idea, policy, or action.

Ad patronum: *It Is True Because My Backer Wants It So*

Of the many errors of resort to authority, the most pernicious are those in this entry and the next, basing the claim of truth on the interests of the client or on the interests of the money. When the lawyer protects the patron's interest at the expense of the truth or of the law, the lawyer cannot be said to serve the law. This

---

[105] For example, in 2007, former Surgeon General Richard Carmona reported to Congress that he had not been allowed to issue reports on health issues, such as the health risks of tobacco smoke and the use of stem cells; complaints of similar pressure were offered by prior surgeons general and have been raised by scientists dealing with climate change and the environment. Gardiner Harris, "Surgeon General Sees 4-Year Term as Compromised," New York Times (July 11, 2007). Similar charges have been made not only by the officials but by experts in several fields of government research. See, for example, Andrew C. Revkin, "Climate Expert Says NASA Tried to Silence Him," New York Times (January 29, 2006).

[106] See, for example, *Renfro v. Kentucky*, 893 S.W.2d 795 (Ky. 1995) (expert on accident reconstruction cannot give opinion on ultimate cause of accident). There are hundreds and hundreds of opinions along the same lines.

is a greater difficulty for lawyers employed by companies and the government, in which the client is indeed the boss, yet the employment cannot be allowed to overcome the professional commitment for which the employment is made, without the lawyer violating personal, moral commitments to the institution of the law. Lawyers cannot be genuinely and morally lawyers if they perceive the job as giving the boss what the boss wants. The lawyer must be willing to tell the client, even the employer-client, "No."

Financier J. P. Morgan is often quoted as saying, "Well, I don't know as I want a lawyer to tell me what I cannot do. I hire him to tell how to do what I want to do." This line is often misread to suggest that he sought lawyers to help him evade the law rather than to conform to it,[107] but the misreading speaks to a suspicion that lawyers merely give the client the counsel they want to hear, regardless of the law. This is a sufficient threat that a provision of American Bar Association Model Rule 1 forbids lawyers from assisting clients in doing anything criminal or fraudulent.[108]

This fallacy is the kindest explanation I can think of for what I believe is one of the most outstanding moral failures by a lawyer to give objective legal counsel in modern times: the opinions of Jay Bybee and John Yoo, then lawyers for the government, that the president of the United States was not bound by the Geneva Conventions and could endorse interrogation methods that would meet others' definitions of torture.[109]

---

[107] The quote was already famous in 1927, when it was remembered and qualified by Morgan's lawyer, Elbert Henry Gary, who gave an interview to the *Saturday Evening Post* in which he said,

> "I was engaged in the practice of law in Chicago. . . . Mr. Morgan was interested in the Elgin, Joliet & Eastern Railway, known as the Outer Belt Line of Chicago. . . . Having information which was not in possession of Mr. Morgan or his legal staff, I saw instantly that his plan would not work. 'You can't do that under the law,' I explained. 'I don't hire lawyers to tell me what I can't do,' was Mr. Morgan's [famed] retort. 'I hire them to tell me how to do what I want them to do.' . . . [From this, some have wrongly inferred] that he was willing to do an illegal thing if a way could be found to do it; safely. But such," said Judge Gary, "was never the case. His statement to me was merely typical of the challenging way he adopted at times. One was supposed to know that what he planned to accomplish was not in defiance of the law."

"Concerning Morgan," Time (March 21, 1927) (www.time.com).

[108] Model Rule 1.2 states, "A lawyer shall not counsel a client to engage, or assist a client, in conduct that the lawyer knows is criminal or fraudulent, but a lawyer may discuss the legal consequences of any proposed course of conduct with a client and may counsel or assist a client to make a good faith effort to determine the validity, scope, meaning or application of the law."

[109] I am not alone in this opinion. See Harold Hongjuh Koh, "A World without Torture," 43 Columbia Journal of Transnational Law 641, 654–5 (2005). The torture memos, from Jay Bybee to Alberto Gonzales and from John Yoo to Alberto Gonzales, on August 1, 2002, are reprinted in Karen J. Greenberg & Joshua L. Dratel (eds.), *The Torture Papers: The Road to Abu Ghraib*, 172–217, 218–22 (Cambridge University Press, 2005). Yoo's

One last aspect of the *ad patronum* fallacy, which is shared with the fallacies *ad popularum* (discussed earlier) and *ad crumenum* (discussed next), is the idea of legal truth being dependent on the interests of those atop the social hierarchy. Even with only potential or indirect influence upon them, some officials will go to great lengths to establish claims of the truth as social leaders would have it. The crimes of the powerful are simply left unchecked. This is hardly the stuff of myth but the fact of too many miscarriages of justice.[110]

Ad crumenum: *It Is True Because the Money Says So*

The client pays the bill but, more importantly, is seen wrongly by some lawyers to be the boss.[111] This is certainly not to say that there is anything wrong in believing that the right answer to a question might be one in which everyone is better off financially, or even someone is better off financially; the protection of the coin as a stake in the law is important and is furthered by ensuring that the economy is healthy. Rather, this is to believe that the correct answer to a moral or legal question is what the person with money desires, because it is desired by the person with money; or the right answer is what the boss wants. The error that a lawyer ought to give the money the advice it wants extends very easily to the error of giving the boss what the boss wants, which was discussed earlier.

Some Fallacies about the Performance of Moral Obligations

False Binarism: *There Is Only One Choice Between Two Options*

We often see the world divided into a single choice of just two options. The policeman, for instance, is confronted with drills requiring a decision to shoot or not to shoot. A prosecutor must decide to indict or not to indict. A president must decide to pardon or not to pardon. This in known to philosophers as the disappearing (or excluded) middle – eliminating all choices but the most extreme. Yet seeing decisions in such a truncated way both rejects moderate options and ignores the hundreds of predicate opportunities for decisions before such a moment of decision is reached. And, seeing decisions in such an unimaginative way elides other options available. The policeman might warn before deciding whether to shoot. The prosecutor might indict on lesser offenses or might seek further investigation before making a decision. The

---

defense of his memorandum, "Commentary: Behind the 'torture memos,'" was published in the UC Berkeley News on January 4, 2005, and is at http://www.berkeley.edu/news/media/releases/2005/01/05_johnyoo.shtml. The Supreme Court's rejection of his wholesale misreading of the Common Article 3 of the four Geneva Conventions is in *Hamdan v. Rumsfeld*, 126 S. Ct. 2749 (2006) (Stevens, J.). The dissents of Justices Scalia, Thomas, and Alito were based on jurisdiction.

110   An example that was famous in its day and still instructive in ours is in Thomas Toughill, *Oscar Slater: The 'Immortal' Case of Sir Arthur Conan Doyle* (Sutton Publishing, 2006).

111   See also the discussion of institutional obligations in Chapter 4.

president might study the sentence in the light of other sentences or reduce the sentence rather than pardon the convicted person.

Stonewalling: It Is Best to Hide Our Errors and Misdeeds

We do not like admitting mistakes, even to ourselves. We don't like admitting them when they are made by our colleagues, either. Whether out of shame, fear, loyalty to our friends, or fear of guilt by association, officials tend to hide official misdeeds. Often the injustice of a bad decision is covered up in the name of preserving trust in the state or in the law. This was the main reason French generals preferred to keep a German spy on the general staff rather than to admit they had court-martialed an innocent man for the espionage.[112] This is a similar sham to the idea that government would not receive the best advice if anyone knew how self-serving the advice is. On this basis, Vice President Cheney has fought for years to avoid admitting which oil company representatives helped form American energy policy,[113] and the president has interfered with testimony to Congress on potentially criminal acts related to the firing of U.S. attorneys and politically motivated leaks about the identities of spies.[114]

Yet, the truth is eventually had, and while we wait, the skepticism and anger that such secrecy arouses does as much harm to trust in the law as routing out the villains could do. Moreover, it is simply not the moral province of the official to hide the error or the abuse. Officials have an obligation to confess their abuses of office, their errors and their misdeeds, because it is incumbent on others to correct them. This is most clearly seen when officials keep evidence of their errors from those who are harmed by them, as when prosecutors or police withhold evidence of innocence, or when a litigant hides relevant evidence.[115]

Exceptional Case: The Rules Do Not Apply in This Case or to This Person

If law is to be fair, it must treat everyone the same way. This is not to say that officials do not confront many questions for the first time, in which case the official must create a unique answer. Nor does it presume that the law is

---

[112] The court-martial of Albert Dreyfus is very briefly considered in Chapter 4, in the section entitled "Institutional Obligations."

[113] See *Natural Resources Defense Council v. Department of Energy*, 191 F. Supp. 2d 41 (D.D.C., 2002).

[114] See Robert Schmidt, *Bush Claims Privilege to Shield Cheney Interview in Leak Case*, http://www.bloomberg.com (July 16, 2008).

[115] Durham County, North Carolina, District Attorney Mike Nifong brought rape charges against several Duke University students, apparently suppressing DNA evidence that would have exonerated them. See Duff Wilson, "Hearing Ends in Disbarment for Prosecutor in Duke Case," New York Times A21 (June 17, 2007). Such suppression is not unique. See, for example, *McGhee v. Pottawattamie County*, 475 F. Supp. 2d 862 (S.D. Iowa 2007).

inherently just and should be applied without considering that it has already been applied unjustly and that it would be unjust to apply it in the same way later. Rather, fairness requires officials to recognize that every answer ought to be one that could be applied again in all similar questions in the future. If an official seems bound to apply a rule that appears unjust, the remedy is probably to change the rule, not to make an exception. If the official is about to exercise a power that seems too dangerous to be allowed generally, the remedy is to not use this power rather than to pretend that it will not be used again.[116] If we cannot confidently apply the law to our friends, then we should change it before we apply it to our enemies.[117]

None of this suggests that officials may not make very fine distinctions in exercising their discretion, for instance by giving a benefit to a subject who the official believes has the character not to abuse that benefit while denying the benefit to one who the official suspects would abuse it.[118] Universality does not require utter uniformity, lest the law become so rigorous that it would create injustice through unforeseen or subtle circumstances.[119]

One of the most dangerous forms of the fallacy of the exceptional case is in thinking that official conduct that breaks explicit laws can be justified by a unique or changed situation. Situations change all the time, but they are rarely as exceptional as those engaged in them believe. Moreover, the laws are often created to work particularly in times of crisis.

There are only two courses of action in such situations that meet the official's moral obligation to follow the law. Either the law must be obeyed or the law must be changed. For the official to violate the law in order to avoid admitting to other officials what the official has done or is doing is a gross disservice to the legal system, no matter how self-righteous the secretive official might be.

The fear created among the subjects owing to dangers of the veil is tremendous. This is the lesson of secret police in America's past; the real threat is not what they do, but what they are thought to do.[120] Further, what few gains are made through illegal procedures cannot offset the harm to the legal system when officials come to believe that they are not bound to obey the law, and citizens know they believe it. For instance, when President Bush condoned a "Terrorist Surveillance Program" in violation of the Foreign Intelligence Surveillance Act, he undoubtedly believed that we were in unique times that

---

[116] See the brief discussion of the attempt to write *Bush v. Gore* as if it were not a precedent, above in this chapter.

[117] See the brief discussion of the commutation of the sentence of Scooter Libby, above in this chapter.

[118] See, for example, Steven Maynard-Moody & Michael Musheno, *Cops, Teachers, Counselors: Stories from the Front Lines of Public Service* 5 (University of Michigan Press, 2003).

[119] This is the function of equity. See Steve Sheppard, "Equity and the Law" (Subject Article 6.31.4.2), *UNESCO Encyclopedia of Life Support Systems* (www. eolss.net).

[120] See *ACLU v. Mabus*, 719 F. Supp. 1345 (S.D. Miss. 1989).

justified his actions.[121] Still, his actions violated his moral obligations to follow the law not only to obey the letter of the act but to inform the Congress of his actions.[122]

Emergencies and wars test this fallacy to the extreme. Cicero's maxim *Silent enim leges inter arma* (During war, the laws are silent)[123] is routinely brought out to justify measures beyond the law in wartime. Yet, Cicero coined the phrase during a trial, attempting (though failing) to cast a murder as a matter of self-defense, in an application of legal doctrines that precisely were meant to apply in times of crisis. There is a grave danger in imagining that war exonerates officials from following the law. As Lincoln observed, allowing the executive untrammeled discretion in wartime invites perpetual wars.[124]

Moreover, such a gathering of power is prone to opportunism, in which officials take advantage of an emergency to gather authority that would be denied them, but for the shock or threat of the moment. The only assurance against such threats to the law is that other officials will resist such aggrandizements of power. Yet, time and again in American history, an emergency, real or manufactured, has been successfully thrust into the political sphere to aggregate legal powers to the executive.[125] At times, these aggregations have been essential to the survival of the nation, such as Lincoln's emergency measures and the rise of the New Deal, yet those that are genuinely needed are inevitably

---

[121] See James Risen & Eric Lichtblau, "Bush Lets U.S. Spy on Callers without Courts," New York Times A1 (December 16, 2005). See also *White House Statement on the Terrorist Surveillance Program, August 17, 2006,* http://www.whitehouse.gov/news/releases/2006/08/20060817-2.html.

[122] The two judges to reach the merits in the first case to challenge the legality of the program both found it to be unconstitutional. *ACLU v. NSA*, 2007 Fed. App. 0253P 145 (6th Cir. 2006) (Gilman, J.); *ACLU v. Nat'l Sec. Agency/Central Sec. Serv.*, 438 F. Supp. 2d 754 (E.D. Mich., 2006) (Taylor, J.). The case was dismissed on the shameful basis of standing unproven because a defendant could not know the extent of harm from a secret program, by Judges Batchelder and Gibbons. *ACLU v. NSA*, 2007 Fed. App. 0253P 145 (6th Cir. 2006).

[123] Cicero, *Pro Milone*, Part IV, at 11.

[124] See "Abraham Lincoln to William Herndon, February 15, 1848," in 1 *The Collected Works of Abraham Lincoln* 451–2 (Roy P. Basler, ed.) (Rutgers University Press, 1953).

[125] Political opportunism is hardly new, and seemingly every executive has practiced it to some degree. Three recent studies cross the presidencies of both parties. On the use of crisis to change economic laws, see Naomi Klein, *The Shock Doctrine: The Rise of Disaster Capitalism* (Picador, 2008). On the use of threats to domestic safety as a tool for executive power, see Jonathan Simon, *Governing through Crime: How the War on Crime Transformed American Democracy and Created a Culture of Fear* (Oxford University Press, 2007). On the use of war powers, see Gerald Astor, *Presidents at War: From Truman to Bush, The Gathering of Military Powers to Our Commanders in Chief* (Wiley, 2006). On the role of the 9/11 attacks as spur to new authority in the current administration, uniquely in disregard to individual rights, see Jack L. Goldsmith, *The Terror Presidency: Law and Judgment inside the Bush Administration* (W. W. Norton, 2007).

accomplished by appropriate changes in the law, with the acceptance of the range of officials involved.[126]

War challenges officials like nothing else to ensure the strength of the shield for the subjects of the law, and a reaction that all must be done is a reasonable one. Yet, *all* is not all, for any sense of all that contemplates the destruction of those things and people who are protected is patently unreasonable, and the freedoms and laws of the people are one of the things that are to be protected. In this light, the much chronicled effort by lawyers for the second President Bush and Vice President Cheney, especially David Addington and John Yoo, to accumulate power for the executive, regardless of the constitutional principles of checks and balances, individual rights, or separation of powers – and in defiance of other officials – risks legal violations but surely violates a moral duty to defend the Constitution and the laws.[127]

Treason: Questioning Officials Is Disloyal

There is a fine line between loyalty to an official or national commitment and the abdication of official responsibility. In 2001, responding to critics who said that the Department of Justice was unnecessarily invading civil liberties in the name of counterterrorism, Attorney General John Ashcroft attacked the critics, saying, "To those who scare peace-loving people with phantoms of lost liberty, my message is this: your tactics only aid terrorists."[128] Such arguments have extended even to questioning the acts of government through official processes. In 2007, Deputy Assistant Secretary of Defense Charles Stimson gave a radio interview in which he attacked lawyers representing detainees held in Guantánamo Bay, suggesting that corporations should not give business to these lawyers.[129] Although it is hard to know for certain that government lawyers and other officials who have argued against policy have been penalized

---

[126] See James G. Randall, *Constitutional Problems under Lincoln* (University of Illinois Press, 1997); Barry Cushman, *Rethinking the New Deal Court: The Structure of a Constitutional Revolution* (Oxford University Press, 1998). A reigning theory of these sorts of constitutional change remains Bruce Ackerman, *We the People: Volume I, Foundations* (Harvard University Press, 1993).

[127] The literature critical of the excesses of lawyers in the second Bush administration grows daily, but a chronicle by a very careful journalist summarizes the story known to date, and both sides of its arguments, with calm and care. See Jane Mayer, *The Dark Side: The Inside Story of How the War on Terror Turned into a War on American Ideals* (Doubleday, 2008). These arguments demonstrate, at least, an immoral disregard for the legal limits of office, and, perhaps, deliberate violations of the criminal law. See Philippe Sands, *Torture Team: Rumsfeld's Memo and the Betrayal of American Values* (Palgrave Macmillan, 2008).

[128] Neil A. Lewis, "Ashcroft Defends Antiterror Plan and Says Criticism May Aid Foes," New York Times (December 7, 2001).

[129] Neil A. Lewis, "Official Attacks Top Law Firms over Detainees," New York Times (January 13, 2007). The controversy that arose over his remarks led to Mr. Stimson's resignation. See "Official Quits after Remark on Lawyers," New York Times (February 3, 2007).

for pursuing the truth over policy, such executive penalties are not unknown, and it seems likely that military lawyers have particularly paid for their criticism of policy and their defense of their clients and the law.[130]

Such a view mistakes one official's loyalty to another official, thinking of it as the equivalent of fidelity to office or loyalty to country. The independent obligation of every official to weigh the moral implications of every act of the legal system cannot be compromised by the commitment of other officials. The law does not care what the president has said. It cannot care what a department chief has said. The officials tasked with the duties of law must independently determine that what is said is true, and what is being done is morally appropriate. Nothing else can satisfy the trust that official has been granted in the office.

Tu quoque: *They Did It, So We May Do It*

The old formal fallacy of *tu quoque* is an allegation of hypocrisy, along the lines of the familiar objection that someone's complaint is "the pot calling the kettle black." It is a fallacy because, of course, the underlying truth was that the kettle was black. *Tu quoque* has another sense, though, in which it can be asserted as a justification for otherwise wrong action because it was retaliation in kind for another's wrongful act. This sort of thinking underlies the perpetuation of ancient feuds, and it is forbidden as a defense in international law.[131] Officials

---

[130] Some evidence of reprisal against the lawyers at Guantánamo includes:

> 1. Lt. Col. Stephen Abraham, USAR, helped convince the U.S. Supreme Court to reconsider its denial of certiorari in *Boumediene v. Bush* and *Al Odah v. United States*. Relieved of duty.

> 2 and 3. Major Michael Mori, USMC, counsel for David Hicks, and Navy Lt. Cmdr. Charles D. Swift, USN, counsel for Salim Ahmet Hamdan. Passed over for promotion and forced to leave the service.

> 4, 5, and 6. Capt. John Carr, USA; Maj. Robert Preston, USAF; Capt. Carrie Wolf, USAF, all prosecutors who requested transfers owing to complaints with proceedings.

> 7. Col. Will Gunn, USAF, supervising attorney; resigned commission effective end of assignment, stating, "What we're doing is far more important than anyone's career. I can't ask people to do what they're going to have to do if I'm protecting mine."

> See Victor Comras, *The New Guantanamo Military Commission Debate*, http://counterterrorismblog.org/2007/08/the_new_guantanamo_military_co.php (visited August 30, 2007). See also the discussion in this chapter of the maxim "good officials must act with courage."

[131] See, for example, ICTY, Case of Kunarak, Kovac, and Vokovic, Decision of Trial Chamber II, 5 July 2000, at http://un.org/icty/kunarac/trialc2/decision-e/00703EV213055.htm. See also Frits Kalshoven, "Reprisals and the Protection of Civilians: Two Recent Decisions of the Yugoslavian Tribunal," in *Man's Inhumanity to Man: Essays on International Law in Honour of Antonio Cassese* (Lal Chand Vohrah et al., eds.) (Martinus Nijhoff, 2003).

may not adopt the methods of criminals to fight crime or of terrorists to fight terror, without threatening the legitimacy of the law itself. As with the discussion of the ruse of dirty hands,[132] as a practical matter, the arguments that doing so is necessary to thwart crime or terror are, usually, mistaken.

---

[132] See Chapter 6, the section entitled "The Occasional Ruse of Dirty Hands."

Epilogue: What the Official Ought to Do
Law and Justice

Consider again the scene described in the Introduction. When Sir Edward Coke spoke to James I, he believed he knew exactly what a judge was to do. The judge was independently to exercise the powers of the law according to the restraints the law itself imposed, and according to the dictates of reason and right. Such decisions were then to be discussed and criticized by other officials, and the good decisions were to be followed and the poor ones rejected.

In the century past, we have grown accustomed to ignoring the problems of moral action, of the good and the right, so much so that to speak of official morality seems quaint or foolish. We have grown accustomed to the Phipses of our world using office for personal advantage and to the smugness of the Stoughtons, and we accept the thoughtful service of the Sewalls and, thankfully, the faithful service of the Joneses. We have learned to accept our world as governed by their laws, and we have come to believe the people have no recourse but a limited ability of political reaction.

It is therefore no surprise if the tools by which such moral assessment of official conduct can be made have grown unfamiliar. We lack a contemporary vocabulary to sort our views of the modern successors to Jones and Sewall from those of Stoughton and Phips, and we fall back on judgment of a result as right or wrong, or we fall into a partisan game of preference for our champions and resentment of their opponents.

Still, tools for the moral assessment of officials persist, and they may still serve, with widespread agreement, as a measure of the justice or injustice of officials' actions. The best of these tools are obligations that can be stated as maxims, basic principles by which each of us, both official and citizen, can assess the decisions and actions of officials. What we seem to lack yet is a public culture that turns on the empathy of shame rather than the interest of offense, one in which a corporate understanding of responsibility requires both subjects and officials to be invested in the retail justice of each official in the legal system. This requires confidence that such justice can be the basis of social consensus, which could arise all the more readily if the Klaxons of the interests pursuing power or profit at the expense of justice can be muted.

For those whose lives are deeply affected by the powers of the state, exercised through its officials by sword, shield, balance, guide, coin, commons, mirror, veil, and seal, it is the responsibility of all officials to act both for the discharge and for the constraint of these state powers by morality. The actions of these officials, including both what officials write into the archive of law and what official culture accepts as conduct appropriate to the office, become part of the law. Each official therefore influences the moral ecology of officials, encouraging better or worse behavior by other officials. Thus each action has a moral dimension in the action itself and its direct effects on those subjects and officials bound to it, as well as a secondary influence on the legal system as a whole. Officials are personally responsible for the moral significance of their acts forever.

This personal obligation to moral action in each official is the true meaning of justice. All ideas about justice must reduce to specific and individual arguments upon officials. Officials must act justly, or justice is impossible. Justice is personal, or it cannot be institutional.

The study presented in this book is necessarily preliminary, even cursory. It presents a view of law as what is done, not merely what is or what is known. Once the action of the law is the object of our study, the morality of the actors is fair to consider. This is all the more appropriate owing to the variety and significance of the effects of these actions in the lives of others.

To develop this study, a more thorough consideration must be given to the intersection of moral judgment and the actions required in legal roles. Maxims and fallacies must be considered and developed. Further, more work is needed to develop the theory of corporate responsibility that officials have for the conduct of other officials. The legal enterprise creates a group responsibility in a variety of manners, and the problems of moral ecology and group responsibility must be further unpacked in this context. Development along these lines will best be done through the study of actual cases from history, in the light of ideas about the law and about the right and the good.

In the meantime, we might consider again the problem of morality in office as considered in the preface. Even if we fear the broad dangers of morality in office, would we not fear more officials without morals? Officials who lack charity, pursue their partisan agendas, seek wealth, grab power, and alter the laws to these ends must be open to judgment by some standards, and moral obligations provide them. Granted, the standards are controversial, overlapping, and subject to debate at their margins, but at their core, the requirements of fidelity to the law, charity to those subject to the law, knowledge, truth, effort, procedural clarity and the rest are really not at issue. The time has surely come to pursue clearer understanding of the personal, institutional, procedural, and substantive obligations that officials must meet to perform their tasks. The assumption is false that officials must do no more than follow the law, hewing to the narrowest constructs of their legal obligations. They have promised to do more. They must do more. We, and they, must hold them to more.

We, both as citizens and as officials, must hold each and all officials to their best, to do it in good faith, to seek the least unjust result, and to do so in every single case. In short, we must have justice in every case, because if we do not, the very reasons for any person – citizen or official – to follow the law are weakened. Any argument for justice that seeks a greater good than this risks ultimately being betrayed by its own contradictions: justice is retail – personal and individual – or it does not exist.

Appendix: Taxonomy of Headings

The Lawes and Libertyes of Massachusetts (Discussed in Chapter 1)

OVERVIEW

The facsimile has 61 pages, including a 2-page introduction and 59 pages of text, of which one-third of page 1 is a statement we would now call a claim to due process of law, and the last $4\frac{1}{2}$ pages are oaths. There are 54 lines per page. On page 1 there are 50 lines, and on page 55, there are 29. Each heading is given one line, and there are 122 headings. Thus, 53 pages at 54 lines each, plus 36, plus 29, less the 122 lines for headings, suggests that the code has about 2,820 lines. Certain of the entries have prefatory language, which is not discounted. Blank lines in a single entry are rare but are counted here.

The taxonomy here is quite rough. Headings are grouped into eleven categories, which were framed in order to present them in rough analogy to modern American categories of law. In attempting to place each heading into a single summary category, preference was given to views of the legal relationship of such headings that would be meaningful to a modern lawyer. The categories created are Commonwealth, Rights of the Person, Law of the Person, Religion, Crime, Court Procedures, Officials, Obligation & Oaths (not counting oath texts), Property, Debts & Collection, Commerce, Licenses, and Taxes, and Natural Resources.

In order to compare the significance by length of the categories, each heading is allocated to only one category. (There is one exception, in that "Liberties common" is too disparate to locate into a category, and its paragraphs were divided between the categories Rights of the Person and Natural Resources.)

There is therefore some skew in the overall weighting; every entry is not to be multiply counted. For example, "Death untimely" is here entered under Crimes, but it could have been listed under Officials, Persons, or Commonwealth. Matters of family, such as marriage, are listed under Property, but they could as easily have been within Religion, Commonwealth, or the Law of

Persons. It is hoped that the skew will affect most categories equally and more or less cancel its effects across the board.

It is also important to remember that the code did not exhaust the standards of the law, particularly for matters of private law. The *recto* of the introduction leaf notes that some special laws and some general laws have been left out. Moreover, certain entries make no sense without implying considerable background knowledge of the common law. For example, Manslaughter and Usury are presented only as defenses; the causes of action must be defined elsewhere.

The last five pages include the language of the 32 oaths that were required by law. Oaths included summonses, and a few oaths for attachment, bond, and replevin, then oaths for the Commissioner representative to the united colonies, an oath of fidelitie to the Government of the Common-wealth, and a Freeman's Oath, then 24 oaths of office, ranging from governor through juror and witness to pipe-stave inspector.

Counting all of the lines in the entire code yields the following weighting: Commonwealth, 436 lines (15%); Rights of the Person, 68 lines (2%), Religion, 169 lines (6%), Law of the Person, 170 lines (6%); Crime, 244 lines (9%); Court Procedures, 393 lines (14%), Officials, Obligation & Oaths (not counting oath texts), 340 lines (12%), Property, 247 lines (9%), Debts & Collection, 104 lines (1%), Commerce, Licenses, and Taxes, 578 lines (20%); Natural Resources, 77 lines (1%).

Weighting alone, of course, is hardly conclusive of significance. Some matters are so serious that few words are needed to describe them. Murder took only three lines. Others are merely too technical to be addressed tersely. The regulation of constables was 13 times longer, at 39 lines. Still, the length of the prose committed suggests something of its importance. Military Affairs required 217 lines, a not unworthy entry for a colony that was so often at war.

CATEGORIES, HEADINGS ASSIGNED, AND LINES PER HEADING

Rights of the Person, 62 lines

Preface (due process) (14), Arrests (11), Bond-Slavery (outlawed except for captives) (6), Justice (4), Liberties Common (¶¶ 1, 3, speech and travel) (9), Oaths, Subscription (only as required by Council) (6), Punishment (no double jeopardy or cruel punishment) (4), Votes (every freeman's vote according to conscience; right to abstain or be neutral) (14).

Law of the Person, 170 lines

Abilitie (3), Age (3), Children (literacy, religion, debts, orphans) (49), Freemen, Non-Freemen (10), Fugitives, Strangers (5), Impresses (16), Indians (70), Strangers (14).

Commonwealth, 436 lines

Benevolence (4), Colledge (25), In-keepers, Tippling, Drunkenes (108), Militarie Affairs (217), Poor (6), Schools (20), Townships (35), Treasure (public expenditures) (6), Watching (town guard) (15).

Religion, 169 lines

Ana-Baptists (20), Ecclesiasticall (118), Jesuits (22), Protestation contra Remonstrance (9).

Crime, 244 lines

Burglarie and Theft (37), Capital Lawes (fifteen offenses subject to death: Idolatrie, Witch-craft, Blasphemie, Murther, Poysoning, Bestialitie, Sodomie, Adulterie, Man-stealing, False-witnesse, Conspiracie, Child curse, Rebellious Child, and Rape) (55), Condemned (4), Criminal causes (4), Crueltie (to animals) (3), Death untimely (5), Forgerie (5), Fornication (5), Gaming (12), Heresie (16), Idlenes (8), Imprisonment (5), Inditements (7), Lying (37), Man-slaughter (self-defense) (5), Prisoners, Prisons (2), Profane swearing (8), Tobacco (use banned except in private room) (11), Torture (banned unless already convicted, no whipping more than 40 lashes) (10), Usurie (defense if not at least 8% apr) (5).

Court Procedures, 393 lines

Action (17), Appeal (25), Appearance, Non-apearance (6), Attachments (12), Causes, Small causes (63), Clerk of writs (14), Courts (91), Damages pretended (4), Juries, Jurors (35), Magistrates (including contempt of court) (43), Prescriptions (no action for breach of God's law) (3), Replevin (5), Summons (12), Suits, vexatious suits (5), Trespasse (no trespass if fault of owner) (4), Tryalls (20), Witnesses (34).

Officials, Obligation & Oaths (not counting oath texts), 340 lines

Barratrie (4), Charges publick (officials' expenses) (102), Constables (39), Councill (18), Deputies for the Generall Court (36), Elections (49), Generall Court (12), Governour (4), Marshal (15), Records (49), Secresie (no duty to reveal nondangerous secret over oath or conscience) (5), Secretarie (7).

Property, 247 lines

Bounds of townes and persons (22), Cattel, Corn-fields, Fences (commons) (97), Deeds and Writings (3), Dowries (36), Escheats (4), Farms (3), Fyre

(11), Lands, Free lands (5), Marriage (53), Wills intestate (5), Wrecks of the Sea (8).

Commerce, Licenses, and Taxes, 578 lines

Bakers (26), Cask & Cooper (9), Drovers (5), Fayrs & Markets (12), Ferries (36), Hygh-wayes (39), Impost (76), Leather (86), Masters, Servants, Labourers (50), Mills, Millers (4), Monopolies (3), Pipe-staves (35), Pound, Pound breach (corral) (25), Powder (11), Ships, Ship-masters (24), Straies (animals & lost goods) (35), Swyne (28), Weights & Measures (40), Wharfage (23), Workmen (11).

Debts & Collection, 104 lines

Bills (as debts) (6), Conveyances fraudulant (29), Distresse (5), Fines (9), Levies (for fines and assessments) (27), Oppression (overcharging) (6), Payments (7), Rates, Fines (15).

Natural Resources, 77 lines

Ballast (6), Fish, Fishermen (18), Hydes & Skins (10), Liberties Common (¶2, fishing and fowling) (16), Tile-earth (clay) (4), Wolves (suppression to protect cattle) (13), Wood (10).

Index